ONCE IN THE MIDDLE OF NOWHERE
~ The Center of the Universe ~

A Collection of Turtle Mountain Tales

JACK OLSON

Assembled, Edited and Published under the direction of :

Robert (Kip) L. Malaska

Copyright © 2003 by Georgia E. Olson and Robert (Kip) L. Malaska

All rights reserved

Without limiting the rights under copyright reserved above, no part of this publication may be reproduced, stored in or introduced into a retrieval system, or transmitted, in any form, or by any means (electronic, photocopying, recording, or otherwise), without the prior written permission of the copyright owner of this book.

ISBN 0-9774124-1-5

Printed in the United States of America

Drawings, Illustrations and Paintings including cover Painting by Jack Olson

Dedication

This book is dedicated to my late stepfather 'Jack Olson' who I owe so much for all he has taught me. "Jack...your dream to share your stories has finally been realized!"

- Love Kip

Acknowledgement

To those with whom I once lived these experiences.

I owe many people, family and friends who encouraged me to write down these stories.

They know who they are and have my deepest appreciation.

- Jack Olson

About The Author
John (Jack) Jacob Olson

Jack was born October 24, 1922 in Bottineau, North Dakota. He grew up on the family farm bordering Canada in Souris, North Dakota. He graduated from Bottineau High School and the North Dakota School of Forestry (now Minot State University-Bottineau). He then attended the University of North Dakota in Grand Forks before enlisting in the Army Air Corps. In 1943, he completed bomber training at Washington University in St. Louis, MO and was awarded his silver pilot wings, which he considered to be his proudest achievement.

He served in the Army Air Corps in World War II as a B-17 pilot and later became a pilot instructor in B-24 (Liberator) bombers. Jack successfully landed his four-engine B-24 bomber after losing over 15 feet of one wing in a midair collision, saving 14 crewmembers and passengers onboard. Later he was promoted as a pilot in command of a B-29. At the end of World War II, Jack left the service and graduated from the Minneapolis College of Art and Design. He later received a bachelor's degree in Aerospace Science from Central Washington University.

In 1950 he joined Brown & Bigelow as the chief designer in metal and plastic products. While working there he received 120 mechanical and design patents and in 1951 his design of the now famous Tupperware Party favor, "the pickle plucker" received the National Design in Plastics award.

In 1958 Jack joined the Boeing Aerospace division ultimately holding the title of Principal Engineer in Concept and Design. His first project at Boeing, before joining the Aerospace division was a mass-transit system in Morgantown, W.Va. He soon became widely recognized for his visionary concept designs, and illustrations of spacecraft and space exploration. His projects involved a concept that paralleled the later design of the Hubble Space Telescope, the design of Boeing's bid to NASA on the Moon Lunar Excursion Module (LEM), a manned Mars outpost, and a solar power satellite project. He considered the concept of using the barren land beneath the solar power satellite as a greenhouse, which could provide food for a city of a million people, as one of his most exciting projects. Jack was also responsible for the concept and detail design of the Boeing Jetfoil, now plying the waters of the English Channel and Hong Kong, the design patent of which he shares with another engineer.

Forced into early retirement in 1984 because of medical problems, he continued to do consultant work for Boeing and NASA. In 1985 he was honored with a one-man show of his spacecraft design illustrations at the

Smithsonian's Air and Space Museum in Washington DC. Twenty-one of these paintings are now part of the permanent Smithsonian collection.

Jack enjoyed flying sailplanes and earned all three legs of the Diamond badge from the Soaring Society of America. He was a pilot and instructor for 20 years. He also enjoyed painting, photography, woodworking, music, and was a history buff. His illustrations have been included in several textbooks and coffee-table books and have appeared in numerous periodicals and products globally. Among other achievements, he was a master Photographer in the Photographic Society of America, a member of Epigraphic Society and of the Soaring Society of America and occupied a chair on the National Space Society Board of Governors.

In 1994, he retired to a summer home on Lake Louise in Bottineau County, North Dakota. He joined the Bottineau Men's Choir. He became active in civic affairs promoting the city of Bottineau. Among many ideas to bring attention to the city, he designed an informational Kiosk and organized a national soaring contest in Bottineau to promote gliding in North Dakota. In December of 2000, he and his wife returned to their home in Normandy Park near Seattle, Washington. On August 28, 2001 Jack lost his 14-year battle with cancer.

Jack Olson – A personal view of myself

Somewhat like Robert Fulghum's observation in his book, "All I REALLY NEED TO KNOW I LEARNED IN KINDERGARTEN," all I really learned about designing things was learned in my father's farm workshop with a forge. There, in remote country away from city distractions, away from playmates my own age, essentially an only child, I was given freedom to do anything I pleased with my father's tools. Having no plans I made model planes, boats, ships, sleds, and ultimately, a full size sailboat of my own design. There I learned woodworking, metal forming and casting, the strength of materials, structural design, what would blow up, and what wouldn't. Going to college only gave scorecard formality to what I had essentially learned already.

Reading the record of my education away from the farm, it would appear that I was confused about what I wanted to do as an adult. This is true, I was. I started out to be an engineer, but I really wanted to be an airplane pilot. World War II came along and gave me that skill. After discharge and returning to school, I switched from mechanical engineering to industrial design (product design), a new profession in 1945. This course of study involved art illustration, human ergonomics, factory mass production techniques, arrangement of mechanical parts for the most efficient use, etc. In other words, just by dumb luck, I had taken a combination of the right courses to be a designer of manned spacecraft, or boats, or cars, or merry-go-rounds for that matter. By 1959 I was chief designer for a factory making a variety of innovative metal and plastic products. I was sick of designing things a person could carry in one hand. Sputnik had been squeaking its message of a new age long enough. I wanted in.

Foreword

How well I remember the first time I met Jack Olson. It was the fall of 1997, and I was working as the dean of the two-year college in Bottineau, North Dakota, when Mr. Olson was announced as a guest to see me. He had recently contributed some of his artwork to the college's Foundation upon his retirement and relocation to nearby Lake Metigoshe, a short distance away from his 1922 birthplace. To get acquainted, I accepted his kind invitation to join him and his wife, Georgia, for lunch at a local establishment. Over the meal, Jack recounted some of his life's events as inventor, wood smith, painter, US Air Force flier, glider pilot, engineer, conceptual designer, illustrator of spacecraft, and the Boeing jetfoil. Jack was articulate and witty. Jack's passion for his life experiences emanated from him. Gradually, I realized I had become spellbound in his company. Completely beguiled, I became aware over coffee that I had to love this man. I had fallen in love with this fascinating, gentle spirit over this lunch with his wife and him. I knew I wanted to keep Jack and Georgia in my circle of friends from that point forward. It was a decision from the heart. He had that kind of effect upon me.

And I have come to learn Jack Olson has had the same effect on so very many people over the course of his life. As talented as he was, he was certainly no braggadocio. In fact, he was often self-effacing, which made the process of 'discovering Jack' full of wonder and surprise. Jack was honored with a one-man show of twenty-one of his space paintings, which are permanently displayed at the Smithsonian. The paintings were the product of his years with Boeing where he conceptualized and drew lunar craft, telescopes, and satellites. These were, however, just the tip of the iceberg. In visiting his Seattle home shortly after his death in 2001, I was astonished by the sheer quantity of his paintings. He seemed to have worked in every medium and with all manner of subjects from portraiture to landscapes to the fantastical. He was known for his humor and his infusion of the unexpected into otherwise serious presentations of art and literature. He was a copious writer of letters, essays, and short stories. He was a renowned and prolific photographer, who catalogued thousands of his own prints over his lifetime. He held many patents. A classic example of the "Renaissance Man," Jack Olson profoundly touched many lives in his seventy-eight years and was well loved.

This collection of short stories is a little jewel to be shared with others posthumously by Jack's family. *Once in the Middle of Nowhere* consists of tales of the North Dakota Turtle Mountains, Jack's boyhood home. He opens with the observation that "almost no one outside of North Dakota has ever heard of the Turtle Mountains." But, these are short stories that pull the reader into that rather magical and historical place--an oasis of deciduous forest in the vastness of the Great Plains that straddles the US border with Canada. Jack uses his vocabulary and his artist's eye like he would a brush; to paint rich descriptions of the landscape that both entice and envelop the reader. Indeed, the collection's illustrations are his. His retelling of personal stories of his youth captures the essence of the people and lifestyle of the rural, pre-World War II Midwest. Today, gravel and macadamized roads have replaced some of the old wagon trails. SUV's, pickup trucks, and snowmobiles cover ground once traversed by cutters and dray horses. But in many other ways, life is lived seasonally today in the Turtle Mountains as it always has been. These tales intrigue and compel the reader to 'step into' Jack's past and to recall and compare their own experiences to his.

A delightful diversion, this compilation is certain to enchant and amuse. As with his paintings, this is another wonderful legacy left to us by a most uncommon man. Happy reading!

Kathleen A. Corak, PhD

Synopsis of Stories

PREFACE (page 13)

Why I bothered to write this collection of tales.

THE PLACE (page 17)

Stealing a style from James A. Michener, herein is a description of the location and geology of a unique oasis in the upper great plains, an area of our country that scarcely anyone has ever heard of. First were the Indians. Then "White Eyes" came to change everything forever.

THE CAST (page 32)

Though I didn't want to be just another old man writing memoirs, I had to have some sort of a base to hang my stories on. My parents had something to do with my being born. My recollections of events involve them. They were typical of the people who once lived there.

ON DISCOVERING THE WORLD (page 39)

As late as 1924, verdant meadows of grass and wild flowers were still to be found. In such a meadow, as a baby, I first observe the process of haying and also discover a bubbling spring complete with tadpoles. I decide to join them and do. Mama was a little upset.

SEX AND DIRTY WORDS (page 47)

What a six year old boy doesn't know about sex he learns from his eight year old cousin, Virgil. The whole business seems revolting. Another older friend fills in some missing information. More bad news.

ASPEN GROVES, ISLANDS OF THE PRAIRIE (page 53)

This story also involves haying time. Once, the prairie had islands of aspen groves. As a young boy in a such pleasant oasis of trees, I find more than wild strawberries. Observing a pair of hawks soaring upward to cloud-base, I learn what I want to do when I grow up--fly.

DAKOTA CUTTERS (page 64)

About an adventure in a unique type of horse drawn vehicle designed to cope with the harsh winters of North Dakota. These enclosed cutters, cozy and comfortable, heated by a small stove, were commonly built by farmers who wanted to go to town or visit neighbors.

BORDER BOOTLEGGERS (page 83)

A goofy time of rum runners and the border patrol. Our farm on the border gave us a grandstand seat.

THE BUCK STOPPED HERE (page 94)

A neighbor gives us a newborn fawn. As he grows up he exhibits some unexpected behavior for a deer:

- A passion for riding in automobiles
- Hijacking candy from the mailman
- Causing general mayhem.

BARNLIFE, CIRCA 1930 (page 111)

A good barn was, at one time, the most important building on the farm, even more important than the farmhouse. This is for those who remember, or those who have unluckily missed the experience.

THE JUGGERNAUT (page 131)

A twelve year old farm boy builds an enormous vehicle of hodge podge parts on top of a hill. Too large to be hauled back up again, he knows it can make only one downhill trip. He waits for many days to demonstrate his creation to someone he deems important. Patience wearing thin, he has to settle for my mother and me. After seeing the wild ride, we are truly impressed.

DUST AND HARD TIMES (page 142)

The era of the Dust Bowl clobbers North Dakota. Thrown in for a good measure are grasshoppers, army worms, wheat rust, and the Depression. Despite the misery, farm folks found ways not only to endure, but to have a good time.

A VISIT FROM UNCLE OLE AND SONS (page 167)

An occurrence carried to the extreme of uneventfulness. A story about dull and boring being brought to the level of an artform.

LO, THE MIGHTY HUNTERS (page 172)

Jake, my father, is the finest hunter in the area. Unfortunately, he dislikes hunting and only does it as an unpleasant but necessary chore. My mother insists that he teaches me how to do it. "Every boy must know how to hunt." His methods are unorthodox. Nothing like the stories in hunting and fishing magazines.

THE LAKE (page 189)

Straddling the Canadian border is Lake Metigoshe Washegum--North Dakota's answer to Lake Placid or Tahoe. This charming, intimate lake has a shoreline so irregular that a chart of it looks like a Rorschach inkblot. With its many bays, coves, --places to build a cottage or just hide away – it provided fertile ground, (water?) for mischief. So, naturally it has a rich history including bootleggers, resort rivalries, special social events, romantic trysts, and other amusements. Some very odd folks actually went there to fish!

THE BEAST OF BIG SANDY (page 213)

Uncle Carl hooked and lost a big one in Lake Metigoshe. Every time he retells the story the fish gets bigger. His friends no longer believe him. Obsessed to prove his prowess as a fisherman he talks a friend into going to Canada for its fabled fishing. He finally ties into a monster, but much to his traumatic surprise it turns out to be a beast of a mechanical, not animal, nature.

ENTERTAINMENT, 20 BCT (page 228)

<u>B</u>efore <u>C</u>ommercial <u>T</u>elevision people had only each other for entertainment. Folks had a lot more fun then. They worked together and played together. Hard times didn't mean not taking time to have a good time. Now as people hunker down in front of the glaring tube, whether on the farm or in the suburbs, they may wonder why they still feel lonely. Read this and learn why.

THE GREAT WATERMELON HEIST (page 248)

My cousin Virgil and I share a passion for watermelon. It is difficult to grow watermelons in North Dakota but Ole Indvik has a patch ripe for the picking. Virgil has a plan how to swipe a couple by using riding horses. It almost works.

BUCK FEVER (page 256)

World War II is over. Before resuming college studies I'm back at the farm visiting the folks. Deer hunting season is about to open. Civilian ammunition is scarce. Knowing that some hunters go nuts during deer season, I build a deer out of sticks and cardboard, and set it up in an illogical place. From a hideout, I watch the insanity.

A BRIEF VISIT HOME, 1944 (page 271)

Now as an Army Air Corps pilot I have a great need to show off a B-24 bomber to my folks and my hometown, Bottineau. It is strictly forbidden on threat of court martial to do so. Besides that, the farm is 800 miles or so away. What the hell, flying is chancy business anyway so why not try to get away with it. Luckily I do.

IMAGES (page 288)

To present a clearer view of a special time and place, a collection of scenes or events recalled, worthy of description in a few paragraphs if not a long chapter. I remember events or scenes encountered as a lad now a little older. Some are pleasant. Some make me wish I could experience it again. Some not.

THE TURTLES NOW (page 307)

The hills are still there. The Lake still sparkles, but much else has changed. Only a third as many people now live in the area as there were in 1930. Some villages have disappeared entirely. Yet the urge to revisit the place once called home causes people to come from Florida, Arizona, California, and elsewhere to again explore "The Lake." Perhaps to remember the time... some, tired of the rat race, come back to stay.

PREFACE

Almost no one outside of North Dakota has ever heard of the Turtle Mountains. The countryside has changed and will never be the same. Nearly all of the people who made the place and times interesting are dead. These characters should not be forgotten.

Prefaces tend to be boring and are usually read only by avid readers. If you skip this one I don't really blame you. However, to skip reading the preface is somewhat akin to not reading the programming instructions on your VCR. You may be stuck with a blinking 12:00 forever. No picture.

In the first place, I had no intention of writing a book. Writing is a lot of work, and work is something to be avoided. I'd rather just tell the stories.

Story telling--that's what got me into all this trouble--telling stories to friends or anyone patient enough to listen to my Turtle Mountain tales.

Though I didn't know it at the time, I was very lucky to be born in a very special place at a very good time. Later in my life, after meeting people whose lives were woven elsewhere, I came to realize how different my beginning had been, how unknown to Americans was this remote and unique place of my birth. No stories, either fictional or true had been written about it. Nowhere, USA.

While visiting friends, I would sometimes be asked to tell one of my Turtle Mountain tales. Sometimes I suspected they thought I invented them just for entertainment value. Actually, I'm not good at inventing fictional humor. All I did was to be a raconteur of whatever childhood event had impressed me--my knack for mimicking foreign accents helped.

As a retired old man, I had become rather useless around the house and I knew it. I had even given up soaring, the sport of flying sailplanes. Georgia, my exceptionally indulgent wife, who has put up with me for many years and is stepmother to my two sons, said to me one day, "You seem so aimless, why don't you write some of your stories about growing up in the Turtle Mountains for the children; they are, after all, stories of your youth. You were raised on a farm at the ending of the age when horses pulled the plow, served as a bomber pilot in World War II, and finished your career as a designer of spacecraft. You've had many adventures. I know that someday they would like to know all about them. Besides, your stories are fun." At first I doubted they would be all that interested, but I thought it over. My adult adventures didn't seem to be all that important. However, there were things I had witnessed in my childhood, the like of which has never been seen on TV.

Sometime later, I was sitting at the desk in my rat-hole den. There, in front of me, was a personal computer that I had impulsively purchased for no reason other than wanting to learn about computers. After staring at it rather dully a thought slowly formed. "Perhaps if I were to use it other than to play solitaire, I would come to understand why the computer craze was sweeping the country."

A blank sheet of paper in front of me had often bugged me before. Now, the gray fog of the display screen was doing the same thing. Since I had a word processing program, Georgia's suggestion to tell about my real experiences came to mind. However, I was determined that I would not write a dull memoir about my flying days in the Air Corps, my midlife crises or career. It seemed every old guy about to buy the farm is writing his memoir. No, this would be fun stories--no dreary stuff. That would be easy--events of my childhood were mostly fun. Some not a whole lot of fun, but at least interesting. It would be offbeat because it would be about long ago in a locality and of people generally unknown. I would write about a way of life and a time that only few folks now living would recall. Most of the people alive over seventy years ago are now dead and not talking; and it is unlikely that any of those now still alive will ever bother to write anything. So, it was up to me.

For starters a couple stories came to mind...

When I had finished the first efforts--"Dakota Cutters and Aspen Groves"-- I gave them to my sons, one a published poet, the other a graphics designer. They were polite about accepting them, and may even have read them, but I knew in my heart they were under whelmed. Was it my writing? The stories? OK, perhaps it wasn't exactly Thoreau, Hemingway, or Twain stuff and they were just too polite to say so, but I knew 'veneration gap.'

My reaction, to their reaction was, "To hell with writing, I'll dump the project. It had been hard work anyway." So now what? Here I was, stuck with an extra copy or two. What to do with them? Then I had the notion that perhaps my old erudite and literate friend, Will Stageberg, living in St. Paul, Minnesota, would enjoy the stories. Perhaps he would read these tales and proofread them as well. I hadn't done much writing since college, a hundred years ago and I suspected that my punctuation and spelling would be found lacking. I sent Will a copy.

My suspicions were correct. A week later Will returned my copy with corrections properly and tolerantly done in red pencil. More importantly, he included a note of great encouragement. He, being as old as I am, apparently could relate to the stories, even if he didn't grow up on the Canadian border of North Dakota. Will also remembered some of the stories I had told him years ago. Included in his note: "How about writing that story you told me about the farm boy who built that colossal juggernaut on top of a hill?" I recalled the story, wrote it, and sent it to him. He sent me a note saying he liked it with the comment, that besides being funny he said it had "psychological significance," "a bright kid in the outskirts of a ghetto of siblings."

I kept on writing and sending copies to Will. Four years later, and now more proficient at the computer keyboard, I have a collection of tales. They are as true as my memory is capable of, and I admit I've had to do considerable research. This mostly has involved reading books or writing to the few folks who are still living in or near the Turtle Mountains to confirm facts. The dead, though fondly remembered, weren't much help except as the characters in this play of several acts. Sadly, since I started this effort, some of my reliable old-timer friends who had helped me remember events or verify details have died.

Their loss has spurred me to hurry up, not only might I run out of references, but out of me.

This collection of tales of the Turtle Mountains, as far as I know, is the only attempt of a book of sorts that is not just a factual history of the region or a paragraph in a textbook about the climate. No nationally known magazine has had articles about this unique part of our country. THE NATIONAL GEOGRAPHIC SOCIETY, historians, or noted authors could have saved me a lot of trouble with an article or two about the Turtle Mountain country and its people, but they have let me down. You're stuck with my version. Anyway, it all took place a long time ago. In very few places have I forgotten or changed the names.

Even though I tried not to make this a memoir, I found it impossible when writing from the point of being an objective observer not to include my parents or myself in the story. Look at it this way. My parents were more or less typical of the folks who once lived there. I simply saw, smelt, felt, heard, and the impressions will be representative of nearly all.

The chapters are arranged somewhat in chronological order but it's OK to skip around. In reading the stories, the clue to the time period in which the story takes place is how I refer to my Parents, Jake, and Lena. From 1922 to approximately 1930 I called them "Mama and Papa," from 1931 to 1936, "Ma and Pa," from 1936 on as "Mom and Pop, or Dad." Perhaps it is a bit strange, but even as a child I frequently called them by their names, "Jake and Lena," and my Uncle Carl, who lived with us, as just plain "Carl." Everybody else did too. Formality was never a big thing on the plains. My Aunt Mina was an exception. She was big on elegance and the latest play on Broadway.

If you have read this preface, I'll just add that I've sometimes included a map or two and some drawings that were easier to make than to write the verbal description.

THE PLACE

The Turtle Mountains: Hollywood filmmakers have not seen fit to make a movie here, nor has NATIONAL GEOGRAPHIC magazine featured an article about this modestly unique locale. Therefore, it may help the reader to visualize the setting if it were described. Many pages could be devoted to this task but that might be boring, so I'll skip it and leave the unsaid stuff to your imagination.

The noted author, James A. Michener, sometimes starts his lengthy novels with a description of the geological origin of the land in which his story is about to take place. To get a feel for the setting, it is a great way to begin. Since I am no author the likes of Michener, I will resort to cheap, unabashed plagiarism of a good idea.

The place in my collection of tales lacks the glamour of Hawaii, the crystal waters of the Caribbean, or the mystique of Egypt. In fact, the land is devoid of geological wonders, noteworthy conflicts, historical significance, or famous characters. Most people, however well educated, have probably never heard of it. They will be more apt to have heard of Mali Africa, or the republic of Tuva, than the Turtle Mountains of North Dakota. NATIONAL GEOGRAPHIC magazine has printed and pictured articles of every land and culture in the world except this locale. By cartological mensuration and calculation, this region is almost dead center in the middle of North America. The name "mountains" is a misnomer. Hills, or plateau, better describes this geologically insignificant bump on the plains.

If one were to be elevated in a helicopter over this area to allow viewing in all directions, except for the hills and forest beneath, the distant scene would be one of endless prairie in all directions. The horizon would be as unbroken as that of a vast ocean. Understandably, a person might feel that he or she was in the <u>middle of nowhere</u>. However, for me as a Boy, it was the center of the universe.

Enough palaver, I begin.

Mountains in North Dakota?

A modern day, road weary traveler is approaching Bismarck on I-90. Bored from the flat distance across plains, he or she again checks the map to see how long it will be before the road will bend. There, on the upper edge of the map is a faint oval marked "Turtle Mountains." The tourist's facial expression changes, imparting a quizzical look. "Mountains? – Turtle Mountains? – Never heard of any mountains in North Dakota--must be a joke."

Why the Earth Pile on the Border?

Straddling the USA/Canadian border is a mesa like mound of hills about six hundred feet higher than the immediate surrounding prairie. Why should there be such a formation isolated here on the vast plains? True, there are no craggy rock peaks here; but to a geologist it is no less an interesting landscape for the lack of them. Indeed, to deduce the geological history of subtle prairie terrain may be more challenging to understand than the birth of the Alps.

According to astronomers, paleontologists, and geologists, about five billion years ago our planet was one very hot stew pot consisting mostly of a glob of nickel-iron surrounded by magma. The 'light stuff,' basalt and granite for example, floated up like slag in a crucible forming the crust of the earth. This eventually formed one big and scummy landmass into one monolithic lump. This super continent has been tagged with the name "Pangaea" regarded as a combination of "Gondwanaland" and "Laurasia." Taking its own sweet time, this large landmass eventually split up, forming a few continents, one of which is North America. The oceans originally were fresh water. Where all the water came from is still up for scientific grabs. Somewhere in the primordial soup, perhaps four billion years ago, microscopic life began. For the past several million years or so, the area known as the Great Plains has alternated between being dry land and sea bottom. The Great Plains are devoid of real mountains. Deep under the upper soils are many layers of sedimentary and metamorphic rocks.

Planet Earth, trying to settle down to an orderly existence in its orbit around the sun, has had to put up with a lot of changing chemical and physical conditions. One of these involved a cyclic change in climate. From time to time, North America and Europe got loaded with an ice sheet similar to the one covering Greenland--only bigger.

Gravity makes ice sheets move and they are then called glaciers. Glaciers grind rocks, warm water melts ice, etc. Glaciers are the global 'Mix Masters,' which altered the many-layered cake that the people of the plains live on. For a geologist to explain the morphology that shaped the subtle undulating terrain of the plains is a far more difficult task than reading the revealing flank of a stone mountain. In the Grand Canyon, the water-driven chainsaw known as the Colorado River has neatly exposed all the layers. In the plains, most of the evidence is buried thousands of feet underground. Therefore, in North Dakota the geologist has to rely on borings, deep holes augured from underground. Even the varied layers of soil types must be studied. As for the surface clues such as the Turtle Mountains, it isn't easy to explain why there should be an island of earth piled there.

The enormous glaciers performing like bulldozers and earth movers came down from the north and brought vast quantities of soil, including boulders, rocks, gravel, sand, clay, and plain dirt (glacial till) For some reason a part of a glacier loaded with all that stuff became stagnant and just sat there as if it had a flat tire. As the glacier melted all the debris was dumped. According to some authorities in geology, the more appropriate term for the resulting pile is Collapsed Glacial Topography, a special form of moraine.

Water also played a role in shaping the scenery, or lack of it. Since the upper Great Plains slope to Hudson Bay, drainage would normally be in that direction. However, at times the receding melting ice formed dams, and huge glacial lakes backed up. These glacial lakes are responsible for much of the deep, rich soil of the area. The first of the last two times that North Dakota was covered with water was a large sea in the eastern part of the state, geologically named Lake Agassiz. The last glacier which muscled its way south to the Missouri River encountered the stalled stagnant glacier. It nudged it, creating a few thrust ridges, then gave up, and went around it. As it receded, a body of water referred to as Glacial Lake Souris formed on the west and southwest side of the Turtle Mountains.

It has been proposed that eventually glacial Lake Souris sprang a leak and suddenly emptied into the Hudson Bay drainage system. This caused a period of severe and rapid erosion leaving the hill country high and dry.

The lakes and ponds of today were formed by glacial ice from several processes. The easiest to understand is that of a large chunk of ice depressing the earth. When it melts it leaves a dent full of water. Rainwater for thousands of years has kept the pothole going, much to the delight of flora, fauna, and duck hunters.

To the layman, the Turtle Mountains are an oval shaped blob of glacial till measuring about 20X30 miles in size. If one were to view this low, muddled oval of earth from very high altitude, it would appear to have the form of an enormous cow pie on a vast prairie.

On normal color photos from space, the Turtle Mountains show up as a green-blue blot. A closer look by an astronaut may reveal numerous sparkling lakes and ponds reflecting sunlight. The wrinkled topography is that of many tree filled ravines in the foothills, circling a higher plateau of gently rolling terrain. Some of the area has no surface drainage. A few major creeks drain the hills on all sides. Water in these creeks, as well as the waters of almost half of North Dakota; will eventually find its winding way to Hudson Bay, Canada.

Viewing the Turtle Mountains from the ground, any resemblance to a cow pie vanishes, for here is a pleasant island of rolling hills in the vast fertile sea of the surrounding prairies. Here is wildlife, trees, berry bushes, clean air, many lakes, and ponds of unpolluted water. Typical of glacial moraine, the land varies from soil suitable for small grain fields, to large areas of soil laden with gravel, rocks, and small boulders that defy the plow. Thus, much of the hill country resembles the hardscrabble forest countryside of Vermont and New Hampshire.

Climate

Mention to someone who never lived there, that you hail from North Dakota, and the first thing that may come his or her mind is a treeless, flat, boring, land with terrible weather extremes. As the preceding paragraphs about geology have revealed, now you and the folks who live there know that the land isn't flat and treeless. Even on the prairie the terrain is sometimes broken with a gentle ravine, a stream, and willows. As for the country being boringly flat, the lowest elevation just in Bottineau County is 1400 feet mean sea level and the highest is Boundary Butte, in the Turtle Mountains, at 2541 feet mean sea level. True, this is only a 1141 foot differential, but even that is almost three times the elevation change in Florida, where the highest point is only 345 feet above sea level.

Best of all is the climate even if it is extreme in winter. It is sometimes so bad a person can tell outrageous stories with very little exaggeration. The summer time on the Canadian border is wonderful. We, who once lived there, never needed to consult a calendar to know what time of the year it was. Winter is winter. Spring is spring. No doubt about the four seasons. No wishy-washy, sissy climate change for us. In my fond memory, the so-called, miserable weather was the most fun. Who can deny the adrenaline rush of survival? An invigorating climate is character building. Therefore, the country is replete with characters. Characters are the stuff of stories.

Winter in the Turtle Mountains brings a unique beauty. Though the hill plateau averages only six hundred feet above the foothill flatlands, it is just high enough to touch the bottoms of low scudding winter clouds. The moment the super cooled moisture touches a twig or branch, it condenses into sparkling crystals. Soon, the forest is heavily clothed with white frost. In the still air of a cold night, frost needles grow to an inch or more in length. What a few hours before was a dull gloomy scene of bare branched trees, is now a wonderland forest of ice crystals. When the branches get overloaded or assailed by battering wind, the frost will cascade to the forest floor and remain until spring. Branches will be bare again until a new load of frost arrives. Most of the 'snow' in the forest is actually fallen frost. It can accumulate to sufficient depth that snowmobilers seldom complain about trail conditions in the hills.

Springtime brings thawing snow and brook music, budding aspen and willow catkins. Before the last patches of snow are gone, the downy fists of the blue pasque flowers will unclench to hold the sun in white palms. From overhead, in springtime, can be heard the melodious sound of returning wild geese. Downwind from hillside shrubbery, nostrils will be treated to the fragrance of chokecherry and juneberry blossoms.

In summertime, probably the most pleasant climate in America, the daytime wind makes waves in the tall, yielding cereal grasses of the prairie grain fields. When it's summer in the hill, country turtles sun on a soggy log, and insect sounds mix with the rustling gentle clatter of aspen leaves. A summer evening on the shore of a remote lake may bring the echoing, haunting, laughing-cry of a loon. Summer is when the water is warm enough for swimming. Summer is when the Indians once made pemmican from chokecherries, highbush cranberries, and cured bison meat.

Fall is the time of collecting; squirrels collecting nuts, migratory birds collecting to form precision echelon squadrons for their journey south, farmers collecting their harvest and school children collecting russet bouquets of autumn leaves. Unfortunately, all too often the most colorful red leaves turn out to be poison ivy. We know that fall is near its end and the first snows of winter are about to begin when V-formations of geese fly southward again.

Admittedly, all these sights and sounds are familiar occurrences in other parts of our great land. For some reason, there is a special intimacy when it occurs in the Turtle Mountains. Perhaps it is the lack of city noise and turmoil. More probably the truth of the matter is that, for each individual, nothing beats memories of home, whether it be the benign and boring paradise of Hawaii or the rigorous, seasonally changing life of the Turtle Mountains. Retired persons, affluent enough to afford two homes, would make an excellent choice if they chose to buy and live in a home during late spring, summer and fall in the Place of Many Turtles. For those who dislike sub-zero temperatures it may be wise to select a place near Brownsville, Texas for the winter.

Origin of a Quaint Name

Not only outsiders but the people who live there have wondered, "From whence the strange, but colorful, Turtle Mountain name?" I had always assumed it was due to a whimsical mood in the mind of the first surveyor marking the invisible line of the 49th parallel. In my mind, I pictured a man tired of wading through the seemingly endless waist-high grass of the plains and impatient from the tedium of waiting for a bison herd to pass. Looking to the west, he mistook the distant blue rise of hills to be mountains. Taking out his trusty pencil, he marked this optimistic observation in his logbook: "Tomorrow we may reach distant mountains." Then, upon discovering only large hills-- lacked an eraser.

The truth of the matter is that the hill country had been named "Turtle Mountains" by someone long before the surveyors--but by whom, I haven't been able to learn for sure. Why the hills were referred to as mountains are puzzling enough, but why the humble name, "Turtle?" Perhaps because the hill mounds of the foothills have the profile shape of a turtle? Perhaps because the maps contour outline of the hills resembles the oval carapace of a turtle? Perhaps because the 'mountains' are full of Painted box turtles? Take your pick. Some say that the hills were named by the French explorers or English-speaking people. Supposedly there is a map showing one end of the mountains as the head, the other the tail.

From a logical point of view, what I believe is this: Native Americans have lived there for thousands of years. Indians tend to name places for a unique local feature. The unique feature of the Turtle Mountains is that they were loaded with Painted box turtles, a colorful little creature. I'm guessing that it was the Indians who named it something like... "The Place of Many Turtles." Then came the Metis, people of mixed Indian and European blood. *(More about the Metis later.)* They were the first to explore and occupy the hills to collect furs. They were expert linguists, fluent in French, English, and Native languages. They then translated the native name, and it stuck.

In retrospect, we who once lived there or those who still do should be grateful the name is "Turtle Mountains." The name could have been more aptly descriptive of the true shape, that of a blob of cow manure. For example, if asked where I came from, I would have hated to reply, "Cow Pie Hills," or "Buffalo Chip," North Dakota.

For the pioneers homesteading on the flat prairie surrounding the Turtle Mountains, life was harsher. There was little to stop the blizzard winds except barbed wire fences. There was not the profusion of berry yielding shrubs or readily available wood for fuel or shelter. Nevertheless, the prairie also had a native abundance to support its creatures. Before the steel sod-busting plow, there were waist-high native grasses, myriad wildflowers, varied wild game, and fish in the creeks and rivers. After the plow, the grasses were replaced by grain fields--wildflowers survived only in pastures and fence lines, ponds and sloughs were drained to make more cropland. Rapid runoff from bare fields meant the streams no longer flowed steadily and fish no longer made silver flashes in the shallows. My farm home was on the prairie. Thankfully, the foothills were only a mile and a half east. Not all the land had yet been changed to sterile grain fields, so I grew up with a chance to enjoy the best of both worlds.

People

(Many more people once lived there than live there now.)

It is a pity that so little historical attention has been paid to this area so rich with potential to history buffs. Perhaps it is understandable because the most interesting era occurred before anyone could or would bother to record it. For another thing, no glamorous Indian vs. "White Eyes" wars were fought there.

Long before European immigrants came to Dakota Territory, Native Americans representing a great number of different nations, including evidence of "Mound-builders." Various tribes had held the Turtle Mountains in high esteem, and no wonder. Isolated on the plains, the hill country offered a variety of wild game such as bear, moose, elk, and deer. In the sheltering forest were lakes teeming with fish and fowl. It was hunting grounds worth fighting for. The great amount of finely made flint arrowheads, spear points, and stone war clubs that have been found in the foothills and interior, suggest that not only hunting but hostilities between various Indian nations must have occurred here for centuries.

Henry Klebe, a Turtle Mountain farmer of Germanic heritage, was an eager amateur collector of Indian artifacts. He alone collected enough material to fill a large museum. In the 1930's he had his own museum in a small building on his farm--open on request. The place was packed with everything one could hope to find in the Smithsonian Institution.

He displayed only the best of the flint points. When asked about how many arrowheads he had found – "Don't have room for zem all. In zee back, washtubs full, I got." The fact that they were not all merely hunting points became clear when he would hold to view a human vertebra he had found, with a flint arrowhead still deeply imbedded in the bone. From the position of the arrowhead it had been a gut shot. I recall him saying, "Zat must haff hurt...ya?" A fine storyteller, he related having talked to some very old chiefs and warriors who had informed him of many legends of great battles fought over territorial rights to the area, possibly for a thousand years.

Before "White Eyes" came, the Turtle Mountains were held by the Chippewa and/or a band of Native Americans who called themselves the Midinakwadshiwininwak. *What a wonderful name!* If I understand it correctly, these folks were basically Chippewa, (also called Ojibwa), and Algonquian Indians of the Lake Superior region. Here is a question for an anthropologist: Why were they out here on this forest island on the plains, surrounded by many enemy nations, and three hundred miles from their usual lake and woodland country? Normally, Chippewa are supposed to be handsome, peaceable, forest folks, floating around in birch bark canoes, and inspiring artists to paint Indian maidens at Minnehaha falls. These were the romanticized Indians that inspired moviemakers to have Nelson Eddy sing "Indian Love Call" to Jeanette MacDonald. These were the canoe builders that lived in wickiups and recited inspiring poetry to each other.

The Sioux1[1] warrior, on the other hand, couldn't get sound nights sleep unless he first meditated on a good hell-raising battle. Contrary to the normal easy-going nature of the Chippewa, the people who called themselves the Midinakwadshiwininwak must have been meaner than wolverines and tougher than a soggy willow root. How else could they have maintained supremacy against the hell-raising warring Sioux in their quest to take over the hill country hunting grounds? Tough as they all were--alas, they were no match for European germs.

The first European to report of seeing and passing the Turtle Mountains was Pierre La Verendrye in the year 1738, a French fur trader on an exploratory mission to find and visit a tribe of Indians known as the Mandan[2]. He had heard that they lived in large log and earth lodges; that they practiced agriculture by growing crops native to Central America. This, of course, was true. The Mandan grew nine varieties of corn, (maize) five varieties of squash, as well as pumpkins. These plants are certainly not native to North Dakota. They also cultivated beans, sunflowers, and tobacco. To the south, the Arikara,

---

[1] *No wonder the Sioux were hostile. They called themselves the Dakota or Lakota, meaning friend or ally. Their enemies, the Ojibwa, called them "Natowessiwak," an insulting name meaning snake. The French then corrupted this to, "Nadowessioux" or, "Nadouessioux" which ultimately got shortened to "Sioux."*

[2] *Mandan, possibly a corruption of the Dakota word, Mawatani. Prior to 1837, they had called themselves the Numakakaki. These were not the only Indians of the plains to live in permanent lodges. Almost all the Native Americans had villages, at least permanent to some degree, to where they returned after the hunt. The Mandans had the most elaborate, well-constructed log and earth homes somewhat similar to the hogans of the Navajo, only much larger.*

a Pawnee name corrupted to "Rees" also lived in log and earth homes similar to the Mandan.

There is a possibility Verenrye hadn't visited the Mandans at all, but the Hidatsa on the Souris *(Mouse)* river who had, many decades before, mostly given up their nomadic ways to settle down in the manner of the Mandan and Arikara.

Of great curiosity to those interested in pre-Columbian history is the account of what Verendrye had found on his journey; something very strange and unexplainable to this day. He didn't record the exact location, but said he had found a tall upright rock, a stele, on which was implaced a stone tablet with an engraved epigram in characters he believed to be Tartaric. It could have been Norse runic, which appears similar. Evidently somebody from the Old World had been there long before him. He took the stone back with him. Since he couldn't read it, he sent it to France where it was either ignored or lost. Perhaps in some dusty basement of a French museum there still rests a nondescript stone with a message still waiting to be deciphered.

The Mandan seemed to be of special interest to all of the early explorers, artists, and adventurers. George Catlin and Karl Bodmer, artists who painted pictures of Native Americans, visited them--Bodmer in 1833, Catlin 1834. Their paintings and notations are fine references to the appearance and life of the native people living on the banks of the Missouri.

Generally, all early explorers found them to be a fascinating and handsome people living rather comfortably in a harsh and unforgiving country. Reports that some of them were found to have blue eyes and fair-skinned led to the speculation that there was a bit of European blood in their veins. The sounds of their language and historical lore hinting of stories from the Bible also fanned ideas of European contact. A few years before Lewis and Clark dropped in for a winter's stay in 1804, a Welshman named John Evans had heard the Mandan spoke a language reported to be Welsh and went to visit them[3]. So far I haven't the foggiest idea what he learned and decided, but I doubt none of them had heard of the counties Dyfed, Gwynedd or Clwyd.

---

[3] *Welsh words in the Mandan language? Far-fetched* as *this may seem, here is a germ of possibility not to be scoffed* at--*unless one is a university graduate in anthropology. In which case, anything printed in a textbook after* 1882 *is scoffed* at.

Dr. *Barry Fell, linguist, of the Epigraphic Society of America spent many years collecting* and *translating evidence of Celtic ogams,* an *ingenious form of writing, carved in stone* and *found in various localities across the breadth of North America. According to Fell, Celts were here long before the Vikings on* a *regular trading business for copper. If you can't buy Fell,* how *about Thomas Jefferson? Jefferson, literate in many languages, noted* a *similarity of the Algonquin language to Portuguese. The Algonquins, root of the Cree, Ojibwa, and others,* had a written language *on birch bark. Evidence of the Atakapa Indians, of the lower delta of the Mississippi, speaking words in common with Egyptian* and *Coptic Egyptian is currently being examined by linguists. The Pima of Arizona language* and *legends is very similar to Libyan Arabic. So much for the immigration hypothesis proposed by anthropologists, that prior to contact with Columbus or the Vikings, all the people living in the Americas had come via the Bering Sea land bridge only.*

Another notable person of Canadian history, to set foot in the Turtle Mountains was David Thompson, explorer, geographer, and surveyor for the Northwest Fur Company of Montreal. In November 1797, (a very dumb time of the year to travel in that country) he left MacDonnell's trading post on the junction of the Souris and Assiniboine rivers, to go 200 miles south and visit the Mandan. A howling blizzard was about to wipe out his party when they luckily found shelter in the oak tree forest of the Turtle Mountains.

The trails past the Turtle Mountains, between the Indian Nations on the Missouri and the trading posts in Canada, were well established at least sixty years before Lewis and Clark. One of the trails crossed was later to become the homestead farm of both my grandparents.

It was from the Hudson's Bay Company fur traders of the north that Lewis and Clark obtained rudimentary maps of what was further up the Missouri River to the west. The Turtle Mountains and the many rivers of Canada were known to Europeans more than a hundred years before the Oregon Trail or the homesteaders of the upper Great Plains.

Except for the fur traders and explorers, the first men of part European blood to make contact and live with the indigenous people of the Turtle Mountains were the Metis. For Verendrye to have heard of the Mandans they were obviously there before him. They were the fur trading voyageurs from the lake country of Ontario, Minnesota, and Michigan.

The Metis were of mixed blood; primarily Indian and French, with a scattering of Scot, Swiss, and Irish to spice up the mixture. They were said to be born in, grow up in, and spend their normal lives in canoes. A large number of Metis once lived along the Red River of the North, near Pembina, North Dakota. They constituted a nation onto themselves and ultimately were treated as badly by the governments of Canada and the United States as were the Indians. The rivers of Ontario, Manitoba, and Minnesota were their highways, particularly for the fur trade. They tended to be a volatile lot, on one hand quick to laugh, quick to fight, quick to dance at the sound of a fiddle, on the other, very devout.

Several historical accounts of their physical appearance report that a massive, muscular upper body, due to constant paddling and less developed legs, marked the Metis man. The only walking most of them ever did was on a portage. Having to walk twenty miles from the nearest river or from God-knows-where-else to get to the Turtle Mountains must have made them rather grumpy.

The Metis were skilled linguists, usually able to speak English, French Swiss, and many Native American languages. In general, they didn't keep written notes but did report, casually, at the Pembina trading post, that the Turtle Mountains were heavily populated with Indians, primarily Chippewa.

This was probably the band that preferred to be known as the Midinakwadshiwininwak.

The Metis hunted bison, but respectfully for their own use. Small fur-bearing animals, beaver, otter, mink, etc. was their main quest in the Turtle Mountains to be sold to the Hudson's Bay Co. Bison were only of value primarily as a food source, since the pelts of small animals were more valuable and easily transported. Bison were so plentiful that the supply seemed endless. Perhaps, it was a Metis that wrote a note that I recall reading. In 1949, while doing research on Dakota Indians for a mural that I had been commissioned to do, I found an old unpublished journal in the Minneapolis Public Library. To the best of my ability to recall, the words were to this effect: "...Standing on a hill, on the west side of the high ground, [Turtle Mountains] I looked west to the horizon. It was an awesome sight. As far as I could see, the prairie was black with buffalo slowly moving north... we could smell 'em, apparently so could the damnable mosquitoes because they were gone, gone to the herd..."

To the American Indians of the plains the importance of the bison was quite another matter. They held the bison herds as being a sacred gift from the Great Spirit Creator. No wonder, to them the plentiful bison was a primary source of food, clothing, and shelter. Then sadly, to Dakota Territory came the commercial buffalo hunters. Vast as the herds once were, buffalo hunters, in a relatively short time slaughtered the herds to the brink of total extinction. With wanton disregard, spurred by a deliberate, sadistic, intention supported by the US government to starve the Indians, the buffalo hunters took only the hides, leaving the carcasses to rot away.

The vehicle for hauling the hides was a two-wheeled vehicle, known as a Red River Oxcart. Lacking metal parts, it had a wooden axle, rimless wooden wheels, and hub. It was made of the toughest slow growth oak that could be found. At first, the drivers had applied grease to the hubs, only to find that sand and dirt stuck in the grease and ground the bearings into sawdust. Omitting the grease solved one problem, but created another. That of sound! The dry wood rubbing against wood made it a devilish earsplitting device. The moving cart produced a squealing, shrieking noise that could knock a flock of ducks out of the air at a half mile. A heavy metal, amplified rock and roll band of today, couldn't match the terrible din. Deafened by noise, to cross-eyed stupefaction, bison would be easy prey to a buffalo hunter's rifle. — Well, OK, a little hyperbole.

After the buffalo hunters came the bone gatherers. Bison bones had industrial value back east. Many old photos show bison-bone mountains waiting to be shipped out. How many bison had there been? No one will ever know. By the time I was growing up, bison bones could rarely be found. Once in a while, someone would find a bison skull preserved by mud in some creek bottom or spring, but that was all.

Pierre Bottineau, "Dean of the Guides," a highly regarded hunter and guide, for whom the town is named, was a Metis. He had been born in Manitoba in about the year 1810. His knowledge of the vast region and hunting skills proved very valuable to many expeditions, government or otherwise.

The locals pronounce Bottineau as a short "Bahtno." Some might prefer to hear the melodious spoken sound of "Bahty-no." This might sound "Frenchy" but why not? We should be grateful. Just imagine the difficulty we would have if the band of Midinwakwadshiwininwak had named that 1880 white settler's village on Oak Creek?

Final Curtain for the Indians

Sometime, after Verendrye's visit, after the Metis were mostly gone, the Midinakwadshiwininwak were gone. In 1837, from a cargo of blankets brought on the steamboat *St. Peter,* the Mandan caught the white man's disease, small pox, for which they had no resistance. It was a horrible way to die. Many committed suicide or men killed their loved ones to end the suffering. The Mandan, Arikara, and Hidasta were almost totally wiped out. Only the Native Americans that lived in small separated remote bands were spared.

Lacking reliable historical accounts, it isn't certain where, when, or how the local bands in the Turtle Mountains caught smallpox, (or the measles, which was almost as deadly to Indians), but in one year they were essentially finished. According to one report, from one band of four hundred there remained but ten people.

By the time the European homesteading immigrants arrived there were not enough Indians left to resist any invader. Colonel George Armstrong Custer might have argued that point, but the Siouan Indians he encountered were now farther west. The American Indians of the Turtle Mountains could offer no resistance.

The first settlers to the area were primarily Scotch, English, French, followed later by Scandinavian, and German people. As for the original people, they were supposed to have been allotted a large area of prairie mountain land to continue their way of life. Instead, with the standard practice of promises and treaty breaking by the government, the Chippewa were confined to a very small area of non-farmable land in the Turtle Mountains for their reservation. In a land where a quarter section, 160 acres of good soil was the minimum to support a family, the Indians were told they had to get along with about 15 acres of miserable rocky land per person. The food, which the government had been promised, 'somehow' never got there. Terrible starvation followed, decimating the tribe. A wilderness priest, Father Belcourt, desperately tried to intercede on behalf of the Indians but his entreaties to the great white fathers in our nation's capital were ignored. A terrible period of starvation reduced Indian families to a pitiful few. Sadly, the plight of the people on this Chippewa reservation was shamefully ignored. Privation and starvation was the lot of those people.

As for the Midinakwadshiwininwak, about the only lasting heritage of these Native Americans is that they probably were responsible for naming what is now a popular resort lake, "Metigoshe Washegum." (spellings vary) The name translates as "Clear water surrounded by oak trees." It is now known simply as Lake Metigoshe.

Archaeologists or anthropologists have never bothered to extensively explore the history of this remote hill country on the prairie. After his death, Henry Klebe's wonderful collection was scattered. Part of it is now in a museum in Rugby, N.D. The rest of it?

Because the shape and quality of arrowheads can yield information as to the Indian groups that made them, and roughly when they were made, it is a shame that records weren't kept as to where they were found. Even today, arrowheads, spear points, and stone club heads can still be found in the countryside by a diligent searcher.

Now

The area has changed very much from when Verendrye, Thompson, or the fur traders saw it. Instead of a prairie of tall waving grasses stretching to the horizon or passing bison herds, grain fields and summer fallow now reach endlessly. In the Turtle Mountains, much of the land is farmed. The original dense forest is gone. A forest fire in 1886 destroyed most of it. Some of the few old trees to escape the fire are on Masonic Island in Lake Metigoshe. One was supposedly core-drilled and the age found to exceed 800 years. Of the new growth timber following the fire, much has been lost either as firewood or simply cleared out. Yet, there are places which still remain of quiet ponds and rustling aspen to sooth the troubled soul. For the person wanting to get in touch with simple wildness, many "Walden Ponds" can yet be found to please a modem day Thoreau.

It was into this place that my grandparents came rumbling in their covered wagons in the eighteen eighties. In the wagons were the children that were to become my mother and father. My mother's parents came that year following the forest fire that had swept through the Turtle Mountains leaving a desolate landscape of smoldering stumps. My father and his parents came a year or so later. Despite the burned-out desolation, here the pioneers homesteaded and broke the prairie sod, a grass-bound black soil enriched by loam-building centuries. The waist-high native grasses were eventually displaced by waving crops of grain. Except for a patch of prairie flowers or a grove of aspen, almost all the original wilderness was gone when I was born. I came barely in time to see the end of everything and the beginning of everything.

The adventurous tourist who enjoys traveling some trails less traveled may find it rewarding to leave the interstate to visit the little spot marked "Turtle Mountains."

For map lovers I have included a map of sorts. Many of the small towns and villages that existed in 1922 are gone or diminished to a few remaining homes.

There is something I left out. If I were to mention that in addition to the once thriving villages of Souris and Carbury in North Dakota, there is also a Souris and Carberry across the border in Manitoba, Canada. If I were to write that the Souris River was called the Mouse River once it entered North Dakota and then renamed the Souris again when it returned to Canada, it would perhaps confuse things. Therefore I won't mention it.

THE CAST

Once vibrantly alive, the people in this collection of stories are dead, except for me, and perhaps one or two others. Only my memory can bring them to life again. Long ago, they were part of a unique community of people in an area hardly anyone has ever heard of. The soil of the land is still there, but everything else has changed.

To quickly get acquainted with the main characters involved in these tales, these few pages are offered. Once the players are known, perhaps the stories will be easier to follow.

ONCE IN THE MIDDLE OF NOWHERE

The place, known as the Turtle Mountain area of North Dakota, has changed; the spirit of the special time of the nineteen-thirties can never be repeated. Nearly all of the people who lived this time are gone. The only way the time and place can be revisited will be by stories told by those who observed the events. Written material of the human side of the period is scant. We must depend on the memory of those who once lived there, and now they are scant too.

If this were a novel, the physical and psychological characteristic of the characters could be developed as the story went on its merry way. This collection of true tales is meant to be such that the stories do not need to be read in sequence--a start anywhere book--therefore I will resort to a straight forward, brief description of the main participants.

Reading about someone else's family is usually boring. These stories are about a place and its <u>people, not a specific family</u>. However, since my parents provided me with the nest from which to observe, they will now serve as once living subjects to hang my stories on. I could not avoid employing them in the cast. Besides, the names "Jake and Lena" are so fitting that if this were a novel they would need to be invented.

My mother was 39 and my father 41 when I was born. I was an October surprise. The year was 1922.

Lena, (Pauline) Short Description:

My mother: depending on my age I called her Mama, Ma, Mom--sometimes "Lena" just like everybody else. Short (5'2"), 120 lbs. Brown hair, workaholic and spunky. She was a wee bit cross-eyed. Talkative, loaded with nervous energy, and opinions.

Lena, Longer Description:

Everybody called her Lena, even I frequently did. Otherwise I called her "Mama" until I was about nine, then I switched to "Ma." When I was about fourteen, my oldest sister, Evelyn, told me that "Ma was country-hick talk" and told me to use the term "Mom," like city boys would.

Pauline Krogen, (no middle name) was born March 1885, to Norwegian immigrants in Starbuck Minnesota. She, at little more than the age of one, came to North Dakota as the youngest passenger in a covered wagon. It must have been an impressive journey for she claimed to remember some of it, particularly when she reached for some pebbles in the bottom of a brook and fell in. Her sister, Josie, had fished her out.

Five feet two inches tall and weighing about a hundred and twenty pounds, Lena was a stewpot of nervous energy. She was spunky, opinionated, and more outspoken than her small size should have deemed prudent. She hated cooking and housework but liked to work outdoors in the fields. Her greatest lament was her gender. "If only I could have been a man ...I would do nothing but work outside if I were a man, I would beat the '–' out of that lazy, overgrown '–' ...I would shake some sense into," etc.

Despite having only a third grade education, she was an avid reader of the newspapers, could debate political issues, and frequently would, with any willing listener. (Willing listener does not describe my father.) Lena was somewhat vain about her looks, when her hair started turning gray she dyed her hair dark brown up until the time of her death at the age of eighty-five. She was careful not to look someone straight in the eye, especially strangers; to avoid it being noticed that her left eye was a little crossed. When being photographed, she would turn to one side, presenting a profile view only.

Musically gifted, Lena was church organist at the Turtle Mountain Lutheran Church for thirty years. In this respect, among a host of others, she and my father, Jake, were incompatible. He sang quite often, always off-key. Never once was the tune recognizable. This drove my mother bonkers. It drove everybody bonkers.

Supposedly, every boy loves his mother, so it may prove difficult to be objective, but I'll try my best. She was a courageous woman, optimistic, and but for her I would never have been educated beyond grade school. The most negative comment I can make about her is that she scared the hell out of me when it came to the subject of girl friends. She might have been right about that.

Lena was quick of motion, but slow to catch on to a joke. Enter now her opposite, a person slow of motion, but quick of wit--Jake, her husband.

Jake, (John Jacob) Short Description:

My father: short and wiry thin (5'4") 145 lbs.; weather-beaten, wrinkled, big rough hands. He walked slowly, talked slowly. Never ate anything that I can recall. Never laughed out loud, only chuckled. Loved animals, children, and a glass of beer. He was a gentleperson.

Jake, Longer Description:

John Jacob Olson (Jake) was born in June 1881, in Thorsby, Varmland, Sweden. He remembered coming with his parents on a sailing ship, a cattle ship converted to carrying immigrants. He was seven years old. The seas were rough on the whole voyage, every passenger was sick except himself and a few other children. One day, the foul air of sickness below deck caused Jake to seek the fresh air topside, despite the crew orders not to. He found his way to the wind-lashed deck. Leaning over the leeside rail, he was intently watching the spray and spume of the wind-driven sea, when a sailor saw him. To scare the boy and thereby prevent further foolhardiness, the sailor seized the lad by the seat of his pants and extended him over the rail and over the churning water, with a threat to drop him to the sharks. The scare worked. Jake didn't do it again.

In Sweden, at a very early age Jake had learned to walk on his hands. He would soon learn that this rare skill would serve him well in his new homeland. One day, he discovered an encampment of Indians near a creek, some distance north of his parents sod house. He could see within the circle of tepees, children playing and laughing. The idea occurred to him that a visit might be fun; even more fun, he thought, if he were to come walking into the circle on his hands.

If modern day gymnasts score a perfect 10, it is the equivalent of what my father-to-be scored with the Indians. As he related the story to me, the children and adults alike were at first confused and almost frightened at the bizarre appearance of a little boy walking upside down into their camp. Then, they broke out into rollicking, rolling-on-the-ground laughter. Soon, all the Indian children and some of the younger men were trying to learn this unusual trick. The little 'paleface' was hero of the day. He was treated to a snack, probably pemmican. Very few Indians spoke Swedish and Jake couldn't speak much English, even less Ojibwa, Sioux, or make signs. Normal communication was out. However, the elder Indians somehow made it clear that they were moving on in the morning. As Jake started to leave for home, one Indian restrained him for a moment. Then the immigrant farm boy was given presents to take home, consisting of a small bag of .50 lead balls and a tiny leather pouch of something unidentifiable, which by hand-sign indications, was very important (probably a good medicine token.) Little Jake had scored with simple gymnastics.

Why did I go into this long discourse when I'm supposed to be describing my father? Well, I think I did describe my father. His outward appearance--baggy overalls, worn shirt, frayed straw hat, wrinkled face, his slow, long-step walk, his ever present pipe, were poor indicators of the real quality of this gentle man who should have been a veterinarian, not a farmer. Lena was impatient with his slowness, and disinterest in world affairs. One of the very few compliments my mother ever had to say about her husband was given as she washed his back in the Saturday-night washtub. "Look at your Pa, beautiful body, not one blemish, hard muscles, but I wish he would eat better." When he died, at the age of 72, from a heart attack, Lena was greatly embarrassed when the doctor informed her that malnutrition had aggravated his condition. It really wasn't her fault. Jake hated eating. She was a good cook, even though she hated cooking.

Uncle Carl, Short Description:

Uncle Carl was 5'6" and strong as an ox. He laughed loudly at every joke. He became my second father when at my age of three, his wife died in childbirth and my parents offered him a place to stay to recover from his sorrow. He died at the age of 82 in my home in Seattle.

Uncle Carl, Longer Description:

Carl Ludvig Olson, born on the farm in America. Because he was the youngest boy, he was expected to remain on his parent's farm to work it. As a young man, he worked almost at slave status on the farm in the foothills. The compensating joy in his life was his INDIAN motorcycle and later, his SAXON automobile. To enjoy some measure of freedom from his parents, he moved into the Garden place, which abutted the home farm. This house he shared with some other young bachelors.

In the first year of their marriage, when the young women that Carl had lost his heart to miscarried and died, Carl was devastated and blamed himself for her death. Jake and Lena, concerned that he might do harm to himself, convinced him to stay at our home until he felt better. Thus, at the age of three, I acquired a second 'father'. He never dated another woman again. He stayed at my folk's farm the rest of his life, even after Jake and Lena were dead.

Carl was physically very strong, loved hunting, and fishing. He liked people, enjoyed sharing jokes and laughed loudly and often. He would discipline me when I deserved it. He established clear boundaries of behavior for me as a child. Whenever he was near, I felt secure and loved.

Many years later, when he was eighty-two years old, he came to visit my home in Seattle and to have some minor surgery. After the surgery everything seemed fine, but three days later as I went to awaken him from his nap, I found that he had died in his sleep. Part of me died that day too.

One odd thing about both Carl and Jake is that both cheated "Father Time" when it came to eyesight. Eye doctors have informed me that it is impossible to avoid the need of glasses when one gets older. Neither Carl nor Dad ever wore corrective eyeglasses. Carl could do crossword puzzles without glasses. His hunting friends were amazed at his ability to see game even when he was in his eighties. Oh, he had hunting glasses alright; I still have them--clear yellow glass with no correction.

Luella, Short Description:

My sister: eleven years older than me. Born in time for the flapper age. Brunette with spit curls. Short-5'0", Romantic, emotional, dramatic, good singing voice. A real pain to her little brother.

Luella, Longer Description:

Luella Karoline: Born May 1912, 5'0", 120 lbs., brown hair. After I was nine years old she wasn't home very often, nor did she stay long. We, like a lot of brothers and sisters, were usually at odds with one another. At every opportunity to sneak away from housework or other duties she would avidly read and reread love stories in the dime romance magazines. I hated them. She liked only popular music, so I decided to tune in Texaco's Saturday opera program just to drive her nuts. She liked to ride horses. I thought horses were stupid. She liked to go to dances. I thought dancing was a dumb way for grown-ups to act. She was a schoolteacher. I hated school. Local boys thought her to be a cute little number. I thought, "what...her? She treated me like her dear, sweet, little brother. I hated it.

Evelyn, a tolerable no-nonsense Sister:

Eva, 5'4", smart, tough, good looking, married to Arnold Wunderlich. They lived on a farm three miles away in the foothills. When I was there for a visit she worked at the difficult task to take the rough edges off of me (or anyone else who she thought deserved it.) She never babied me. I liked that. Thanks Eva.

Arnold, Brother in Law:

Arnold, a handsome guy with black hair, brown eyes, medium height, hailed from Minnesota. He first came to our farm as a farm hand. Athletic, a good ball player, swimmer, and a dude who dressed well. Good-natured and a capable farmer, it was natural that Eva would fall for him. It was a great marriage to the end.

Gene, Nephew, Offspring of above:

Mature beyond his years, Gene was only five years younger than me but generally far more responsible, he was the kind of a kid that would carry in wood from the woodpile without being told to do so. Plumb unnatural. Smart in school.

Myself:

John J. Jr. Called "Jackie." Average blond kid. Dumb in school.

Others:

It didn't seem unusual to me at the time, but I should have been rather confused by the names of relatives. I had two Aunt Ann's, Ann Woods and Ann Moody, two Aunt Selmas, Selma Moum and Selma Norell, and two Uncle Carls, Carl Olson and Carl Krogen. Of course, in the days of big families, there were other normally singular named aunts and uncles and all their children.

Also mentioned will be friends and neighbors--people who won't need any special description to get started with the stories. Looking back I now realize how wonderful they were. If I were to list all that played a role, I'd discover that I left out at least one important person, so I'll leave a big bunch out.

By the way, my mother and father sometimes had 'racial' arguments about the merits of Swedes vs. Norwegians. It was just a holdover from parentally installed traditional prejudice. My father was Swedish. To the Norwegian parents of my mother this was akin to being a leper, in fact, being a Swede was almost as undesirable as being Irish. Therefore their courtship had been a Romeo and Juliet situation. So, Jake and Lena eloped to Minneapolis. On June 6, 1906 they were married. I want to believe they had a good time while they were there. The going wouldn't be easy for such a 'mixed marriage' upon coming home. Luckily, my Swedish grandparents were far more tolerant.

ON DISCOVERING THE WORLD

As an eyewitness describing the scenic remnants of the virgin frontier of the Dakotas I must go back as far as it is possible for my memory to bring into focus. The first experience I can remember occurred before my second birthday. In 1924, there were only a few little scraps of unaltered prairie or forest remaining; a pond here, a spring there, or a copse of aspen. Several images retained from childhood involve a meadow and the process of haying with horse-drawn equipment.

Through my eyes and ears coupled with my memory we can go back and have a look at a place now changed and people long gone. I will begin with the first image I can bring into focus.

On October 24, 1922, in Aunt Ann Wood's home in Bottineau I got myself born. Getting born must be easy. I did it and I was only a baby. Frankly, I don't remember the event. Early memories are limited. The artist Salvador Dali once wrote a chapter about his prenatal memories. Either he was stretching a story somewhat or I am a dullard. The earliest event I can recall with clarity probably took place when I was twenty months old--haying season in a meadow.

(A note: Except for talking to strangers, local dialect Scandinavian was the at-home language of my childhood, until I started school.)

Haying Time

Obviously I didn't know the names of all the things herein described at the time. I just remember the sights, as things to be named later.

My mother has spread a thick gray blanket, in the shade of a clump of willows, at the edge of the meadow. She places me on it and removes the tiny walking shoes, my first, to leave me barefooted. This way I won't be tempted to toddle far in the stickery spears of mown stubble hay. Mama then places the wicker lunch basket and straw filled box at the base of the willows. As I am to learn later when I'm old enough to understand, straw packed under, around, and over the coffeepot will keep it reasonably warm until noon.

In the glaring sunlit meadow, Papa is hitching the horses to the multitined hayrack with the large diameter metal wheels. A short distance away rises the ravined foothills of the Turtle Mountains. Trees fill the bottoms of the ravines. Tannish green grasses cover the rolling hills between. Mama goes to help my father with the business of haying, a process unknown to me. She is wearing what I will come to know as her favorite working attire--a white cotton jacket over overalls and a white dishtowel formed into a hood-like bonnet on her head.

Windrows of hay have previously been made for dry curing a few days ago. They now lie in scented ranks on the stubble grass of the meadow. Mama climbs up and sits on the perforated metal seat of the hayrack. It will be her job to drive the horses and gather the windrows one by one to where Papa is standing. Jamming his pitchfork upright in the middle of the meadow, he says only two words to Mama – "Lena, here!" Two words apparently constitute sufficient information. She drives the team to the first windrow. At the end of the row she actuates the trip-lever which drops the curving spring-tines into gathering position. The steel tines hit the ground--ching! A chorus of metallic sound.

Lena gathers and drags the first windrow of hay to where Jake is standing. She then presses the foot pedal, which raises the tines. Again--chinngg! This time the pleasing sound lasts a moment longer. After a few more dumps, Papa starts building what will be the haystack bottom. He packs the hay down by tramping on it. I continue to watch as the haystack grows, but my attention span eventually plays out. It is warm. Sunspots filtering through the willow leaves perform a dance on my blanket every time the gentle wind nudges the leaves above. The occasional chinng reassures me that my parents haven't wandered away. This sweet smelling bright world is safe and secure.

Mama awakens me--it is lunchtime. I discover that I've been covered with the free part of the blanket. Papa sits next to me under the willows and lights his pipe. Mama then opens the basket holding the sandwiches and chicken drumsticks. For me there is milk, for my parents, coffee. My first picnic.

Mama and Papa go back to work. The haystack is a lot higher now.

"Jake," as my mama calls him, has pulled the hayrack next to the stack so he can climb on top of it. He first pitches the hay on the stack then he climbs on top, spreads the hay just so, and packs it down by tramping on it. The stack is taking shape like an emerging mushroom. When I've watched long enough to get the idea of what is going on, I become bored and restless. It is time to escape the blanket, shoes, or no shoes. Added to the sounds of insects, I hear a wonderful tinkling sound coming from a patch of weeds and rushes.

Leaving the blanket, I find that by watching where I put my feet that I can walk without too much discomfort. Soon the grass is tall, soft, and mixed with weeds and wildflowers. Then I discover the tiny rill making water-music. It is coming from a small spring surrounded by low bushes. The water in the spring is like a flawed mirror, its surface broken only by the dents made by the feet of water-skimmers. Underneath the surface, popeyed tadpoles and other wiggly things. I have discovered a heaven of things to play with.

The tadpoles fascinate me. I want to hold one in my hand. By lying on the very edge of the damp bank I reach for one but it doesn't want to be held, it scoots away--perhaps if I walk into the water I can get closer. I step in and the mud under the surface feels cool. The next step and my foot sinks down deep into ooze. In pulling my sinking foot out, I fall backwards and find myself sitting in mud and water. The surprise over, it doesn't feel too bad at that. In fact it feels very good. Mama won't let me splash in the washtub. Here I can splash to my heart's content. "Take that, you uncooperative little creatures!" Suddenly, I become aware that Mama is running toward my friends and me.

"Jackie! Neimen! What are you doing!" Mama is scolding me as she hurriedly yanks me out of the water. Why should she be so upset when I was only having such a great time? How can I tell her that I was just trying to catch a tadpole, when I don't even know the name of it yet?

The spring dried up when the years of the Dust Bowl came. The meadow disappeared sometime after World War II. It is now a grain field with no hint that a spring, willows, wildflowers or meadow was ever there.

Tornado

First impressions can be very lasting. The first tornado I witnessed made a very profound impression indeed. Because Uncle Carl hadn't come to live with us yet, I deduce that I was about three years old.

Even as a child, I can sense that suddenly something in our house is badly amiss. The mood of my parents has changed to one of imminent danger. I don't know what is occurring--but I sense that something terrible is about to happen. It has to do with the unfamiliar word "cyclone!" that Mama shouts to Papa. "Let's go under the bridge." *(Then folks called tornadoes, cyclones.)* Since I am too small to run fast, Papa picks me up and runs outside. Mama is hurrying him along.

My mother and father are running down the road toward the creek. It is a strange experience. I have never been carried by anyone running before. The sky overhead is very dark. Just below the massive dark cloud, a strange greenish, cylindrical cloud is moving like a steamroller horizontally, north to south.

Mama frets, *(talking Norwegian)* "I hope the Backmans have seen this coming in time." She is concerned about my older sister, Luella, who is visiting there. My parents wade quickly through the water into the protective shelter of the small wooden bridge. "This must really be serious," I think… "They didn't even stop to take their shoes off."

Papa and Mama are now standing under the bridge in knee-deep water. The south opening of the bridge is a big rectangle, framing the scene of the ominous cloud outside and overhead. The roll cloud has passed leaving a lull in the wind. With me held firmly in his arms, Papa wades to have a closer look at what is going on. The cloud above is a dark greenish gray and changes to dark blue-gray at the horizon that is if we could see the horizon. We can't. Only the gurgling water of the creek we are standing in seems darker.

There it is!--the thing that Papa and Mama are worried about. A huge gray-white snake is writhing from the cloud to the ground. Where it touches the ground, things jump and swirl into the air. A flash of sheet lightning behind the strange form momentarily turns it into a dark, ominous, slimly tapered, and twisted column of mysterious power. Unlike the loud rumble of thunder it doesn't make a loud noise--just a steady hissing sound.

"Where's it going?" asks Mama.

"Too early to tell," says Papa

The flood plain of our creek is little more than a hundred yards wide bordered by a bank of low hills on either side. The snake of fury comes down the west hillside. It comes on across the flat part to a bend in the creek where the water is deep. Momentarily there is a white puff of spray as the snake touches the water. It continues eastward, along the shallow ravine on a course for the barn.

"Where's it going?" asks Mama, knowing as much as Papa does.

"Might hit the barn," says Papa, knowing as much as Mama does.

I don't know anything but watch in fascination.

The voracious tube is making a snake trail up the hillside toward the barn. It barely misses the pig house and continues on its threatening course. At the last moment it swerves southwards towards the well and small milk house where the cream separator is. We can't see this little building from where we are standing under the bridge so my father wades out for a better view. We get to where we can watch just in time to see the milk house exploding into the air. Boards fall from the air like fluttering autumn leaves.

"It missed the barn," says Papa in Swedish.

"Blessed God," says Mama in Norwegian.

I don't remember the walk back to our house, but I do remember the relief my parents voiced of having such a close call and losing nothing but the small building and a few milk pails.

A few years later, the folks are talking about a recent tornado destroying a local barn. This reminds me of the incident of the tornado at our place so I ask my dad about it. Considering my age at the time, he is very surprised that I can recall visual details of the encounter with the tornado. My memory seems to be better than his are except he tells one interesting detail that I didn't know about:

"Edvin Gustafson found one of our milk pails in his pasture," said Pa.

It had been hung with the others in the milk house. Gustafson's place is over two miles away, east in the Turtle Mountains.

Very Strange Behavior

At the age of four and a half I am treated to an unforgettable adventure and witness a bizarre event which is somehow involved with my sister Evelyn getting married to Arnold.

Mama hasn't been acting normal for a couple days. Last night she put a lot of stuff in Papa's car. This morning she got me out of bed when the sun was just barely lighting the side of the milk house. She dressed me in going-to-town clothes, so I asked if we were going to visit Grandma in Bottineau or going to

Souris. "We're going on a long trip to a place near Brainerd, Minnesota," she answered.

"Where's that?" I wondered.

"Many miles southeast from here," she replied.

I didn't need any more information than that--it would be far, so I would simply keep track of where we went.

After hours of driving on a graveled highway, it was obvious that Minnesota was a far greater distance than I had expected. On the way I had kept asking, "What's the name of this town? How much farther to go?" It wasn't just me bothering Papa. So often Mama told Papa that she had to stop for coffee in the next town that he finally said that we would never get there before sundown unless she could hold off a while. There were toilet stops too.

Late in the afternoon we were in Minnesota and now there were more and more evergreens. As the sun got even lower, Papa said we didn't have much farther to go. He also said that we would have to stop and ask somebody how to get to Star Lake because the map didn't show little country roads.

It was sundown when we came to the Wunderlich place on the northeast shore of the lake. This would be easy for me to remember because it was the first sundown I had ever seen reflecting on the surface of a lake. People came out of the house and everybody was smiling and asking questions in English. A smiling lady reached down and shook my hand.

"So this is Jackie – how are you Jackie?"

"Hungry."

"Well, we'll fix that, won't we?" and she did. Somebody also put me to bed long before I wanted to go.

The next morning, a tall young man named Arnold, the person that my sister Eva was somehow linked with, asked if I would like to see a big hunting lodge that his father had been building for some rich guy. Since I had no idea what a hunting lodge was, I was eager to see it. The lodge was only a long walk down the beach. When I first saw it I was surprised. It was a huge building made of logs. I thought it odd that a rich guy couldn't afford lumber like the folk's back home. We walked up the steps of the big porch and went inside.

"This is going to be the dining hall. It isn't quite finished yet," said my new friend Arnold. "Here, look at this." He put his hand on a boat. It was pointed at both ends and rested upside down on two sawhorses. "This is a real birch bark Indian canoe – it's a very old one but it's still in good shape – it's going to be kept in a special boathouse." The canoe impressed me, but not as much as the next thing he showed me.

We had walked to the wall on the right-hand side of the fireplace. The wall had big empty bookshelves separated by what looked like a skinny floor-tobeamed ceiling closet, with a little paneled door about waist-high. Arnold opened the door. There seemed to be nothing inside except a bell rope to one side. Outside hung a tasseled cord dangling from a brass fixture.

"This is a 'dumbwaiter'," he explained. "When everybody at the table is ready for dinner, the real waiter pulls on this cord. The cook downstairs then loads the food onto the dumbwaiter tray and pulls another cord to let the waiter know the food is ready to go. Then the waiter pulls down on this rope that goes over a pulley and hoists the food up to this floor. Then he takes out the grub and serves the table."

At first I thought, "What a fun idea." Then I thought more about it and decided that this rich whoever person, wasn't a very nice man. "Here he is, up in this fancy big dining room and his poor wife is down in the cellar cooking for him and his friends. She at least ought to have her kitchen next to the dining room like decent people who treat their wives better."

Whatever happened after our visit to the lodge, I can't recall but I do remember that for some reason my parents left the next day for Duluth. At Duluth I see big buildings and a crazy looking streetcar that went up a very steep incline to the top of the hill and then down again. There is a steel bridge built between huge towers that can be raised to let ships pass. In the neighboring town of Superior, we visit a girl named Genevieve, who I am told is Eva's close friend. Visiting is boring, but a super treat occurs when I get to go to a movie and see an animated cartoon starring Felix the Cat.

On the way back to North Dakota, we stop at the monstrous man-made ore pit in the Mesabi iron range. The puffing steam shovels loading iron ore fascinate me. From the rim high above the bottom of the crater, they look smaller than toys on the bottom of the crater.

It seems that the excitement of this journey will never end. As we approach the outskirts of Thief River Falls, Minnesota, Mama says that the smoke column we see isn't a bonfire. Papa agrees and says a building is on fire. He then drives faster than he ever has before or ever will again. We turn up a street and at the top of a small rise we can see that a house is burning. Papa stops close to the house and hurries out of the car. There aren't a lot of people there yet, just a few milling around in the street as if they didn't know what to do. He asks someone if the fire department has been called. The answer is **ya, ya.**

It is a pretty gray-green house with white trim, and fancy woodwork around the porch and near the peak of the gabled roof. Fire is pouring out of the window near the peak and is now burning the pretty scroll work. That makes me very sad. We don't have decorated stuff like that on our house. The fire is getting worse. Papa is helping to carry furniture out of the house, and is still at it, when the firemen come in a big truck and start pulling hoses out. They yell at Mama to move the car. She says she can't drive. A fireman comes into our car and backs it away just as Papa is coming back from the house. Papa now gets in the car and says we might as well continue on our way home. We are just in the way here.

All the way back I worry if the firemen could have saved the rest of that house. Then I start worrying that our own house might have had a fire while we were gone and we don't have firemen to save it. We get back late at night and I'm very glad to see our house is still there, safe and sound.

A few days later Eva and this new person, Arnold, show up at our farm. I ask Mama how come Arnold is along because it isn't harvest time. Mama tells me that Eva and Arnold are married now. I'm not sure what that means but I get the idea that she isn't my sister anymore. Mama says they will be staying only for a day or so. They will be sleeping in the bedroom where Mama and Papa normally sleep. Mama and Papa will use the milk house, which is also kind of an emergency bunkhouse.

The next morning, I woke up late and started to get out of bed when I saw something through the bedroom door of Mama's room. I saw something so strange, I knew I'd never get over it. Eva and this Arnold person were standing together with their arms tight around each other. They were next to the big white wicker rocking chair. She was in a pretty dress the color of the keys on our piano. He was wearing white pants, white shirt, and a cream-colored V-neck sweater without sleeves. They were studying each other's faces, yet somehow not finding anything. Then they put their mouths together. Their mouths together! They were kissing, but I didn't know about kissing then. I had never seen anyone kiss before. All I knew were those two grown-ups were doing something very disgusting and unsanitary, but it must be OK because they both seemed pleased about it.

Before they could catch me having seen them, I ducked under the covers and pretended to be asleep. After I heard them go downstairs I got up and went down too. The image of them doing that was very puzzling and I wanted to ask mama about it. I made up my mind that I wouldn't tell Mama what I had seen. It wasn't any of my business and so it wouldn't be any of hers either. Something about it made me feel I had intruded on a very private matter, a matter connected in some way to this business of being married. I decided I would never tell anybody and I haven't until just now as I write this.

It wasn't until I was much older and in high school, and had changed my attitude about young ladies, that I fully understood the strange behavior that I witnessed that summer morning.

SEX AND DIRTY WORDS

    This business of sex and other bodily functions has been going on for a long time. Because of animals, farm children get their introduction to the reality of it all early in life. Perhaps my discovery may have been a little different from others. I hope so.

    If you don't like 'dirty words,' skip this story.

'F--,' 'S--,' 'P--.' Aha, Aha! If you filled in the missing letters, you obviously already know the words, but do you know why they are considered dirty words? Continental snobbery, that's why. Fornicate, defecate, and urinate are acceptable words. Even preachers and TV evangelists use them on occasion. That seems to be OK, they almost make the words sound cultured, sophisticated. That's the whole point in a nutshell. Those words, which mean exactly the same thing, are CONTINENTAL words. F--, S--, P--, are ANGLO-SAXON words used by lowbrow, inferior Anglo-Saxon people. Well, I think the Anglo-Saxon words are handier, more useful. Fornicate you!...doesn't seem to be very effective. Oh defecate! Sounds dumb. I'm urinated off! doesn't convey the level of anger I may feel. If you don't mind, I'll spell the Anglo-Saxon words out to tell this short tale.

At the ripe old age of almost six years I learned the meaning of the word 'f---.' I had heard the word before many times, but didn't know its meaning. It seemed to be a handy, expressive word used by hired hands, older boys, and joke tellers. "Where's that f---ing hammer?" "What the f--- are you up to?" "I don't give a f---." It seemed to be a general-purpose word covering many situations. Somehow I knew, felt, that I shouldn't use that word in front of my parents. I would have to wait for the proper moment to demonstrate my expanded, enriched vocabulary.

The folks needed to make a trip to Souris, and of course, I went along. While they went on their errands, I had been left at the Moody's. Victor Moody was married to my Aunt Anna. They lived upstairs over the restaurant they owned. They had two sons and one daughter much older than I. They also had one son, Virgil only two years older. It was Virgil who educated me. Good old cousin, Virgil.

When I was dropped off to play with Virgil, I was told he was out in the back lot playing with some town boys. Always a little nervous at meeting new boys, I decided to employ some bravado by using that handy word. Coming to the group of boys shooting marbles, I boldly said: "What the f---ity-f--- are you fellas up to?" The boys at first looked a bit startled and then, started to roll on the ground laughing. Virgil then came up to me and asked: "What did you say?" I slowly repeated what I had said. "How old are you?" he asked. "Six and a half" I replied. "Don't you know the meaning of that word?" "What word?" I said somewhat hesitantly. "F---" said the grinning Virgil. I replied, "Guess not," shamed at my ignorance. "F--- is – F--- is like – F--- a lady. – You know, like bulls f--- cows." The revelation was overpowering. Until then it hadn't occurred to me how I happened to get born. People were no different than animals! They did 'breeding' too! Feeling really embarrassed, nauseated, stupid, I just stood around while the boys went back to their game of marbles. I had to seriously give this business of f---ing a lot of thought.

On the farm, I remembered the event when my folks rented a purebred bull from somewhere to breed the cows that were in heat. The whole process seemed strange and disgusting. Strange, because the bull snorted and dug up some ground with his hooves, and acted very intense about whatever he was going to do. Then a revolting thing happened. When the cow urinated, he sniffed her urine. Then, coming up behind the unsuspecting cow, he mounted her. His skinny, long penis slid out from somewhere and he stuck it into the poor cow. I was surprised a sword like that didn't kill it. All the while my stupid folks just stood there, unconcerned. Finally I came to the conclusion that this was normal, part of the breeding act, how a calf gets planted.

The same thing had to be true about horses, pigs, and chickens. Chickens?! So that's what the rooster was doing--all that running after a fleeing hen. When the rooster jumped on top of the hen and grabbed her by the back of the neck, I had thought he was just being a bully, or punishing the hen for doing something that irritated him. "Wait a minute – chickens lay eggs... how does the rooster get his thing through that hard shell?" Another puzzle needing answer.

To plant baby seed, humans did something too. Yeah, so what about humans? What time of the year does the woman come in heat? How does the man know when she is ready? Remembering image of the bull pawing the ground, sniffing urine, I couldn't believe my father would do things as disgusting as the bull. Nor could I believe my mother would willingly get on her hands and knees and let my father mount her. Yet, I was here. Other people are here. I had to admit to the reality of people copulating. The more I thought about it, the idea of my parents doing that act was so repulsive I swore I would never say the word 'f---' again.

No different than any other kid, I soon got over my trauma about people doing it. However, I had noticed something about my penis. *(Penis, another acceptable CONTINENTAL word.)* For some strange reason, it would sometimes harden and stick out. Weird! I found this to be so fascinating that I decided to draw pictures of penises. The problem was that I had decided to do it while I was in school.

Like all rural schools, ours taught eight grades in the same room. There were other older boys in Mountain View No. 1 when I was in the first grade, Harold Backman, Art, and Olaf Berge. Ira Lee Miller was a first grader like me. They needed entertaining and I was the boy who could do it. Sitting where I was, near the back of the room, the teacher couldn't see what I was drawing. It hadn't occurred to me that she would mind about my choice of subject matter in the first place. What possibly could be wrong with drawing penis pictures? I might be dumb at arithmetic, but I could draw better than anybody could; so I drew a side view figure of a boy with an enormous penis. I didn't want anybody to see my work of art until I was ready, so I hid my effort as best as I could.

Not satisfied with my first attempt, I drew another. Somehow, the penis looked dull and uninteresting, despite its generous size. It needed colors to brighten it up a bit. A flash of inspiration lit my creative mind. I marked off sections dividing it up into about eight parts. Then I took my Crayolas and carefully colored each section with different color. It was a chromatic success, a rainbow. I included testicles, testicles with polka dots. I made another, even better. Proud of my artistic achievement, I decided it was time to expose my gaily-colored stained glass penis art to the world. I'd start with Harold. He was across the aisle and a seat behind one of the Berge girls. I handed my best masterpiece over to him.

Harold unfolded my drawing and looked at it. By the way his eyebrows raised I knew I had made a fine impression. Desperately, he tried not to laugh, but exploded. At first I was disappointed, I had intended it beautiful, not funny. Then I felt a ground swell of pride. I was making Harold laugh harder than I had ever entertained anybody. Now all the boys and girls looked over to see what the laughter was about. The teacher, alerted to trouble, left her desk and was on the way to the trouble spot--me. Harold quickly handed my art back while whispering "Get rid of it quick, hide it." Too late, the teacher saw the evidence and seized all my drawings and scanned them. Obviously she had no appreciation for art. The room became deathly quiet. Jackie was in a heap of trouble. She took me by the ear and we were definitely headed for the wood storage room, which was also part of the school entry. I had never been spanked, nor had anyone else, but I knew I was a goner.

Once in the entry room, its interior much darker because of the single little window, she closed the door on a very quiet class. The kids were concerned for me, obviously no one had ever committed a crime of this magnitude before. The punishment would leave me with hideous scars, perhaps maimed.

Just inside the door leading to the classroom, my teacher stood towering over me. Looking up into her furrowed scowling brow and angry eyes I was very frightened. I anticipated a lot of pain coming my way. Hoping I wouldn't cry, I steeled myself for the coming blows. She held exhibit one, my masterpiece, in her hand and slowly unfolded it for closer examination. The look on her face was one of bewilderment mixed with anger. At that moment, I wished the world would swallow me up. Then her expression changed. She looked as if she was about to laugh. Hope of divine intervention flickered. If not an art connoisseur, at least my teacher had a sense of humor.

She studied the picture again and then covered her mouth with her hand to stifle laughter. I wondered, "What was so damn funny about my picture?" Her body swayed backward against the door. Leaning against the door, she slowly sagged downward to a sitting position on the floor while still gazing at my work of genius. After a few moments, she composed herself and stood up. She tried to work up anger again, but didn't make it. Then, under much control, she said, "Don't you know this is very shameful and a bad thing to draw?" I innocently shook my head--no. "Don't ever, ever, draw private parts again." Much relieved, that I wasn't going to be spanked after all, I promised that I would not.

After coaxing her face back into a serious appearance, she turned to reenter the schoolroom. She paused turned again to me and bent down to my ear. "I'm going to send you home – don't tell the kids that I didn't punish you," she whispered forcefully. I promised. Thank God, how I promised. After gathering my coat from the hook on the wall, she then sent me on my way home, early. This was a Friday afternoon. Still, somewhat baffled by the unexpected uproar over my colorful pictures, I headed for home. It was too early for me to be home. My ma would ask questions and I'd have to answer. By playing in the creek or something, I could delay getting home until the regular time to do so.

At first, I wondered why the teacher had sent me home early. Then I suspected she was uncertain I might talk and let the other kids know I had gotten off easy. Since this was Friday, she was hoping that by Monday, the kids would have forgotten the incident.

At the creek I had one final thought that upset me; "Dang it...she kept my pictures." *If my first grade teacher is still alive, I wonder if she still has them hidden somewhere, tucked away among her teaching keepsakes.*

Even when I became a little older, I never had the nerve to ask my folks about sex. Despite the reality of my getting born, I still could never imagine them ever doing it or be inclined to give instructions. My sex education would have to be the responsibility of my friend Harold. He was five years older than I was. I regarded him as a man of the world, my guru, and my key to great knowledge. *(More about Harold later.)* One day, I decided that the next time my folks would go visiting the Godfrey Backman's, I would ask Harold about sex stuff straight out.

He patiently answered, (quite accurately incidentally) all my questions. From him, I learned that there isn't an in heat season for humans. From him, I also learned the danger of 'knocking up' a girl. Hearing about venereal diseases didn't scare me as much as having some young lady become pregnant and be stuck with a squalling baby and the ensuing shame of it all.

Having Harold scare me was one thing, but even my mother made sex seem like an evil conspiracy invented by the Devil. Ma had reinforced Harold's warning about pregnancy and added a few more upsetting facts. Birth control devices always fail. Do 'It' and the girl becomes pregnant. (Which I interpreted as immediately.) The girl's parents will then demand with shotgun in hand, "Marry her or else or go to jail."

The information was very discouraging and ominous. With no job, uneducated, immature, indigent, unskilled...how could stupid teenager meet parental responsibilities? Suicide would be a coward's way out--but then again, still worthy of consideration. I came to regard my penis as a potentially treacherous, one-way ticket to disaster. My paranoia was so intense that if I ever were to be faced with social obligation to shake hands with a girl, I would make certain that I was wearing rubber gloves.

All the pleasant aspects of sex, love, and romance my friend or anyone might describe from then on would fall on deaf ears. Harold and my mother succeeded so much in scaring me, that I remained a virgin far beyond normal experimental sex time for boys. As a late teenager full of raging hormones it was mighty frustrating. Once in a while I'd see a pretty girl and yearn to be with her. Then the warnings would come to mind and I'd wonder, "How can such a lovely creature be such a booby trap?" No pun intended.

It took World War II and the prospect of soon getting killed, and a 'what the hell' attitude to overcome my fear of the dreadful sexual gamble.

There was an element of truth in the warnings.

ASPEN GROVES
ISLANDS OF THE PRAIRIE

It may seem strange to write about something as mundane as groves of trees. Well, these groves were special, at least to one farm kid in the 1930's. They are gone now and won't be coming back. They deserve being remembered. It is unlikely anyone else will write about them, so here's my two bits worth.

These little groves of aspen, which once dotted the prairie, are nearly all gone. They are a little more numerous on the Canadian side of the border. The reason, perhaps, settlers on the Canadian side were predominantly of English, or Scottish origin. They came from a land where gardens and preservation of scenic places is an important part of their heritage and tradition. As late as 1960, while flying in a Piper J3 Cub over the border, I could see, in Canada, many of these little clumps of trees encircled by curving patterns of summer fallow furrows or growing wheat fields. On the USA side, it is almost barren of native groves on the prairie. Even now, in the '90's, if flying over the border in the Turtle Mountains, a difference can be seen. On the Canadian side, more of the native trees are still growing. On the U.S. side, much of the hill country has been cleared for farming.

Perhaps, it seems strange that I should bother telling about little groups of trees, especially about a seemingly insignificant species of tree--the aspen. Locally it is called "popple" or "poplar." This tree deserves more appreciation than that. What would summer be like without a tree that gaily rustles in the lightest breeze? What would autumn be like without its yellow leaves, which will later fall to paint golden polka dots on pathways and in the roadside water puddles. North America just wouldn't be the same without aspen.

aspen (as' pen) Any of several poplars of the genus *Populus*, having leaves attached by flattened leafstalks, so they flutter readily in the wind. *P. tremuloides* and *P. grandidentata* of North America, is often called "Quaking Aspen."

A dictionary definition is understandably short. Botanical textbooks are more comprehensive. Aspen trees may be humble but not ordinary. Obviously, dictionary writers can spell perfectly and make concise definitions, botanists can describe how to identify, classify, and stupefy, but they lack heart and imagination. Their descriptions remain coldly colorless and fail to reveal the true nature of this friendly and unpretentious tree. For example, there isn't any reference to how great the young trees are for a boy to climb, not to mention the joy of tree swinging. *(Tree swinging a fun and hazardous sport once known to spirited youngsters lucky enough to live near a grove of aspen. Later on in this story, I'll get around to describing the fine art of tree swinging.)* Nor does the dictionary or textbook say anything about it being the perfect tree for picnics. Under its dappling shade, no girl ever looked prettier or swain more handsome. What other tree can so quickly, with spattering sounds similar to that of a sudden summer shower, warn of the unwelcome visit of a capricious hat-blowing, skirt-lifting breeze? The velvety smooth trunk of an aspen is almost as white as birch, and presents a much easier surface in which to carve initials or graffiti, more so than any other tree. Even an awkward klutz with a dull knife can do it. Many people did and do, as evident by often initialed aspen trees in picnic areas. The wound will heal with black scar tissue. Years later, the initials or words will stand out boldly. To some people this may turn out to be a little embarrassing, e.g.: "Jim & Jenny, forever, 19 –." Jim of course is now married to Darlene, and Jenny married the local minister. Jim and Jenny, now with new partners, are careful to avoid being near the revealing tree.

Aspen trees still grow in the Turtle Mountains as elsewhere in our nation. However, the special groves of this story are almost extinct.

The first aspen thicket I saw disappear was just across our creek on the Backman farm. When old man Peder Backman, or more likely one of his boys, David or Edner, cut it down. I asked my mother why they were doing it. She said something about them insisting it acted like a snow fence, causing the road to be blocked in winter. In her mind they offered another phony reason, claiming they needed it for firewood. It didn't matter; they owned it, so they cut the trees and turned it into another acre of cropland. She and I both really hated to see it go. The firewood story I didn't buy any more than my mother did. After all, there was plenty firewood available for the chopping just two miles east in the Turtle Mountains.

As late as 1930, many clumps of trees still dotted the prairie, creating many tree islands. These groves spread out from the hill country for many miles. At the age of ten, I was old enough to begin seriously exploring the groves near or on our farm. Sometimes small discoveries were found another of nature's surprises-- almost always a pleasant experience.

Before telling of my experiences in visiting such places, it would be well to describe these arboreal oases in greater detail; how they were formed as they were. A photograph would be wonderful, but to my knowledge there aren't any; probably because a hundred years ago, about the least important thing on a settler's mind would be a picture of what he considered nothing more than an ordinary wood lot. Apparently, most homesteaders didn't give a damn about landscape scenery. They seemed to have an attitude that if the land couldn't be plowed or used as pasture, it was worthless. They would have really hated Yellowstone or Yosemite National Park. A grove of aspen was only an irritating impediment to plowing a straight furrow. *(For some reason, plowing a straight furrow was very important.)* As for beauty, to them the aspen grove was nothing more than a visual nuisance interrupting the plain unbroken line of the horizon. These folks, in general, also seemed to hate potholes or sloughs of water, since they spent a lot of time draining them.

By the time I was old enough to use a camera and develop film there weren't many left. Little did I know then, that now 60+ years later, I would lament not having a photo. Obviously, I hadn't thought of photographing them either.

My parents happened to like trees, so our few groves remained until my folks were too old to farm. The tenant farmer that leased our land had a different view of the aesthetic value of trees. There were a few extra acres of cropland to be had, so the three groves that remained – vanished.

Aspen trees in the hill country, where they are mixed with other kinds of trees, grow in seemingly aimless fashion. The groves of Quaking Aspen on the prairie grew in separate orderly groups, generally circular in form. The average copse was about 30 yards in diameter.

Referring to the title of this story, comparing these clumps of trees to islands is an unavoidable simile. Visualize acres of prairie, fair weather flat, or gently rolling swells. On this land, tall grass or wheat gently waves in a river of wind. Some distance away can be seen a tight cluster of trees rising abruptly out of the sea of wheat, or sometimes, plain summer fallow. Instead of aspen, it isn't hard to imagine palm trees of a small South Pacific island. If seen from aloft, the numerous groves would resemble an archipelago of islands. The comparison can be enhanced even further because the shape of some of these islands had the form of atolls. A few of these groves were actually rings of trees enclosing a glade of grass or brush much like a coral reef encircles a lagoon. Perhaps, a New Yorker would rather compare the form of such a grove to a bagel.

Two questions may come to mind. Why just patches of trees on the prairie and not a large forest of timber? Why aspen trees sometimes grew in the form of a ring? To answer the first question briefly: Trees can grow in poor ground. Most forest soil is poor. Grass needs good soil, and in good soil grass its twining ropelike roots choking the tree, eventually takes over. As to the second question, the reason a ring of trees is sometimes formed is due to the way aspen propagate.

Given a reasonable climate, trees can grow almost anywhere, For example, trees grow in the hardscrabble soil of Vermont, between cracks in the rocks in the Rocky Mountains, on sand dunes in Oregon and the glacial till of the Turtle Mountains Grass flourishes best in rich loam or loess. Half of North Dakota was once the bottom of ancient Lake Agassiz, its silt bed now ideal for grass or grain. The Great Plains lack trees because the soil is too good. Competing for growth in good soil, grass usually wins. For one thing, grass can tolerate a prairie fire. It simply grows back from the roots. Grass also gets first-rights on rainfall. Grass is sneaky and greedy. Each year its roots will encroach more and more among the tree roots, which eventually expand into the tight, ropelike web of grass fibers and choke.

The reason there were any trees at all on the prairie surrounding the Turtle Mountains is that the land is not uniformly rich and perfect for grass. There are gullies and gravelly hillocks, sloughs and streams, and occasional piles of boulders dumped by the ice age glacier. A typical grove of aspen probably got started when an aspen seed, carried by the wind, fell in the shelter of a rock pile. The seed germinated and a seedling grew. Protected from prairie fires by the rocks or an upwind slough, it grew to maturity. A few years later, a grove or ring of aspen is formed.

Why sometimes a ring? Aspen trees propagate *(vegetative reproduction)* not only by seed, but more often, by roots spreading horizontally outward to send up shoots to reemerge as new trees, actually clones of the original tree. *(In fact, it is not a good idea to plant an aspen in your yard unless you and your neighbor enjoy cutting down unwanted aspen suckers.)* The life span of the particular subspecies of aspen that grow in North Dakota is 30 to 40 years. Eventually the original tree dies and so do its first clones. Aspen is not durable wood. It falls and rots quickly, turning to duff or soil. Meanwhile, the following clone trees for generations continue to grow from the original connected root system, sometimes forming a ring around an empty clearing--a glade. Because nature abhors a vacuum, new growth will fill the void. Oddly enough, even though growth above ground is renewed periodically, the old root remains as a monolithic living system. Perhaps, a very old aspen grove will someday prove to be the largest living thing on earth[4].

The reason for the long explanation is so you will understand why, on a seemingly empty prairie, these groves were such a treat for a young boy to visit.

Children raised in a city like New York or Des Moines may cherish grander, more exciting memories--the circus coming to town, big-league baseball, or gangland massacres. Country kids have to find pleasure in more subtle ways. In the course of my growing up I, like other neighbor kids, visited aspen thickets many times. The first impression is sometimes the clearest, so I will begin there.

Perhaps, I was eight or nine years old--I don't recall exactly, just that I wasn't old enough to drive the horses pulling the hay mower but old enough to take lunch *(8:30 – sun time)* to Pa, who was mowing grass for hay. This hay meadow was on Uncle Carl's land about a mile southeast by east of home. The first part of the walk was on "the grade." "The grade" was our name for the road that passed our farm. For that matter, "the grade" was a common name for any road that had been graded to shed rainwater quickly. Grading left a deep ditch on both sides of the road where rain puddles could be found after a shower. They were fun to chuck rocks into, making a satisfying gallumph sound. This day it seemed to me that last year at this time there were more and deeper puddles. Already, there were subtle signs that a long period of drought was coming, but few paid much attention. These signs could only be read in retrospect. This same ditch, four years later, would be full of very dry dust, instead of runoff water.

A shortcut getting to the meadow where Jake was mowing meant crossing a plowed field. No problem in bare feet, which is standard summer wear. My father saw me coming and stopped the horses, got off the mower, stretched in a backward bending motion, walked about a bit, adjusted a buckle on the harness of one of the horses, then finally, lit his pipe. A few moments later I had delivered the lunch. We sat cross-legged in the shade of the team.

---

[4] Since I originally wrote this story in 1991 an aspen grove in Utah has been found to be the most massive living organism. Its mass is estimated to be 4.5 million pounds. The largest organism in area is a fungus in Washington State covering 1500 acres. (Ref. DISCOVER magazine Oct. 1994)

Jake, who never did eat much, seemed to take a long time opening the lunch box. First, he took out the Thermos bottle of coffee and poured himself a cup. Coffee first, it seemed forever before he got to the sandwiches. I had been waiting for him to pick one out, before I felt I could take one. Neither one of us had said anything to one another. Pa never did know what to say to me or me to him for that matter. About half way into lunch he finally asked:

"Where's Luella?"

"Visiting Selma at Backman's" I told him.

"Probably helping Tilda *(Selma's mother)* by reading TRUE STORY magazines" was his reply. TRUE STORY magazine, full of gossip and love stories, was the NATIONAL ENQUIRER of the thirties. Naturally, I didn't know, or care what Luella was up to. She was after all, only my old sister and a spit curled twenties Flapper to boot--certainly an alien to me.

My lunch delivery obligation over, Jake went back to mowing. I had nothing to do except walk home again, which didn't appeal to me. Something caught my attention. In the thicket of aspen trees, about a hundred yards south of the hay meadow, I saw some very agitated noisy crows flying over their nest in the top of one of the trees. This activity deserved investigation. Visiting one of these groves had not, until now, been one of the big ambitions of my life. However, this time I was curious as to what the fuss was all about, so I walked toward the thicket. A strip of summer fallow separated the meadow from the grove.

Ordinarily, crows never seemed upset about much, even the approach of man or boy unless he was carrying a gun. *(How crows could tell the difference between a boy carrying a gun or a boy carrying a big stick, I didn't know until much later in life. Since then I have learned that, unlike other birds, crows are very intelligent, having an I.Q. of at least 180. Possessing superb eyesight, they not only can tell the difference between a gun and a stick a quarter-mile distance away, but can tell what kind of a gun, whether shotgun or rifle. They will even know the caliber, range, manufacturer's name, and can read the serial number.)* I wasn't old enough to carry a gun. That would have to wait until my twelfth birthday. Therefore, it wasn't me that was agitating this black pair of cawing and squawking complainers. It turned out to be a Broadwing hawk. It was sitting on a branch near the crow's nest. The crows were dive-bombing the unwelcome intruder to no avail. As I got closer to where I could see more clearly, I guessed that the hawk must have been checking out a potential lunch in the crow's nest. Seeing me walking into the edge of the grove made the hawk reconsider having a crow egg snack at that moment, so it took off. The grateful crows decided that small boys can be useful at times and settled down in the upper branches to console each other about the close call of losing their ugly children.

The summer fallow had ended in the shade at the edge of the grove. Buckbrush was growing and fighting for root space under the aspen. *(North*

Dakota farm kids know that the only useful thing about buckbrush is that its woody stems are sometimes hollow and can be used to make the stem for a boy's smoking pipe. I would have stopped to cut a stem, but observing the activity in the trees was more important.) Thinking there might be something else worth observing in the trees, I sought a path through the underbrush.

The greenish white trunks of the aspen were numerous, and I had to be careful where I stepped, dry pointy twigs can hurt bare feet. Much to my surprise the center of the thicket was open to the sky. Except for a few rotting logs and a couple of boulders, here was a clearing free of anything but grass and a profusion of wildflowers. The grass was tall but not tall enough to hide an orange sprinkling of tiger lilies, the light blue, delicate flowers of wild flax and many other flowers I didn't know. Near the shady side of the glade grew bluebells. Ever on the lookout for wild strawberries, I looked closer to the ground. After lifting the green leaves of the sprawling plants, I found the little red berries. No domestic strawberry can ever match the pungent sweetness of wild strawberries. The breeze was just strong enough overhead to produce a delicate clattering sound from the fluttering aspen leaves. Here was heaven on earth! A sunlit glade, summer clouds, and wild berries.

As usual, my mother, Lena, had provided more lunch than Pa ever ate. Since I still had the lunch pail, I sat down, opened it, and took out the extra sandwich. Sitting cross-legged in the grass, I watched grasshoppers, bugs, and butterflies doing their nature thing as I ate it. Afterwards, I got up and gathered strawberries in the lunch pail. There was a spot where the grass was very thick and I flopped down on my back where I could comfortably look up at the ever-changing cumulus clouds and see what faces or other images the clouds were shaping today. One at a time, I savored each little strawberry. It was a most enjoyable moment. Moments later, as I lay on my back, I became aware of an unexpected sound coming from the sky; the sound of a lost mewing kitten. No, not a kitten, more like that of a high-pitched whistle. The tone descending and then extended in duration. It was a haunting, pleasant sound from above--what the dickens was doing it? Then I saw them.

Two circling Broadwing hawks had caught the rising air of a thermal somewhere over the plowed fields upwind. Anyone who has ever heard the sound of a Broadwing hawk will never forget it. Apparently, these are the only hawks to make this sound as they thermal[5]. The hawks, in their airy carousel had now drifted over my glade. For some reason, the new presence of hawks didn't seem to upset the crows. They either recognized the sound as unthreatening thermaling music, or just assumed that as long as the dumb farm kid was

---

[5] *Thermal: Meteorol. A mass of warm air, that has been heated by solar insolation upon dry earth such as a summer fallow. This air will rise in the same way a hot-air balloon rises. Circling within these air mass enables 'soaring birds' sailplanes to climb upwards. This is called thermaling.*

lounging around, there was no danger and kept quiet. Considering the pleasant sound from the hawks, I was grateful the crows shut up.

As a small boy I had no knowledge of thermals and wondered how those circling birds could gain altitude with every circuit without so much as a single flap of their wings. It was pure magic. Although, they were fairly low at first, only a hundred feet or so every turn sent them higher. Soon, I could no longer hear them, then two or three minutes later; the hawks were mere specks in the sky at the base of a cloud. How I wished I could do that! What a thrill that must be--to climb upward, higher in the sky, so high that they must be able to see to the edge of the world and not strain a muscle to do it. Airplanes I knew about, but not gliders and sailplanes. That knowledge would come later.

To be a bird must be the ultimate experience. However, being an airplane pilot would be as close as a human could get to soaring. From that moment in the aspen glade, riding horses, John Deere tractors, racecars, boats, and clipper ships, lost their appeal to me. I wanted to fly. *(Twelve years later I would be flying, thanks to the U.S. Army Air Corps. Over sixty years later, I still fly sailplanes for recreation. It is common for glider pilots to fly in the same thermal with hawks, gulls, or eagles. Every time there is a soaring bird sharing my thermal, especially a hawk, I watch with fascination still, at how we climb with so little physical effort, and remember the first time I witnessed powerless flight. I still can't make that mewing sound, but I would if I could. It is the joy--sound of soaring.)*

When I was twelve or so, and more proficient at the sport of tree climbing, I decided to climb an aspen tree in a grove next to our pasture. Not yet being able to fly like the hawks, I had to settle for the next best thing to get off the ground--climb a tree. Here, was a crow's nest, which I thought I'd look into. Every aspen grove had a resident crow family and this one was no exception. The nest was an easy climb above the ground. Looking into the nest I made a discovery. Crows have criminal minds! Until then, I hadn't known about the strange character flaw that crows have. The term "Thieving Crow" had had no real meaning to me. Now I found that crows are felons, burglars. They steal things! Along with baby crows, the ugliest fledgling critters I had ever seen, was stolen loot. Here was a small white marble, a pop bottle cap, some crumpled tin foil, and remarkably, a small silver salt spoon! After fishing the spoon out of the nest, I climbed down and took it home to show my mother. After I showed it to her she asked:

"Hvor fant du den?" Norwegian for "Where did you find it?"

"Out of a crow's nest," I told her in English.

"Neimen!" – An all-encompassing, general purpose, Norske word, signifying great astonishment or disbelief.

Even after I explained how I came to find it, she had trouble believing me. In fact, I'm not totally sure she ever did.

Not all encounters with aspen took place in prairie groves. There was this business of tree swinging.

It was haying season, and since I was now a gangly-armed fourteen year-old, it was expected that I help my dad. *(I had dropped the use of "Pa." My older sister, Evelyn, had told me that "Pa" was strictly country kid, hick-talk. No matter, half the time I called him "Jake" anyway.)*

Due to the drought, the hay meadow we were using was up in the hills. After tying the hayrake to the back of our hay wagon we clattered up the grade going east for a mile and a half. We didn't stop to visit the Moody's, relatives now living on the old Olson place, which had once been my grandfather's farm. The road first wound up the foothills past chokecherry and juneberry bushes. Then came the small burr oak trees, which everyone used for cutting fence posts. A couple of miles east, the trees were taller, and included ash and birch. I wasn't sure where the meadow was that my dad was going to, even though he had told me it was on so and so's land. Finally the road became just a trail through tall aspen. We broke out into a clearing. The meadow, which had once been a slough, lay spread before us. It wasn't a big meadow, just enough hay for one haystack. What attracted my attention was a stand of young, slender aspen surrounding the meadow. They were of wonderful size and shape for tree swinging.

Because of the low boy population in our part of the country, we couldn't experience team games like baseball. Therefore, when three or four boys got together, one of the games was tree swinging. In this game there was no serious competition, other than seeing who could produce the most spectacular swing. It began by looking for aspen of just the right size, preferably tall and skinny. Such trees were to be found in shady places, where branches reach upward for the sun. The object was to climb the aspen as far as one could, just before the tree would bend of its own accord. Then just at the right height, taking a firm hold with our hands, we would swing out into space with our feet. If we had judged correctly, the tree would bend like a fishing pole and lower us to the ground. At times our judgment wasn't too good. A tree too limber and the swing to the ground would be fast, terminating in a hard bang, and a headache. A tree too strong or stiff and the swinger would be left hanging from a bowed treetop, several feet above the intended landing place. Then the other boys would laugh and wait to see what the frustrated, still airborne pilot would do. If too high, the swinger would try to climb back up the bowed limb. If the tree had a lot of spring, it would then come back nearly to its original position, sometimes with the swinger upside down. Then the option was to climb back down, or try again. OK, to modern kids, this sounds mighty dull. Elvis wasn't born yet and the only rock and roll we knew about was loosening a big rock to roll down hill.

Jake stopped the team and untied the hay rake. Hitching the team to the hayrake, he told me to drive the team and start raking while he took a smoke break. The first step was to get the hay neatly piled into windrows[6]. This was a fun job requiring some planning and foot coordination with the trip-pedal. After a while my dad took over the job to finish windrowing. We would soon start the stack building process. He was to drag the rows of hay to where I was supposed to start building the stack. There would be a while before the stacking began; enough time for me to try out one of the super looking aspen trees just waiting for a champion tree swinger. My dad went about his business and I went about mine. I picked out a dandy. The ground under the tree was full of bumpy big hummocks, too rough for haying.

The tree was a tall one, taller than I had ever tried before. Up, up I climbed. Jake hadn't seen me depart for the tree, or seen me climb it. I was hoping he would watch my swing and be impressed. The tree was ready to sway with my weight. This was going to be spectacular. It was. Having taken a firm grip, I made a mighty swing outward. The tree top bent out about ten feet, then, with a resounding snap, it broke. The broken limb twisted out of my hands as I plummeted, face-up, legs and arms outspread, to terra firma. The hummock I impacted hit me square in the back. I was no longer breathing, I couldn't. The wind had been knocked out of me. Stunned, I couldn't move anything. All I could do was stare at the blue sky. "Oh God," I wondered. "Am I going to die?"

Jake hadn't seen me fall, but he did see me, supine, in the weedy grass, and walked over to where I was lying, still staring at the sky. My first awareness of his presence was seeing his face and hat come into view against the blue void above. Maybe he can help me," I hoped. "Maybe he can do something so I can breath again." Instead I hear his voice, filled with bitter disappointment in his son.

"You were supposed to help me today... and here you are, laying around doing nothing." Then he walked away! Walked away! – and his son was dying!

After what seemed minutes, a wheezing, wisp of a gasp admitted a trickle of air into my lungs Another wheeze, the sound of a coarse file drawn over the edge of a corrugated cardboard box. I was going to live – maybe. After a couple minutes, I was able to actually breathe. Getting to my feet was hard, but I had to explain to my dad what had happened. He was at the haystack site doing my job.

"Dad – I gotta explain what happened." He was still disgusted with me but stopped what he was doing and listened. I pointed to the culprit tree with its still dangling, broken top, to confirm my story. He looked at the tree, then at me and then, very slightly, smiled. "Let's have a look at that tree of yours." He then slowly walked over to the treacherous tree. When he got there he took a

---

[6] *Windrow: A row of hay raked up to dry before being gathered into cocks'. (haypiles)*

leaf from it, rolled it between his fingers, squeezed and smelled it. Then he looked at the bark. "Serves you right for not knowing a 'black popple' from the others... brittle as glass, no wonder it broke." Thus, I learned there are many sub-species of aspen. I had been taught a breathtaking lesson. This variety should be called *"Populus tremuloides busts-easi."*

The aspen groves on the prairie weren't any good for tree swinging. With no big shade trees to encourage tall spindly growth, they grew too stocky and stiff. However, they did harbor more creatures than just tree swinging boys. Once in a while we would see a Virginia Whitetail deer in the aspen groves. For those so inclined, the groves were a good place to set traps for weasel, badger, fox or other creatures looking for an oasis in the barren lands.

One by one, these prairie islands vanished. Not all were lost because of farmers cutting them down. Many were lost in the drought of the Dust Bowl Era. This terrible period wiped out not only trees, but crops, pastures and thousands of farms and farmers as well. Of the local groves, among the last to go were on our farm. Like I said, my mother liked trees.

"Cleaning up the prairie" has not been limited to just aspen groves. To survive economically, farms now must be large in acreage. Many farm children opt for moving away, thus leaving the old folks behind with no takers. When a farm is abandoned not only are the farm buildings sold and moved but also those few left are burned and ashes buried by bulldozer. Even the farm water well is filled in, this understandably, for safety reasons. Finally, the farm windbreaks of cottonwood, box elder, other trees, and miscellaneous shrubs, are cut down, burned, and buried along with anything else left over. No trace of prior human habitation will remain. If someone were to ask me where the Thorsgard's house or the Garden place, or even the Mt. View School No.1 had once stood, they would just have to take my word for it. I wouldn't be able find a nail, board or shard of glass to prove it. Three fourths of the original farm homes and buildings of my youth are gone. Only large grain fields remain. The prairie country has become neat, clean, and sterile as a well-scrubbed hospital corridor--and except for half- mile long planted windbreaks, equally uninteresting.

DAKOTA CUTTERS

This story is about a type of winter vehicle unique to the far north border country of the Great Plains many years ago. The last of these vehicles were still in use in the 1940's. Since then, this charming bit of Americana has simply faded away and their existence unrecorded. Therefore, I have written this story of a typical adventure in one of them, because no one else, to my knowledge, has bothered to do so.

Perhaps the average person, upon hearing the word, cutter[7], will probably either have an image of a coastal sailing vessel or some bloody aproned guy in a butcher shop. My dictionary's second definition states: 'a one-horse sleigh.' In New England, this particular kind of cutter would mean a sleigh similar to the cute little job that "Santa Claus" whips around in. These sleighs may have been popular in Vermont or Maine, but not in North Dakota. The driver of such an open snow buggy would not have made it alive through the first blizzard. Up near the Canadian border, what we called 'Cutters' was much sturdier stuff. Only a few, made of lightweight plywood, would be light enough to be pulled for any great distance, in deep snow, by just one horse. Ours were built to carry passengers plus a little cargo space. Each was a homemade, singular creation. The quality of each vehicle was dependent on the design skill, ingenuity, and building ability of its owner. Since creative skill levels vary in people, the cutters varied as well. Some were crudely built and some were well made.

A well-worn axiom states that Necessity is the mother of invention. Thus the great necessity of coping with North Dakota winters caused the birth of the special cutters of this story. The need to go to town didn't end when the first snowstorm hit the farm. There were supplies to be gotten and emergencies like another baby to get born. Automobiles could not be depended upon, not with deep snowdrifts and oil in the crankcase the consistency of cold tar. A four-wheeler 65 years ago could only mean a lumber wagon or buggy. A common winter conveyance was a big bobsleigh, staked for hauling logs. It could also be fitted with a rack for hauling hay, or a tall-sided box for grain, or a low box for hauling manure. It was not the most elegant vehicle for a trip to town. The great solution was an <u>enclosed and heated</u> cutter. Whether the enclosed cutter was invented by a single individual or just evolved, who knows.

Regretfully, the only photograph of a cutter that I have is not of a typical cutter. It is of one used to carry rural mail and so it is larger than average. Therefore, I will attempt to describe the more standard enclosed cutter.

Imagine a six-foot high box on a set of runners. It was usually less than six feet long and just wide enough to seat up to three passengers. A few larger cutters, school buses, could seat more. In front was a big window and on the sides, smaller ones. For heat, a small stove sat in one corner with its smokestack poking up through the roof. Behind and under the seat, there was space for groceries or whatever. A single door opened on one side. In some cases, a feed box for the horses was stuck on the back, like the trunk of an automobile.

Cutters were cozy and pleasant to ride in. My first trip in my father's cutter remains as one of my most cherished memories.

Cutter Ride To Souris

In 1930, Souris was a small prairie town about ten miles away. Its population was less than 500, yet it had about all the stores and professional services a farmer needed. The name Souris is French, pronounced "sooree" (more or less), meaning mouse. Since French speaking folks were scarce as molars in a frog, we simply pronounced it "surris" and didn't

---

[7] *Cutters gradually disappeared with the coming of better-graded roads, snowplows, and better automobiles. Some cutters, a 'school bus' and 'mail cutter' was still in use in the Turtle Mountains, as late as 1944.*

care one way or another what it meant. The town is still there but nearly all the stores are gone and only a few people remain.

The new cutter stood near the blacksmith shop where Pa had built it. To me, a boy nearing eight years old, it held the promise of new adventure. After looking it over, inside and out, I was impressed and thought it must be the best one in the whole county. I knew my pa could build things, but not this dandy. Had I been a little older, I would probably have known that my pa was a skilled carpenter. True, Jake was good at building things--once sufficiently motivated.

Motivation was Lena's job. My mother had a lot of practice at motivating my father--a very tough job. It couldn't be denied Jake was a man who frequently needed a very firm push to get started. However, once started, he would put his heart into the project until it was finished.

Like a lot of farmers, he had used the front runners from an old bobsled on which to build the cab. Shiplap siding had been his choice of materials for the sides. Barn siding would have been cheaper but shiplap made a smoother, more professional looking surface. Overlapping joints made it more draft proof. The roof was gently curved and covered with blue sand asphalt roofing material to shed water. Rain in the winter is not expected, but snow will thaw occasionally, especially with heat inside the cutter. For the side door he really splurged and used a small sheet of plywood he had been saving for some special, but until now, still unknown purpose. In this door he cut a square hole and installed a small window. On the left side, opposite the door, he installed another window to match. The front windshield was a multi-paned window, perhaps scrounged from an abandoned chicken coop. It had been re-puttied and cleaned. In the center, just under the window, was a slotted hole just big enough to pass the reins through for steering the horses. Layers of corrugated cardboard, neatly wrapped in old gunnysacks, cushioned the pine board seat.

The crowning jewel of this rig was a store-bought, tiny briquette-burning stove. The original purpose for such stoves must have been for some small stationary room or very little building. They had a tiny, flat, top surface, and stove lid just big enough for a coffeepot. Obviously the miniature stoves weren't originally designed for a moving vehicle. Nobody in their right mind would attempt to boil a pot of coffee in a lurching, swaying cutter. This stove sat in the front left-hand corner just under the window. A skinny three-inch stovepipe extending straight up through the roof, was capped with a wee 'coolie' hat to keep the snow out. A sack of charcoal briquettes for fuel and metal scoop was held in an old wooden eggcrate near the door and away from the stove.

The progress of its building had not been totally smooth. There was the minor irritation that Pa always encountered. Whenever Jake built anything, Lena insisted on painting it. Painting would have been OK. The problem, much to Pa's frustration, was that she painted <u>while the project was still in process</u>. Jake would no sooner get a couple of boards in place than Lena, paintbrush in one hand, paint bucket in the other, would be slopping paint over it. The inevitable result would be that he would get paint on his hands or overalls from accidentally grabbing a freshly painted board or brushing against it. He would then swear in Swedish. Lena would loudly cuss him out in Norwegian for being careless. Jake would then mumble an insult about the Norwegian race being mentally retarded. *Oh Oh,* Lena never took jokes all that well. Jake quickly learned another lesson: A woman with a loaded paintbrush in hand should never be insulted.

The color of the finished cutter and the stains on Jake's overalls, hands and cheek, was that of the enamel left over from painting the kitchen, pale yellow ochre. The finished cutter was then parked behind the milk house to await the snows of winter. It seemed like a long wait, it was. By the time the deep snows came, I had almost forgotten about the cutter.

Having received a coaster sled for Christmas, coupled with a recent blizzard that packed the drifts into hard surfaces ideal for sledding, I had come to fully enjoy the delights of winter. On school days it would be dark when I had finished supper, but that didn't stop me. Before the folks had even finished their coffee, I would put on my 'Lindy airplane helmet,' coat and overshoes, and go sledding in the moonlight. The snow seemed even faster at night.

One Friday evening, as I was about to go out sledding again, Ma told me that tomorrow Pa would be going to Souris in the cutter. She put her hand on my head to get my attention as she spoke to me in English. "You're old enough now to go with Jake to town – he needs some company – maybe he can teach you some words to Swedish songs – maybe you can even help him to carry the tune and stay on key." I couldn't have heard words more potent with the lure of a great adventure, but to tell the truth, that part about singing didn't appeal to me. I had no burning desire to learn Swedish songs. Furthermore, expecting my father to carry a tune and stay on key would be an impossible task. Despite years of coaching, neither my mother, nor my sisters, Evelyn and Luella had ever been able to teach Pa how to stay on pitch.

To heck with Swedish songs – ten miles of white arctic snow, across a gently rolling prairie, in a horse drawn cutter was a joyful prospect almost too wonderful to bear. That evening, the outside temperature was nearly twenty below zero, Fahrenheit. Perfect! At that temperature there would be little likelihood of a sudden blizzard. Blizzards rarely occur under the high-pressure dome of a cold arctic air mass. Even better, chances were it would be sunny with little or no wind.

Later that evening, sitting at the kitchen table after supper, Lena handed Jake the shopping list. Overhearing her talking about it in Norwegian and my dad occasionally grunting – ya,ya, I got the gist of the list: A sack of flour, a sack of sugar,...dry beans, split green peas,... Oh, if there was any left from the Christmas buying season, lutefisk and pickled herring...some raw wool from Australia, a carton of kitchen matches, a can of Allspice, a gallon of kerosene for the lamps, etc. There were some open-ended items discussed where Jake would have to use his own judgment. These would be special treats...lingonberries from Norway-- maple syrup if it wasn't too dear and so on. Ma didn't have to remind Pa to get tobacco. It would be the first thing he would buy. Prohibition or not, I knew he would also try to find a bottle of beer.

The sun with its two companion sun-dogs[8] almost as bright, had been up almost an hour. The sky was the clear sparkling blue known to those who live in the far north. The team was hitched up to the cutter outside the front gate and waiting to go. The horses with their coat of long winter-hair and horse blankets temporarily tossed over them, seemed downright eager. For them, the opportunity of getting away from the dull monotony of the barn and the humbling job of pulling the manure sled, would be motivating to any noble steed.

From the smokestack of the cutter, curled a lazy spiral of smoke and vapor, an unraveling skein of white yarn rising upwards in the still air. Actually a high hard snowdrift blocked the gate through the lilac hedge. No big deal, it was always blocked in winter. We just cut steps in the steep part and walked over it like a stile. In the cutter, extra blankets were folded on the seat just in case we were wrong about the unlikelyhood of a sudden blizzard. Pa got in first, grabbed the reins, and lit his pipe. Awkwardly, due to being overdressed, I followed. Under my layers of woolens plus a coat, Ma had first made me put on clean long underwear. She stressed that this was of <u>utmost importance</u>. They had to be clean in case some accident should happen. I might have to be undressed by a stranger, perhaps a doctor or undertaker. There would be no excuse on earth for me to be found wearing dirty underwear. So I learned an important lesson that day. There is something worse than death after all--being found dead with dirty underwear.

I was put in charge of taking care of the lunch bucket and the big thermos of creamed and sugared coffee. Since I was coming up on eight years of age, I was considered old enough to share some coffee with Pa. It was cozy warm inside the cutter; we were ready to go. Jake relaxed the reins and with a sharp tug-signal and "yiidap" to the horses, we left. The horses, already impatient to get moving, took off almost at a trot. With jingling harness bells we were on our way. First, north out of our yard and onto the road where we go west for a half-mile, then we would turn south for a while. Adventure ahead!

Very soon we came to our first obstacle. A gentle hill slopes downward from our farmyard to Boundary Creek. Over the creek is a wooden bridge on a road--grade lined with willows. The willows act as a snow fence and if there is a

---

[8] *So-called 'sundogs' is a weather phenomenon meteorologically called perihelion. Very bright spots, sometimes called 'mock suns,' almost as bright as the sun itself appear on either side of the sun. Occasionally, in very cold weather it is not uncommon to see one above the sun.*

snowdrift anywhere, it will be on the grade and sometimes completely over the bridge. Clearing the willows out would have solved the problem but Lena wouldn't put up with cutting them down. Her argument was: "They look so nice in summer and it's just as easy to shovel a little snow, as it is to cut them down." No counter argument was acceptable, even from the neighbors.

The recent blizzard had left a big drift over the bridge. Jake had seen it from the top of the hill and stopped the horses momentarily to study the problem. To go another way would mean a long detour. Once committed to drive over, it meant we couldn't change our mind and turn around. Cutters have a basic design flaw; they can't be backed up in deep snow. He knew there was an old ice-hard drift under the new one, he guessed that the horses would only sink knee deep on the new one. We would go for it. He was right. In a few heaving moves from the team we had scaled the drift and were on our way across the ravine and up the gentle hill on the far side. We passed the mailbox for the Peder Backman place on our right, just across the creek. A half mile later we were at the corner where we would turn south. After another half mile we passed the next farm, the Thorsgards. Most of the journey from here would be on flatland, only occasionally broken by drainage ravines, nothing to be concerned about until we had to cross Boundary Creek again.

Another half mile further down the road, we were passing Mountain View School No. 1, the damnable, stupid, miserable, I-hope-it-burns-down, rural school that was interrupting my serious education. It was pure pleasure to pass it. Now Jake decided to save a mile or two and go cross-country across the flatlands for a while. We didn't need a road in a cutter. He was familiar with the fences and gates we could go through. We would have no problems – 'no problems' the stuff an unexpected adventure is made of.

It is easier for me to simply describe a typical prairie in winter, than to write it as a narrative of what I remember about that day. Flatland grain fields of tall stubble, capture drifting snow to leave a very special scene. This isn't the powdery soft, undisturbed snow seen in Christmas cards. This snow has been wind-driven in open country. It has rapidly snaked along in countless, little sinuous rivers, coming to rest only on the lee side of anything that can slow its progress, whether it be a clump of tumbleweed, a tuft of grass, stubble rows or sometimes another drift. When it has been driven hard enough, it is almost ice. A person can walk on hard packed snow scarcely leaving a track. It produces chirping, squeaking noises when you do. Before the days of the Dust Bowl and weedless, monster summer fallow mixing dust into the snow it would be clean, white-clean, icy blue-white clean. Whatever the complex aerodynamic reason may be, I can't explain, but the wind will sculpture the snow to look like a frozen white sea. Unlike the ripples of a sand dune, this is a choppy ocean of sharp crested waves suddenly frozen in time, translucent white waves instead of blue or muddy green. However, in the snow shadows of the crests opposite a low sun, indirect light from the sapphire sky will impose a full spectrum of blues blending to blazing white again. Against the ' three suns' sparkle the facets of countless snow diamonds.

We were afloat on a sea of sparkling snow and my father was taking the current where it would serve best. Only a gate or two was closed to temporarily impede our progress. When I wasn't strong enough to open a gate, Pa would get out and do it. He carried a pair of fencing pliers in case he had to cut and then reconnect the barbed wire if the gatepost had frozen into the ground.

A mile or two more and we came to the small hills of the creek again. Not being near a road, Jake followed the rim of the ravine for a while looking for a place where he could chance going over the leeside snowdrift, which followed our side of the hill. Unlike the snowdrift on the bridge at home, about this drift he had no accustomed knowledge of its structure. He didn't know if it was a new drift or an old one with new snow. He didn't know how deep or solid it was. He could only make an experienced guess. It was new territory. The topside of the long drift had the icy look of hard snow; but then again, it might be only a thin crust.

Finally, Pa found a place that he judged we could go over--even if the horses were to break through it wouldn't be too deep. It was important to cross the drift perpendicular to its breaking edge so the cutter wouldn't tip on its side. If the cutter were to tip unto its door side it would be a serious problem. To line up square with the edge, Pa made a looping 270 degrees turn to the right and steered the horses to the edge. The horses seemed apprehensive for a moment but went on.   At first, the drift was hard, Pa was holding the team back from going too fast by pulling on the reins and 'talking' to them. Once over the cornice, the horses broke through the crust and into the softer snow on the lee side. The cutter nosed down at a steep and uncomfortable angle. Shortly thereafter, the cutter broke through as well. Now it was no longer a sleigh but a clumsy barge half-sunken in a pond of powder snow and crumbly icy crusts. The drag must have been very heavy, but our team was not a pair of citified buggy ponies, they were honest-to-God draft horses; big, powerful, strong-boned horses, with hooves the size of a frying pan. Pulling was their main talent and like the professionals they were, they lunged forward in a coordinated effort of a series of heaving motions. With harness bells jingling and great teamwork they pulled us through.

At the bottom of the ravine where the snow was thin, Jake let the team rest a bit and to let the horses congratulate each other for a job well done. After a short wait, we were on our way again. Going across the creek was no problem as it was frozen solid to the bottom and would have supported the entire mass of the Empire State Building. The hill on the opposite side had blown clear of snow, so bare that we went up the hill on frozen turf. The big snowdrift challenge had been passed and the rest of the way to our shopping town of Souris, town population 278, would be easy.

We were about two miles northeast by east of town, when we heard the long, melodious, wailing whistle of the passenger/mail train. Without bothering to take out his watch, Pa looked at the sun and said in Swedish: "Eleven

O'clock, the train from Rugby is on time. The 'Goose' must have broken down, they're using the old steam locomotive." I was elated and yet disappointed at the same time. It meant that I would get to see the engine at a distance, but not up close as I would if I were in town at the depot. Despite the heat from the stove, part of our window was frosted up. Not having a clear view, I became apprehensive about missing the sight of a lifetime. I squirmed around trying to stand in a position so I could see through the clearest pane. Pa saw me straining to get a good view. He solved my dilemma by steering the team in a direction so I could perhaps see the oncoming train through the unfrosted window nearest the stove.

Because of a slight rise in the terrain blocking the full view, the first thing I saw of the train was only the big white and gray steam-cloud trailing behind the up-blasting stack of the racing locomotive. This was a special treat, for normally the "Galloping Goose," a diesel electric locomotive pulled the train. Again the whistle--what a marvelous sound! Suddenly, in clacking rumbling fury, appeared a collection of railcars, connected like a string of wieners to the locomotive. The engine, tender, mail car, passenger car, and three freight cars in a sea were seemingly suspended as they sped over the roadbed in a sea of glistening snow. As it glided on its way, Jake kept aiming the team at the now coasting train until it disappeared behind the maze of trees, the few visible houses, and stately grain elevators of Souris. What a day and it wasn't even half over yet! For me, the train had truly been the sight of a lifetime.

A half-hour later we were passing the first homes on the edge of town. Staring through my side window I studied the street side houses. Once, behind a partially frosted window, a curtain parted. A face briefly appeared to observe who was coming to town. We were apparently judged unimportant, for the bored face turned and disappeared. The curtain swung back into a state of listlessness.

Two blocks later we passed the hotel on the corner and turned onto Main Street. Here was all the bustling activity of a Saturday in town. The chimneys of homes and stores had smoke and steam going almost straight up in the frigid, still air. Cutters were everywhere, their little smokestacks steaming. On the packed snow of the street, a few piles of horse manure, also steaming. Farmers were walking briskly from store to store. Little puffs of steam came out of their mouths as they panted. It was too cold for anyone to stop and talk, but briefly. As bundled up as these farmers were, in their long overcoats, ear-flapped fur caps, scarves, overshoes, and mittens, it was a wonder they could recognize one another in the first place.

Sidewalks had been shoveled to provide an inviting path into the stores. This left a snow ridge on each side of the street. Some horses, tied to the back of parked cutters, were poking their noses into the feedbox. Only a few automobiles were present, their engines idling to prevent freeze-up. Obviously, the owners must live close to town or they never would have risked using anything as unreliable as a car.

Pa found a place to leave the cutter, unhitched the team, tied them in back, threw a blanket over them, and opened the feedbox. They were unimpressed with city life but definitely interested in oats. Horses have very little curiosity about urban life.

The first stop would be the pool hall. It had once been a saloon or, in the local idiom, a beer parlor. Prohibition had almost ruined the business but it struggled on somehow with the pool tables, tobacco sales, and soft drinks. Prohibition or not, back in our farm home, the gun cabinet was well stocked with hard liquor. It had been given to my folks from our Canadian friends across the border. Some had just been left by bootleggers some place on the farm where my folks would find it.

These daring local entrepreneurs, braving the law to serve the thirst needs of our country, sometimes used our farm for a little cross-border, off-road traveling, and were either repaying us for some flattened wheat or for not 'ratting' on them to the border patrol. Considering the price of wheat, they could have flattened the whole farm and we wouldn't have lost much. Pa's only complaint was that the bootleggers never left any beer, which is what he really craved, even in wintertime. Oddly enough, Jake didn't like hard liquor very much.

We stomped the snow off our four-buckle overshoes, before going into Tony's Pool Hall. Inside was a row of pool tables with a score-keeping wire above each of the tables. On this wire were counting buttons strung like beads on an abacus. The beads counted by fives, four black, one tan, etc. To slide the buttons, a cues tick would be used. A couple of young guys were having a game at the back table. They took a brief look to see who had come in the door, then went back to concentrating on the game. A long bar, on the left with punchboards scattered randomly on its varnished surface, held little evidence of brisk trade. After all, with nothing but soda pop, tobacco, snacks, and coffee to be sold, business was slow. There is not much demand for pop in twenty below weather. Coffee and snacks had to bear the burden of business. At strategic locations on the floor were brass spittoons – yech.

The owner, an amiable, handsome man of Armenian roots walked toward us behind the bar. Smiling a broad grin he looked directly at Jake and asked the standard greeting: "Well Jake, what brings you into town?"

"To get some beer," replied pa slowly; his Swedish accent a contrast to Tony's linguistic heritage.

"Can't get it here, until this damn prohibition law is repealed."

"Ya"–The best snappy answer Jake could think of at the moment.

"What the hell would you want with a beer anyway – It's twenty below for God's sake – what kind of a person would drink beer in winter?" opined Tony. "Besides, you live on the border and should be able to get some of the hard stuff from one of the bootleggers."

Jake looked at him a moment and then said "Oh ya – we got whiskey, scotch, a couple quarts gin, apricot, and plain brandy, aquavit, but no beer."

Tony looking a little nervously askance at the door said: *"Jeezuz* Jake, if anybody from the border patrol would'a heard that, you would be sent to the pen five years for just saying it."

Jake then told him quietly, in his matter of fact, low voice. "Oh they already know I got it. They drop in for a warm-up snifter now and then."

Tony looked at my pa incredulously for a moment, then changed his expression to a big grin and said: "Jake...up till now, I thought 'Windy' Larson was the biggest liar in North Dakota." Tony laughed out loud, Pa only chortled, and he never laughed loudly. Then a bit more seriously, Tony asked: "Well, what'll you have Jake, best I got is near-beer." Pa ordered a near-beer and a couple of cans of Prince Albert tobacco. Tony then turned to me, "And what'll you be having boy?"

"A glass of milk" I replied timidly, not quite sure he would have milk. He did. After pulling a glass jug out from an ice box, he poured a tumbler full.

Milk in a pool hall? Yup--back in those times, life was civilized. Even after prohibition was repealed and booze flowed normally again, pool halls didn't bar children from entry, just from drinking booze. Pool halls (later taverns) served as social centers for the men folk in small towns. Boys were expected to accompany their fathers wherever they went. Young daughters went with their mothers. All children were expected to be seen and not heard. In winter, the potbelly stove area in a general store was for smaller groups of town men. Generally farmers didn't have time for the leisurely sojourn by the stove. Barbershops were reserved for serious political discussions. Womenfolk traded gossip over bolts of cloth in the dry-goods stores.

After we left Tony's and were outside again, I was upset at hearing about how my pa could go to jail for having all that liquor in the house. What Jake had said was true every bit of it, including the part about the border patrol stopping by for a warm-up. Further adding to our larder, the Canadians would give us a bottle of whiskey now and then just to return a special favor. Cream sold for more money in the States, so we would sometimes take our neighbors milk cans to town along with ours. Occasionally, when Jake returned the cans he would be handed a bottle of some kind of spirits. The police must have assumed we got it all from our neighbors across the border because they never asked anything about who the bootleggers were. Anyway, I don't think they ever really wanted to know, fearing that the warm-up supply might be cut off.

I knew rum running was illegal, but then so was poaching and that went on all the time, except during hunting season. Nobody I knew had ever gone to jail for that. As for cops chasing bootleggers, this had until now, had seemed to me just a fun game for grown-ups. After the warning words from Tony, the thought of Pa being arrested by some serious, pinch-mouthed officer of the law for just talking about it worried me a lot. Finally, I just had to ask: "Pa, why did you tell the man about the whiskey in the gun cabinet?"

"It was true what I said, wasn't it?"

"Ah–ya" me agreeing, but still worried.

"He didn't believe me – people seldom believe the truth" Thus Pa let me know there was nothing to worry about.

A few steps north up Main Street and we came to the butcher shop. Meat we didn't need, we never did. It was fish, lutefisk, or herring my pa went in to get. As we entered we heard the voice before we saw the man who said:

"What brings you to town on such a warm day Jake?" a slight variation on the standard greeting from the butcher, who was a powerful looking man with big hairy forearms.

"Lutefisk, got any left?"

"Too much, I'm gonna be stuck with some unless you buy the barrel."

"Save what's left over till next Christmas" Pa suggested. That idea seemed reasonable to me, that stuff couldn't possibly spoil any worse than it is already--my opinion of lutefisk. The butcher came around in front of his counter, lifted the lid from a new oak barrel, and then lifted out a slab of white, glutinous looking fish. Ugly stuff.

"How you Norskies can eat this stuff is beyond me" chided the butcher. I agreed. Pa spoke up, with a stem tone of indignation. "I'm a Swede."

"Christ forgive me – if I cut the price will you forgive me?"

Then Pa said, "For calling me Norske I should get it for free." By their chuckling, it was evident both thought the banter funny. Jake ordered some of it, the exact amount, I can't recall but from the size of the gray gelatinous mound on the scale, I would guess about five pounds.

In the meantime, I had lifted the lids of a couple of other barrels until I found the pickled herring barrel. Herring appealed to me so I called my father's attention to it. He ordered some herring after sampling a chunk. Then I spied some jars of pickled pig's knuckles--Uncle Carl's favorite delicacy. Pa bought a few pounds of that too.

As the butcher weighed out the fish on his scale and was wrapping it in brown paper he said: "It beats me how you Swedes and Norwegians are always throwing insulting jokes at each other."

Jake replied: "A Norwegian can't insult a Swede." The butcher paused a moment in the conversation, as he tried to get the gummed-tape dispenser to work before he answered: – "Oh yeah – how come?"

Jake lit his "Prince Albert" and took a couple drags on his pipe, then – "Norwegians can't think up anything to say." I thought – "Boy, am I glad Ma didn't hear that."

As we left the butcher shop, Jake said we were next going to the E.L.Garden Furniture and Hardware Store. For a very good reason, this appealed to me even less than going to school.

My cousin Virgil, who lived in Souris, was two years older than I, and therefore, a man of the world. Last summer he had told me that the E.L.Garden hardware and furniture store doubled as the community mortuary. *(Believe it or not, this was true.)* Virgil told me never, ever, to go into the weed-filled lot behind the store. Supposedly there was a big concrete cistern covered by old rotting boards. He said this cistern held spoiling, moldy old blood, blood drained from dead people. This dreadful cistern, hidden in the tall grass was a death trap. He said an unsuspecting kid, even as small as me, could accidentally step on the wrong board, break through, and drown in blood. At first I thought he was just trying to scare me, maybe he wasn't, but scare me he did. For weeks after that, I had nightmares of the most hideous death that anyone could imagine.

As we approached the dreaded store, I recalled that just last summer, I heard the folks tell of some man who had fallen into a water well and drowned. Wishing I could somehow talk to this man through some angel go-between, I would tell him it could have been much worse. I would tell him he had actually been very lucky, he could have met his fate in the cistern behind the E.L.Garden Hardware and Furniture Store.

The front of the store was filled with display cases of women's things. There were fancy buttons, needles, thread, sewing machines, dinnerware, pots, pans, teakettles, etc. Floor space was dedicated to racks of pitchforks, axes, spades, and garden rakes. On the floor sat chicken incubators, anvils, kerosene heaters, nail kegs, and other heavy stuff. Hand tools were on display shelves; such as hammers, hand planes, saws, bits and braces, fencing pliers, blacksmith tongs. Kegs of nails occupied all leftover spaces.

On the south side, a wall of varnished oak drawers ran the length of the store and floor to ceiling. Big drawers on the bottom, medium size in the middle, and little ones on the top, at least twelve feet up. Access to these drawers was by means of a traveling vertical ladder, which rolled on a track on the floor and was steadied by another track at the top of the case. To order something from the drawer section meant the clerk had to look up the right drawer and push the ladder to the right location, then climb up and fish it out of the bin. They held Model "T" coils, spark plugs, coil springs, lamp globes, nuts and bolts, harness fittings, anything a person could possibly imagine. Odd things that a customer didn't call for very often filled top drawers. Seldom was a customer told "We don't have it, I'll have to order it," and even more rarely, "We don't have enough." The whole place would have been heaven to me if it weren't for the knowledge that somewhere in this building, they drained, patched, and refilled dead people.

Dead center in the floor of the store was the heat register from the furnace below. Here stood my father and I, letting the melting snow drip from our overshoes. Pa was asking who had died lately, a subject that I didn't need to be reminded of. My thoughts immediately went to that blood-cistern in the back lot. Hopefully, it was frozen over by now and a kid wouldn't have to worry so much about drowning.

The new chilling concern that now occupied my mind was – "Where in this building does the horrible deed take place. Where does the blood-letting happen?" Then I noticed that the inside length of the building wasn't as long as the outside. Then I guessed the answer. Behind the back wall would be a big dingy room with a cutting table and lots of medieval, gruesome instruments. There would be jars of different colored wax to rebuild smashed faces. Leather awls, thread, and needles for sewing dismembered arms or legs back on. My imagination started getting the better of me. I pictured that, even now, there was some corpse on a table with tubes draining blood to the cistern. Did the undertaker remove the guts too? Guts spilling into a big galvanized washtub, like the one I was staring at. Did he dump the innards into the cistern along with the blood? Things were going from bad to worse. What do morticians replace the blood with? Kerosene? No, that would leak and I hadn't smelled any kerosene at funerals, just roses. It would have to be something that would be liquid when warm and solid when cold. It couldn't be gelatin that would get moldy too quick. Then, on a shelf, I saw the paraffin cartons. Wax! That's it, melted paraffin, like my ma used at canning time. Then I imagined a big kettle of wax warming on a stove. Hideous visions were getting the better of me-- surgical saws, steaming kettles, meat knives, bloody aprons, rubber gloves--my head was spinning, I felt sick. My stomach wasn't handling this very well; my staring eyes fixed on the ominous door to the back room.

Startled by a big hand on my shoulder, I became aware of the hardware dealer / mortician's voice: "What's the matter boy – you feel alright – you look a might pale." He turned to Jake who hadn't, until then, noticed my condition. In Swedish, Pa asked me if I was sick. I was, but too embarrassed to admit the cause so I said I felt fine. Still not reassured by my answer, Pa was concerned. He didn't want me to throw up in the hardware store, so my dad used an excuse by saying we had to go to Monkman's, a confectionery store and coffee shop. If I was going to throw up, Pa would rather I did it outside. Escaping the hardware store and the shock of cold fresh air revived me.

Monkman's was on the other side of the street, next to the bank on the corner. We walked across and had to step over a small snow pile in front of the store. In addition to all kinds of candy or other sweets, the store had patent medicines, horse liniments, magazines, and gumball machines. Best of all, Monkman's had sodas and ice cream--served at a marble-topped counter, and a new-fangled malted milk mixing machine. By now my stomach had recovered enough from my overactive imagination in the hardware store to consider the treat of an ice cream cone. The more I thought about it, the more the idea appealed to me. I asked Pa if he'd buy one for me. No matter how broke Jake might be, he could somehow always come up with a nickel. As usual he found one in his pocket and gave it to me so that I could buy the cone myself as a display of maturing responsibility.

To have ice cream in winter seemed more natural to me, than ice cream in the heat of summer. In winter, we could make our own ice cream just by setting the bowl of flavored and sugared cream out in the entry porch for a while. After eating it, all that fat and sugar would heat a kid up from the inside. City folks only ate ice cream in summer, an odd habit that I couldn't understand.

Mr. Monkman spied me sitting on the tall stool and came over to me. He was about the same age and size of my father, but not as wrinkled. Although he wore glasses, he looked over the steel rims as if to see me better. I wondered why he didn't just take 'em off. After I ordered a vanilla cone he asked me "Are you glad you don't have to go to school today?" That had to be the dumbest question anyone had ever asked a normal boy. However, I was polite and merely said, "You bet." Meanwhile, my pa had spent some time selecting various kinds of candy, mostly leftover Christmas sweets, to bring home. These were measured out on a balance scale and put neatly into small, white, paper sacks.

It was almost noon, and we still hadn't left our list at the grocery so we headed up the street to the grocery store. Next to Monkman's was the Souris Opera House. There had never been an opera performed there to my knowledge, but in summer there had been some vaudeville performances. Actually, it was a small movie theatre showing silent pictures. Talkies were yet to come. A billposter caught my eye as we passed the box office--something about a Zane Gray story. No chance of our seeing a movie in wintertime. So I put that fantasy out of my head as we continued up the sidewalk.

Outside Frykmans garage, a car was idling roughly and steaming. "Froze up" Pa said. In my opinion, so was the mechanic who was stabbing the carburetor with a screwdriver. He was cussing and shivering, while referring to the car's legitimacy of birth as if it was a human being instead of a machine. It was too cold to stop and talk cars. We cut across the street to the grocery store. Again the foot-stomping ritual before entering.

"Not a long list. I can fill this in a few minutes" commented the clerk. He also added that the store now had some apples from Washington and oranges from California. We couldn't afford that luxury so I wasn't surprised when my pa ordered none. Pa now said we were going out to have something to eat at Moody's, then get the team and cutter to load up. He told the clerk we would be back in a short while.

Jake fetched the empty thermos out of the cutter and we went into Moody's restaurant for a quick dinner *(now called lunch)* Here I had a combination of food strange to me, a hot roast beef sandwich with mashed potatoes and gravy. While eating it, I wondered why Ma didn't make this good stuff at home. I'd have to talk to her about that. Pa had the thermos refilled and we headed back to the cutter where he added more briquettes to the few glowing embers and opened the draft.

We took the blankets off the horses, hitched up the team, and made the rounds to collect our purchases. First we picked up the fish at the butchers, then the kerosene, and a new sack of charcoal briquettes from the hardware/mortuary. Jake put the kerosene into the feedbox in back. It would have been stupid to put it up front next to the stove. Actually, I thought he should have put it next to the lutefisk hoping some would spill and improve the flavor of that awful stuff. Next we drove the team and cutter to the grocery store. The groceries were ready when we got there and Jake stowed them behind and under the seat. We had started on our way out of town when Jake said he had some money left over, so we turned and pulled up in front of Monkman's. He gave me a dime and told me to go buy the Sunday edition of the DENVER POST. Great day, Hooray! The funny papers! It would be a week old, but so what? "…the Katzenjammer Kids are timeless. To fully savor the joy of having the funny papers, I would wait until after supper to read them. Even the faint inky smell of new newsprint appealed to me, so I held the precious paper on my lap all the way back to our farm.

On the return home, we followed the regular roads. Jake had had enough of cross-country adventure and strange snowdrifts. About half way home, we shared some steaming coffee from the thermos. Italian kids may get a little wine at a tender age. Scandinavian kids are allowed a little coffee. Sipping coffee, heavily laced with cream and sugar, while gliding along in a cozy cutter is about as good as life gets.

By the time we got back to Mountain View School No. 1, the sun was very low in the southwest. The shadow of the team and cutter stretched far out on the snowfield. This shadow seemed to have a sporting life of its own as it climbed, skipped, dipped, divided, reassembled up and down the irregular snowdrifts. Instead of sun-dogs, there was now a glowing halo around the sun. Where the sun-dogs had been in relation to the sun, were just areas glowing brighter than the rest of the faint halo. Pa said this meant it was a good thing we went to town today because there was probably going to be another big snow by Monday, perhaps even a blizzard. A blizzard, a heaven-sent blizzard?! I wouldn't have to go to school if the blizzard was real bad. How wrong Ma was to call Jake a pessimist. Pessimist indeed! He couldn't possibly have given his school hating son better news.

At last we turned onto the driveway and stopped by the lilac gate, that is, where the gate opening would have been but for the snowdrift covering it. I headed out of the cutter with the DENVER POST, but Pa yelled at me to carry some groceries while I was at it. As I climbed over the stile snowdrift, the sun was about to set. It was a red-orange ball, just beginning to slide under the horizon by the spire of the Swedish church. Only the spire was visible. The rest of the church was hidden by the small hills also hiding the real horizon. Lena, looking from the kitchen window, had long ago observed that the spire served as a marker of the winter Solstice. She was right, as usual. Already, I could see a difference from where the sun had set three weeks ago, the sun was moving north again. In about three months sledding would be over, however life has its compensations, so would school be over.

We carried the smaller packages into the kitchen, then Pa drove to the milk house, which was about a hundred feet south of our house and deposited the flour sack inside. After parking the cutter close to the old auto shed, Pa unhitched the team and took the horses into the barn to be unharnessed. Then they were ushered into a warm stall to be fed a well-deserved mound of hay and a feedbox of oats.

Inside the house, the lights were on. Unlike most farm homes, we had electricity from a 32-volt generator/battery system. We may not have had a big farm, but our light system set us apart. Carrying a package into the warm bright kitchen, I noticed the GRAND FORKS HERALD spread on the kitchen table where Carl had been working the crossword puzzle. From the sound of a crackling aspen wood fire in the stove and the heavenly aroma of frying pork chops, I knew supper was almost ready.

After eating our meal we went into the living room. Carl turned on the Atwater Kent battery-operated radio. Jake sat down in his favorite easy chair. Lena and I divided the paper. She got the news section and I, the funnies. There on the front page of the comic section were the stylized banner words: Happy New Year... 1930. Though I wouldn't admit it out loud, school had its benefits-- I now could read the funnies myself without having to ask Uncle Carl to do it.

Stretching out on the floor in front of our fancy coal-burning stove, I spread the comic section fully open. Hardly had I found the Katzenjammer Kids when I heard a loud 'pffst' sound from the direction of where my father was sitting. Turning to see its source, I saw my pa slouched down in his easy chair, which was half hidden by a book cabinet. Jake was tilting a bottle to his mouth. He had popped the cap off a bottle of beer. Because of the fancy printed label, it wasn't home brew either. Puzzled, I wondered "Where and when had he gotten it?" I had been with him all the time. Tony hadn't sold him any. The cutter! It had been standing unattended on the street while we were shopping. Obviously Jake had a lot of friends.

Another "Cutter Story" as told by Carl

Uncle Carl visited our home in Seattle in 1972. *He had come to visit and have surgery, supposedly minor. After the operation everything seemed fine. However, he died peacefully while taking a nap ten days later. The evening before, he had related the following story. (Time period: circa* 1916) *It seems, quite naturally, that romance also was to be fostered in the confined quarters of a cozy cutter. At the time of the story Carl was still living with his parents on the Lars Olson farm.*

Carls' story:

One evening after the chores were done, Carl decided to visit the family living on the Garden place. This small farm was only a half-mile away. Since the family had three young men constantly full of mischief, it usually meant some kind of fun could be expected. The brothers also had a good-looking sister, which served as bait to attract victims. *(Carl told me the name of this family, a name I have forgotten.)*

The boys had been teasing their sister about a date she was about to have with a young man. He was coming to take her for a ride in his cutter that evening. They either didn't really approve of her choice in boyfriends, or were just being overly protective. Whatever, they decided to play a little joke.

Not to reveal that they were up to no good again, the boys went about some routine chores like cleaning their rifles or playing cards. Meanwhile they took turns looking out the window to spot the approach of the boyfriend's cutter. When one of them saw the team, cutter, and swain coming up the lane in the moonlight, the brothers took immediate action. They seized their loudly protesting sister and carried her upstairs where she was bound, gagged, and tied to her bed. One of the brothers, the one closest in size and facial features to his sister then dressed in her outer garments. Considering how everyone dressed in the winter clothing of shawl, hat, overcoat and overshoes, disguise, would be easy. The unsuspecting beau was met at the front door by one of the brothers who held the door open as the bundled up girlfriend shyly held her head down and headed for the cutter. Protocol normally meant that the caller would politely visit the folks a while before leaving. A little confused with the eagerness of his date already in the cutter, he barely had time for a quick hello and – "I guess I'd better get going," so didn't notice a brother was missing. He hurried out to the cutter and his waiting inamorata.

After a snap of the reins, the cutter was on its way. The brothers went outside to have a better view. The cutter, gliding along in the bright moonlight, its small smokestack leaving a wispy smoke trail, seemed to go a long way before anything occurred. The brothers were beginning to worry that it would be out of sight soon before the action started. Suddenly, the cutter rocked a bit and the startled team turned sharply off the lane and raced erratically into the snow covered stubble field. Carl and the brothers, howling with laughter, ran outside to see what would happen next. The cutter came to a sudden stop. The door burst open and a fleeing figure ran back toward the house. The driver now headed the team back to the lane and headed out, obviously determined not to confront this mad household. Luckily, one of the brothers who had run down the lane caught the bridles of the team and stopped the team. After considerable loud, laughing conversation, he convinced the chagrined victim to come back to the house and have a cup of coffee where he could pick up the real article as soon as she was untied and calmed down.

Come back to the house he did, most likely to prove he could take a joke as well as anyone. He and the genuine sister even followed through on the date. One can only imagine that it wasn't quite the same romantic evening they had anticipated.

BORDER BOOTLEGGERS

Whether the liquor smugglers performed their illicit escapades across the Canadian border for profit, the challenge of thinking up schemes to outwit the Border Patrol or just for fun of being chased--we will never know for certain. Whatever their motive, for a decade during the prohibition era, bootleggers provided some great entertainment for at least one farm boy. The events are true. Well, perhaps the dates and quotations may not be exact.

ONCE IN THE MIDDLE OF NOWHERE

In Gilbert and Sullivan's operetta, THE PIRATES OF PENZANCE, *the pirates are really decent good-hearted guys after all. The police, whose "lot is not a happy one," are revealed as bumbling Bobbies, dedicated to public service with no real conviction that they are doing anything all that important. So it was, in the bootlegger era of the border country of the Turtle Mountains, of North Dakota.*

The Eighteenth Constitutional Amendment prohibiting the manufacture, sale, and transportation of intoxicating beverages went into effect Jan 16, 1920. Almost immediately, in the spirit of American tradition vaunting free enterprise, a host of entrepreneurs went to work manufacturing, transporting, and selling intoxicating beverages. Nationally, it was a zany era lasting thirteen years. One could say it was a fun time, if it hadn't been for big-city gangsters who didn't have a sense of humor.

The Year? I'm guessing 1930

It is summertime and the night temperature at midnight is still stifling. As usual, I am trying to sleep next to the snoring body of Uncle Carl, in our tiny upstairs bedroom. My mother, Lena and my father, Jake, were in the next room. Lena had gone to bed complaining of the heat. If it weren't for the mosquitoes, she had exclaimed, we would be sleeping outside. To get a little air circulation, they had left the door open. For some reason, Pa seldom snored. Ma made up for that tranquility by cussing complaints in Norwegian about the damn misery of heat. There is no sound from the weather vane on the lightning rod, on the roof. Its dry bearings would normally respond with loud groans throughout the house, to every errant breeze, or change in wind direction. It is dead calm, no sounds outside from anything. The last sound we had heard in the evening afterglow was that lonesome who-oo hoo–hoo wail of the Mourning doves.

Suddenly, a beam of light came through our west upstairs window accompanied by the roar of an accelerating automobile engine. Then more lights, the roar of another engine adding a riotous rumble to the night air. The bootlegger-chase was on. The border patrol had spotted a bootlegger coming down the little road from Canada, along willow lined Boundary Creek. This time the bootleggers had spotted the cops waiting in ambush and turned on their headlights to attempt a high-speed escape. Turning the corner onto the main road had caused their light to flash into our window. They sped past our farm, the tone-changing sounds of engines working, as well as the Doppler effect sound of the whistle of a passing train. Carl didn't even stir.

From the bedroom where Jake and Lena slept, I hear Ma say: "I wonder if the damn hoodlums will get away again tonight?" Since Lena thinks prohibition is a dumb law that isn't working anyway, she is more opposed to the nightly disturbance than opposed to the flow of booze across the border. Besides, as Ma says, "There were not as many drunks before they made a law against drinking, than there are now." Privately, I wonder if my lack of sleep from all this nightly activity will stunt my growth.

For some strange reason, I rarely hear of anyone being arrested. Come to think of it, there have been a few guys caught, but they probably deserved it. Getting caught is considered too careless and dumb to earn any respect from the local neighborhood. I recall hearing Godfrey Backman, who lived two miles away, saying, "...got caught, stupid damn fool – he should'a known better."

How come the activity on our farm and that of our close neighbor, Peter Backman? For one thing, our farms lie along the border. Canada doesn't have a prohibition law, the U.S. does. Since the north side of our farms end at the Canadian border, legal booze means just one step across the line. The county road, which runs through our land, begins at Highway 14 in the foothills of the Turtle Mountains, and runs west parallel to the Canadian border, a half-mile away. This road goes for several miles before it becomes more trail than road. It is along this road that the bootlegger-hunting United States Border Patrol patrols.

In the early days before the U.S.A. became persnickety about nationalism there had been no custom offices worth paying attention to. Many little roads, lanes or trails crossed the border. To visit a Canadian neighbor, one simply walked or drove across and visited. The idea of having to drive to Carbury, nine miles away, and check in with a customs office to visit a neighbor a mile away, seems a very silly notion. My folks choose to ignore the rules.

Because most of the area to the west is an open, treeless, prairie with very little cover for the hiding of a rum-running vehicle, there isn't much activity there, as up in the Turtle Mountains. However, Backman's farm across the creek and our place is probably, compared to the hills, the second best place for a bootlegger to cross the border. Boundary Creek snakes down from Canada into North Dakota, and first cuts through Backman's, then our pasture. A small road follows the creek to our Canadian neighbors, the Stewarts. There are willow trees, and other places to hide a car, in the shallow draws along the creek. It is here the Border Patrol hold most of their nightly chases. My folks have a grandstand seat at the racetrack.

The best place to smuggle liquor across the border is in the Turtle Mountains. There must be a hundred trails through the woods being used by the rumrunners. Smugglers prefer trails that are well-hidden and reasonably negotiable by vehicles. The smuggler trails run roughly, and I mean roughly, north and south. The police have been told to patrol east and west near the border. Since there is no road paralleling the border up in the hills, naturally, they drive on the one they can--by our place, on the prairie. This brings to mind the old joke about the man looking for his lost keys under the streetlamp. When asked what he was looking for, he replied, "My keys."

"Where did you lose 'em?"

"Across the street."

"Why not look there?"

"It's dark over there, no light."

The police apply the same logic to finding "hootch haulers."

Remoteness appeals to bootleggers. North Dakota, if anything, is a land of remoteness; so remote that big-time law enforcers take this attitude: "Whoever heard of the Turtle Mountains?" "Wherever that is, it can't amount to much." "There can't be much liquor traffic in such a backward, nowhere place. Now take Chicago for example, that is real bootlegger country. It has famous gangsters, sophisticated restaurants serving lobster and escargot. It has speakeasies, operas and dark, sinister men in pinstripe suits carrying Tommy-guns. In our part of the country only bankers and preachers wear suits. Chicago has Elliot Ness, making headlines in all the daily newspapers. How's that for something! Forget this small town and rural stuff."

Compared to Chicago, certainly activity in our vicinity is strictly small town stuff. Local bootleggers are not inclined to shoot holes in fellow bootleggers. Instead, they are more likely to share information on the best trails to take through the hills, the best time to make a run, ingenious places to hide the hootch. Our rumrunners are unarmed, drive 'jitneys' or beat-up old cars. The border patrols know our local entrepreneurs are basically harmless. Bootlegging in our community is, in general, considered a victimless crime. If a 'whiskey wheeler' blunders and gets arrested with a rumble seat full of scotch, it's no big deal. It hardly even gets the name of the arresting officer on the inside last page of the weekly paper the BOTTINEAU COURANT. No awards, no honorable citations, no fame. "A policeman's lot is not a happy one."

As for bootlegging, even as a kid I thought the whole thing was a dumb adult game. If somebody is all that thirsty for a drink of hard liquor, all he has to do is cross the Canadian border and have a shot or two. Oh well, I guess what the bootleggers are doing is to save the would-be drinker the trouble of getting in his car and wasting gasoline on a long drive. One bootlegger with a big truckload can provide the booze for the whole county. One truckload, versus fifty cars. Think of all the needless driving that is saved. Come to think of it, the bootleggers are providing a service, saving petroleum as a natural resource--it should be considered an unselfish act of community service in the national interest.

What kind of a person was the average illicit liquor supplier? Perhaps we can look at this character this way. H. Allen Smith wrote a book called the COMPLEAT PRACTICAL JOKER. In it, he extols the virtues of the genuine practical joker, as opposed to the party jerk that plays mean tricks on people. This individual, he claims is a fine and extraordinary person. A person who has all the best qualities that a human being can hope to aspire to. He wrote that, contrary to opinion, the true practical joker is not a sadist. He intends no real physical harm. In the first place, he never pulls a joke on someone who doesn't deserve it. In fact, the ideal practical joke will not work at all on a person of virtue and honesty. For the person who has it coming, a well-engineered joke will work only at the moment the victim has it coming.

The skilled practical joker has to be inventive, be a master of timing, be a psychologist, and be courageous. As a person of great sensitivity he would rather not see the outcome, preferring instead to contemplate the result of his trap in a meditative state, away from the scene. Our local bootleggers sort of fit this category. They too had to be inventive and careful of timing. Resolute, daring, and dedicated, they exhibited courage to do what they believed the righting of a public wrong--and made a few bucks to boot. When successful, the daring liquor suppliers were further rewarded by contemplating the happiness of a customer, cozied up by the fire with a fifth of his favorite Canadian whiskey.

Present day dope smugglers have tried a lot of ways to circumvent John Law. So did the "lads of likker" in 1930. Except for an idea involving beehives, I didn't personally witness any of the ingenious schemes, but I couldn't help hearing about some of them. For example, I overheard a story about some guy who went to Canada and filled the inner tubes of his tires with whiskey. It turned out to be a poor idea. Perhaps a blowout wasn't possible, but a washout was. The sharp gravel of the washboard roads proved to be too much for the hard filled thin tires. It was probably just as well. Vintage wine is bottled in a good year. The booze that came out those tires was tainted with the essence of "GOODYEAR."

As for Bootlegger Inventiveness, My Personal Observation Involved Beehives

Our neighbor's land ran north all the way to the Canadian border, a half-mile away. One day, I decided to walk north along the creek in their pasture and see if I could spot more than just frogs in the deeper pools. Ma had told me that in the old days fish once swam in great numbers in the creek. Hoping to see if, by some miracle, some had come back this year, I stopped at every little pool and looked intently. There were no fish, but I did see bigger than normal minnows, so I kept going. Soon I realized that I had crossed the Canadian border into Canada. To my surprise, I saw a short distance away, tucked behind a clump of buckbrush and willows, a row of white painted boxes gleaming in the sunlight. This collection of stuff hadn't been there a month ago and looked totally out of place. My curiosity led me to looking closer.

The boxes turned out to be a big number of beehives. Actually, I had only seen pictures of an apiary before, but I recognized it as such. Curious and eager to see some real bees, I cautiously walked closer to the hives and looked. There didn't seem to be any. Somewhat disappointed, I wondered how I could get them to come out. Then the brainstorm hit me. All I had to do was what the Katzenjammer Kids would do.

The comic strip KATZENJAMMER KIDS *(perhaps called CAPTAIN AND THE KIDS)* is my favorite of all the comics. In one episode, I laughed at the antics wherein Hans and Fritz try to stir up a beehive expecting the bees to attack the bumbling Herr Captain. The bees come out but chase the pranksters instead. The boys save themselves by jumping into a creek. This antic seemed like a fun thing to do--be chased by bees and escape. Here are hives, there a creek.

Summoning up my courage, I approached the nearest hive and took a firm grip on the box. I shook it. Instead of bees coming out, I heard a tinkling sound, clink, clink--no bees. Harder this time and ready to flee, I shake it again... clink, clink. Still--no bees. Very strange.

Carefully I opened the lid and inside, neatly packed in gleaming rows, were dozens of bottles. Booze! The next hive was also filled with bottles, only with different colorful labels. There must have been thirty or more hives all packed with bottles, but no bees. Boy, was I disappointed. The thought crossed my mind that I could easily take a bottle or two home for the folks, but that would be stealing. Then it occurred to me that the bootleggers deserved to have a trick played on them. If only I could find some real bees to put in one of the hives.

When I came home I didn't tell my parents about what I had found, but I asked a lot of questions about where I could find some bees. No luck. My prospects for finding a bee swarm was pretty dim. However, that evening at the supper table, Ma mentioned to Pa that maybe they should look into getting some bees and a hive from Sears Roebuck or somewhere. "Jackie has taken an sudden interest in bees. He should be encouraged. He isn't interested in normal farming." It was not exactly what I had in mind. Bee farming doesn't interest me either.

Maybe Pa knows who the rumrunners are, maybe he doesn't. Nevertheless, he has never mentioned it. However, the bootleggers must think he does and Jake is just being a good guy by not telling anybody. Apparently, in appreciation for his keeping mum they sometimes leave a little present where Pa can find it. Once I was with my father as he opened the granary door and walked inside. There, sticking up in a pile of seed wheat in the bin, was a bottle of whiskey. He picked it up and studied the label. "Wish they would leave some beer for a change," was all Pa said.

Not only do the bootleggers leave liquor gifts, so do our Canadian neighbors. Prices for cream are better in the U.S. than Canada, so, as a favor to our Canadian friends, Jake will drive up to the border and pick up cream cans from the Morrisons and the Stewarts, to sell in Bottineau. Pa then returns the empty cans to the border and leaves the cream-money inside the can. Sometimes our neighbor will meet him at the border with a 'wee gift.'

The only problem is that neither Jake nor Uncle Carl drink very much. Our gun cabinet is full of spirits, as are some of the shelves in the cellar built for holding canned goods, holding sauce of another kind. There's hardly any room for the juneberry sauces, chokecherry jellies, etc.

Being denied legal access to alcohol seemed to increase the desire for it. This is human nature I suppose. The desire became so acute that certain people would drink anything with alcohol in it, even if they hated the taste. It appealed to them because it was forbidden. Liquor had no appeal to me. There was all kinds of it at home in the gun-cabinet for the taking. Sure, as a matter of curiosity, I had sampled some from a number of bottles. The one labeled, "Apricot Brandy," I expected to be great. It was a disappointment like the rest. Therefore, I couldn't understand what the appeal in drinking liquor was. Once, while accompanying my folks on a trip to Souris, I learned of another source of obtaining the forbidden elixir. Vanilla flavoring.

Last Saturday, I went to Souris with my folks. Once free of parental watchfulness, I decided to visit the poster displays of the Souris Opera House, actually a silent picture movie theatre. I wanted to look at the theatre-bills announcing Coming Attractions. Just to the north of the theatre was a small space between the commercial buildings where a group of older boys--late teenagers, were gathered into a small secretive group. They were laughing and jostling each other as if they had shared a most wondrous act of rebellion next to pushing over a privy at Halloween.

I hate to admit it, but I'm scared'a town-guys a lot bigger'n me. I'm also curious about what town kids do. As unnoticeable as I could, I sidled over to them to hear about their adventure. It turned out that they were bragging about how they had bought several bottles of vanilla extract, using the ruse that their mothers had sent them on an errand involving household cooking. Even at my young age I'm thinking, "Are store-keepers really that dumb?" The bottles, perhaps by intent, contain a lot more alcohol than vanilla juice. The boys had learned, from reliable sources, that a fella could get a 'happy feeling' by drinking the stuff. The way to do it was first squeeze your nose like taking medicine, then drink the whole bottle and wait.

Ha, ha, ha, what fun they had giggling, telling, and bragging, about what had happened to them. First they had drunk the stuff, then felt goofy-giddy, and then got sick-throwing-up sick. Each story about getting dizzy, getting sick to a greater degree than the other. Great fun.

On the way home from our shopping trip to the cosmopolitan city of Souris, I was mentally trying to sort out this business of drinking something which would make a person giddy, uncoordinated, sick, and still call it a fun. What was I missing? City boys sure baffle me.

There weren't many illicit stills (Moonshine) in the Turtle Mountains, because Fancy labeled liquor was so readily available across the border. Transportation wasn't the big problem, hiding the supply was. Waterwells, haylofts, wheatbins, and empty pickle barrels were the obvious places. It was rumored that there was an ample amount of.. 'heavenly spirits' hidden in a certain church steeple. Typical of the up-front nature of my father, Jake never hid any. He felt he didn't need to. Preferring beer, he wouldn't have cared if the cops had a raid and took the hard stuff. Lena might have objected though. She enjoyed an occasional ounce of brandy.

Lake Metigoshe was special beyond just being wonderful, magical, mysterious, sinful place. The lake, with its incredibly contorted shoreline of hidden bays was the perfect place to celebrate and exercise the secret desires of normal human beings. Because of its many coves it afforded many hiding places. Therefore, it was a fine place for bootlegging.

One end of Lake Metigoshe extends into Canada. Historically, waterways had been the original highways of America. Lake Metigoshe revived the inland water transportation trade for a while. It became a short highway of sorts. A water highway connecting legal Scotch whiskey to a place where scotch was illegal. On moonless nights, more than one rowboat with muffled oars plied the dark waters of the lake between Canada and the American shore. "The Lake" has always been a special place. It was a natural magnet for those wanting to supply some 'mood-enhancer' to amplify the romantic moment or party revelry.

At one time there was a special large cabin, a watering hole built to straddle the US/Canadian border known as "Cooper's Place." Inside there was a long bar divided by the "line." If the American revenoors should come, all the liquor was quickly moved to the Canadian side. It was a very popular place for the folks who had come by way of Burnett's launch, an outing known as the "Booze Cruise."

One day, during the bootlegger era, the lake had visitors--the kind that wears pinstripe suits and carries violin cases even if they can't play a note.

Big Time Boys from Chicago

This evening my folks have come to visit the Godfrey Backman family and, of course, I've gone along. The first thing I asked of Mrs. Backman, Anna, was "Where's Buck?" "Upstairs" she said.

Visiting upstairs in Buck's room has always been a real treat. He's not only my best friend, even though he is five years older, which makes him a man of the world and exciting source of knowledge about it. His room is a wonderland of wonderful junk and oddities that I would like to have, if Ma would let me. He had a real revolver for practicing quick-draw, cowboy novels, a collection of tobacco cans, airplane magazines with stories about flying aces in the Great War, an arrowhead collection, and souvenirs from places neither one of us have ever been, like Fargo or Minneapolis. In fact, his room is so full that things are under things, hiding more treasures to be found.

Upstairs, I find Harold cleaning his .22 rifle. His greeting is a grin, an incandescent smile capable of lighting up even the gloomiest of places. Then he asked, "Did you hear what happened at the lake last Sunday?" I shake my head "No." Of course I don't know the short road through the hills hasn't been built yet, so our trips to the lake are very infrequent. Nobody has visited us in a week, so how would I know what had happened? Buck went on to say that he and his folks had been to the lake on a fishing trip. His story, I know is going to be interesting, they always are.

"We were just finishing eating a bunch of perch when 'Mossy Norman' came up and told me about the monster car with Illinois plates parked next to the Dygert's East Side hotel. This got my curiosity up and I decided to see for myself." Buck then told me that he and Mossy walked up the hill to see this mystery vehicle. He had anticipated that Mossy had exaggerated a bit. It turned out that Mossy hadn't stretched it at all.

"There, in front of Dygert's was the biggest damn car that I have ever seen. Even the hearse at the Bottineau funeral parlor couldn't match it!" Buck said that a bunch of farmers and a few of the storekeepers from Bottineau were standing, or slowly walking around the strange car, giving it a lot of attention. It was the biggest car anyone's seen in the whole state. Black and shiny, the hood alone seemed longer than an ordinary local car. Everybody agreed that it was impressive. Some of the nervier locals were looking under the car at the suspension system, at the hood ornament, the spare tires sunk in front fender wheel wells, the huge chrome-plated headlights and so on." Already I was sorry that I hadn't been there to see it. Buck could see I was impressed already.

"Wait'l ya hear this," he said. "There were three guys sitting in the car looking straight ahead, as if trying not to see anybody. They seemed to be very glum and sour-lookin." Buck then told me that, despite the day being so hot, they were wearing pinstriped suits, and felt hats with a wide headband. The plates on the car were from Illinois. One of the spectators got so curious he couldn't stand it any more. So he got up enough nerve to go to the driver and ask if he could look under the hood. These guys were, in Buck's words, "Damned unfriendly." All the driver growled was 'no rube,' and kept staring straight ahead.

Buck finished wiping the excess gun oil from his rifle, and looked in the barrel to see how clean it was before he would put it away. He stopped talking for only a couple seconds, but it seemed a long time before he went on.

"The farmer who had asked the question about looking under the hood had been close enough to see something out of the ordinary. The windows had been rolled down so nobody else noticed a certain detail. He didn't say anything right then because the fourth man was coming out of the East Side hotel, carrying a paper sack, probably sandwiches and pop. He was wearing a pinstriped suit and hat too, just like the others. On such a hot day, that seems really stupid. Even preachers are smart enough to take their coats off at "The Lake." His personality wasn't any better than the rest of them--unfriendly as hell. This guy with the sack gets in the car quick-like and slams the door. They start the engine--dad-burnit! (Buck's favorite expression, something he had learned from a wild west novel.) Dad-bumit! You should'a heard the roar of that big som'bitch. When that big sucker took off, it sprayed gravel like bullets on the guys who had been standing behind the rear end."

Buck hung the .22 on some pegs on the wall like he had seen in a cowboy movie before he continued the story.

"After the dust settled, everybody was still talking about the spectacle. Then the farmer who had asked to look under the hood spoke up. "Did anybody notice the windows?'

'What about 'em?' another voice asked. 'Well, I saw 'em edgewise, damned if they weren't three quarters an inch thick or better'. "Bulletproof," somebody else said. Another guy yells, "Let's go int'a Dygert's and find out what the sonavagun was in the store for," and a couple men went inside. They came out with the news. Mr. 'Pinstripe' had asked about renting or buying a lake cottage, something bigger'n a cabin. They had been told about a cottage that was up for rent--there being a lot of cottages available on account'a the hard times."

The news about the big car had spread faster than a case of chicken pox. Late arrivals appeared within fifteen minutes of the departing dust of the twelve-cylinder giant. A few of the late coming locals who had missed the event in the parking area, were disappointed, and decided that they needn't miss a chance to have a look at 'that car' and drove over to the cottage in question. The car wasn't there and never showed up.

The fancy dressed hoods from Illinois must have decided they made a big mistake in believing they could find a hide-away in the Turtle Mountains. Even an unusually stupid elephant would be smarter than to think it could hide out in a cabbage patch. If the sinister men from Illinois thought they could hide out and be inconspicuous in the Turtle Mountains, they didn't know country folks very well. Buck's opinion: "Must be easy to make money bootleggin' in the big cities – if somebody as dumb as those guys can afford a car like that."

There were no big cars visiting from Illinois after that.

To wrap up this bit of history of local bootlegging, I will add the following.

In winter time the rum-running business ground to a halt. It was just too darn cold for a sane man to be out. Bootleggers may have been a little crazy, but not insane enough to be out in a North Dakota winter. However, government bureaucracy being what it is, the border patrol still had to make their rounds.

On days when it was really cold, the patrol would drive into our yard and come knocking at our door. Neighbors never knocked, they just walked in. We'd yell, "Come in," already knowing who was at the door.

The two uniformed men--always two, with their hands, feet, and noses smarting from the cold, would first come into the storm porch, then unbuckle their overshoes and brush the snow off. After clumping their laced, knee-high boots into the kitchen they would politely take the chairs offered and sit down. As usual, the first polite comments always involved the weather. Other small talk ensued. Lena would offer coffee. They would always accept, hoping, in the meantime, that Jake would offer them a warm-up shot of brandy or something for their coffee. They knew he had hard liquor. Obviously, they never asked where he got it, fearing that such indiscretion would cut off future supply. As Jake's part of the ritual he always offered and was never turned down.

After sipping a shot or two at the kitchen table, eventually one of them would sigh and say, "Well, I figger we better get going, the county is swarming with desperate criminals – somewhere." Buckling their overshoes back on, they would bravely go back into the cold. "See ya tomorrow maybe." No maybe about it. Tomorrow would find the brave Border Patrol back on the road as usual, and a warm-up break at our house.

Dec. 5, 1933 the eighteenth amendment was repealed. Prohibition was over and life on the border has lacked a lot of color ever since.

THE BUCK STOPPED HERE

This story is true. It is about a real deer and real people. It is not a "BAMBI" story. The deer in this story spent a great deal of his time getting into crazy kinds of trouble, usually with humorous results. The story location is the northern border of North Dakota. The time period is 1932 to 1933. This animal came into my life when I was ten years old. That he was an unforgettable character is evident because after sixty years I still remember him.

Right off the bat I'm going to tell you this: Unless you have had a deer for a pet, you probably don't know a whole lot about deer. Perhaps my pet deer, a variety commonly called a Virginia White tail, was unique--but I doubt it. I strongly suspect that all deer, if given the same opportunity of being raised from birth, would exhibit the same inclination for getting into trouble.

When Walt Disney made a movie called "BAMBI" he blew the whole scene. He should have contacted me to provide consultant services and then his story would not have been a saccharin tearjerker. Instead, it would have been a revelation of the goofy antics and mischievous mind of a ruminant mammal, of the family Cervidae. A member of this family came into my life for little more than a year, when I was hovering around the age of eleven. It was to be a fun filled visit.

Late Spring of 1932

One afternoon, a neighbor came to our house carrying a small cardboard box. In the box was a spotted fawn not much bigger than a raw-boned alley cat. Obviously, it had just been born, perhaps had never even suckled its mother. The neighbor said, "Found it in the woods – must'a gotten lost – maybe its mother lost it."

Claiming he didn't have the heart to just leave it, he had decided to give it to my father, Jake, who had been recently appointed as a local deputy game warden. He also said, in many guilt loaded words – "I figgered you, Jake, would know what to do with it." Even I, gullible as an almost eleven year old boy can be, didn't swallow the "Lost its mother bit." The little creature quivering in the bottom of the box could hardly stand up, much less, wander away to get lost!

A doe does not forget where its fawn is nested. Fawns don't lose their mother. Pa and I guessed that the doe had had an accident involving a high velocity bullet. Despite his suspicions, what could my father prove? It didn't matter now. Here in the box was a newborn spotted fawn. To give credit to the conscience of our suspected guilty neighbor, it was obvious he felt bad about killing the mother. Only a very hard-hearted man, upon finding a helpless fawn, would be pitiless enough to leave it curled in its nest to die. The wise thing to do would be to give it to Jake, or some other softhearted animal lover--which he did and, much to my delight, we were stuck with it.

My father had been popularly welcomed as the local game warden. Local hunters chose not to hunt during deer season. Legal season was considered dangerous time due to having wild-eyed, big-city hunters in the woods. Local farmers also knew Jake was a soft touch. They 'figgered' that "good-old-Jake" would never arrest somebody for putting meat on the table. Of course, they were correct in that assumption. Even Uncle Carl provided some, occasional out of season venison, to offset the monotony of pork or chicken, at our dinner table.

As for the probable illegality concerning the little fawn's arrival, it didn't matter a whit to me. Nestled in the straw was the most appealing, potential pet any boy could hope to have. As he grew up, he revealed a behavior one wouldn't normally expect from a deer. It soon became obvious that there was more to this creature than just being an animal, suitable for posing as a model for a cute lawn decoration. He would prove to be a car-freak, full of curiosity with a penchant for mischievous antics, thrown in for a good measure.

The Name "BUCK"?

"Buck" is the kind of an unimaginative name you would probably expect an eleven-year-old kid to give a pet deer. Oddly enough, the fawn wasn't named Buck because he was a male fawn. I named him in honor of Harold Backman, who was nicknamed "Buck."

Harold, or "Harrol," as his mother called him, was five years older than I. He was my local friend, guru, and hero. He knew <u>everything</u> that was important and interesting. He knew that any person of keen eyes, superb coordination, and brave heart, could learn to fly an airplane merely by reading the latest "How to Fly" article in his FLYING ACES magazine. Although he had never actually flown anything other than a kite himself, he knew all about flying airplanes.

Buck knew more than the stick and rudder exercises of flying. Buck knew how to rope a calf, set a broken leg, and get maximum price out of fur buyers by stretching skunk, weasel, or mink skins just right. He knew all about the sophisticated world of Hollywood entertainment. He knew all the facts about cowboy stars of the silver screen. He knew about Ken Maynard, Tom Mix, and Hoot Gibson. As an authoritative source of western history, he couldn't be beat. He had all the statistical facts about the 'real gunfighters' of the old west. Best of all, as I became older and in the process of reconsidering the value of girls, he knew about sex. He disclosed a redeeming quality about girls, a form of life that I had hitherto considered basically useless. He informed me that girls if properly approached, and certain rituals performed, could provide a very special source of pleasure. This special pleasure could provide a lot more fun than the game of spin-the-bottle. Certainly, the only possible way a fella could repay that kind of free tutoring would be to name your very special pet fawn, "Buck."

If Walt Disney would have had the experience of raising a deer like mine, His movie about a 'fawning' fawn named "BAMBI," would have been a lot more entertaining. There wasn't much in his movie to suggest that deer have a sense of humor, if you can call practical jokes and mischief humor. My deer spent a lot of time thinking up things just to get people annoyed. The movie Bambi looked cute, graceful, and sissified. Buck got over being cute, like a kid goat gets over being cute, when it is four months old. A ballerina is graceful.

Buck was not a ballerina. He would sometimes come running into the house, slip on the slick linoleum and crash into things. Seeing him bound effortlessly, over a seven foot high lilac bush, was more on par with watching an Olympic high jump event. As for being sissified, the yearling Buck enjoyed roughhousing like a linebacker. He did have one mental problem, a justifiable paranoia about strange dogs. This phobia he had good reason to have, something that I'll explain later. In the meantime, back to the beginning, his babyhood.

The First Days

Lena carefully lifted the little guy out of the box, and said that he wouldn't live long unless we got some food into his stomach. She wrapped him in a towel, and put the fawn in a padded apple box, while she pondered how to feed it some milk. What we needed was a baby's nursing bottle. On second thought, Lena thought a bottle might not work anyway. The fawn looked too weak to nurse. Milk needed to be injected into its mouth. Then my mother remembered having an old rubber bulb ear syringe somewhere on the junk shelf in the cellar. She sent me down to get it while she warmed some milk. Ma had decided that cow milk wouldn't be rich enough for a deer. Goat's milk would be better. Since we didn't have a goat, she laced cow milk with a liberal shot of cream. The mixture warmed on our wood burning stove. A few minutes later, we were ready to try to feed the fawn.

The deer was frightened and skittery, but since it was so weak, there wasn't much problem handling it. After Ma sucked up a syringe full of milk, she held the fawn's head up and squirted some milk in its mouth. To her satisfaction, the little rascal got the idea that lunch was being served by the third, or fourth syringe full. Soon, it was greedily sucking on the pointed rubber end of the syringe as if it had just found its mother again. Though Lena was holding it in her lap, he even tried to stand up. This didn't work very well. When Ma decided he had enough, she put him back in his box. She then took the box into the dining room, where our open stairway slanted upstairs. Then she placed him under the stairway where he would be out of the way, and we left him to sleep off his milk binge.

Our dog "Tootsie," who had watched the whole affair, looked into the box, sniffed at the creature and looked at us as if to ask, "How come I don't get treatment like this?" From then on, the place under the stairway became imprinted in Buck's mind as his 'safe' place. Even when he became a full-grown buck deer, it would be the place he would head for when frightened. He had great fear of strange dogs. If one were to come into our yard he would, at high velocity, seek instant refuge under the stairway. This was more often than my mother would have liked.

Some hours later, it was time for a second feeding. This time he could stand up and even twitched his tail a few times. By the next day or so he recognized the syringe on sight, as lunchtime.

On Saturday, Jake had to go to town. One of the things Lena asked Jake to get was a baby's nursing bottle. This caused my dad a few problems with his friends, who were always looking for an excuse to do some ribbing. According to a later report from a neighbor, even the store clerk raised an eyebrow, and gave Pa a hard time as He, at age fifty-three asked for a nursing bottle.

The baby bottle worked a lot better than the ear syringe. At every feeding he not only wagged his tail furiously, but would gently butt the bottle as if to speed the process up. He was on his way to boisterous good health. One thing I noticed was that, as he nursed, his hind legs were locked together into a knock-kneed bipod. Looking at him from behind, the hind legs made a steadying triangle. Inside the elbows of his hind legs, were small tufts of stiff hair similar to a bristled miniature hairbrush. These tufts acted something like "Velcro" and prevented slippage at the apex of the triangle. What a marvelous solution for a structural stability problem. Perhaps our deer was unique in this feature--I don't know. Our deer, is the only one I have ever seen close up as a fawn that young. Most of the time, after feeding, he just slept in his box under the stairway. About a week later, he began to explore the house, his feet slipping sometimes on the linoleum. Deer droppings, neat little marbles as they were, soon became a problem, and so my mother said he would have to be moved outdoors.

In 1933, the era of the Dust Bowl had already turned much of our farm into a desert. There weren't many places where a nice patch of grass could be found to build a pen for Buck. Uncle Carl decided that the best place would be in the shade on the north side of our windbreak near the mailbox, half of the enclosure to be in the trees and half in some tall grass and weeds. It seemed ideal. Lena, chief of any and all operations, approved, so Carl built a deer pen about thirty by thirty feet in size. He used the kind of wire mesh we used for the pigpen. I hated to see the fawn get stuck in an enclosure like some caged zoo animal. Buck didn't seem too keen on the idea either. The box under the stairway was his idea of home. He would never change his mind about that matter.

After we had left him in the pen, he frantically ran from side to side looking for a way out so he could follow us. Finally giving up, he found a place to stay curled up under a bunch of weeds. He established a nest where he would stay all day until we showed up with his milk bottle. The milk bottle and I had become his mother. At the sight of his bottle he would get over his depression instantly. I still didn't like the idea of Buck being cooped up. He should be playing with Tootsie, that's where he belonged. My folks said that deer and dogs don't play together. Heck, what did they know? I had seen Tootsie and Buck sniffing noses every now and then. For some reason, he had no fear of our dog. Maybe they weren't exactly buddies, but they got along OK.

Two or three days later, one night we were awakened by the noise of barking dogs. We didn't pay a lot of attention to it at first because, every now and then, neighbor dogs would show up to raid the chicken coop or something. However, our chickens were locked up and safe. We hadn't thought of the deer. Finally, my dad went out and yelled at them to go home. Apparently, they understood the Swedish language and obeyed.

The next morning I went out to feed Buck, and he didn't show up at the side of the fence with his tail wagging in anticipation. Then I saw small tufts of deer hair caught in the fence wire, and a path of downtrodden grass around the fence. Dog tracks! The damn dogs had been chasing my deer. Then I saw him; he wasn't curled up in his normal nesting place, just sort of stretched out in the weeds. Was he dead? Thankfully, he wasn't dead, but mighty beat up looking. Here and there a torn patch of skin on his head and flecks of dried blood in his hair. From fear of the barking dogs, running outside the pen, he had darted from one side of the wire enclosure to the other, only to smash into the fence. Damn, damn. I hated those dogs! Buck didn't seem interested in my being there--or in the milk bottle either.

Gathering him up in my arms, I took him into the house and told my folks what had happened. I was angry because they had put him in that pen. Defiantly, I put him on an old hooked rug under the stairway again. Later on that day, Buck's hunger overcame fear and he gulped down a quart of milk. He never went back into the enclosure again. That night we put him in the barn, which, in summer, was empty of other animals except at milking time. During the day, he would follow my mother or me wherever we went. He would even occasionally follow Tootsie.

Somehow, he never associated Tootsie with being a dog. However, the experience in the enclosure had frightened him so much that, upon encountering other dogs, even a Pekinese, he would panic and run to his 'safe place' under the stairway.

A Strange Obsession

Buck adapted to living on the farm so quickly; it was as if he was never meant to be a creature of the wild. As it turned out, Buck developed another trait that seemed plumb unnatural. He had become a car-freak! Looking back, it became clear that we were to blame for this idiosyncrasy. It began when we took him for a ride in our '28 Dodge to see the neighbors. We took him for rides when he was a fawn to show him to neighbors who wanted to see the little 'critter.' For another thing, after the dog incident, we didn't dare leave him home alone unattended, so we took him in the car. He behaved well the first few times. He just curled up behind the back seat, with his ears back and snoozed. Then once, while standing on the rear seat, he discovered the landscape moving by at thirty-five miles an hour and he was hooked! From then on, if Pa took the car out of the garage, he would be first to enter. He wasn't fussy about whose car it was.

Any automobile pulling into our yard would get his instant attention. Buck would do everything, but kick the tires and look under the hood. If he had had a thumb, he would have hitchhiked. If a door were left open, he would be in the car in a flash. The neighbors soon learned about our deer's obsession, and were careful when opening the door with Buck around. He would even hide in the Lilac bushes to ambush the unwary. Sometimes an uninformed stranger would unwittingly open the door, then be extremely startled to find a deer in his or her lap. Women tended to yell a lot.

While riding, he had discovered the mysterious fun that dogs seem to enjoy that of sticking the head outside the car, and letting the wind peel the ears back. Once in a while, I was able to talk my folks into taking both Tootsie and Buck with us in the car. There we would go, driving along the highway, a dog's head out one window, and a deer's head out the other.

If we were going to town, we didn't want him with us. Once in the car, he refused to leave it. When he was still small enough to have fawn spots, removing him from the car was no problem, we could just carry him out, but when he grew to be a 165-pound monster, he was impossible to dislodge. Tug on his ears, pull his head, push him from behind, it was incredible how strong and slippery he was. He could place his feet against the door posts, seat corners, and threaten to poke his sharp hooves through the overhead panels, whatever measures were taken, we lost. To him, it was a big fun game. Buck seemed to enjoy the siege. He always won. The only way we could dislodge him from any car or truck was to fill a bottle with milk, and entice him out. This removal ruse was to serve us well, since his sudden presence in a visitor's car was never by invitation.

In the summer of his first year, our fawn didn't assert himself very much. In general he stayed out of trouble--except for cars. Neighbors were amused that we had a pet deer, and remembered to get out of their cars quickly.

Buck had more curiosity about things happening around our place, than Tootsie did. One day, a mother skunk showed up with a retinue of baby skunks following. He cautiously followed them as they headed for shelter under the milk house. Mrs. skunk didn't seem all that concerned. However, the baby skunks, following their mother in trail formation, became aware of Buck coming to examine the review. Then quickly, as if obeying a command from a drill sergeant, they did an instant flank right, and attempted to do a spray job on the deer, even though their spray equipment hadn't developed yet. Not only did their glands fail to perform, also their coordination. Running 'skirmish-line-forward' toward Buck, they suddenly planted their feet, and flipped their tails only to tumble in somersaulting disarray. Some natural instinct about skunks caused Buck to make a mighty leap sideways. This event was typical. It was always amusing to watch this so-called dumb animal, explore the strange world surrounding him.

Uncle Carl had discovered that our dog had a sweet tooth. The previous Christmas season he had offered some hard candy to Tootsie. She had enjoyed it mightily, getting overweight in the process. Then, in an inspired moment of scientific experiment, Carl offered a sugar cube to this innocent deer. Instant addiction! From now on, next in priority to a bottle of milk, and a ride in a automobile, a lump of sugar was most important in Buck's inventory of worldly delights. Our pet was adjusting to modern human society rapidly; he had now become a sugar junkie!

School began in September.

"Welcome children," the teacher had intoned, as if reading from some manual, "Your seating assignment will be..." Damn! How depressing. Somehow, I got through the first day. The only other boy in the school that year, was Vern Berge. All the rest were girls. How am I going to survive this coming year? It was the custom of the local school board to start the school year at the end of harvest, and finish at the beginning of spring plowing. The purpose was to make sure children would be home to work, or help out when needed. This meant that the school year was usually about seven months long. How I hated going to school! Every child there was smarter than I. My mother had erroneously decided that one is never too young to learn; therefore she started me out in first grade, when I was still five years of age. It never occurred to me until I was much older, that I was almost two years underage for the grade I was in. Of course, I couldn't keep up with the others, but I didn't know why at the time. The Berge and Thorsgard girls were so much brighter, and quick to learn. I felt like a stupid retarded moron. Until I was eleven, I didn't have anything I could boast about to the other kids, but now I had a pet deer.

Sometime in October, Buck followed me to school. The children were delighted and envious of my pet deer. The teacher hadn't expected this intrusion in her plans for an orderly year of education. Vigorously clanging the school bell, she ordered the children into the schoolhouse, and told me to send the deer home. Ordering Buck to do anything was an exercise in futility. Nevertheless, I pointed northeast and said: "Go home Buck." He looked at me as if I was speaking a foreign language. Buck's attitude was more like a cat than a dog. He never obeyed any command except milk call. Leaving Buck outside, I went into the bleak white edifice of Mountain View No.1. Buck hung around for a while, and then headed for home, a tan streak disappearing into the distance. My heart went with him.

Perhaps a month or so later, Buck followed me again. This time he didn't go home right away, and hung around till the recess bell rang. The schoolyard had no playground equipment; nevertheless all the students went outdoors to play a game of nip-stick[9]. Buck welcomed the kids as they came out the door. They delightedly approached to pet, and fondle him. Some of the girls had opened their lunch buckets for a recess snack. The odor of jam wafted into Buck's nostrils. Sugar! The girls giggled and treated him to sugary snacks. From then on, he put up with all the attention. At the sight of a lunch bucket, visions of sugarplums danced in his head. He was not easily to be put off.

At noon the schoolmarm rang the dinner bell. The children grabbed their lunch buckets and headed outdoors. Buck, for some patient reason, was still there. Apparently he had holed-up in the empty horse barn on the north side of the school lot. *(Small horse barns were provided for children who had to come a long way to go to school. In the case of Mountain View No.1, it was seldom used.)* When we came out, he casually walked over to meet us. Sitting on the steps of the schoolhouse, the girls and I had opened our lunch buckets. Then Buck drawn to the odor of sugar in the form of chokecherry or strawberry jam followed his nose right into lunch buckets. The girls pulled the buckets away. No matter, Buck discovered jam near the edges of their mouths and slurped his tongue on their faces. He found the sweet surplus no matter how they turned their heads away. Buck was gentle but obnoxiously persistent. His tongue tickled. A lot of giggling and yelling ensued. After the school bell rang 'return to classes,' Buck hung around for a while and then headed swiftly for the farm.

For some strange reason, Buck seemed to have a perfectly timed clock in his head. Back at the farm a mile and a half away, he would know to the minute when the lunch bell would ring at school. A couple minutes before the noon bell was rung, I could look out the window and see a small tan speck coming over the low hills between our farm and the school. It would be Buck, running and bounding over fences on his way to join the pupils, and whatever they had in their lunch buckets. Even our teacher began to look forward to his visit. Outside he would intrude into whatever game we were playing, frequently getting in the way of an organized game by the teacher. Pushing him would only result in playful resistance. Country girls can roughhouse as well as any boy. Sometimes we would make a snow pile to play King-of-the-Mountain, a game of roughhouse battle, the winner was whoever remained on top of the pile against all comers. Buck got the idea and would join in. He would enjoy the pushing and pulling, yet somehow managed never to step on a fallen child. Once in a while, we would put the smaller children on his back, which he would dump off unless we held a strawberry jam sandwich in front of his nose. In this case, he could be led in a circuit, ignoring the child on his back. Thus, the school year passed. He didn't visit every day. When he didn't, we were disappointed.

---

[9] *Nip-stick: This was a game using two sticks. A long stick called the 'nipper' and a shorter one, about six inches long. A narrow groove would be scratched in the ground. The short stick would be placed crossing it. The nipper would be used to flip the short stick into the air to about waist high. Then using the nipper the player would try to keep the short stick in the air, every hit counting. The player scoring the most hits won.*

Winter is a wonderful time for a boy with a pair of skis and a hill nearby. North Dakota is not known for its hills but, luckily, we had one near our barn. One day, I had been skiing down this little knoll and decided to build a jump, made of snow piled up and shaped into a ramp. Buck had watched me build it and had waited as I made the first run. On my first attempt to jump, I crashed on landing and decided to try it again. Then as I was about to start down the hill again, I saw Buck was standing on top of the jump as if daring me to try. I ran down and tried to chase him away. He ran to the top of the hill and stood there as if nothing had happened. Putting my skis on again, I started the run to the jump. He beat me there, and I had to fall down to prevent crashing against him. His sharp hooves had broken my carefully made jump into clumps of packed snow. I had to repair it with the shovel. Climbing back to the top of the hill I put on my skis again. Again, there was my obnoxious ornery pet, intentionally trampling the jump, nosing snow-clods away! What a lousy way to get attention. All my yelling and cussing was music to his ears. All the chasing I did was just his favorite exercise.

My mother, Lena, had less patience than I did. One day, after doing the laundry she hung the clothes out on the clothesline to dry. It didn't matter that the weather was below freezing. First the sheets would freeze solid and then, by sublimation, they would dry out to wave in the wind as if on a summer day. Lena went back in the house assuming all was well. What could possibly go wrong with the laundry on a cold, calm winter day? Then she happened to look out the window and saw Buck, chewing on a corner of a sheet. Perhaps he was just enjoying some dripping water before it froze. My mother didn't care what his reason was. She grabbed the broom, and tore out of the house to chase him away. Buck now discovered a new game called "Chew-the-Sheet and Get Chased." He made tantalizing circles just out of reach of my mother's swinging broom. From then on my mother made sure he was locked in the barn when her clothes were on the line.

One day, somebody blundered and Buck got out of the barn. He soon found that washing had been done, and clothes already hung and frozen. He stood by the clothesline to get Lena's attention in the hope of being chased. She didn't see him but I did. Thinking he would just get bored and go away, I didn't mention anything to Ma. After a while he walked up the sloping cellar door, covering our 32-volt power plant, beneath our kitchen window. He looked in the window, and wiggled his head to get my mother's attention, then turned and walked towards the clothesline, taking a backward glance now and then to see if the 'broom-lady' was coming. Then Buck positioned himself near the array of clothes. After looking back towards the house to make sure my mother was still looking, he then reared up slightly and raked his foot down the frozen sheet. It tore as if slashed by a knife. Lena knew some powerful cuss words, and put them to good use. She grabbed the ineffectual broom, and ran out of the house without bothering to put her overshoes on. Buck had a wonderful time leaping over the lilac bushes, caragana hedge and picket fence, all the while followed by

Ma racing through the snow, swinging the broom and damning the deer to perdition. Later, we were all cross-examined as to who had let the deer out of the barn. As punishment, supper that evening was mighty bad.

Here is a personal zoological observation: Compared to a deer, a dog is stone deaf. To reveal this discovery I will begin with Mr. McArdle, our mailman. McArdle had the rural route, which came by our farm. He was one of the first to know about our deer, and kept his car doors closed. Somehow, he learned that not only our dog, but our deer loved candy or sugar, so he treated them both with a sugar cube every mail day. The deer and dog would recognize the sound of his balloon-tired Model "A," and be waiting at the mailbox long before he got there. Buck would always be first to arrive. Tootsie could recognize the sound of the mailman's car a half mile away. Buck, much farther. How much farther? The answer deserves explanation.

The discovery of his long distance hearing capability involved our party line telephone. Due to road conditions in winter, the mailman came at varying times of the day. We didn't know when McArdle would show up. His arrival time was important because we had to be at the mailbox to meet him if we wanted to buy stamps or mail a package. Waiting for the mailman out by the mailbox in a temperature of ten below, ranked low in pleasant things to do. We didn't want to run out to the mailbox at every car sound that we heard either. Like the rest of the folks on the route an alert system was needed. The answer was to call a neighbor down the road and ask them to tell us when the mailman had come. (That is, if they had noticed.) That way, we could anticipate his arrival at our farm more accurately.

Just outside our south kitchen window was a small knoll. On top of this wee knob, Tootsie and Buck would wander from time to time, to listen for the approach of the 'candy man.' They could tell the difference between McArdle's Model "A" and other coming cars. The dog would walk to the listening spot, sit down, point her nose to the west, and if she heard the mailman's car, would head for the mailbox. Buck would do the same thing; only he would stand very still with his nose to the west, and move his ears slowly like a scanning radar dish. When he heard McArdle's car, he would flick his ears as if to turn off the scanner, and head for the road. He was always first to hear the 'right' sound, and be first to the road. Watching Buck and Tootsie was as reliable as the telephone, but we couldn't keep staring out the window all day when there was work to be done. When it was really important not to miss the mail, we called back down the line to a neighbor.

One day, Lena called her telephone-and-gossip buddy, Gunda Berge. Mrs. Berge had a good view of her mailbox from her kitchen window. Lena asked Gunda if she would keep a sharp lookout for McArdle because she had to mail a big package back to Sears Roebuck. It was real important to tell us if the mailman had been there. Gunda, of course, agreed. The conversation, to be polite, went on from there to other things of local importance – who had a gallstone operation – who was pregnant again, etc.

The mail was later than usual that day. At least four other cars had driven by. Buck had walked to the listening spot a few times, so had the dog. Both had recognized the on-coming car as a dud. Late in the afternoon, I happened to see Buck, who was taking his turn at the listening post. He was scanning. Then I saw him flick his ears in "McArdle, Model "A" recognition and head for the mailbox. Then a minute later, the telephone rang, and Gunda said the mail had just been by. Gunda Berge lived <u>three miles away!</u> Five minutes later, Tootsie went out to the road.

Whenever I see hunters, carefully being quiet while stalking deer, I can only smile at the futility of such antics. Buck could hear the sound of a snowflake crashing into the ground. A hunter, even wearing moccasins, would to a deer, sound like a clumsy rhinoceros in a hubcap factory. A deer hears all sounds. It only tries to sort out the benign sounds, from the ominous. *(I would tell the benign sounds to make, as opposed to ominous, but some hunter might read this and I don't want to be responsible for wanton deer slaughter.)*

One day Mama *(I called her mama in private. In front of my more worldly friends, I said "Ma.")*, asked me to bring a few extra loads of wood into the house, because there was going to be a blizzard. Nobody argued with my mother when it came to weather forecasts. She had the weather vane on the roof, a barometer in the living room, and records of the wind direction for the previous days. If she had heard the weather forecast on the radio, she rarely agreed with it. Lena was always right. Weather reports from KFYR, Bismarck, had predicted fair weather. "Damn fools – don't they ever look out the window?"

We hadn't even finished milking the cows, when snow began to fall. Flakes the size of popcorn slanted toward the ground in a light wind. It was time to put Buck in the barn, but he was nowhere to be found. This caused me to worry. Carl said it was nothing to get upset over, not one wild deer had the luxury of a barn, and they survived just fine. True enough, still I wished I knew where he was. Buck hated to be put in the barn. His desire was to be under the stairway in the dining room.

An hour later, all the snow of Canada and Alaska seemed to be roaring horizontally past our house. Unlike the stupid, whining sound tracks used in movies, the sound of a real blizzard is a shuddering, house-shaking rumble. Where, in all this fury was Buck? After supper, we settled in the living room. Dad tended the lignite burning stove, then flopped on the sofa for a snooze. Mama relaxed with her favorite occupation--the spinning wheel. Uncle Carl was trying to coax some sense out of our static plagued Atwater Kent radio. He was hoping to hear the Eddie Cantor show. I was trying to build a model of the clipper ship "Cutty Sark." My heart wasn't in it--where was Buck? Then a deer face appeared outside our window in the lee side of the storm. It was Buck, looking as pathetic as he could. Dusted liberally with snow, he managed to project the forlorn image of an orphan, abandoned to a cruel fate by a bunch of Sadists. I begged my mother to let him in. After all, Tootsie was in the house getting served leftover Christmas candy, furtively doled out by Carl. Mama said the deer belongs in the barn, but it was too dangerous to attempt to do that in this storm. Carl said it served him right. Finally, Mama relented and said he could come in to the narrow confines of our entry storm-porch. In summer, this was a small, 4'x 10' screened enclosure, in winter; panels were put up to make it a transitional sheltered room in which to take off our overshoes. It was also used to store milk or cream just above freezing point. In here I put an old hooked rug, and let Buck come in. He tried to nose farther inside when I went back in the house, but seemed grateful to settle for the corner where the rug was spread.

Two days later revealed a brilliant snow sculptured landscape. Sundogs held the sun in parenthesis, and a huge snowdrift heaped up near the Lilac hedge. This drift was perfect for making a snow cave. Igloos are hard to make, snow caves easy. After locating a spade in the garage, I dug an entrance doorway, then a room big enough to stand up in. It was surprisingly cozy inside. Buck and Tootsie joined me, and I truly felt like a real Eskimo with his arctic pals. My parents thought my energy could have been better spent digging a path through the gateway to our driveway. Two weeks later, a Chinook wind came and melted my igloo to the point I had to repair it with some snow blocks. It lasted almost a month. Buck preferred my snow cave to the barn for shelter.

It is still winter. Keep in mind the passion Buck had for riding in automobiles, as I relate the following events.

I have long forgotten his name, but our community was served by a rotund, very near-sighted traveling salesman. He was, primarily, a "Watkin's Products" dealer. His home base was the thriving town, Souris. His thick-lensed glasses gave him an owl-like look. Always properly dressed in a company-approved suit, he sold spices and flavorings, natural and artificial, to rural households. Four times a year, spring, summer, fall and winter, he would come rattling by in his Model "T" sedan Ford. He provided farm wives the zippy essentials, which would make the difference between an ordinary meal and something exotic.

The big seller was the Scandinavian favorite, Allspice. Other popular flavors were cinnamon, cardamom, cumin, and sage. Bottles of vanilla extract, lemon and coconut, as well as spices were neatly stored in tiny drawers--drawers neatly fitted into factory approved, rosewood cabinets.

Any novelty in a rural community spreads like measles, so he already knew we had a deer. <u>What he hadn't heard</u> was Buck's obsession with automobiles. He was destined to learn the hard way. On a dazzling bright winter day, came the innocent Watkin's Products salesman.

Prior to the arrival of the spice peddler I had been sledding on the barn hill. Disappointed with the snow conditions, I abandoned the slope. I was carrying my "Flexible Flyer" sled back from the barn-hill, when I saw a Model "T" coming up the driveway from the road. Out of the rear window of this box-like car, stuck Buck's head pointed into the breeze. A piece of cardboard attached by one edge to the window opening, flapped in the wind. At the lilac gate the car stopped abruptly. The round body of Mr. Salesman burst out of the driver's door, and headed angrily over the snowdrift covering the walkway to our house. He banged on our porch door. As soon as my mother answered, he started yelling angry accusations. Lena never was one to be yelled at. I interceded and told my mother that Buck was in his car. Ignoring the angry man with the frost misty glasses, she told me to get Buck's milk bottle and coax him out. Mr. Salesman, his thick glasses still fogged over, loudly said my mother owed him a lot of money for destruction of property, and near cardiac arrest. War clouds. To avoid further collateral damage, I hurried to get the milk bottle.

Back outside, I opened the salesman's car door with one hand, and held the bottle in the other. Buck considered the new option thoughtfully, and came out of the car. The back seat was a mess. Elegant cases were tipped over, and many drawers had fallen out. Spice cans and flavoring bottles were scattered in disarray. Very few things seemed to be broken, except for the lid popped from a Cinnamon can or two.

When I got back in the house, our peddler was sitting, a bit more calmed down, and a cup of coffee in his shaking hand. My mother had agreed to pay for anything broken, and nothing else. This seemed fair enough to him. After a second cup, and a few sandbuckles he related what had happened. Every winter the problem area near our farm was the road and bridge across Boundary Creek. The willows, acting like a snow fence always left a drift over the grade. This is what our Watkin's Products man had encountered. He got stuck. Curious as Buck was, upon hearing the fuss down by the bridge, had gone to investigate the possibility of a potential ride.

Taking the shovel out of his back seat, Mr. Watkin's Products had impatiently shoveled the impeding snow in front of his car. The strenuous effort had steamed up his glasses so when he threw the spade into his back seat, he hadn't noticed that a 165-pound deer now occupied it. To his surprise, the spade came flying back out the door. Still not aware of the deer because of fogged up glasses, he threw the spade back in again. Same result, out came the spade again. Startled, he became aware that an ornery beast was implanted in the backseat of his car. Startled? To say he was startled is an understatement. Buck was standing in a sea of spice cans and bottles. His nose was poking into the mess, checking out exotic flavors.

Partially recovering from his heart-pounding trauma, the spice salesman remembered hearing about the Olson's having a pet deer. Then he got mad, damn mad. "I've got to get this accursed beast out of my car before he wrecks everything." Then he tried to take the bull by the horns. Only this was no mere bull. Grabbing Buck by the head he tried to pull him out. Buck only braced his feet and resisted. More bottles rained out of the cases. Next, our frustrated Watkin's Products man opened the opposite door, and tried to push him out. Same result, none. As far as Buck was concerned it was a big game. "I'm in this car to stay. The odors are marvelous." Finally, in futile desperation the spice dealer slammed the rear door on Buck. The right hand rear window of the car had been broken and replaced by a piece of corrugated cardboard. Buck didn't duck quickly enough and his head punched the cardboard out. This explained the view of my happy smiling pet as the Model "T" came rolling into our yard.

After he had related the full story, my mother and the Watkins man began laughing about the incident. Lena considered it fair to pay for actual damage, which didn't turn out to be much. She bought some Cinnamon cans she hadn't planned on having. Thus indirectly, Buck had added to the flavor of hot cocoa and spiced Brandy for the rest of the winter.

Spring came without any particular event, save one. Buck was in the barn at milking time, and a neighbor came by followed by a harmless dog. The neighbor had entered the barn looking for Jake. Buck, upon seeing the strange dog, bolted and tried to escape. The other door was closed. In panic he streaked into a stall occupied by only one cow, and jumped through the small, four paned window over the manger. We couldn't believe how he could have made it through that tiny opening. He didn't escape unscathed. A piece of glass carved a chunk of hide from his back. Later, when the wound healed, the hair grew back as a black patch of hair.

One day in late spring, Victor Moody, married to my Aunt Anna, came into our yard. His dog "Bo" was along. This was a German Police dog, but not a particularly hostile dog. However, Buck didn't know that. To him, any dog was cause for panic, and panic he did. He took off for his 'safe place' under the dining room stairway at full speed. It didn't matter that the porch screen door was closed. He came through it at about forty miles an hour. Lena was just carrying a kettle of soup in the kitchen. Buck's route to the dining room required a 90-degree turn. He didn't make it. He slipped on the slick floor and momentum carried him sliding into the legs of Lena. The kettle of soup flew in the air as Lena, and deer piled up against the far wall. Buck scrambled to his feet first and made it to his place under the stairs. There he stood quivering, too big for the small niche looking frightened and stupid. As soon as Lena got to her feet, she ran to the deer and pounded him with the kettle to chase him outside.

Summer eased along without any outstanding events, just the occasional ruckus and yelling heard from the driveway when a strange car had come for a visit, and we hadn't gotten to the driveway in time to restrain Buck. However, there was one memorable weekend involving my Aunt Mina, Ma's younger sister.

"Minnie" was married to Sig Sigurdson, a pharmacist who owned the Sigurdson Drugstore. She was a refined lady, elegant, sophisticated, educated, cultured--a person who knew all about the latest hit Broadway musicals and plays in New York City. My mother, a farm wife with peasant, work-worn hands, felt inferior and intimidated in the presence of her sister. Above all, Lena hated being caught at home wearing her paint stained overalls. She would become very embarrassed whenever Mina dropped by wearing a fashionable dress, stylish shoes, and smelling nice. Ma would stand there, in her beat-up overalls, wanting to die on the spot. In truth it probably didn't matter that much to Minnie. Mina and Sig would sometimes show up unexpectedly for a visit. This Sunday, in particular, Mina arrived with Sig driving in the front seat and Mina and her friend, Luella Stewart, in the back. Sig was in his Sunday-outing best, a boater hat with a wide black band, white shirt, tie, and gray slacks. Mina and Luella were decked out with fine summer hats, ruffles, lace, parasols folded.

On hearing the sound of a strange car in our yard, my mother hastily said to me "Where's the deer?" It was too late. At the sound of screaming ladies I ran outside. As I ran through the gate, I saw Buck in the back seat on the laps of some very upset women. Sig was out of the car trying to extricate the intruder by pulling his head. In the meantime, Ma was frantically filling a bottle of milk. Sig was losing, the women were yelling, Buck was having a very good time.

Thank God, the bottle worked. Buck came out of the car with his ears waggling in anticipation. Aunt Mina and Luella Stewart bravely struggled to recover their composure. Hats askew, they came down our walkway making sounds of dismay, and discomfort. For me the whole episode had been better than watching Laurel and Hardy. Buck seemed unconcerned about the ruckus.

A later visit from Sig and Aunt Mina was responsible for Buck being sent to the zoo in Wahpeton, North Dakota.

One day in late summer, Sig and Mina, now much wiser about our deer's car habits, decided to risk another trip to our farm. After coming into our yard, Sig sounded the car horn to announce their arrival. Then he waited to get out of the car until we came out to the driveway to reassure Mina that Buck was properly restrained. He was. As usual, once people were out of their car our pet behaved decorously. First he would check the car to make sure all the doors were truly closed and then knowing his entrance was barred, would casually follow the visitors down the walk.

In the meantime, unknown to us, sexual instinct had reared its ugly head. In the previously innocent mind of our now, almost mature deer, he was no longer a cute little spotted fawn. He was big. Horns had begun to sprout. Little did we know that a rage of hormones had addled Buck's mind. However, the restrained Buck behaved himself as a well-brought-up, refilled aristocrat. He even politely stood still, almost bowing, as Aunt Mina patted his head.

In one corner of our inner yard, Sig was talking to my dad about the crops. Buck was following Lena as she was showing her sister Minnie the profusion of the flowers she had growing in different patches. We assumed that the attention Buck was giving my aunt was mere curiosity. Little did we know what wild fantasies had been going on in his unsophisticated little mind. He had never seen a female deer, or even a goat for that matter, in his whole adult life.

There must have been something about the perfume aunt Mina was wearing--maybe the pat on his head--perhaps there was musk in her exotic scent... Whatever it was, it stirred primordial instincts in Buck's glands.

Aunt Mina, in her Sunday best, adjusted her glasses, bent over to look at the Asters. Buck, solidly convinced that this must surely be the doe of his dreams, lost all sense of propriety, seized the opportunity, and mounted Aunt Minnie who screamed, and pitched forward into the flowerbed.

Another Sunday shot to hell.

Two weeks later, Jake was building a shipping crate to hold Buck. Mama said we had to send him to a zoo in Wahpeton. She assured me that he would be happy there with other deer of his own kind.

About a month later, we got a letter from the zoo manager. Buck and several other deer had been killed by a pack of big dogs that had somehow gotten into the compound. There had been no stairway for him to hide under.

Buck had been right to fear strange dogs.

BARNLIFE, CIRCA 1930

This isn't a story exactly. It's more like what sport announcers call 'Color.' That is, writing about a barn, and its animals in the 1930's won't have much of a plot. Even so, enough activity went on in a typical barn to merit telling it, hopefully without it being too dull. Nevertheless, as part of history in a place almost no one has heard of, it needs telling.

The first task a homesteader, interested in survival, had to face, was that of providing a barn for the well being of his animals. The barn, from the start, was the key to survival. Every farmer was judged by the quality of his barn, and how he treated his horses, cattle, wife, children, dog, hogs, cat, and chickens. Often in that order.

ONCE IN THE MIDDLE OF NOWHERE

Tourists today, in the 1990's, often pass abandoned barns in their travels. If it should happen to be a round barn, or perhaps a barn with some other unusual form, perhaps the observer may casually mention to his, or her, traveling companion: "Look dear – What a quaint old barn – wouldn't aunt Alice just love to paint a picture of that one?" Perhaps, some of the more aware and sensitive travelers, speeding by, may wonder what it was like when the now crumbling barn was occupied by living animals. Most however, will give it only a quick glance. More likely, they will regard it only as a potential subject for an arty photo, or watercolor painting.

Usually, little serious thought is given to the vital role these barns once played in our past. Some still function, but much fewer in numbers. Across our nation, whether it is in Vermont, North Dakota, Montana, or the Palouse country of Washington, only a small percentage of the original barns are still in use.

The barn of the early settlers was far more than just a quaint structure. It was the prime source of family survival on the farm or ranch.

The barn of my childhood was very ordinary, smaller than that of my grandparents. However, it contained all the standard essentials common to all barns. Simply put, it had the basic shelter, tools, and animal supplies used by people dependent on animals, and for animals dependent on people. Entering a barn, say on a cold January day, was not only a routine necessity but offered a relatively pleasant time. Of course there was a lot of work to be done, but at a measured pace allowing for a relaxed visit with the animals. Here were the sights, sounds and smells of life. Even the smell of manure from grass-eating herbivores wasn't all that bad, just uniquely different.

The barn of my parents, Jake and Lena, was modest compared to that of either of my grandparents. The success of a farmer, let's say in 1917, was measured not in terms of money in the bank, or the car he drove, as much as the quality and size of his barn. The barn of my grandfather, Lars Olson, was huge. For practical reasons, it sat nestled against a hillside, as did most barns with a hill or slope available. The height of my parent's barn was about thirty feet. Even a young child could throw a pebble over it. The height of the Lars Olson barn was more challenging. In my memory of childhood accomplishments, I still remember the pride I felt at discovering that I was old enough, and strong enough, to be able to throw a stone over the massive roof of my grandfather's barn.

Our barn was not only much smaller; it didn't have cupolas on the roof, as did most barns. It didn't have lightning rods, or a fancy weather vane. It was more like the size of barns in the far-western states. In these states where winters are milder, there isn't as much need to store enormous quantities of hay inside. Therefore, barns were usually smaller. Our barn was smaller, not because our winters were mild, they weren't, but our farm was smaller in acreage. The whole farm was just a little more than a quarter section in size, about two hundred twenty acres, including twenty-five acres of pasture. Nevertheless, unpretentious as it may have been, it represented what life in a typical midwestern barn was like, regardless of size.

One of several things that distinguish a typical midwestern, or eastern barn, from those of the west, is that all midwest barns, big or small, were painted. Many of the barns out west, where lumber was more readily available and replaceable, have never seen a coat of paint. Barns in our locality were usually painted red, perhaps with white trim. Only a few barns in our county were painted white and an occasional maverick, blue or tan.

Immigrant Northern Europeans in North Dakota. seemed to have an obsession about painting buildings, or anything else for that matter. The general philosophy seemed to be – "If it happens to be an object not currently of use to the farm, get rid of it. If it's too big to move, paint it." This may even include a boulder. Another general difference is that many western ranch barns tend to have vertical siding. East of the Rockies, barns usually have horizontal siding made of boards especially milled for barns or wooden granaries.

In the days of diversified farming and before tractors, the barn was the most important building on the farm. To survive the first winter, most homesteaders, upon arriving on their barren tract of land, would immediately start to build a sod house for their families, and a shelter for the animals. This first barn would be built of readily available materials, such as sod or plain logs. Few homesteaders could afford, or had access to store bought lumber. Whatever the sod buster could use for the animal's protection, and survival from the weather would be used, but it had to be done quickly to beat the first snows.

Because the first crude shelters usually lacked a hayloft, hay would be stacked up next to the barn for additional insulation, or nearby for easy access. In reality, the survival of the animals was of paramount importance to the survival of the whole family.

If the homesteader survived the first winter or two, and if the crops were good, then he may be able to afford to build a better building. The first substantial structure would be a good barn. The house came last, not because the farmer preferred his horses or oxen to his wife and children, it was simply a pragmatic matter of survival. Perhaps next year or so the family could expect to move out of their sod house, into a new house or the beginning of one. Only a few new arrivals to North Dakota would have the financial means to build proper farm buildings, right from the start.

Life in the barn varied with the seasons. In fall, the hayloft (also properly called a haymow) would be stacked to the rafters with hay. Winter nights, would find all the stalls full of horses and cattle. Spring brought the newborn calves or colts, the little 'critters' at first somewhat stupefied and surprised to be here. In summer, the barn was primarily a place for a cow to get relieved of the pressure of milk twice a day. Working horses were fed in the barn, especially during spring plowing and fall harvest. Other barn occupants, especially in bad weather, would be the family dog and cat. Pigs and chickens were never allowed in a barn, they would get separate buildings of their own.

Stupid sheep were rarely found in North Dakota. No farmer that gave a damn about taking care of the land ever had sheep.

Our barn was situated on the downhill side, of a shallow ravine, about a hundred yards south of our house. For a practical reason, farm buildings were always separated by a distance sufficient to minimize the danger of fire spreading to other buildings. Farm fires were not uncommon. A barn or house fire was the farmer's greatest dread, with tornadoes a close second. The idea of a bucket brigade to put a fire out is strictly Hollywood stuff. No way could neighboring farmers be organized quickly enough to put out a fire, especially when one considers the water supply limited to that of a watering trough, and a hand pump.

Tornadoes and farm fires have a lot in common. They are very unreasonable when it comes to stopping them. To emphasize the importance given to the value of a barn, I can recall hearing a neighbor telling my folks about a farm fire near Souris. "What burned?" my mother asked. "The house," was the answer Lena replied, "That's really too bad--well, good thing it wasn't the barn and animals." Starting at the south side of our barn was twenty-five acres of rolling hills, and bottomland. It was an ideal pasture, for in addition to native grasses, in normal years it was supplied water from Boundary Creek. We had an additional twenty acres of pasture a mile east where, later in summer, the cattle would be driven every morning after milking. Here and there, scattered in our wheat fields and in the Turtle Mountains, were meadows to provide our winter hay.

The hayloft had to be filled with about sixteen to twenty hay loads, every summer. All the hay, which wouldn't fit into the loft, would be made into haystacks, and left in the meadow until needed. Hay bailers were unknown to us. Hay had to be handled, and piled with a pitchfork. A lot of hay was required because in the twenties, horses had not yet been completely replaced by John Deere or Mc Cormick Deering tractors, and hay was horse fuel. The term 'horsepower' had real meaning then. Not long after horses were phased out, so were cattle on most Dakota farms. Farmers gradually switched to strictly raising grains.

I was lucky enough to be born before the end of the barn age. My parents had ten horses, counting one buggy-horse[10], and a riding horse. Perhaps, I don't have a romantic view of horses, because of the daily chore of having to fork manure from the barn gutters into the manure wagon. I soon realized that a horse is primarily a conveyor belt for rapidly, and inefficiently processing sweet hay into malodorous, balls of olive-brown crud.

Our medium sized barn had fifteen double occupancy stalls, five stalls for ten horses, and ten stalls for twenty cattle. The north center of the lower level, which equaled a stall space, was occupied by the hay drop area and a feed

---

[10] *"Buggy-horse"—'meaning a horse for pulling a buggy,' not meaning insane, although in my opinion, all horses are mentally retarded*

bin. These occupied almost half of the total space. The feed bin extended upwards nearly to the ceiling. It would be filled from outside the barn through a small trap door, near the hayloft door. It was built somewhat like a king-sized bird feeder. Access to the oats and barley mixture, was through a hinged lid, which could be held open by a wooden catch similar to the type used on outdoor toilet seats.

Just as no baseball game would be complete without a hotdog, a movie theatre without popcorn, or Norwegian without a cup of coffee, no barn would be complete without its resident cat. Farm cats were not allowed in the house, at least in ours. Rarely was an animal regarded or kept merely as a pet. The cat had an essential job as a rodent killer. Cats, even though assigned a menial task, have a way of taking over, and making it look as if the world was intended for their privileged, and personal use.

In the first place, cats regard rodent killing as pure pleasure, almost a privilege. Secondly, by the time a new cat has occupied the barn for a week, the barn and all its creatures now belong to the cat. It will have picked out its favorite animal to sleep on when the weather is cold. Our cat usually could be found snoozing on the back of one of our draft horses. Certainly, this was the best choice, since horses sleep standing up, and can be relied upon to not move around much and disturb a catnap.

The third bonus for the cat--free lunch. At milking time, our cat, tail erect, would saunter over, and rub against the leg of the milker, and meow expectantly. The standard ritual followed: The cat-trained milker, after gently kicking the cat a short distance away from the milk pail, would then bend a teat in the direction of said cat, and squirt milk into the cat's happy face. Milk spattering all over, the cat seemed to bite, lap, and swallow all at the same time. It would even paw at the stream, as if trying to intercept the milk in midair. When sated, our cat would find a clean, sunny place in the straw to sit and clean up. First, it would use one paw to rub the side of its head, then lap off the milk, then the other side. A milk bath, no less. This practice apparently was common to all cats. A close friend of mine, who encouraged me to write this story, reminded me of this universal nature of barn cats. His barn cat also used this peculiar method of ingesting milk. When or where cats, in their evolutionary development learned this, I have no idea.

Our cat was named "Gämmär Kät," pronounced somewhat like 'gummar cut', meaning 'old cat.' To us, the name meant much more. It meant old, important, venerated, barn-owning, super-hunter cat. She had the top part of her ears missing. As a younger cat, she had been caught outside one cold night, and her ears had frozen. Once she had been caught in forbidden territory--inside the house. In her hasty retreat she had been a mite slow going through the screen door. The door spring was faster than she was. Her tail got caught going through the door, and from then on, her tail had a permanent kink in it.

A problem with cats is that they have kittens. A necessary problem, I suppose, or there would be no cats at all. Gämmär Kät decided the best place to bring her kittens, a week or so after birth, was under the feed box. It was supported about a foot above the floor and it had a dark space underneath, ideal for our old cat to hide her annual kindle of kittens. These healthy kittens were doomed. When big enough to come out and play from under the box, my father would have to capture, then reluctantly take over the hill and dispose of them. Cute, cuddly, curious bits of life as these kittens were, they had to be disposed of. They weren't needed. It was agonizing to watch my father gather up a batch of little kittens, and put them into a burlap gunnysack. Then, shotgun in one hand, gunnysack in the other, he would walk over the hill to the manure pile in the pasture. Soon, I would hear the sound of the shotgun blasting the kittens into oblivion. The reality of life is learned early on a farm.

Jake loved all animals. I believe it was harder for him to kill them, than it was for me to accept the reality of the need to do so. The farm needed only one or two cats to take care of mice, rats, and gophers. Gämmär Kät was too good a rodent killer to consider replacement even if she was getting old.

Sometimes our kittens had a break. Once in a while, a neighbor, needing a cat to take care of his rodent problems, would stop by. For me this was good news! This neighbor, needing a rodent-eliminator, had brought reprieve from death row for at least one kitten. How pleased I would be to hear that my pa didn't have to kill all of them. The neighbor would take his time on picking out the one he wanted. I'd urge him to take two. There were usually five or six in the litter, each one mewing its credentials. The neighbor would lift the tails of each to check whether they were male or female. Then he would decide whether to take a tomcat or a female. Actually, it was a decision to be made thoughtfully; tomcats don't have kittens, but females are generally better hunters. It didn't matter much to me--just so he would take one. Please.

Accepting the reality of farm life was one thing, but it bothered me that a cat was kept only for its capability of killing other little creatures. There didn't seem to be room for anything in farm life, except that which offered practical value. Cats were kept, not for their cuteness, charm, or comical antics, but for their usefulness in killing mice and rats. Mice too, are cute, but can raise hell with a burlap sack of seed wheat, or packaged food in the pantry. It was simply a choice of mice or keeping a cat handy.

Cats were considered useful not decorative. No cat was permitted to be pampered, and allowed to stay in the house. There was one exception--our cat was permitted to stay for a short duration if Lena had seen a mouse somewhere. A cat that failed mouse catching would be replaced. Cats were not the only animals subject to the rule of practicality. With rare exceptions such as my pet deer, no animals were kept merely as pets. Every creature on a farm had to earn its right to stay alive.

Our Gämmär Kät was an expert at having her kittens in a secret hiding place, which we never found. Only after their eyes were open would she carry them down from the loft, or wherever, and put them under the feed box and introduce them to us at milking time.

One year there were only two. Lena then said to Jake, "We better save one of these kittens, I don't think Gämmär Kät is going to have any more kittens." Lena was right. Gämmär Kät didn't have any more kittens, and it took a while before the young cat had any. The decision of which one to keep was up to me. The loser would still have to die. The one I chose was a female, a tabby with white undersides. Uncle Carl said she looked like a "Maxine," so that's what I named her – "Max," for short. When Max was almost a year old, Gämmär Kät took on the job of teaching her daughter the fine art of gopher hunting. At this occupation, the old cat was unexcelled.

First, a word about gophers. North Dakota auto license plates have a slogan proclaiming itself the "The Peace Garden State." At one time the subtitle appropriately read "The Flickertail State," because these little animals seemed to be everywhere. "Flickertail" is another common name for a ground squirrel most people called a gopher. This rodent looks and acts like the prairie dogs of the west. The Flickertail is smaller, but has the same habits and same type of habitat– that of living in underground burrows. Instead of barking they make a high pitched peep, to warn other members of the colony. They can be a serious problem if they become too numerous. Our pasture was full of these rascals. For convenience, I'll just call them gophers from now on.

One day, I saw Gämmär Kät followed by her neophyte trainee, strolling nonchalantly down a cow path onto the hunting ground. As if given a signal to stay back, Max sat down on the path to watch. With her kinked tail erect in the air, Gämmär Kät walked by a gopher mound, exhibiting total disinterest in its occupants. Oh yeah? To understand the following hunting strategy, I must explain the shape of a gopher mound. They are not as neat or large as a prairie dog mound, but are generally the same. The gopher digs a hole and the dirt piles up around the hole leaving a shallow funnel similar to the caldera of a miniature volcano. Gophers erectly stand watch on the rim of the crater and peep at the approach of danger, then rapidly scamper back into the hole if something gets too close.

The old cat knew the exact distance of 'too close.' After walking the 'safe- for-gophers' distance away from the mound, she stopped, sat down, and started to groom herself. Then she started walking again, this time at a 90-degree angle to her original path, but on a course which would bring her a little closer to the hole. Again, she carried her tail at maximum upward, a deceptively nonchalant extension like a flagstaff. The curious gophers retreated back toward the hole, keeping just enough below the rim so they could watch. Again, Gämmär Kät needed to groom herself. What an actress, portraying ultimate boredom, that old cat was the Sarah Berhardt of cat-dom. After a patient while, she resumed her walk, the path had changed again. Then it became obvious what she was doing. She was walking an ever-diminishing spiral!

The gophers followed her progress, all the time staying behind the near side rim. When Gämmär Kät had made a complete circle she was now much closer to her quarry. Not only was she closer, but behind a convenient tuft of grass and weeds. This time, instead of grooming she lay down as flat as possible. The dumb gophers no longer had a good view, and stood erect on the rim to see better, a very bad move. All gophers couldn't get into the same hole at once. One pounce, one dead gopher. Did the other gophers learn anything? Apparently not.

When Max had her first batch of kittens, Gran'ma decided the new babies needed some real protein, and went hunting. After a week, our barn and barnyard was so littered with dead gophers that Jake had to get a shovel, gather them up and dispose of them. Gämmär Kät, having earned her keep for many years, was allowed to live out her life without threat of disposal. She lived to be eighteen years old. For some reason, I had special fondness for our cats. A few years later, when I was in the Army Air Corps, homesickness didn't bother me very much-- that is until the day I got a letter from my mother telling about the new kittens she had seen coming out to play from under the feed box.

Dogs also were seldom kept as mere pets. Our dog was expected to help herd the cattle. Therefore, when we needed a dog to replace Fido (yes, Fido), Ma insisted we get an English Shepherd. This is a breed known for its ability to keep the cattle in good order, grouped as a disciplined platoon, as we moved them from one pasture to another, or sent to round up an errant heifer. The English Shepherd has an uncanny instinct for herding. From an advertisement in a farm magazine we ordered a pup. A couple weeks later we got a phone call from Mr. Shelton, train station manager in Carbury. He said there was a hungry puppy waiting to be picked up at the depot.

Uncle Carl named our black and white English Shepherd puppy "Tootsie." This name was probably inspired by a song title. Carl was a fan of the radio comedian Eddie Cantor, who along with the song "IDA", often sang the song Al Jolson made popular--"TOOTSIE."

After a year of patient training, there was little need to shout orders to Tootsie. She would simply look to us for hand gestured instructions. Pointing at a straying heifer would be sufficient for the dog to change the heifer's viewpoint concerning a clump of clover off the road. If the creature were a little dim-witted or slow, a quick nip at the heels by the dog would speed the return of the AWOL steer or heifer. Older cows had already learned to be obedient.

Tootsie took much of the boredom out of herding our cows to and from the east pasture. The dog was phenomenal in her ability to interpret the subtlest of directions, whether by voice or hand signals. Sometimes, only the quietly spoken word, "Tootsie," and a directive look of disapproval at the errant heifer or steer would be enough to send her on her way to correct the issue. After putting the critter in its place, she would return to my side for a congratulatory pat on the head. After several trips to the pasture, the dog didn't even need any commands at all; she knew what to do without being told. How could one not admire a dog like that? This bit about driving cattle to pasture is perhaps only a sidetrack issue, but it should be told somewhere in the story about barn life. Meanwhile, back to the barn.

"Time to do the chores," usually heard three times a day, this statement meant it was time to go to the barn, and attend to the animals. Twice a day, in the morning before dawn, and evening after sundown, the cows had to be milked and fed. The third visitation was the rather onerous job mucking out the manure from the gutters. This task could take place anytime during daylight hours. After loading up cow and horse manure unto the manure sled, we would take the load of steaming dung to the pasture manure pile.

As winter neared spring, the hay in the loft would be getting low. Sometimes upon returning from the manure pile, if it were a pleasant day we would unhitch the manure sled and hitch up to the hay sled. Then we would go to one of our summer haystacks and get a load of hay. Returning home we would transfer it into the hayloft. This was always a pleasant journey across the snow to the sun sparkled meadows. The hay smelled fresh and sweet, a refreshing contrast to the manure sled.

In summer time; cows were called into the barn only for milking; thus the manure didn't pile up fast enough to require cleaning out daily. The sled would now be exchanged for a manure wagon, used perhaps once a week or even less.

As for the chore of milking, the folks never complained about it. I made up for their lack of complaining. I hated to milk cows. They actually seemed to enjoy it. At least my ma did. My mother, Lena, said it was a time to relax with the animals. More likely, it was an excuse to get out of the house. She despised housework. "Why wasn't I born a man?" was her often-stated complaint. Ma was happiest driving four horses pulling a reaper. As far as I was concerned, I was raised by three fathers; Jake, Uncle Carl, and my mother, Lena.

Cattle are strange animals. They are deceptively stupid looking. This is a sham. If a cow is giving you a dim-witted look, it is actually checking to see if you closed the gate properly. Leave a strange object in the pasture, and the first animal to check it out will be some heifer sniffing at it. A horse, if it sees it at all, may shy away from it--perhaps get startled, and run headlong into a tree.

Cows can even tell time. Whitey, our queen boss cow had a built in clock, comparable to the official clock of the Naval Observatory, in Washington D.C. At precisely 05:26 P.M. she would head for the barn from the pasture to be milked. The other milk cows had to follow, or else. If chickens have a pecking order, then cows have even a more strict 'horn-poking' order. In this hierarchy, Whitey was Master Sergeant. Outside the barn door, Whitey would sort out who was to follow her regal entry. Any cow that would transgress by not entering in proper order, would have to answer to Whitey's horns. The heifers and steers were PFC status, and yearlings mere recruits to follow last.

Inside the barn each cow, heifer, and steer had its assigned space, and woe to any heifer that got into Whitey's stall by mistake. The cow next to Whitey was tolerated as second in command. Any human army sergeant would admire the order, and discipline that Whitey instilled. Yet, she was a gentle cow who inspected all newborn calves, sometimes with an approving slurp across the ears. As you may expect, Whitey[11] would be the first to be milked, by Lena. It was her favorite cow.

Believe it or not, as a young boy, just like our cats, I liked to drink warm milk fresh from the cow. Only I used a tin cup. Having it squirted in my face may have worked, but I didn't have the built in self-cleaning capability of cats. At milking time, I would sometimes grab my tin cup and run down to the barn for a snort. There would be Ma and Pa in the barn milking, while the cows were happily munching hay from the manger. First, there would be the gentle ringing sounds of streams of milk hitting the inside of an empty milk pail. Later, the sound changing to the softer, foamy, deep tone of a pail nearly full. Sort of a liquid doppler effect. Extending my cup to Ma, she would quickly fill it, and I would drink the stuff.

While milking, Lena seemed always to be jabbering away. She would be telling Jake about the latest gossip or talking politics, weather or whatever. Jake, a non-talker, rarely responded. If he had gone too long without mumbling some answer, Ma would speak up a bit more loudly and say, "Why don't you answer me once in a while – Why did I have to get stuck with a man who won't talk?"

When all the cows had been milked they would then carry the pails to the milk house, where the cream separator would be used to separate cream from the milk. Before the electrification of farms, a cream separator was a hand-cranked centrifuge with continuous flow. It was cleverly designed to separate the lighter cream from the milk. In a county of thousands of cows, cream could be sold, but not milk. Cream would be made into butter at the local creamery to be sold elsewhere. The skimmed milk would then be taken back to the barn to feed the calves and pigs. Surplus milk, if any, would be thrown away. The cream we sold was how we survived the drought years of the Dust Bowl Era. Little as the money was, with it we could buy groceries...flour, sugar, dry beans, etc.--just the bare necessities.

As I have already stated, I didn't enjoy the chore of milking. In fact, I bitched about it. Yanking on milk-slippery teats, with my head leaning against a stinking cow was not my idea of a good time. Added to the list of unpleasantries

---

[11] *In 1934, the worst year of the Depression* and *Dust Bowl era, my folks were desperate for grocery money and had to sell a cow. Whitey* was *the oldest* and *with her milk yield dropping,* was *the most logical to be sold. It* was *the first time I saw Ma really cry hard.* We *got almost three dollars for her*

of milking, were more than just the horse flies that buzzed about or stung the back of my neck. It was the matter of the cow's tail. This device, a heavy hawser with a frayed end, could add considerable misery, to the already miserable drudgery of milking. It seems that the Creator of cows installed this cudgel as an afterthought, more likely as a quick fix for His screw-up of inventing flies in the first place. While its primary purpose might have been for swatting flies and other insects, either He overlooked something, or... had no concern for the milker of cows. Perhaps He never considered the bad aim, and gross manners of a cow.

Example: There sits the milker, his or her head close to, or perhaps leaning against the cow. A horsefly lands on cow, close to milker's head. Cow reflex takes over, and she swiftly swings hawser-tail with the velocity of a baseball bat swung by Joe DiMaggio. Brush end of tail bashes back of milker's neck. Loud noise comes from milker. Hopefully the end of a cow's tail is dry, and the swat is nothing more than a stinging irritation. However, there were times when the brush was loaded, still wet from a summer shower or worse. Prior to being milked, some cows liked to stand in the muddy creek to escape the irritation of mosquitoes. Then the tail would have some residual mud to apply. If the mud had dried out, the tail would be loaded with ceramic marble sized pellets. Bad enough, but sometimes things got a lot worse.

As anyone who has observed a herd of cattle for more than a minute knows, cattle wisely raise their tails prior to expelling the by-products of grass conversion and water. Normally, they accomplish this job without fouling the fly swatter. Cows have been doing this for centuries, and are quite proficient at raising their tails just high enough. However, evolution hadn't prepared them for the desert dry years of the Dust Bowl. Eventually, even the green grass of the creek bottomlands was almost totally gone. We struggled to find substitutes for the cattle to eat. We fed them coarse marsh grass from the drying lakebeds or sloughs and a few times we fed sugar beet peelings, shipped in from the Red River Valley. In desperation, the cattle experimented with new food on their own. Letting them out to graze in our failed crop wheat fields, they ate even the green, but still a bit stickery Russian thistle. The result was not good. In fact, it gave them a bad case of diarrhea, which would squirt out in a stream as from a fire hose. No poor-suffering cow could raise her tail high enough to avoid the olive colored stream. The only hope for the would be milker was that the dunked appendage would have dried out before milking time. The law of averages didn't always work in the milker's favor. More loud noise with cussing thrown in. Only one such encounter would be enough to drive the milker into getting some twine to tie a cow's tail into a state of immobility. Fortunately, no one tried tying a brick or some other weight to the end of the tail, or I suppose there would have been an unconscious person stretched out in the gutter.

Milking had other drawbacks. Occasionally a cow would have a stinging fly land on her undersides. In this case the cow would attempt to use her leg to clobber the pest. This time, instead of the milker being in the way, the milk bucket would get it. It never seemed to happen when the pail was empty, only when it was full. If she didn't knock it over she could manage to step in it. Perhaps my parents enjoyed milking but don't ask me why. At least I have explained reasons for my dislike of the process.

All things considered, mucking out the manure was, to me, a less unpleasant job than milking, so I complained to my ma about milking the "damn cows." For a good measure I went to my pa about it and said I'd do anything to get out of milking. If I haven't already said I was a spoiled rotten kid, I'll say it now. Spoiled rotten to the core. I didn't know which parent let me off the hook, but it was probably Jake. A deal was made. If I would do other work of equivalent time, like mend fences, or odd jobs in the blacksmith shop I could get out of milking. To tell the truth, while I may have occupied our shop the equivalent time, I didn't do much useful work. Instead of casting a babbit bearing for our cultivator, I'd maybe cast a keel for a model sailboat I was building. When caught in the act, my mother would find some excuse for me, saying something about my learning to work with my hands. Perhaps I should feel guilty about getting away without milking, but I don't. Again, I digress. Back to the barn.

A more or less continuous chore was the business of watering the thirsty livestock. In summer this was no big deal. If there wasn't any water in the creek we used a small internal combustion engine to pump water from the well into the trough *(water tank to city folks)* since a tornado had dismantled our windmill, the folks had replaced the wind-driven pump with a one-lunger gasoline engine. This primitive engine was a lot bigger for the power it put out than needed to be. It had two flywheels and a belt pulley. A cast iron water chamber, open at the top, enclosed the single cylinder. The primitive ignition system and carburetor was an example of how simple things could be and still work. It had to be started by turning the flywheel. Most of the time, it had to run a while before one put on the belt. When the engine was warmed up, the belt could be slipped on using considerable manual dexterity while hoping to avoid mangled finger. The engine was water cooled without an adequate way of draining the jacket, therefore, we didn't dare to use the engine in the chronic twenty-below temperature of winter for fear of water cracking the block. So it sat there until spring while we pumped water by hand.

The water trough, made of galvanized metal, was also in danger of freezing up and splitting a seam. There were two practical answers to this dilemma. One, pump just enough water so the cattle would empty the tank and two, heat the water. Regardless of how carefully one monitored the water quantity; ice would form on the inside of a metal tank at thirty-below. Water from the shallow well wasn't much above freezing even as it was pumped.

Heating the water was the desired solution. For this purpose a submarine stove was available commercially and we had one. It was an odd shaped affair. Resembling a sheet metal duct about six feet long, bent at an angle, it had a square cross section with a smokestack at one end and an opening to insert firewood at the other. This sheet metal heater was small enough to fit submerged in the water trough. It had a sloping square duct conning tower that stuck up out of the water. Into this, wood could be stuffed and fired up. To keep the stove from becoming a boat and floating up out of the water it had to be held down with boulders. The stove dealer did not supply boulders, but large rocks were free from the pasture. The wood insertion and air supply duct had a lid with a draft control vent. A periscope chimney poked up through the water at the other end.

Firing up was no easy job, considering the draft had to go downhill. Wood soaked with a little kerosene helped. There were times when even the kerosene was hard to light. On really cold days, the stove had a struggle trying to melt all the accumulated ice on the inside of the metal tank. There would be a melted pool of tepid water above the stove and six inches of gray-white, stubborn ice, clinging to the sides of the water trough. At this point, we had to resort to using an axe to chop away chunks to speed up the process. Because this whole procedure involved building a fire and chopping with an axe, it reminded me of camping out. It was actually fun, so I didn't dodge this job whenever I was home from school to do it. Of course, I preferred anything to school, even cleaning the barn. Maybe even milking.

Sometimes beauty came to the barn. On very cold days, 25-degrees below or more, a visit to the barn often found the interior changed. Instead of drab, dusty, spider-webbed walls, they would now be white with frost. Not just the velvety, flat kind of frost on windowpanes, but long needle shaped crystals of sparkling ice. Body heat expelling moisture from the hides of horses and cattle would condense on the uninsulated walls. In the calm environment of no wind, the vapor would grow long ice crystals. Near the doors and windows, the coldest areas, it would be more than an inch thick. Drawing pictures or writing naughty words, or initials in the frost was fun because it was so tempting and easy.

In coming to the barn to do the milking it would be dark outside. Whether it was morning or evening. In very cold weather the sky is almost always crystal clear and the stars of winter seem brighter than those of summer. There would be no problem seeing the path to the barn with only the bright evening afterglow on the horizon. If the display of the Aurora Borealis was acting up, so much the better. With the moon up, there would be more than enough light to cast distinct shadows on the snow. Here on the Canadian border, Polaris is 51-degrees above the horizon. Though we didn't know their names, the many constellations were as familiar to us as the barn itself. Eyes of older people may only see the star cluster Pleiades as a little celestial smudge, but young eyes are better. Sometimes I would pause on my way to the barn, then look up and try to see how many more pinpoint stars could be seen in addition to the seven sisters.

Coming to the barn a vigorous shove was usually required to slide open the barn door, not only because of frozen bearings in the rollers, but snow and ice at the bottom of the door. Before turning on the lights, the interior of the barn would be as dark as an unlit coalmine. The muffled sounds of animals stirring and an occasional snort of welcome could be heard. A flood of warm air loaded with combined smells of sweet hay, manure, and animal odors would wash over us as we reached for the lightswitch. After turning on the lights the barn would be much brighter than usual. Even the feeble 50-watt light bulbs of our 32-volt system reflected a million sparkles of light from the white frost on the walls. Despite the icy cold of the exterior walls, the interior of the barn, oddly enough, would be quite warm. Many animals do a good job of heating. Though I have never been in an Inuit (Eskimo) igloo, I have read that they too, in spite of icy walls, are warm inside. The same effect occurred in our barn, I guess.

Late summer, when most of the hay loads have already been put in the loft, the barn sometimes had another guest or two hired hands. Our bunkhouse had only a single bed. If we had more than one hired hand to do the wheat shocking, ("stooking," in Canadianese), or bundle hauling, the extra man was given a sheet, blanket and pillow and put-up in the haymow. Who got the barn was determined by the flip of a coin. Actually, most hands preferred the barn. The bunkhouse had poor ventilation for a stuffy August night. In the Depression Years more men would come looking for a job than we could hire. The folks gave them a meal anyway and let them spend the night in the barn before walking on to look for work elsewhere.

Entertainment in a barn? Of course everyone, including city folks have heard of barn dances. None ever happened that I experienced, so I can't comment about them. Unlike New England barns which sometimes had a separate area for storing buggies or wagons our barns didn't have a space that could be cleared readily. As for boy/girl entertainment, the phrase, 'A roll in the hay,' is based on something more than mere rhetorical invention. I can't comment on that either. However, some of my more worldly friends had pointed out that hay is useful for things other than animal feed. For one reason or another, I just missed out. Damn! It should come as no surprise that quite a few people were conceived in a haymow. A more innocent form of fun that the neighbor boys and I had, required a hayloft a lot larger than our barn. While I mentioned before that my grandfather's barn was big, I need to give an idea of how big. Our whole barn would have fit into the hayloft of the Lars Olson barn with room to spare on all sides, and the top would have been several feet below the hay-sling track. This barn, like a lot of barns in the foothills, was built with one side nestled into the side of a small hill. The reason for this was that it provided drive-in access to the loft without building a special ramp. A whole hay load stacked on the hay wagon, twelve feet high or more could be driven inside. Before going to the hay meadow for loading, a hay sling, a cross-webbed affair similar to the cargo-sling for ships would first be put into the rack of the hay wagon.

With the hay wagon full of hay and in the loft, the sling would be attached to the hook of the overhead double-block hoist. The horses would be unhitched from the wagon and hooked up to the hoist line that ran through a sheave fastened to a floor beam. The team would then be driven to pull this line and lift the entire load of hay from the hay wagon. Once up near the peak of the roof pulling other lines fastened to the trolley suspended from a track could move the load. The interior of my grandfather's barn had massive crossbeams, but there was enough opening provided for the load to pass through. When the load got to the desired position, a quick jerk of the trip-line freed one side of the sling and the load was dumped. This way a pile of hay twenty-five feet high could be put in the loft. It would be extremely difficult to pile hay that high with only a pitchfork.

The foundations of barns built into a hillside were always made of granite fieldstones. This job was beyond the skill of most farmers so stone masons were hired to cut and fit these durable hard stones. Even some of the large barns of the flatlands had stone foundations to support the massive load of the loft. Why all this explanation? One, to give an idea of the size of the loft interior and two, to plant in your mind the potential that such a device as a hay sling with all its ropes, blocks and trolley track could offer a bunch of boys full of vitamins and adventuresome spirit.

In late spring and early summer, the hayloft of a barn would be nearly empty. There would be a time before the summer hay would be loaded again into the barn. The interior of the loft was a natural playground. Crossbeams for daring someone to walk the high beam. Built-in ladders at either end to test the nerve of high climbers. Best of all, there were the hay sling ropes at the Forsberg barn. The Forsberg barn was almost the same size as the Lars Olson barn and, it too, had a stone foundation built into the side of a hill. The notable difference was that it didn't have any crossbeams to get in the way. This meant a great opportunity to do some giant swinging from the sling ropes. With a little effort by the Forsberg boys, Eugene and Gordon, a single line of large diameter (hawser) rope now hung from the trolley track to the floor and a bit more. A knot had been tied about six feet above the floor. There was just enough hay left in the barn that could be moved to the right spot for landing, or crashing as the case may be.

My cousin, Virgil Moody, introduced me to this fun game going on at Forsberg's barn one day. After explaining it to me, I eagerly went with him to try it out. The Forsberg's lived only a mile away from the Moodys. The kids were home and were happy to show us to their giant swing. Gordon was a little too small to demonstrate the swing but Eugene was eager to show off the awesome ride. Taking the knotted rope and draping it over one shoulder, Eugene climbed the ladder at one end of the barn. He kept taking up slack in the line as he climbed. Finally when he got high enough, the knot was at his shoulder that he grabbed with one hand as he hung on to the ladder with the other. Then with a yell, after seizing the rope with both hands above the knot he swung free of the ladder. He whizzed by us and swung upwards letting go in time to plummet, following a trajectory path into the pile of hay.

Of course, Virgil had to try it next. Then it was my turn. Eugene cautioned us not to let go too early or late or we might miss the hay. We had a little trouble at first. Both of us let go a little early or late and found out the edge of the hay pile had a very hard bottom. Although somewhat bruised, it was too much fun to quit until we got the timing down just right.

Arriving home late that afternoon my mother asked how I could get so dusty, bruised, and my hair full of chaff. "What have you been doing, for heavens sake?" "Nothing, just playing at Forsberg's." To tell her may have brought down a ban of some sort. The fun lasted till haying season began.

Having explained some of the aspects of barn life, it occurred to me that I ought to lighten up and relate an incident of a less serious nature.

Bob Sigurdson, one of my city cousins, first son of Aunt Mina and Uncle Sig wasn't cut out to be a city kid. ("City?" at the time Bottineau had a population of only about 1850 souls, some city.) He truly loved horses and other animals for that matter. Because his father was a pharmacist, he was destined to become a pharmacist too, whether he wanted to be one or not. (Eventually, he got his way and wound up raising racehorses.) I envied my city cousins. I didn't want to be a farmer and I felt somehow inferior to my culturally advantaged cousins. In my mind – "our fathers should have traded sons. I would gladly become a pharmacist to avoid a future involving the milking of cows."

The Sigurdsons would visit our farm once or twice every summer and Bob would come along to see the animals. Their automobile would barely have stopped when the car door would fly open and he would make a beeline for the barn or pasture without more than a quick, politely, mandatory "Hello Aunt Lena," as he sped by. His younger brother, John, was content to walk down and play with toy boats in the water trough. Bob couldn't be bothered with toys. He would try to pet every calf or cow, scratch the pigs with a short stick. Most of all, he wanted to get involved with the horses. Our horses weren't ponies but that didn't matter to Bob, they were horses.

We had two big horses, and I mean massive, that had a perverse nature. With a lot of idle time on their hooves, they evidently had nothing better to do than to think up a practical joke they could play on the unwary. Can't say as I blame the horses either. It must be very boring to just stand there in that confining stall and wait to be fed, wait to be harnessed, wait to be let out. Now please understand, horses aren't all that bright so any joke they could play would be somewhat unsophisticated. Carl had named these two Percheron mares,

"Manda and Sophie." Ma claimed it was in remembrance of some of Carl's old girl friends. Probably true.

Whether it was a brilliant inspirational flash or something that just evolved, Manda and Sophie came up with an idea. "Since whoever is feeding us has to walk between us to get to the manger with his pitchfork load of hay, all we got to do is to lean together at the right time and we can catch the sucker!" A couple of horses weighing a ton apiece can squeeze mighty hard by just leaning if they put their minds to it. In practice their idea proved effective.

Uncle Carl must have been the first victim, because one day as I was feeding the animals, he warned me to walk very fast when I went between Manda and Sophie. Well, I didn't quite understand how fast and I got nailed. There I was, caught between the sides of Manda and Sophie. Their bellies trapped me, I could hardly move. To be fair about it, the horses may not have been doing this as a joke. Instead, what the goofy horses had in mind was getting scratched. Perhaps my wiggling served the practical purpose of scratching some itches the horses had as I struggled free. To them, people were nothing more than animated scratching posts. Once in a while, even when were expecting the clamp from these two hay burners, we still got caught if we were a bit slow delivering hay.

The day the Sigurdsons came to visit was during the beginning of threshing season, a time when the horses were being fed in the barn. As I recall, Bob was probably twelve years old. Anyway, he was at that gangly age. The first thing he did, as always, was head for the pasture, and I followed. The cows were out grazing in the creek bottom so cow petting was out. Then he asked, "Where are the horses?"

"In the barn, they just came off the field."

"Swell[12] --have they been fed yet?"

"Nope" I answered, knowing what the next question would be.

"Can I feed'em?"

"Sure, but first we've go to throw down some hay from the hay mow." Which we climbed up into and did. Then we climbed down and I showed Bob the knack of getting a big forkful and how to hold it just right as he went between the horses to dump it in the manger. I started him out on the dull-minded horses that looked forward more to hay than playing stupid jokes.

Everything went well, Bob had the knack of feeding hay down pat. In fact, he was so competent that I thought he might even escape getting caught by Manda and Sophie, the last horses to be fed.

At last, there he stood, poised with a big forkful of hay about to go through the canyon between Manda and Sophie. And nearby I stood, hoping for the big squeeze. If he walked fast, he'd make it. If he walked at the standard

---

[12] *"Swell"--a fad word, equivalent to "cool" in 1990s.*

rate, he'd get the vise. How shameless of me not to warn Bob. Shameless--Yuk, Yuk.

With his eyes focused on the barely visible manger, he attempted to walk through at the standard rate.--Clump! There was Bob, clamped in an animal vise, his arms pinned down at his sides. He kept yelling "Hey! Hey! Leggo, dammit, leggo!"

Feeling a little guilty, I helped shove the horses apart. Finally freed, he looked at me and asked, "Do they always do that?"

"Oh no, just a couple of times before." Lie.

"Should'a warned me."

"Yeah – but I forgot." Another lie.

A few minutes later, Bob was laughing about it. He said he had a couple friends in Bottineau he hoped would come out sometime. He would talk them into helping feed Manda and Sophie.

Some fifty years later, my wife Georgia and I visited Uncle Carl, who was then still living on dad's farm. Jake and Lena were both long gone. We all decided to have a look around the old Lars Olson place. The barn was still standing but since the farm had long been abandoned, the barn was now falling apart at the seams. The cupola had blown off and was lying in a broken heap in the tall grass. Georgia remarked that it was a lot bigger than she had expected. "It must have been the size of a gazebo." I told her that at one time there had been a tall lightning rod with a horse and buggy weather vane on the peak of the cupola.

Walking up the gentle slope to the entrance of the hayloft, we found the hayloft door, fallen from its track and lying flat at the entrance. As we walked inside, the rustle of some bird was heard somewhere high in the rafters. Georgia said something to the effect that the barn loft seemed as huge as a cathedral. She wanted to know what the big room attached to the back of the barn was. Carl said it was the foaling shed, a private place for the mares to have their foals. It was large enough for the expectant mare to exercise. It had its own hayloft and feed chutes from the oat and barley bins. Georgia, who had been raised on a farm in Utah, was impressed. Her father's barn had been smaller than the foaling shed.

Uncle Carl died a couple years later. Eventually the Olson barn was sold for fifty dollars. Somebody wanted the upper structure cross beams--each worth fifty dollars easy. The barn then just disappeared. On a recent visit we again visited the site. Nothing remained except a small board we found, part of the sliding door. On it were Carl's initials, C.L.O., carved when he was a boy. We still have it, a board cut to about ten inches wide and sixteen inches long. This board means a lot to me personally. It not only brings to mind the image of Carl as a young farm boy carving his initials, but serves as a souvenir of a time long ago when the heart of every farm was the barn.

My parent's barn is gone now as is the big ones of my grandfathers. After a farm is abandoned, it is common for the community to get rid of unused buildings and clean up. It is very offensive for the local folks to see unpainted, unrepaired buildings. Now, it is difficult to even locate where the buildings once were.

The next time you pass a barn, unused but still standing, I hope I will have answered some questions even if you may not have asked them. The few barns still in use are still important and I expect each will also have a cat that owns it.

ADDENDUM

My close friend, Will Stageberg, who encouraged me to write these tales me sent a letter telling of a cat on his farm in Minnesota. I thought it too good not to share, so I asked for permission to include it here.

Letter from Will Stageberg, Aug 20, 1991

More About Barn Cats

When I was about eighteen years of age and living on the farm with my folks, we had a female cat that was worthy of scientific study. She was plain--mostly white with patches of light gray and a touch or two of beige. Not a pretty cat, and she knew it. I don't think she was ever in the house. (The house might be our domain, but every place else was hers.) She was a spinster--never had any kittens and wouldn't have anything to do with the mechanics of producing them. She kept us in the category of cordial acquaintances rather than dear friends. She would tolerate a little petting in a weak moment, but would cut it short to avoid any emotional entanglements. The only food she ever got from us was her ration of milk in the barn. I don't know where she slept. She would touch base with us now and then. She had no name.

I don't know how we happened to come by a kitten at that time. When the spinster cat saw it, her expression was one of outrage and disgust. She went away in a huff and didn't come back, even for milk, for a couple of weeks. When she did and the kitten was still there, it was obvious that she was having a problem trying to decide whether or not to cross us off her list of Persons Worthy of Visitation. She obviously compromised, because she spent about half of her time around the area, but avoided close contact with any of us.

One day I was sitting on the back steps and in a condition that farm kids know pretty well absolutely nothing to do. Just sitting there. The kitten was happiest at times like this because it got whatever attention I was capable of giving.

In the distance I saw a movement in the tall grass. An animal was moving through the grasses, not in a hurry. It was moving toward the house. When the animal emerged from the grass, it was the spinster cat, chin-high, and dragging a gopher that it had caught and killed. (We called them striped gophers.)

For a space of about 150 feet she walked straight at me, stopping when she was about ten feet away. Then she swung her head and threw the gopher at the brainless kitten. With the hauteur of a grande dame, she stalked off. Even though she detested the irresponsible kitten, she didn't want it to go hungry.

My dad had a little dog of a breed that we called rat terriers. This goggle-eyed creature, if it had been a human child, would have been characterized as hyperactive. It suffered from a short-circuited mentality--an example of pre-natal lobotomy. The result was that, even though it had absolutely nothing to be happy about, it was always happy. It was passionately fond of me.

The dog had phenomenal hearing. (Not as good as "Buck." Jack's pet deer.) When I came home late at night I would usually have to park my Model "T" Ford at the bottom of the sandy road up the hill to my folk's farm home because the road was customarily washed out. Half way up the hill and still almost a block away from the house, I would hear the scurrying of frantic feet ahead of me. Then a bundle of flying fur would hit me chest-high. Its feet could be muddy and I could be wearing the only decent suit I owned. No matter--I knew I was in for it, and who could rebuff such violent affection?

The farm home looked out over a pretty valley. On a beautiful day I was standing in our alfalfa field and absorbing the serene and pleasant view below. Then I became aware of my brain damaged friend, who came and sat next to me, his head jerking from side to side with spastic motions as he tried to figure out what it could be that I felt was worth looking at.

The next thing that I realized was that the spinster cat had joined us. She sat by her supposed natural enemy, the dog. In a little while, and to my utter amazement, she sat up and started to wash the dog's face. She licked around the

dog's eyes. (He obligingly tilted his head in the appropriate direction.) She licked her paw repeatedly and washed the dog's nose. He acted as if this were boringly routine. She was thorough about the job and did not quit until her self-conceived objective had been fulfilled.

How I wish that that occurrence could have been preserved on film! A person seeing it would still have a hard time believing it. It was another strange show of gruff affection on the part of this altogether unusual cat.

How could I not include Will's story, even if it didn't take place in the Turtle Mountains?

THE JUGGERNAUT

Except for real names of people who may or may not still be alive and some minor details where I have had to guess what happened, this story is true. It happened a long time ago in a place that has changed. The land is still there but the buildings are gone as well as those who lived there.

Definition, WEBSTER'S NEW COLLEGIATE DICTIONARY: jug'gernaut, 3. (not cap) any massive inexorable force that advances irresistibly, crushing whatever is in its path.

Already, at the age of twelve, John had begun brooding about his lot in life. It is damn tough to get some attention when you are only one of thirteen brothers and sisters- -and there was another baby coming. Any chance of his attaining any sense of self-esteem or self-worth lessened with every new sibling getting born. Babies kept coming annually, as regular as the yearly return of wild geese or wood ticks. He just had to do something spectacular to gain some notice. Notice would have to be from someone other than his family. If he didn't do something noticeable he would forever be condemned to be just one more insignificant person in a vast throng of unknown, non-entities.

Then one day he had an idea. A great idea. He could do it. It would be spectacular.

Scene 1: Across the Road from the Skolund Farm

John had finally found his fourth and last wheel for the 'car' he was secretly building on top of the hill. As he had labored to roll the heavy wheel up the hill he had wished he could have found one of a size to match at least one of the other three. The big wooden wheel with its steel rim would have to do, even though it meant again having to cut and fit an axle at some different height in order to have all four wheels touch the ground at the same time. Considering his size and strength, the vehicle he was building was much too big to be built at the bottom of the hill and be pulled up; so he had cleverly decided to build it part by part on top. It was another week of drilling holes, wiring, and finding old bolts to fit before he had his creation ready.

His machine had not turned out exactly as he had planned, but all things considered it looked very big and impressive. He felt pleased and proud of his accomplishment. Once his masterpiece of engineering and craftsmanship was revealed, no longer would he be teased or called "silly" or "stupid John" again by his smarty-pants brothers and sisters. He would be admired and respected. However, the actual field demonstration would have to be shown to somebody really important. 'Really important' didn't mean his own dumb family either. Not by a long shot. He would wait. For a year, if he had to.

Scene 2: The Jake Olson Farm on the Border

Another sunny summer Sunday morning and it was still early. The cattle had been milked and sent out to pasture. My mother, Lena, had just hung up her apron behind the stove. There would be plenty of time for exploring and playing in the creek before we would be leaving for church. I was about to charge out of the house and go down the hill when she had stopped me and announced that we would not be going to church that day. No church? Hooray!--Oh, oh, just a minute--in my mind the news was just too good. There had to be some bad news coming, and it came when Ma said, "you and I are going visiting." The words "You and I" were the wiliappy clue. Whenever Ma said, "You and I are going..." instead of "we are going..." it meant that my dad wasn't going to take us in the car. We would be walking! Walking was bad enough, but when my mother told me who she planned to visit, my outlook for that day was really shot to blazes.

We were going to visit the Skolunds. Personally I didn't have anything against the Skolunds, but their farm was about seven long dusty miles away. A fourteen-mile round trip walking was not my idea of real fun. I don't know why Pa often didn't take us when Ma wanted to go calling. Maybe it's because they had had a fight or something, perhaps to save tires or gasoline. More likely, at the rate of speed my pa usually drove his 1928 Dodge, Ma thought we could get there faster by walking. Then again, she actually liked to walk. Anyway, for whatever reason, we would be walking.

Normal attire for a Sunday visit by my mother was a cotton summer dress, usually homemade. This was always worn, believe it or not, over a stiff corset. Her attitude seemed to be "To hell with being comfortable; one must look proper and erect at all times." On the other hand, farm women rarely wear hose or stockings in summer to visit another farm lady. It would be considered too ostentatious and hot. However, practical matters did not apply when it came to the corset. Another habit Lena had was that of wearing comfortable walking shoes to get there; in a paper sack she would carry a pair of nice shoes for being there. The nice shoes she would put on just before we walked into the 'visitees' house. Over her head, Lena, always wore a white dishtowel formed into a strange kind of bonnet to keep the sun off her face. She wanted to retain her fair complexion and not look like her sister, Josie, who lived in California. "All that sun makes her looks like a wrinkled old Indian." she would mutter. As for me, I wore what all other farm kids wore, clean overalls, a denim shirt, and a straw-hat--period. No underwear or shoes. Shoes were for school and church. In summertime it was thought needless to fritter away so much money just for walking. By the time summer was over, calluses on my feet would be tougher than bison hide. Like any other barefoot boy, I could walk over Russian thistle, sharp rocks, cactus, or stand on live coals, and feel no irritation.

The Skolund farm was located in the foothills. Ma knew where it was. I had never been there. She had told me it was somewhere east of the Turtle Mountain Lutheran church but I hadn't paid much attention. The mention of church again reminded me to be thankful for small compensations. I wouldn't have to go to church that day. For that reason alone it should be worth the long walk. Since we couldn't easily go overland we would follow the roads. We started out by walking on the grade for a half-mile east to the 'Townline.' Here a rutted, north/south road separated Harem Township from Dalen Township. On this road we would go south for about five miles. Actually it wasn't a road in the normal concept of a road. It was an area saved for a real road someday. It separated the two townships. Hence the name "Townline." At our end it didn't even deserve to be called a lane. In reality, it was just an untended neutral zone of native prairie about twenty feet wide, with a trail of two ruts.

The original trail had been made by wagons. Except for harvest hayracks, wagons for travel were now a relic of the past. This was 1932--modern times! The modern age of airplanes, dirigibles, Lindbergh, Roosevelt, bobbed hair, the Charleston. In that new era I really couldn't relate to my mother telling of Indian uprisings. Although once, when I was about eight years old I did see a buckboard full of forlorn Indians clunking along this very town line, perhaps on their way to relocate on the Turtle Mountain Reservation. Apparently they preferred the old town line trail to the 'improved' gravel road a mile east. The likelihood of passing "White Eyes" jeering at them would be less here. Somehow they didn't look like the wild savages I'd read about or been told they were. My feeling of sadness at the time of seeing their poverty and plight was very heavy. It was a sight I would never forget.

Now, in that new age, the double ruts were caused by automobiles rather than wagon or buggy tracks. The road wasn't a perfectly straight line, as one would expect on a surveyed boundary. Scattered boulders, some naturally deposited, some left and forgotten by farmers who had cleared them off their fields, caused the road to meander a bit as the motorists had to drive around rocks which had threatened to put a hole through the oil pan or rip off the differential. Tall grass and weeds grew on the narrow twenty-foot strip separating the two townships. However, on the part between the two ruts, the grass and weeds were cut, not by a mower, but by the underside of moving cars. The actual height of the vegetation varied, depending on the depth of the ruts. In places where the ruts were shallow, the grass was six inches high or more, other places the grass was cut flush to the ground if the ruts were deep. The cars with low clearance did most of the cutting. My dad never drove fast enough to cut grass; the car just gently bent it out of the way.

Model "T" Fords had the best clearance of all. Second best were the Model "A's." The poorest cars for clearance and most likely to bottom out, were Chevies, Nash, Plymouth, or Dodge. Except for the Forsbergs who had a Star automobile, no other brands existed locally. Every now and then, as we walked along that road, I checked the tops of protruding rocks, especially where the ruts were deep. I'm hoping to see if anyone had bottomed out. Much to my satisfaction, I found telltale signs of metal on a mostly buried granite boulder and pointed it out to my mother. "Serves the damn fool right for going too fast and not being careful," was her sympathetic comment.

Anyone who has had to walk down the single narrow gully path of a two-rut road will agree that it is something akin to the challenge of walking balanced on the single rail of a railroad track. The narrow tires of the first automobiles weren't much wider than wagon wheels. They didn't leave a very wide rut. To walk the rut meant keeping your toes pointed forward and placing one foot precisely in front of the other, or risk turning your foot on the edge of the sidewalls. It became a game to see how far I could go without stumbling out. Compared to walking barefoot on lumpy prairie with its hidden rocks to stub my toe on, rut walking was a pleasure. Most of the time the rut bottoms would be dusty-smooth and I could make little puffs of dust by stomping my foot harder. Wherever the fancy pattern of some special tire tread had left its imprint in sunbaked mud, stepping on it provided a tickling sensation. Even through the tough soles of my feet, different designs could be read like Braille, without looking. Best of all, every now and then a rut puddle, left over from a recent shower would provide some cool mud to squish up between my toes. It was almost erotic.

So on down the road we went. Ma, wearing shoes, walked down the area between the ruts. As I kept plodding along, placing one foot in front of the other in the narrow rut, a thought occurred to me. Old frontier scouts claimed they could easily tell the footprints of an Indian from that of a white man. "A white man,'" they said, "walks with his toes pointed outward at an angle on either side of a line. Indians walk with toes forward, placing one foot precisely in front of the other as if centered on a tightrope." Here was the answer to that peculiar habit right under my feet. Obviously Indians grew up walking down Model "T" ruts.

We passed a few farmsteads on the way. Nobody seemed to be home but for a barking dog or two. Lena said that the folks must be off to church. Again, the mention of church reminded me that walking to visit somebody was simply the price to be paid. Except for the occasional startling bevy of Hungarian partridges exploding into the air or the squeaking departure of a pheasant, the journey for this ten-year-old boy became boring. After what seemed hours of being on the trail, I complained to Ma that I was tired of all this walking. "In that case," she suggested, "You can run a while."

After the five-mile stretch we abandoned the town line, turned east, and were walking on a graded road again. We were both thirsty and Ma said we would stop at someone's farm for a drink. There was a farm a short distance ahead. We couldn't see the house very well but we could see the barn roof with its weather vane above the trees of the windbreak. She hoped that no one would be at home so our trip wouldn't get interrupted by a needless visit. We would just help ourselves at the pump. Actually, I think she didn't want to explain to anyone why we were walking when there was a perfectly good '28 Dodge at home.

We neared the farm gate, left the road, and walked up the curving graveled driveway. A shaggy brown dog barked continuously as he shuffled from side to side as if on an invisible tether. It was a sign nobody was home. "Probably in church," ma said. The dog barked for a while until he got sick of his own noise and shut up. Seeing that we were just going to the pump, which was out of his jurisdiction, he considered his obligation was over. He turned and went back to his spot in the shade of the house and lay down.

As on all farms, the pump, windmill and water trough were located a sanitary distance away from the manure drainage of the barn. The pump was hooked up to the vertical lift bar of the fan above. By pulling a lever fastened to one of the legs of the windmill, the tail vane of the windmill straightened out and pointed the blades of the airwheel into the wind. It began to turn. Soon cool water was pouring from the pump spout. We cupped our hands to the stream and drank. Of course we had to utter the common comment about how good plain water can taste on a hot day. As Lena turned off the windmill, she said she reckoned we were still about a half-hour away from Skolund's. As we left the farm, I took another look at the fancy horse-and-buggy weather vane on top of the barn. It was a dandy--I wished we had one for our farmhouse instead of that plain vane we had that noisily scraaawked at every change of breeze.

As we walked along the way, Lena kept talking about how much she felt sorry for Mrs. Skolund. It was all Karl Skolund's fault that she had so many children. "He couldn't keep his pants buttoned, he ought to be neutered, etc. etc." There were already at least a dozen kids or so and probably "One in the oven" again. My mind boggled, "God forbid! A dozen children!" Up until then I had no idea that in the Skolund family there were more than the three children I knew in the Turtle Mountain school. At my age, I hated even the thought of human babies. I was thoroughly repelled by diaper-stinking, drooling, ugly, slobbering, squalling, helpless babies. Except for crows and mice, animal babies were cute and cuddly. Animal babies weren't totally helpless. They could run and play just a few days after birth. There was absolutely nothing about a human baby to justify its existence. To think that the birth of such a miserable creature was preventable and not prevented--unbelievable! By now I was madder at Karl Skolund than my ma was. How could he do that? To his own wife yet. The sheriff ought to put him in jail.

Since the main character of the tale "The "Juggernaut" and the visit to the Skolund's is a boy named John, it would be fitting to write a character profile and perhaps illuminate the essence of this young lad and his dreams.

During the two years I attended a one-room rural school, perched on one of the foothills of the Turtle Mountains, John was one of my classmates. Because he was a grade or two ahead of me, I assume he was at least two years older than I. My sister Luella, eleven years older than I, was our schoolteacher. This explains my going to the Eidsvold School instead of Mountain View No. 1. on the prairie. In rural schools all grades are lumped together, so it was confusing at times as to who was how old or what grade they were really in. John sat in the back of the room, where the older boys sat. Because Skolunds lived so far away, he came to school along with his older brother, Martin, and sister, Greta, by horse and buggy. Martin, being the oldest was well behaved and responsible. Greta was somewhat frail, shy, and always smiling. Sometimes John was in school physically but not really present. His mind was often elsewhere inventing things.

Because country school children were deprived of playground equipment, we were constantly thinking up things to do during dinner hour (lunch recess). Mostly it turned out to be slingshot practice, snow sledding, or running down snowshoe rabbits that interested the boys. All the boys but John, that is. Usually, John would be off in the woods building a wickiup, or trying to kindle a fire by friction using a bow-spun stick and kindling board. One day while the older boys were gathered in a huddle, telling the latest dirty jokes, he made an announcement that he would demonstrate how to make a small hole through a board without using an auger bit. This caught our attention momentarily. Over a fire he had heated the end of an iron rod he had found until it was cherry-red hot. Then by holding the other end wrapped in an old discarded piece of leather for insulation, he neatly burned a hole through an old board. We were impressed and agreed that if we were ever caught out in the wilderness and needed to bore a hole in something, we would remember the valuable lesson. However, iron rods are hard to find in a wilderness. Therefore, carry an iron rod with you at all times.

Inventors, like John, can be mighty entertaining. Even in class when he was supposed to be studying, he drew pictures of inventions, especially cars. We never quite understood his 'improvements.' Generally, he was very well behaved but one day, as he sat at his desk, he broke wind. My cousin Virgil, who sat behind him was unappreciative and loudly banged John on top of the head with a book. My teacher, sister Luella stormed back and gave Virgil a verbal thrashing. Virgil yelled back about John's gas attack. By now, the girls were giggling and boys falling out of their seats with laughter. Virgil and John had to stay after school and, as punishment, write sentences on the blackboard. Fifty times Virgil had to write, "I will not hit anyone on the head with a book." I'm not sure what John had to write.

Perhaps in his struggle to be noticed, or perhaps just because John could not resist the creative urge, he decided to build something to challenge his skill. He had always wanted to own and drive a real car, a real big car with gleaming paint, white tires, big chrome-plated headlights and a sixteen-cylinder engine that rumbled like distant thunder. Even if his folks could have afforded a coaster wagon he wouldn't want it. Coaster wagons were for little kids to haul dumb faced babies in. Since the prospect of having a real car seemed a bit unlikely, he would have to build a reasonable facsimile. Build it, but where? If he built it in the farmyard his folks would probably stop him or his damn-nuisance brothers and sisters would get in the way. He couldn't possibly find an engine to propel it so how would he get it to move? The only energy option he had was gravity. He would build it to roll down hill. It would be full-size replica of a car. Wait just a minute–how would he be able to push his big car up the hill when he finished? After some thought, he had the answer. He would secretly build it on the hill across the road from the farmyard. Nobody in his family noticed him anyway, and with luck, no one would notice the activity in the brush clump near the top.

As a builder he soon learned the difference between the dream fantasy of the ideal design and reality. At first he had hoped to find car wheels with real rubber tires from some abandoned automobile or something.

He had found only one useable discarded wheel on his farm, and it wasn't a car wheel. Now he would have to search the scrap piles of the neighbors. Once he had located the wheels, what would he use for a frame? The only frame he knew about was a discarded and broken old lumber wagon behind the machine shed. It also had one big wheel that still seemed sound. It would have to do. Removing the wheel and rolling it up the hill had been hard enough, but the only way he could move the frame was to take it apart and carry or drag the parts up the hill and reassemble it. This had been no easy task. Luck was with him in one respect; as usual, none of his brothers or sisters noticed his activity.

Finding a matching set of wheels was much harder than he thought it would be. Eventually he had to settle for anything that would roll. If he found a wheel the same size as the one he already had, the rim or the hub would be shot. Obviously this was the reason the wheel had been discarded in the first place. He had to take what he found and somehow make it fit. Not only did none of the wheels match in size but not all were even of the same material. One of the wheels was made of metal from an old hay rake or cultivator or something. Since each wheel diameter was different, the axle height of each would have to be readjusted, that is if he had a matching axle for the hub of the wheel in the first place. This meant boring holes in the frame, adding a filler block or something. Burning the bolt holes with a heated iron rod was the easy part. He had experience. Finding the bolts was harder, he did a lot of scrounging. Failing to find all the bolts needed, he wrapped the parts together using wire, old barbed-wire, untwisted to make a single strand. Nails were used where a nail would hold, like in building a seat for example. He had to use more diagonal bracing boards than he would have liked. They were necessary but spoiled the racy look he desired. The steering mechanism had demanded the most ingenuity. It was solved with some rope, pulleys and a sort of tiller-bar. He would have to imagine having a steering wheel, chrome plated headlights, and a fancy body like the hearse he had seen. It took a lot of imagination.

The project over, he felt physically and mentally drained. He could do no more. His vehicle was as ready as it ever would be. He sat on a near-by rock and looked at it in the soft light of the last rosy glow of sunset. Perhaps it didn't look very much like a real car, even a very big car--it was something else-- perhaps something the army would have. Maybe a tank. Nevertheless, he was proud of it. The next step would be the demonstration.

John's machine had been finished for days. It sat near the top of the hill, its great mass mostly hidden by a clump of silverberry and buck brush.

Wheel chocks were in place, holding its great bulk straining against the pull of gravity. Both chocks could be pulled away with a rope from the drivers seat. He tired of waiting on the hill even though his folks hadn't noticed he was gone. Naturally, that was to be expected. From now on he would work on some other project behind the machine shed.

Several times each day John had gone out to the road to see if somebody 'important' was coming. Daily he had fantasized someone important from some city, perhaps a state senator or maybe even a person as important as the governor.

The vigil had been a disappointment. Without adequate warning, the occasional passing car had gone by too fast for him to make it to the top of the hill in time. For that matter how could he tell by just looking if the person inside was important or not? After another week of frustrated waiting and missed rare opportunities, he concluded there was something wrong with his scheme. From now on he would increase his vigilance by going more often to look down the road. He might have to settle for somebody a little less important than the governor, but even so--still more important than his stupid brothers and sisters.

The Big Day at the Skolund's

John walked out the driveway past the cottonwoods to look down the road again for the third time this Sunday. In the distance he saw someone coming! It appeared to be only a woman and a boy, hardly important, but as dignitaries they would have to do. He couldn't wait any longer. The time for his ride to glory had come. The demonstration hill was opposite the farmyard driveway. The barbed- wire gate would have to be left open so he could coast through. John undid the loop and dragged the post, wires and spreader bars aside and then ran up the hill.

Arrival of Dignitaries

The Skolund place had been in sight now for quite a while. Since turning south Ma and I still had about a quarter mile to go. The Skolund place was on the right side of the road. Soon we were near the windbreak of trees between the road and the farmyard. Even though the drought had been hard on all the trees, and leaves were sparse, they still screened the view of the buildings and the hordes of children I expected to see. We were almost past the first row of cottonwoods and about ready to walk down the driveway. Lena's distance vision was poor, and I had been too occupied trying to look into the farmyard mostly hidden by the scraggly branches to notice the hurried activity on the hill to our left.

We reached the open gate of the lane leading to the house, which stood about eighty yards away and to the right of the driveway. About fifty yards beyond the house stood the open side of a large shed where farm machinery, wagon, buggy, or family car might be stored. Looking slightly against the sun, the opening appeared too dark to see what was in it.

Over to the far left was the barn, a few boards missing due to a recent windstorm. The driveway lane curved left toward and past the barn. Farm buildings were never built close together as a way of cutting potential fire losses. That way if there were a fire perhaps only one building would burn down. A few children were playing in the yard. Some idiot dogs were yapping themselves hoarse. Lilac bushes partially screened an outdoor laundry washtub by the house. Rows of diapers hung on the clothesline. Diapers meant babies. A quarantine warning sign of some terrible disease would have been a more welcome sight.

We had just walked through the open gate when Lena saw the gatepost and wires lying to one side. She exclaimed in a tone of disgust, "Some careless 'treode' *(pronounced tray-hooda, Norwegian for wooden head)*, left the gate open and the cows can get out!" She went to pull it back into place. I helped her pull it tight as she closed the loop over the post. We hadn't taken five steps before I heard a loud clatter and rumble coming from behind us.

The sound was both startling and ominous. I turned to see a massive vehicle thundering down the hill. The ugly hulk was swerving from side to side. A wildly active person was frantically grappling and heaving on some sort of a steering bar. On the way down it plowed through patches of buckbrush and silverberry. Careening wheel rims dug into the dry earth, ripping clods of sod skyward. Clang! A metal wheel rebounded from an imbedded boulder. Boards flew off. Thud! A huge wooden wheel hit another rock. More boards flew away.

For a moment I stood transfixed by the explosion of events. Then the reality of impending doom struck me. The out-of-control mechanical beast, a maze of lumber, rope, wire, odd-sized wheels, and clattering noise was charging towards us with all the fury of a wild bull. The intended course of this tornado was the gate, the one we had closed, and the road beyond. John, the driver, was yelling and screaming repeatedly: *"THEEE GAAYTE! O —PN – THE GATE!"*

By the time I had realized what was going on, it was too late to open the gate. The swerving, bouncing, lurching, clattering monster was almost upon us. Ma heard the ruckus, but never did clearly see 'it' coming. Wire gate or no wire gate, we were in position to get killed. Just barely, I had time to push her behind the protective bole of a nearby cottonwood tree when the fury hit the fence.

The 'juggernaut' didn't even slow down. Whang! Screetch! The double-stranded fence wires didn't break instantly but fence posts did. A row of bone-dry oak posts snapped with the pop-pop-popping sound of a string of firecrackers as the fence wires pulled them down.

John had originally intended to go whistling down the lane past the barn. Unfortunately, barbed wire had jammed the steering mechanism. Totally helpless, pale-faced John roared by--dragging a long string of wires and fence posts behind him. The barbed wires were furiously sawing the bottom of the tree trunks nearest the gateway. If it had slowed down much, I didn't notice it. The noise and huge dust cloud was impressive. At first it seemed he would hit the house and about ten kids. Screaming children ran out of the way just in the nick of time. Even the dogs shut up and ran for life. Our hero fortunately missed the house, but just barely. Unable to steer, it was evident he would not miss the machine shed, its black maw hiding God-knows-what machinery.

It was a marvelous sight to see the machine thundering like a demented rhinoceros toward the open shed. Then John and juggernaut disappeared into the blackness of the opening. The darkness lasted only a microsecond. Suddenly, a flood of sunlight flashed inside the building as a section of the rear wall vanished in a burst of boards. Then came the sound of impact. Boom!!! John, wagon, and previous fence finally came to a stop in the barley field about a hundred feet beyond the previous wall. His little brothers and sisters ran through the new opening and into the field to see the body.

Luckily, there had been no machinery in the way, only a wall. Miraculously, John was still alive. In fact, he had only a few cuts, bruises, slivers, wood fragments, and a lot of dusty debris loosened from whatever had been on the back wall. He seemed a little dumbfounded as if trying to decide his venture had been a success or failure.

From my standpoint the demonstration had been a resounding success and I was glad to tell John that it was the most interesting event I had ever seen. It had been worth every mile that we had to walk to see it. I would have walked it again.

Every now and then I wonder whatever became of John. I like to think of him retiring as a General at the U.S. Army's Aberdeen Proving Ground in Maryland.

DUST AND HARD TIMES

The Dust Bowl era of the thirties wasn't the most fun time a person could experience. However, it did give me the impetus to leave the farm, an occupation I wasn't cut out for in the first place. Hard times must have booted a lot of people. It seems about 90 percent of North Dakotans now live in other states. Half of them live in Mesa, Arizona. Homesick for heat and dust I guess.

This story is true. True that is, as well as I can remember it. If you are a republican, you will hate the part about FDR.

The 1930's were the hard years, not only from the great national depression, but from crop losses due to insects, wheat rust, and severe drought. 1934 was the driest year of the Dust Bowl Era. In spring and summer there had been almost no rain at all. The little precipitation, which did fall (four inches in Bottineau County), had mostly been in the form of snow, dusty-grey, dirty snow. Banks had failed and many farmers lost what little they had left. People, livestock, and even buildings seemed to vanish, farm by farm, as if caught in the receding dust storm.

There were several factors, which led to the terrible era. Ironically, one of them was the 'invention' of the <u>summer fallow</u>, an agricultural farming practice innovation which makes it possible to grow crops in arid areas without irrigation. The idea works like this, ' in areas of little rain, farmers raise crops on only half of their total acreage at a time. For every field raising a crop, there is an equal area of weedless cultivated land. Crop growing and summer fallow fields alternate from year to year. This practice is known as dry farming. The use of the summer fallow, which turned the Great Plains into the most productive grain growing area in the world, is the same summer fallow that uninformed city folks think is 'idle land,' land they still believe the government pays a farmer for not growing anything. Alas, the summer fallow was also the primary 1930's dust source.

Before and after the Civil War the program of the genocide of Native Americans had greatly reduced their population. One of the shamefully inhumane programs condoned by the US government was that of starving the Indians into submission by killing all the bison. This ultimately reduced the herds, once numbering in the millions, to near extinction. Of the surviving Native Americans, most were herded into reservations. In the northern plains a few Indian nations such as the Sioux, still resisted. A vast, rich prairie grassland, now empty of bison and Indians, was opened to settlement by white people.

Settlers came from the eastern states, claimed land, and broke the sod. The first year's planting usually produced a crop. The second year, not so good. By the third year it was evident that wheat could not be grown. Discouraged farmers were pulling up stakes and going back to Wisconsin, Ohio or wherever. The basic cause was inadequate rainfall. At the latitude of Kansas it takes about twenty-four inches of rain to grow a crop of wheat. Unfortunately, the annual average rainfall of the Great Plains is far less than that (Near the Canadian border, it is 16 inches.) Hence the crop failures.

The solution was the summer fallow. Somewhere back in the dark corner of my memory I recall that the principle of dry farming was invented by an agronomist in Kansas. He solved the problem of making the prairies capable of producing crops of grain. As a scientist, he had the logical thought that if rainfall could be saved for one year and added to the precipitation that fell the following year, a crop could be grown. To learn the name of this enigmatic person I asked the help of the reference library of almost every agricultural college or university. The polite answers I got ranged from "An interesting question," "The Mormons developed it," "Dry farming had evolved from the time of the pharaohs," to "Doubt there was ever a singular person."

If a singular person did develop this farming method, he or she would deserve a first-class memorial. Because of the simple solution, the Great Plains provide 1/12th of the bread for the worlds population.

The basic principle of saving water is simply to prevent evaporation. But how does one put a cork or lid over a whole field? The answer is twofold: One, keep all plants, weeds or crop from growing, thus preventing the plants from pumping up moisture from underground. Two, destroy capillary flow (wicking) of water to the surface of the soil where it can evaporate. Capillary flow can take place in porous material in which solid particles or fibers are small and packed together. It takes place in firm soil, but not in gravel, for example. The solution: After each rainfall, stir up the soil with a cultivator, thus breaking it up into loose particles so as to interrupt flow channels. Moisture, unable to creep upwards, will be trapped below the field's surface. This enabled farmers to grow grain in the Great Plains or anywhere else where annual rainfall is less than needed. However, summer fallow is very vulnerable to wind erosion, and blowing dust.

The real culprit causing the miserable dust storms wasn't just the practice of summer fallowing, per se. It was the type of harrow used to cultivate. The harrow commonly used was a large wooden frame crosshatched with many rows of railroad spike teeth. When pulled by a couple of horses, it stirred up the soil just fine. But, too fine. The problem was that it left the soil too level and too smooth. This made the dirt easily picked up by the wind. It took very little wind to start the dust moving from a dry field. Cultivation today is done with disk or spade cultivators that leave not only deep furrows but also sometimes intentionally leaving stubble to discourage blowing dust.

Another factor that led to the Dust Bowl was the draining of wetlands. Every slough, lake, or pond was drained to get more land. Even the Mouse River (original French name, Souris), which had had a meandering course across a river bottom, sometimes a mile wide, was dredged into a straight channel with the intention of getting more farmland. The soil turned out to be unfit for farming, so that was a stupid idea in more ways than one. Later on, the Federal government put the "CCC"[13] boys to work building low dams in several places on the "Mouse," thus restoring wetlands and creating one of the nation's largest waterfowl refuges.

Even to this day some 'experts' argue how much of the drought was due to a natural climatic change and how much was man-caused. I only know that certain measures were taken by an enlightened government to reverse some of the bad land use practices adding to the drought and it has worked remarkably well. However, in the past couple of decades, I have noticed that some farmers are draining wetlands again and sometimes even the trees of shelterbelts are being bulldozed. Historically, stupidity has a way of repeating itself.

Now on to my personal observation of "Dust and Hard Times."

The era of the Dust Bowl may conjure up the image of a forlorn family from Oklahoma heading west in a beat-up automobile to hoped for greener orchards in California. In reality, they were the lucky ones. They had enough

---

[13] *CCC: acronym for Civilian Conservation Corps. Young men, mostly under twenty years of age, who needed work could join the "CCC's" where they would be housed in military-like camps and put to work building dams, parks, etc. They also earned a small salary.*

money to buy gasoline and repair tires to make the trip. Many farmers could not even afford to make the journey west. They were financially trapped to face whatever nature threw at them. Carl Steinbeck in his novel, GRAPES OF WRATH, and many magazine articles showing the heartbreaking scenes of destitute, desperate farmers such as in LIFE magazine, focused the plight to an area much smaller than what was actually involved. The truth is that the misery extended far beyond Oklahoma and Kansas. It stretched from Texas beyond the Canadian border. It wasn't just the drought, or economic depression; there were other miserable factors. Insects--grasshoppers, army worms, and plant diseases like wheat rust raised as much hell as the lack of rain. It didn't matter much how a farmer lost his crop, to him and his family it was lost. This was the world I grew up in.

An Early Memory of the First Big Swarm of Grasshoppers.

The original site of the town of Bottineau was about a mile or two up Oak Creek from where the town is now located. James Hill, builder of the Great Northern Railway sometimes peevishly ignored where a town was already located when his railroad tracks were being laid. Whether this was done to display his power or just to make things miserable for the pioneers, who knows. Certainly the elevation difference for roadbed building between the original site and the present location did not justify his petulant action. Bottineau had to move if it was to have the service of a railroad. It was here at the original townsite, now Dana's Grove that the Old Settlers Picnics were held in the early thirties. Many of the original pioneers were still alive who remembered the original townsite. Here they once came annually to share memories of the early days.

I Can't Remember the Exact Date. I'm Guessing 1931.

A few people were already sitting at picnic benches when our car rolled into the loosely designated parking area. We got out of the car, then gathered up the potluck picnic food we were supposed to share. As we were carrying the baskets to an empty table, Lena commented about the unusual number of grasshoppers leaping out of our way. She said that there seemed to be a lot more here than at home. My parents and neighbors were already concerned about the threat to crops from these insects and this looked very ominous.

At all events such as this, relatives usually tend to bunch up into groups. This picnic was no exception. Our bunch consisted of the folks on my mother's side. On my father's side, my grandparents were dead.

For a kid, the speeches were boring, but the food, especially the watermelon, compensated. Some speech maker was droning on when I noticed someone pointing at the sun. People started looking up, ignoring the talk being given at the moment. At first we saw only a strange, fuzzy, yellow halo around the sun. Then we recognized the cause. The circle of sparkling light was sunlight being reflected from the wings of countless grasshoppers! A look of despair could be seen on the faces of people at the tables. Wherever they lit, a swarm of these insects could mean the total destruction of a farmer's crop. Ants are normally blamed for spoiling a picnic. This day we would gladly have traded the sight above for a dozen anthills. On our worrisome journey back to the farm we encountered large areas where the hoppers had landed, and were devouring the crops. In places on the road the insects were so numerous that it was like driving through a fog. Though that first swarm missed our farm, we lost most of our crop later that year.

Perhaps a more light-hearted way to relate the story about the voracious appetite of the grasshoppers is to tell about a phone conversation that I had last summer. I had attended a high school reunion in Bottineau where I learned that one of the former students, Cliff Marchand, was now living in Moses Lake, Washington. Since this town is in the center of the state only sixteen miles from Ephrata, where our glider club is located, I decided to give Cliff a call one weekend.

On his part, there was considerable surprise to be hearing from me for the first time in fifty years. Following the first exchange of "I'll be damneds..." there was the inevitable series of "Do you remembers?" It wasn't long before Cliff asked; "Do you remember the grasshoppers?"

"Mighty hard to forget" I answered.

"God they were something." He went on. "Ate our whole crop, ate everything, even the weeds and Russian thistle--and when there was nothin' left in the field they even ate the fence posts--left nuthin' but bare barbed wire layin' on the ground." This, I hadn't heard before, but I wished I'd have thought of it.

Later, in a phone call to an old farmer friend of mine, Oliver Magnuson, I told him of my phone call to Cliff. I expected him to laugh in disbelief at the story about grasshoppers eating fence posts. Instead, he said, "Well – I don't know about eating fence posts, but they would eat anything they could chew." "I remember that I had been out on the field when they came." "I had left my blue-denim jacket at the other end." "When I came to get it there was nothing left but the brass buttons." It is obvious that people like Cliff and Oliver should be writing these stories, not me. I can't match 'em.

In case you are wondering how grasshoppers which normally only leap and fly a few yards came flying at high altitude, I don't blame you. I didn't understand it myself until years later when I became a glider pilot. I discovered that insects of all kinds, ranging from mosquitoes to clumsy beetles, were striking and sticking onto my sailplane's wings at altitudes over ten thousand feet above ground level. How did they get there? The same way that my thousand pound glider does, borne aloft in a thermal. Thermals are localized masses of surface heated air that rise upward like a hot-air balloon. It is common for the velocity of rising air to exceed more than a thousand feet a minute. Circling in thermals then gliding to the next mass of rising air make it possible for migrating birds to fly long distances. Some large birds, storks for example, would be unable to migrate without thermals. Insects like grasshoppers do the same--and they only need to be several feet above the ground to be caught in a thermal and borne upward thousands of feet.

It wasn't only grasshoppers; one year there were the army worms, voracious hordes of worms so numerous and thick that automobiles would slip in the blanket of worms crossing a highway. Though they couldn't fly, they came on and on, crawling over everything, buildings included. The olive green and black striped worms were as voracious as the 'hoppers.' They didn't eat fence posts, but after going through a grove of trees, there wouldn't be a single leaf left to flutter.

If crops weren't lost to insects or hailstorms, there was rust. Wheat rust, parasitic fungi, usually showed up as little red-brown spots on the grain, then spread to cover the whole plant. It had the appearance of iron-rust, hence the name. It normally didn't completely wipe out a crop, but greatly reduced the bushels per acre. At harvest clouds of red dust followed and covered the reaper. The development of rust resistant wheat and eradication of common barberry bush, the host plant of rust, greatly reduced crop losses due to this problem.

Fighting insects, plant diseases, and enduring low crop-prices at the market would seem to be enough to keep anyone away from the poor-odds gamble of farming. For me, as a young lad anticipating the future, the final blow to any desire I might have entertained to becoming a farmer was the terrible drought.

The Era of Drought and Dust Storms. July 1934

My sister Luella was a few paces ahead of me as we walked back to our farm. This was typical of us. We seldom walked together side-by-side, but in-line; a habit, I suppose, acquired from walking single-lane cow paths. She, eleven years older than I, was a rural schoolteacher home for a few weeks in the summer. As we hiked down the graded dirt road I was wearing my standard summer clothing-- a pair of beltless blue jeans and straw hat, both in tatters. The searing sun was frying my bare back. Without a shirt, underwear or socks, I could easily feel that already the air temperature at mid-morning was approaching ninety degrees Fahrenheit. Before the day's end, the thermometer in the shade at the north side of our house would show its blood-red line almost to the top-end of the numbers.

We had just driven the cattle to what we called the east pasture. It was the only place where any grasses or normal weeds were still growing. The slough, which had once been there was now dry. Enough sub-surface moisture remained to provide patches of grass fighting to stay alive. The home pasture was barren except for the areas around the now dry creek. In other fields and pastures, Russian thistle[14], a sticker-loaded tumbleweed relatively new to America, seems to be the only plant other than cactus, which can grow with so little rain. In desperation the cattle had even tried to eat this thistle while it was still green and soft, but it caused watery diarrhea. All vegetation suffered. Trees of the distant aspen groves were bare from the tops down to a few fluttering leaves a few feet from the ground. The hardy, tough box elder and cottonwood trees in farm windbreaks were in the same state of despair. Whatever wheat crop we would get would come from the low places.

As Luella and I came down that road, I was watching my shadow effortlessly sliding in the dust. Something about it caught my down-turned attention. At first, I wondered why the shadow edges were in sharp outline near my shadow's feet but fuzzy around the outline of my hat. Not solving this puzzle at the moment, my mind had turned to other thoughts. The seriousness of the drought was finally beginning to sink into my immature skull. "What will become of us if we don't get some rain soon?" I wondered. We will be able to eat fairly well, despite the shortage of store-bought staples like sugar and flour, only because we have the garden and potato patch. The garden is watered with hand- carried buckets of water from the well. Meat would come from cattle, chickens, hogs, and wild game. Dessert would come from up in the hills. Luckily, the Turtle Mountains were only a mile and a half away and although it hadn't rained up there either, there had been many lakes, sloughs, and springs to provide an underground reservoir of moisture for the juneberries[15], chokecherries, pincherries, wild plums and highbush cranberries.

Food wasn't the big problem. Potatoes and free berries were one thing, buying gasoline, shoes, knitting yarn, and paying taxes was another. For that we needed money--hard cash. My serious thoughts led to my mother, Lena. She kept the books on farm expenses and tried to work out a budget. She made an effort to conceal her worry and concern, but I remember one evening that really bothered me--so much so that I would never forget it.

One evening I had come into the house, after sunset. From the darkened dining room of the house I happened to see her as she sat at her writing desk in the alcove. Here, every night before going to bed she would write at least one letter to a friend or relative and keep a daily journal recording the weather, cattle prices, family events, etc. This time she was looking in the Sears Roebuck catalog. Her face had a sad, wistful look as she turned to one section after another. A few moments went by, she slowly closed the pages, put her elbows on the desk, and bowed her head into the interlaced fingers of her hands. A feeling of sadness for her swept over me. It made me uncomfortable, I felt I was an intruder seeing something I didn't really want to see. I tried to

---

[14] *Russian thistle: A form of tumbleweed covered with tiny thorn-like stickers supposedly came from Siberia to the U.S. in a load of rust-resistant seed-wheat in 1885.*

[15] *Juneberries: (Amelanchier alnifolia) shadbush, also* known *as service or sarvis berries, saskatoons, and locally as plain old blueberries*

tiptoe away. Perhaps I made a little noise, for she sensed my presence nearby. She lifted her head suddenly, made a little sniffling sound, turned, and asked, "Is that you, Jackie?"

Quietly, embarrassed, I answered–"Yeah Ma."

"Where's Luella?" she asked.

"Over at Backman's visiting Selma."

Ma then mentioned that Luella hadn't found a teaching job yet. Perhaps she would get one near Roth. Roth! Suddenly I felt sorry for Luella if that was where she had to go this fall. The little town of Roth was on the flat, barren prairie. There was nothing to slow the dust-laden wind but a few barbed wire fences that had snagged ragged balls of Russian thistle here and there. Roth was another word for bleak.

Ma went on:

"She has to have some new clothes to look nice for the school board when she applies for the job. Dresses I can probably sew, but I don't think my machine will handle making a coat for you, and you need a new coat and a warm hat."

"I don't need a coat," I said.

"Yes you do, your arms stick way out of the sleeves, and I can't make the sleeves any longer." With a sigh, she quietly said, "Somehow we got to find the money to buy you some clothes for school. Then too, this is the second year in a row that we won't be able to pay our taxes. I think you're old enough that I should tell you – if we don't pay up, we might lose the farm[16]. For now, we do what we can – I guess we will just have to sell Whitey."

"Sell Whitey? Oh no." I knew this was an extremely painful decision on my mother's part. Whitey was our dominant lead cow, gentle with my mother but tough on the "disrespectful" heifers who didn't know their place in line. True, she was getting old but had always been my mother's favorite cow. I wondered how my mother would have the courage to sell her. *(Later that summer she did sell her--for less than $3.00. Ma really cried that day–not out loud, just tears.)* Then the image of seeing my ma upset faded and my thoughts came back to the present as we walked along.

Looking up, I watched Luella as she plodded down the road ahead of me. I wondered how she would survive the future if things didn't get better. It was hard to think of Luella as my sister because she was eleven years older than I. She seemed more like an aunt. I had another sister, Evelyn, even older than Luella. She was married and living (surviving may be a better word), on a farm three miles from ours. She seemed even less like a sister, more like a second mother. Luella, now a schoolteacher, sometimes found summer jobs as a

---

[16] *Taxes: Going through my mother's papers after* her *funeral* in 1969, *I discovered the amount of taxes* we *hadn't been able to pay for two years* was *only $18.00*.

housemaid or clerk in a store. Jobs for women were even harder to find than for men. Sometimes Luella really irritated me. She teased me about having a girlfriend, one of the Thorsgard girls, Esther. It wasn't that I had anything against blue-eyed, flaxen-haired Esther. She was as innocent of boyfriend stupidity as I was of having girl friends. It's just that I didn't see much value in girls in general. When teased about them, I got mad as hell and hated girls for just existing, thereby giving my sister an opportunity to tease me. The thing I resented most was that she treated me as her "baby brother." The fact that I was her much younger brother didn't have anything to do with it. I just didn't want to be treated with so much emphasis on baby. I wanted to feel, if not as an adult, at least my age.

Well, baby brother or not, this day Luella had been a cow-herder, a lowly status no better than mine. Watching her, I remembered a day three years earlier when my mother told me some news about my teacher/sister. "You know she won't be your teacher at the Eidsvold School in the hills, this fall." (Luella had been my teacher for two years at this school.)

"No, no I didn't" – and I didn't care either.

Then Ma said, "This means you will be going back to the Mountain View School again." This was not good news.

It had been strange, having my sister as my schoolteacher. Imagine having a sister with the official authority to discipline her little brother, me-- something she never dared to try at home. For that reason, not having Luella for my teacher sounded like a real good deal. Luella had had the job of teacher in the rural school up in the foothills, so it was a decision by my folks as a practical matter that I would attend that school. Then the blow struck. Full realization of what my mother said finally got through my thick head. There were several boys attending that little school in the hills. There had been a lot of fun times there in the previous two years. There had been woods to play in, hills for sledding, boy-talk, and doing boy things. Mountain View No.1 on the prairie was on a barren, lonely, flat location. The nearest tree a half-mile away. Worse, it was attended almost exclusively by girls, Berge girls, and Thorsgard girls, all smarter than I was. In the coming school year there would be only one other boy, Vern Berge. Damn! Having had Luella for a teacher hadn't been as bad as I thought.

Luella was about twenty yards in front of me. About a quarter mile from us are our farm windbreak and its dying trees. Again as I watched my moving shadow, my mind had shifted from worrying about the folks to worrying about myself. Thoughts filled in my troubled brain. The present not only seemed bad, but the future even more ominous. "What will become of me?" I wondered. "Even if the drought ends and crops grow again, I'm too damn dumb to be a successful farmer. Besides, I am uninterested in wheat farming, any kind of farming."

Another unpleasant aspect of living on a diversified farm is butchering. Having to kill and cut up animals that you have raised from birth is miserable enough, not even counting the guts and gore of it all. Since it was obvious that I would never make it as a farmer, what else could a stupid farm boy do to make a living? I'd like to be an engineer, a designer of wonderful things like ships, airplanes, bridges, and big dams. That dream seemed unreachable. Engineers had to be good at mathematics. I was lousy at it. A dumb horse had a better chance of learning to sing the National Anthem than I did of becoming an engineer.

As long as I was dreaming of the impossible, what I'd really like to be was a famous pilot like Charles Lindberg. Lindberg was like a god to me. A gold-plated hero. From my current viewpoint, making airplane models was about as close as I would ever get to be a pilot. Pilots had to be real smart, have super coordination, be heroic, know navigation, and watch a bunch of instruments at the same time. I had none of those qualities. The girls in school could beat me at arithmetic hands down. "They can even beat me at spelling and they are mere girls! I am a boy for gosh sakes! Therefore, I must be the dumbest boy ever to get born."

What really disgusted me is that despite their academic superiority, the damn girls didn't even want to be engineers, much less a pilot. It just wasn't fair! Ma would say that I was just feeling mighty sorry for myself, but it was obvious that I was a hopeless case. Someday I'd be just one of those sad looking guys riding in railroad box cars, stopping here and there looking for a handout.

Luella's voice snapped me out of my heavy thoughts. "Oh dear God" I heard her saying as she walked, "Why don't we get some rain? When will this damn drought ever end?" Then she spied a bedraggled, small ragweed on the side of the grade. She pulled it out of the ground. A clod of root bound dirt simply sifted away, leaving its roots completely bare. "Look at this, not even enough moisture to hold the dirt together!" She threw it into the ditch and began to cry. My mood was not improved. First Ma, and now Luella weeping about hard times.

Little did I know that ten years later from that moment on the sun cracked dusty road I would be an Army Air Corps bomber pilot, followed by college and years in varying jobs in concept and preliminary spacecraft design engineering.

Dust Storms, Some Observations Recalled

Persons who have witnessed a total eclipse of the sun agree that it is very difficult to describe to those who haven't seen one. The same difficulty of description holds true for the approach of a monster dust storm.

At one time or another, most people have experienced a dust storm of sorts while crossing an arid area. The dust storms of the Dust Bowl era cannot be compared to the fog like blowing dust of our desert lands. The kind of storm

I'm referring to can best be described with the over-used word--awesome. Awesome, as in total solar eclipse. Then again, unless one has experienced a total eclipse of the sun, even words from the most skillful writer cannot describe the feeling of seeing the sun suddenly turn black. A partial eclipse, even 99.9%, is only mildly interesting. Total is different. It is as if someone walked into a room in daylight, turned on the lightswitch and had instant blackness from the bulb flooding the room. By the same token, to describe the emotional impact of an on-coming wall of churning dust in a 1930's dust storm is almost as futile as attempting to describe a total eclipse. The best I can do is to relate my impression of the storms as a series of observations.

The first indication of weather coming our way was by 'reading' the weather vane on our roof. Before I go on, I must explain the unusual nature of our weather vane. It only looked like an ordinary weather vane. It was not just a wind direction indicator to be observed visually, it made noises about the wind. It was loudly audible if one were inside the house. Its metallic groans were sometimes audible enough to be heard outside. We had an 'audio' wind indicator that my mother could understand and interpret, day or night.

An engineering design flaw was the cause of the noise. On our house were three lightning rods, each with a different colored glass ball at mid-point. Just over the blue ball of the third lightning rod was the weather vane. This vane was a simple arrow, nothing fancy like the horse and buggy vane on my grandfather's barn, but ours had a noise generator, its bearing. The bearing on our weather vane, as all bearings, required at least two parts. Onto the lightning rod a flat washer had been welded just above the ball. On the vane was a short cylindrical section of the same outside diameter as the washer. It had a hole slightly larger than the lightning rod. To this had been welded the pointer and feather section of the arrow. This vane, slipped over the rod and resting on the washer, meant one flat bearing surface against the other. Everything was made of steel, not exactly a self-lubricating material like an Oilite bearing. It didn't turn easily in the wind. When it did, the grating surfaces of the bearing caused the growling noise. Two or three times a year my dad would go up and grease the bearing, but it wouldn't last long before it went back to being its usual loud-mouth self.

Normally the wind had to be at least 3 mph before the vane would change direction and when it did, the vibrations of the bearing would be conducted down the lightning rod and into the rafters of our upstairs east bedroom. The bedroom then resonated better than the soundbox of a bass viol. Very loudly. A change in wind produced a loud SCRAWK!! Guests staying at our house, not forewarned about our weather vane, would sometimes be startled out of their wits with a very loud and unexpected SCRAWK! in the night. My mother, who cherished her talking weather vane, could read these sounds and prognosticate the weather for the next 24 hours, unless the weather vane changed its mind and scrawked again. No scrawk meant the wind was holding steady. Scrawk, scrawk, scrawk, meant the wind was snaking along, a turbulent warning that the weather was up to mischief. A single scrawk after a long duration of no noise meant the wind had changed, the weather system had changed. Time to check the barometer. Sometimes we would have gone to bed with the weather vane reassuringly pointing to the southeast. In the middle of the night--SCRAWK! Then Lena would stir in bed and say, "The wind has just switched to the south-west – no rain again tomorrow."

The weather vane on our roof had been indicating steady wind from the southeast for two days. In normal times, though there were no clouds, a southeast wind, plus a falling barometer, was a good indicator that weather was coming. With these basic instruments and observation, Lena could predict the weather better than a university trained meteorologist.

But these were not normal times. However, desperate hope is hard to kill. Steady wind from the southeast had always before meant a good chance of rain. Lena would go outside frequently during the day to make sure the vane was still holding steady. Jake, Carl and I would do the same. No one dared to mention the likely prospect of rain because of an unspoken superstition. We didn't dare, after so many disappointments, say out loud that conditions were right for rain. We felt that the mere act of saying, "It looks like rain" would somehow offend the pluvial gods and jinx our chances. This morning, date long forgotten, the wind had not only held steady from the southeast but also had increased in velocity. This was an even better sign. Then, shortly after noon, a monster cloud front began to fill the western horizon. Carl had seen it first and called our attention to the oncoming weather. We all walked to the tiny knoll just south of our house, our traditional weather viewing site.

A huge cloud-wall about a mile high, darkly ominous, extended from north to south as far as the eye could see. No billowing clouds to indicate the convective action of cumulo-nimbus rain clouds, just a wall. Sunlight on the top of the wall blazed a dust-yellow ragged thin line. Underneath a dark massive form was bulldozing its way toward us. As it came nearer, we could see no hope of rain. Another dust storm was coming. Disappointment sometime hits so hard that a person can't even feel right about cussing. This was one of those times.

Typical of people, who have weathered storms before, the best thing to do was to do something, anything, even if it might be futile. Pa went to check the chickens and get them into the coop along with our stupid turkeys. Turkeys are so dumb about weather that I often wondered how the species had ever survived in the wild. Carl went to make sure the granary and barn doors were closed and secure. As instructed, I went to the auto shed and rolled some boulders against the bottom of the shed doors to keep them from flopping away in the on-coming wind. Meantime, in the house, Ma put rags into a dishpan of water. At the last moment we would have to close all the windows and stuff wet rags in every possible crack or opening that could admit dust. Effective as this procedure was, we still couldn't keep all the dust out. The dust, talcum powder fine, driven by high winds would find a way in. The heat in a closed-in house in summer would be stifling, but it was the price we had to pay to avoid a lengthy clean up afterwards.

Barn, granary and shed doors closed, chickens and turkeys put in the coop, we could only wait and watch until the 'wall' hit us. Horses and cattle not lucky enough to get to the barn in time would just have to weather it out. As usual they would stand tail-to-the-wind to weather the storm. At the rate of speed that the approaching wall of dust was moving over the ground, it wouldn't be a long wait before it struck. Now we could see a rolling movement of dust in the wall itself, presenting the familiar but still unnatural scene of curling columns of dust moving upwards. The cloud-roller about to crush us, weirdly appeared to be going rolling backward while moving forward. Streamers of dust, rivers of dust, were rising in the face of the wall. The very top of the roller was sunlit and the bottom was in dark shadow. Occasionally there was the deep rumble of thunder. As with many fierce dust storms, static electricity was producing more lightning than the average thunderstorm. The lightning was for the most part unseen because of the dense, dirty cloud. Added to the disappointment of getting no rain there was the added fear of lightning setting fire to one of our tinder-dry buildings.

The storm was close now. It had enveloped the Thorsgard place and Backman's farm was disappearing. The wall was crossing the two-hundred-yard-wide flood plain of Boundary Creek and then rapidly came up the hill to blast our house. Before the dust-roller came, the weather vane had been steadily indicating a strong southeast wind. Just before the storm hit the house, the wind had stopped for a few minutes. After the first whumping blast, the wind now reversed to come from the west. The weather vane squawked loudly as it rotated on its dry bearing to indicate the new wind direction. The interior of the house grew dark as if someone had pulled down all the shades. Outside, only the dim outline of the milkhouse a few yards away could be seen. The dust laden wind blasted the west side of our house. Big balls of Russian Thistle could be seen passing by, airborne or bouncing on the ground. The barn was totally hidden in a dark tan-gray pall of moving dust. The house shuddered from the gale, and the unique smell of topsoil could be detected despite all the wet rag sealing we had done. After a half-hour or so, the stifling heat of the house lessened. Not only had the dust shut out the sun but evidently the storm had been a cold front. Cold fronts normally brought thunderstorms and rain. Again, these were not normal times. We had the thunder and lightning but no rain.

The storm blew out in less than two hours and calm air now prevailed, typical of violent frontal storms. Other less violent, but still miserable, storms would sometimes last a few days.

Outside we checked to see what damage had occurred. There was nothing serious, only the chore of general cleaning up to be done. Russian thistle and other tumbleweeds were stuck in the fences and lodged in the lilac bushes. These would be gathered and burned. Inside were little dust drifts on the windowsills and floor by the door. We were lucky this time, not like the day when a sudden dust storm had come up at my grandmother Krogen's funeral. We had come home to find a sizable dust-drift about five inches deep on our sun porch linoleum floor. All about the house there was dust on the floors and furniture. It had all come in through tiny cracks and under the door of the rag-sealed house.

Of the many dust storms of the thirties, one in particular added not only to the dismal prospect of my future, but set my determination to spend my adult life away from the desolate, dusty plains. Somehow, somewhere, someday, I would live where there would be water in abundance and, hopefully, mountains, or at least healthy big trees--something, anything, to slow the wind better than a barbed wire fence.

Luella had gotten the teacher's job in a small rural school, south of Roth. It was on the flatlands about twenty miles from our farm. Our Pa, Jake, and I were to go and bring her home for the weekend. She boarded out at one of the farm homes. However, once a month she would be coming home to visit. Since it was October, this was to be her first time home. Dust was already mildly blowing as we left the farm. By the time we got near Roth, we could hardly see the road. There was no dark cloud, just gray dust. The yellow-orange spot of the sun could be seen overhead. Pa was to pick Luella up at the school after Friday classes. The graded dirt road we were driving on was only about a foot higher than the surrounding prairie. The ditches had long ago been filled in flush by dust. This dust had once been topsoil on some of the richest farmland on earth. In some places even the road was flush with the rest of the new desert. If it hadn't been for the telephone poles or fence lines marking the side of the road, we might have lost the trail.

We finally came to the school--until then I had thought Mountain View No. 1 was bleak! This place was truly awful. It matched the most depressing Dust Bowl pictures of Oklahoma as seen in LIFE magazine. The dust laden gray- yellow sky outlined a small schoolhouse, a broken-down horse shed, and two outdoor privies. True to local tradition, the buildings had once been painted. Little patches of color still appeared on the lee side. The wind and dust had sandblasted away the paint on the west, or weather side. The windows had been sandblasted into permanently frosted glass. Inside the school, where Luella was gathering up her things and student papers to be corrected, the poverty of school amenities was evident. In my school, at least the maps weren't torn, and the world globe wasn't broken and sitting askew in its cradle, and our east facing windows were transparent. Usually I didn't waste time feeling sorry for my teacher/sister but this time I did. She deserved better than this.

That day had a powerful impact on me. One thing for certain, if I was smart enough to be a teacher, I sure as hell wouldn't want to be one in dust blown North Dakota. The calendar pictures on the wall of our kitchen at home had pictures of elsewhere in the United States, pictures of oceans, mountains, rivers, lakes, and big green trees. There really were wonderful magical places free of dust. "How am I going to tell Ma or Pa or even Uncle Carl that I didn't ever want to be a farmer and take over the farm? What sane person would want it? I may not be very smart, but then again, I'm not that stupid either." In 1934, passenger airplane pilots earned three times more than a doctor of medicine did. In my mind, what hope could a dumb farm kid, who knew he was a moron in school ever have of becoming a transport pilot? It seemed that any profession that appealed to me required serious mathematics and I had trouble with the times tables. What could I do to escape, survive the blowing dust of Dakota? The dream of becoming a pilot seemed incredibly remote. Becoming a janitor seemed remote.

One compensation about living in North Dakota is that it is the best place in the world to observe weather. Without many trees or mountains to block the view, moving clouds, tornadoes, hail, rain, snow, sun, stars, and the glowing aurora borealis, all have a marvelous stage to present their play to an intent and involved audience.

Sometimes the Clouds Looked Like Rain for Certain.

For two days the weather vane had again indicated a wind from the southeast-by south. Lena noted it in her journal and hoped that this time we would get the rain to save our withering crop. On the late evening of the third day a buildup of cumulus clouds appeared to be coming our way. They had the look of clouds bringing a heavy rain. To the southwest, a cloud-street of clouds. To the northwest, a buildup of churning activity was heralding the coming of a downpour, which we so desperately needed. Anxiously, Ma, Pa, Uncle Carl, and I went to the small knoll south of our house to silently watch the path of the approaching rainstorm. The importance of getting rain didn't need to be discussed.

A line of clouds had formed from north to south. Billowing tops indicated strong convection. As it approached we could see rain falling. Only it was just virga!--rain falling in air so dry that it evaporates before it reaches the ground. Lightning was flashing continuously; thunder came in a steady rumble. Since there was no sense in inviting lightning into the house, Carl went inside and disconnected our radio antenna as a precaution.

As the storm came closer there was an ominous looking roll cloud tumbling in front of the massive towering cloud. As the roll cloud passed, tumbling overhead, the wind was calm for a moment, then all hell broke loose and gusts of wind from the west blasted the farmyard. The lightning was unbelievable in its ferocity. As the main cloud came over the farm, the lightning was a continuous flickering blaze of brilliant light. A newspaper could have been read in the continual blaze of lightning. The thunder didn't just rumble, there were continuous explosions of cannon fire. Clods of dirt or dust appeared to jump from the surface in our pasture where the lightning hit. Without rain to diffuse the light, lightning bolts were skinny and extremely bright. Miraculously, none of our buildings were struck.

Once the front of the cloud had passed, the wind changed to calm for a moment, followed by the crackling sound of hail falling on our roof. White pellets were bouncing in our yard. Jake said, "Well, at least something is coming down." Lena was not amused. We didn't even get much hail. Not that it would have mattered a whole lot. We didn't have enough of a crop to be all that upset.

As the storm rumbled its way over the Turtle Mountains, the sky cleared to its normal self. At dusk the planet Venus could be seen in the cloudless west. Another storm had passed without rain.

Not every storm brought lightning, but usually something elecrostatically related. Unlike normal electrical storms, dust storms sometimes produced a phenomenon, which was sometimes eerie, but in general, relatively harmless compared to lightning. Even without obvious thunder and lightning, one of the electrical characteristics of dust storms was the incredibly high levels of static electricity that would build up in ungrounded wires. Dust blown across bare wire produces a high-voltage electrostatic charge similar to the way friction does on the belt of a Van de Graaff generator.

Ranchers know the danger of a lightning bolt striking a barbed wire fence and conducting its fury through a cow or cows that happen to be touching it. This would often result in a very dead cow, or number of cattle for that matter. It would occur even more often in normal thunderstorms if not for the rain wetting fence posts, thus providing a grounded path for the current. During the thirties, because of the extreme drought and powder-dry soil, a fence line or telephone wire may go on for miles without being grounded. Dust blown by the wind across any wire would build charges of static electricity of extremely high voltage. Although the voltage was high, the amperage was generally insufficient to do any real damage. However, the visual display could be not only spectacular but also frightening. Many farmers and ranchers had reported seeing balls of fire racing along the wire. One evening one of these displays of static electricity scared the dickens out of my mother, Lena.

("Ball-lightning" is probably a form of St. Elmo's fire, a flame-like, harmless, electrical discharge sometimes seen by sailors in a ship's rigging.)

Ma had been alone at home. Pa and Carl with me, tagging along had been to a farm near Kramer looking at a threshing machine for sale. When we got home it was about an hour after sunset. Lena was very upset. She had had a very scary experience. We knew that a dust storm had occurred in our absence because, for a while, we had been driving in it. Her story, as closely as I can recall, unfolds thusly:

There had not been much wind when we had left shortly after supper, 06:00 P.M. Later the wind had increased its intensity. The dust began to blow.

Lena started stuffing damp rags in the cracks around the windows. It was going to be another miserable evening, coping with wind and dust.

At dusk Lena happened to be looking out the west window of the kitchen, hoping for a sign that the weather was easing off. She then saw a sight that would have frightened even the most stouthearted. The telephone line coming from the west, dips down on its short poles to cross the wide creek ravine, then slopes up the hill to our farmhouse. On this line formed fuzzy fireballs of blue-white luminosity. A glowing ball would form on the telephone wire near the creek, then come rolling up the wire to the house where it would burst in a flash. Then it would be followed by another assault. This kept repeating for several minutes. Ma, who worried that the house would catch on fire, went through a mental inventory of what she would try to save. Then the fireballs stopped coming when the storm abated. Needless to say, she was glad to see us come home to find the house still standing.

Many years later, Uncle Carl, while visiting us in Seattle, told of ball lightning actually coming into the house of a neighbor. He said that the glowing turbid sphere danced across the room to capriciously disappear out the front door. There have been times when I thought Carl was stretching things for entertainment value. This was one of those times. I have since read similar reports of this occurring in various places around the country. Who knows, perhaps it was the truth.

Dust Storm Entertainment

Even during days of a mild 'duster' quite a charge would build up in the disconnected radio antenna. This was a stranded wire stretching horizontally from our house about sixty feet to an old telephone pole. It had a lightning arrestor to bypass lightning to a ground wire. Carl didn't trust the arrestor, so he would disconnect the antenna when the wind came up. It didn't matter, with the noisy static the antenna produced during a dust storm we couldn't hear the radio anyway. By connecting a piece of wire to the antenna lead, some fun could be had shocking people. In the absence of a person needing to be shocked, the livingroom stove worked fine. Holding the wire close to the stove a blue-white spark would jump the gap. To see how far it would jump was interesting. Sometimes the gap would be as much as an inch.

Before I go on with my recollections of the dry years, the politics and times beyond our troubled locality need explaining. Because of my mother's interest in politics, I was probably more aware of government than most kids my age. Mussolini could be seen strutting in movie newsreels; Hitler could be heard ranting over the short wave radio. I was keenly aware how worried Lena was that there was going to be another big war at a time that her son, me, would be of the right age to be a soldier. It didn't help my mother's mood any when I said, "Well, it's a way to get out of being a farmer."

I will relate my personal observation of what happened politically and the measures taken by what I consider to be an enlightened government to restore sanity, well being and prosperity to the people. Many articles and books have been written about the great depression, the most notable perhaps, John Steinbeck's novel, THE GRAPES OF WRATH. Few have given enough credit to the measures taken to end the depression and the drought by the Federal Government.

Much credit must be given to a New England aristocrat, Franklin D. Roosevelt who became president. It seems strange that a man who had not suffered poverty, had attended upper-class schools, had enjoyed being a privileged person, would do so much to help the oppressed. Strong minded and stubborn in achieving his goals, he did something so revolutionary, so different that it shocked the nation. Instead of appointing cabinet positions and advisors as political favors or rewarding party sycophants to whom he owed something, he selected intelligent, experienced people who actually knew something about the field to which they had been appointed. Something that no other president had done before, or sadly, rarely since.

When Franklin Roosevelt was inaugurated March 4, 1933, that same day every bank in the country had to close its doors. People everywhere were in despair, frightened. The future apparently hopeless, there seemed to be no hope for anyone, the few rich and many poor alike. Even to our remote part of the United States, the "middle of nowhere," indigent men came looking for work. Their previous profession may have been schoolteacher, steelworker, or a bankteller, but here, in a very remote and desolate land, they were willing to do anything however menial to send money home.

Almost every day, the Great Northern branch line, a railroad train coming from Rugby, North Dakota, would have a number of jobless men 'riding the rods' to Bottineau County looking for work as farm hands. Only a small percentage would find jobs, such as shocking[17] wheat or pitching bundles, and that would last only for the duration of harvest. Since crops were poor, harvest didn't last very long. Many men would head north into Canada to look for work there. Canada was having problems of its own.

FDR's cabinet and advisors were given the task of coming up with ideas to restore prosperity. and put the jobless to work. One of the ideas was the National Recovery Administration, (NRA) It was instituted and seemed to work but its implementation had been unconstitutional and was soon dumped. Some Republicans hated Roosevelt's dramatic and forceful hand, a few others thought he was doing the right things for recovery.

Another program that did work, and worked well, was the Works Projects Administration (WPA) The indignity of accepting a welfare check without earning it didn't appeal to proud, honest folks. To support the ethic of

---

[17] *Shocking: Gathering wheat, barley or oat bundles from the ground and stacking them, heads-up* into *neat groups. There* were *usually about fourteen bundles to the* shock. *Canadians called them "stooks."*

work oriented people; the government created legitimate jobs for every profession, whether it be common labor, or a Doctor of Philosophy. Artists were put to work painting murals in government buildings, libraries, and post offices. Authors wrote books; for example, a volume of 48 books about the history of every state. Masons built park bridges and retaining walls for highways. Carpenters built or repaired various community buildings including well-designed outdoor privies for farmers.

My folks needed government relief but had refused to ask because of pride. When the opportunity came for Jake and Carl to work on the Peace Garden road destined to cross the Turtle Mountains, they gladly took the job. It meant digging with a pick and spade, not exactly glamour work. Republican critics of the WPA accused the workers of malingering, leaning on their spades. In some cases there may have been some truth to that but this kind of talk didn't go over too well with the folks doing the job, especially those who came home dog-tired and aching.

Bigger projects, which could use the stoop-labor of younger men, were handled by The Civilian Conservation Corps. The CCC's planted trees, cleaned streams and rivers, built wildlife refuges. They left a legacy we still have and use today.

As for dealing with the Dust Bowl, that was a challenge that seemed impossible to solve since Mother Nature was being given the blame, or it was simply "God's will." Both cop-out thinking.

Luckily, the men of Roosevelt's coterie were more concerned with solving the problem than being re-appointed to office. Among them were Rex Tugwell and Henry Wallace. I don't know much about Rex Tugwell, but Henry Wallace was delightfully different.

He knew something about the post to which he had been assigned. He had experience in agriculture. As I recall, he played an important role in the hybridization of corn, *(maize, to purists)* Unlike his predecessors, he didn't wear double breasted pin stripe suits suitable for Wall Street. Instead, he was likely to show up with cow manure on his boots as well a bunch of bright ideas in his brain. The recommendations he made, with the advice of meteorologists, coupled with intimate knowledge of farming methods, resulted in drastic changes in farming. He insisted that the government had to become involved to change bad agricultural practices. The milling industry had conspired to keep wheat prices low. To compensate for the low prices, farmers planted every square acre they could, thus overtaxing the land. The nation needed the farmers, the farmers needed to survive, and the land needed to rest and recover. Therefore the government established the Agricultural Adjustment Administration, the AAA.

To compensate for loss of income from an idle field, the government would pay for a percentage of acreage left idle. These fields were to be planted with alfalfa or clover and not cut. Plowed over it served as green manure. In such fields, clover not only put nitrogen back into the soil, but as projecting stubble it protected it from the wind, no dust could blow.

A side benefit of the fields of clover, plus flax fields, was one of aesthetics. Yellow clover was the main variety grown in our area. Flaxseed is used to make linseed oil. Until the advent of synthetic paints, flax was one of the major crops grown in North Dakota. Flax blooms in the morning. The bright blue blossoms are usually gone by mid-afternoon. In the morning, from the hills of the Turtle Mountains one could look out over the prairie to see checkerboard fields of blue flax, yellow clover, green wheat, and black summer fallow. A very lovely sight.

Incidentally, my first 'town job' when I was hired by the AAA, at the age of eighteen I calculated farm acreage's from aerial photos. If a farmer had planted too much grain, good-bye AAA payment check. A fellow employee, Raymond Hanson, called me over to his photo table one day. He had been assigned my dad's farm. He grinned at me and said: "Hey do you know that your dad has been farming three acres in Canada?" I couldn't believe it. "See, here is one boundary marker, and a mile away is the other. By drawing a line between them with a straight edge, you can see your dad's field bows into Canada – three acres worth." He was right. All these years my dad had been farming part of Morrison's land. It was understandable, the border is ill defined and the land rolls gently. The two markers can't be seen at the same time from ground level. When I got home for the weekend I told my dad about it. He said, "Well – Don't tell Harry (Morrison), he'll make me pay up."

The major source of precipitation on the plains is a mass of marine air coming from distant seas. Meteorologists said that rain 'leapfrogged.' The hypothesis was that restoring wetlands would help. In other words, rain falling in one area would evaporate and be carried by winds to fall again some other place. The largest area of wetland to be restored by the CCC's in our part of the country was The Mouse (Souris) River. It is now one of the largest game refuges in the nation, a 'duck factory' producing countless birds.

Another important measure to halt the blowing dust was the establishment of shelterbelts. These were rows of trees and shrubs planted to act as a wind barrier and snow trap to supplement annual moisture. They were designed by the forestry experts. Trees were selected for their growth rate, drought resistance, foliage density, and other factors. Horticulture, like landscaping, is one of the few professions wherein design involves the fourth dimension--time. How the shelterbelt would look five, ten, thirty years after planting were shown on cross-section drawings. Many of these shelterbelts are still growing. Greedy farmers to gain more land, unbelievably, have cut down some.

Changing from a toothed harrow to other types such as special disk harrows reduced blowing dust from summer fallows, which left the surface less vulnerable to the wind.

How much credit for the end of the drought and dust storms is due to measures taken by the government and how much due to climatic change is uncertain. It depends on whom one asks, Republican, or Democrat.

There were a lot of things that happened on a national level during the thirties. The ones that directly affected our farm seemed important for this part of the story. Let's go back to the farm on the Border.

1934 Learning to Swim in a Desert

Tarzan. – Johnny Weissmuller – Man oh man, how that sonavagun could swim!

Since my dreams of becoming an airplane pilot seemed remote, there was no need to continue to mope about that prospect. I had lesser, though more reachable ambitions to pursue. One of them was to learn to swim. Since there wasn't any lake nearby, our creek would have to do. Before the drought there had been numerous swimming holes at least waist-deep. Now even Boundary Creek was dry. Learning to swim in that creek should have been as remote a possibility as becoming a pilot. My mind didn't work that way. I would build a dam in the creek just downstream from what had once been a swimming hole. The next time it rained enough for a run-off, I would have a great place to learn to swim. The narrow stream had banks about three feet high. All I had to do was plug it up.

For a week, I carried rocks from the pasture and dumped them into the narrow place just beyond the potential pool. Though the narrow place was less than eight feet across, rocks needed to fill the gap must have amounted to about three tons. When I was finished, the pasture was almost barren of rocks within a radius of two hundred yards. Then it occurred to me that just rocks would leak, so I decided to waterproof it with little sticks of brush and plaster the waterside with mud. The creek was so dry that there was only a little mud. Plain dirt would have to do. I took a few more days to complete the job. Finished with the dam, I decided to build another one in a place I thought would provide deeper water. I had run out of rocks, so I decided to build one out of scrap lumber that had once been a small chicken coop. After pounding about four short fence posts into the creek bottom, I built a wall of boards and backed it up with dirt. Now I had two dams. All I had to do was wait for rain. As it turned out, I had a long wait. Like next year. All summer and fall, there was not enough rain to make the creek run.

The next spring, melting snow in the Turtle Mountains brought enough water to fill my 'Pools.' There were minor leaks and washouts, which I had to plug, but now I had a swimming hole. Unfortunately, the water was just barely above freezing. No matter, I tried the murky water. My feet sank through a shallow layer of mud, which covered a very sturdy bottom, mud-ice. The frigid water surged up to my crotch. Damn! it was cold! Could I let this stop me? This wouldn't have stopped Johnny Weissmuller, star of TARZAN OF THE APES. He made swimming not only look easy but about the most fun anybody could have. Summoning up all the courage I had left arms flailing, feet kicking, I plunged forward. It was shockingly cold. It wasn't easy. It wasn't fun. Water closed over my head. I sank like a brick. My arms and legs were numb. The only thought in my mind was to scramble up on the bank and put my clothes back on. This took about thirty seconds. I ran home to the warmth of our wood burning stove. Standing there, I was shivering, my teeth rattling, my skin blue, when Ma asked me what had happened. I told her. "You mean to tell me that you went into the creek on purpose?" "You could have drowned! – damn fool kid – couldn't you wait 'til summer?"

After the short, spring run-off, the creek dried up again. Again I waited for a warm rainfall. Then I was about to learn another lesson.

When soil is very dry it doesn't absorb water readily. Raindrops seem to encase themselves in balls of dust and roll down slopes like marbles. When it did rain that summer, the rain came quickly and in considerable volume. The dry soil resisted absorption and the water ran quickly down gullies, ravines, and then into the creeks. Boundary Creek was soon full to the brim. A flash flood ensued. My dams didn't last long. Soon there wasn't even a ripple where my dams had been. My wooden dam was gone and the rock dam was now just a rock pile to one side of a new channel the swift stream had cut. Not only were my dams gone but so was the bridge on the road across the creek. Almost every bridge and culvert in our part of the county was either washed out or damaged. Nobody complained. It had rained! My learning to swim would have to wait.

Uncovering the Skeleton of a Rain Shaman, the Rains Begin Again, 1935

A hint that the drought was ebbing occurred in 1935. I believed that I caused the rains to come again by digging up the remains of an Indian rain shaman. It is now with the great shame of a matured adult that I admit desecrating a grave. The grave of no one should be disturbed, ancient or recent. However, being a dumb, insensitive kid, I didn't know any better, I dug up a human skeleton.

How it happened was thus: I had ridden my bicycle over to the Wunderlichs to visit my sister Evelyn and my nephew Gene. Though he was five years younger than I was, he was maturer. In fact, I think he was at least seven years old when he was born. This kid never knew the meaning of childish irresponsibility. Here I was, thirteen years old and he, at the age of eight, was out in his father's field disking with a tractor. Feeling really stupid and embarrassed because my folks hadn't yet even let me drive our tractor, I just said hello to my old sister, Eva, and left. Not wanting to go home, I headed south on the graveled highway, N.D. State No. 14. Passing the old Myhr place I came to a place in the road that passed over a small rise between small hills. For some reason, perhaps only because I had never explored the place before, I decided to dismount and walk to the top of the knoll on the west side of the road.

At the top of the hill I had seen nothing unusual and hadn't really expected to. There was nothing but the same old dead grass and scraggly silverberry. I was about to walk back down to my bicycle when I noticed something out of the ordinary. A number of rocks were lying neatly packed together like paving stones. This was no accident of nature. Someone had done this for a reason. Then it occurred to me that it must be a grave. An Indian grave! "Maybe there would be beads and arrowheads?"

With great expectations I jumped on my bike and headed over to Wunderlichs to borrow a spade. When I came back to the hill, I dug around the rocks until I could loosen and lift them. Chopping at the hardened soil I dug down about a foot when I came to a yellow-brown bone. Carefully digging with a small stick I could see that it was a skull. At this point, I headed back to the Wunderlichs to call home and tell my mother what I had found. Even my sister Evelyn was impressed, but not enough to investigate for herself. After all, she was in the middle of canning. Gene, my grown-up-at-the-age-of-eight nephew, was very responsibly still disking.

To hell with'em all, I went back to the hill to continue digging. I hadn't reckoned on the telephone party line. I had just gotten down to the skeleton's rib cage when a few people showed up. Obviously a few folks had been listening in. There weren't all that many, perhaps a few from Bottineau, but among them were the Shelton lads from Carbury. While I was still scratching around in the shallow hole looking for artifacts, a cloud started to form overhead. It grew and grew in size. Suddenly there were a few blasts of lightning and it started to rain! Rain!

We had almost forgotten what rain was. I was sitting in a hole in the ground, which had now collected a pool of water. One of the Sheltons, I think it was Jimmy, said, "I think you just uncovered an Indian 'Rain Maker'." Of course he was kidding, but then again, come to think of it; it did seem pretty strange that it would be raining here and nowhere else.

After the rain passed, I continued digging but the rest of the body seemed to be missing. A big horizontal badger hole under the body explained the missing parts. There were no beads, buttons, nor arrowheads--nothing of value to a kid. The skull lay beside the hole and Jimmy Shelton asked if he could have it. "Sure," I replied. A skull had no value to me. After all, I was looking for valuable stuff and hadn't found any. It was almost suppertime so I just went home. A couple days later the Shelton's reported that the skull had disintegrated into small fragments. OK, too bad, so much for the rewards of treasure hunting. Come to think on it, the Sheltons were right about the rain shaman.

The rest of the summer we had showers somewhere in the county almost every day. Almost enough to grow a regular crop.

Years later, after I learned more about Native Americans, I realized that the body probably wasn't an Indian after all. Not that that should make any difference, after all, their graves should be respected and left alone as much as anyone else's. Plains Indians and the Turtle Mountain Objibwa didn't bury their dead. They put their deceased up on platforms, either in the trees or on scaffolding. White settlers buried their dead in consecrated graveyards. This gravesite was next to the old Turtle Mountain Trail. So who was this person under the stones? Europeans knew this area sixty years before Louis and Clark came up the Missouri to sponge a winter's stay at the hospitality of the Mandans.

When I became an adult, which took a very long time, my conscience bothered the heck out me. I was ashamed about what had I done. I had been a teenage ghoul, but what could I do about it? Too late forever. Then in the summer, 1993, I visited Milo Shelton who still lives in what was once Carbury. I recalled the story to him and confessed my guilt. He said, "Not to fret, Jimmy took the fragments back and reburied the bones the day after the skull fell apart."

End of Childhood, 1936

"Jackie–come here, I want to talk to you serious now." I had just come in from going to the mailbox and was carrying the GRAND FORKS HERALD. Every time my ma wanted to 'talk serious' it had been bad news. This time was no different.

"You know we got to send you to Bottineau to go to high school this fall." Complainingly, I whined, "Ah Ma, I don't want to go, Virgil doesn't have to go and he's two years older than I am. Harold Backman didn't have to go either."

"You're going to go and that's all there is to it!"

I had to think of another reason not to go, so I shouted, "Why for God's sake, I'm stupid at school work–all the other kids are smarter than I am–I'll just make a damn fool of myself and be a disgrace to the family." This made her angry. She put her hand on my shoulder and shook me.

"Don't swear like that–you are not stupid, look at what you read–Shakespeare's something, a book about inventions, THE WORLD BOOK OF..."

Poor Ma, this was going to be easy. Logically, I had her whipped.

"That's because those are the only books in the school bookcase and what's more, I can't understand hardly any of that Shakespeare stuff!"

"Never mind, you are going–Luella and Evelyn went to high school and more and so are you, and that's that." Ma knew she would have her way, but we both knew there was a problem of a practical nature--lack of money.

We had a small crop that summer. Things were looking up. We still needed money for me to go to high school in Bottineau, eighteen miles away, and that required rent money for a room. Every farm kid that lived any distance from town had to find a room furnished with a bed and a hot plate for cooking. A table and a chair might be an optional luxury. Most of the money we had to spend for my schooling came from the cream we sold. I was old enough to replace a hired hand at harvest time and that helped save money for school. From that year on I would be home only for weekends and summer vacation. The first step to leaving the farm had been taken. At the age of thirteen I started high school. Too young.

As it turned out, I was right about my not being ready for higher education. Academic courses were hard for me. To tell the truth, I didn't spend all that much time studying. My attitude was that I was to dumb too learn anyway. Building model airplanes in my room or going skating at the rink was a heck of a lot more satisfying. As for being a whiz at math, I found out someone had invented the slide rule and that helped. Forty years later, with a pocket calculator, everybody can be a whiz. Without my PC you wouldn't be reading this.

Rain and crops have been pretty steady for many years. If I had stayed on the farm I'm still sure I would not have prospered & this story would not have been written.

A VISIT FROM UNCLE OLE AND SONS

A visit from Uncle Ole is a non-event in the extreme. Close brothers prove that it isn't necessary to talk to each other. If you like reading exciting stuff, skip this one.

Italian brothers who have not seen one another for a long time don't just shake hands. They grab one another, they hug, and they shout "Mario, Vincento, Luigi!" They pound each other on the back. They ask about mama, papa, sisters, sons, daughters, nephews, nieces, cousins, and second cousins, Aunt Sophia. This is not the way of Old World Swedes. At least the ones I observed.

A visit by Uncle Ole and his boys is something my mother could never understand. It was something no other normal person would understand. Only the Olson brothers (my father and uncles) seemed to understand even enjoy this strange kind of family encounter.

As for me, a visit by Ole and sons was as fascinating to watch as the mating dance of the Western Grebe--but lasted much longer. The mating dance of the Western Grebe is full of flourish and activity. To impress the females, the male grebes paddle about one another with much head bobbing and posturing. Suddenly with furious thrashing of their feet, they will rise out of the water and run in formation across the pond, then as suddenly, dive beneath the surface. It is a rich display, full of excitement and amusing to observe. A visit by Uncle Ole was its direct opposite--interesting and amusing only because of the extreme inactivity involved. Turtles basking in the sun would display more action. A sudden tornado could not disturb the incredibly dull tranquility of an Olson brother encounter.

This following brief story is typical of one of the rare visits we had from Uncle Ole.

Uncle Ole seldom visited us, but he seemed to have a talent for picking the worst time to do so. Lena loved the outdoors, hated housework. To her, Sunday meant a day free of the usual drudgery, a day when she might have lunch at a cafe in Bottineau or at "The Lake." Sudden company on a Sunday could spoil everything. It wasn't just that she hated to cook for unexpected company. She especially hated to cook when Uncle Ole dropped in for his rare summer visit. It wasn't that my mother disliked Uncle Ole. How could anyone dislike loveable, gentle Ole? It wasn't just the cooking that upset Lena. It was because she never understood the event, or more accurately, the non-event that always took place. If it wasn't for Ole's son Reuben, the day of the visit would be a total loss. Reuben didn't fit the Olson norm. He would actually engage in a normal conversation.

On Sunday morning a good Lutheran is expected to go to church. The rest of the day is supposed to be one of rest or whatever. Lutherans tend to be obedient when it comes to religion. Besides, the rule is also sensible since six days of hard labor in seven is enough for anybody. Despite hay that may need to be mowed or ripe crops reaped, the only acceptable menial labor allowed on Sunday is the ordained necessity of taking care of the animals. On this warm summer Sunday morning in 1933, care for the animals had already been observed. The cattle had been milked and put to pasture. Any other form of labor would have brought stern disapproval from our more pious neighbors. My parents believed in going to church, but not to puritanical excess. Going to church could sometimes be skipped. This day I had hoped the folks would decide to go to Lake Metigoshe.

Uncle Carl and my dad, Jake, having just finished mid-morning coffee and a cinnamon roll, went outside to snooze in the shade under the maples in our front yard. Being full of vitamins and the vigor of youth, I was eager to stir up some interest in driving to "The Lake." Summoning up my best selling speech I went outside to talk my father into going. Lena was hopefully putting on a dress suitable for any kind of an outing. She just wanted to get out of the house before company dropped in. Alas, before she finished I heard the sound of a car coming from the west. I hoped it would go by without stopping. It didn't.

Through small openings in our windbreak of box elders I could see that a car was slowing down. A Model "T" Ford passed by our mailbox then clattered its way onto our driveway. The top was down. Its radiator was steaming slightly, trailing the odor of an overripe swamp. The four cylinder, coffee-grinder engine was making a sound similar to that of sticking a piece of cardboard into an electric fan set on low speed. Using engine compression for a brake, the Model "T" groaned and complained as it came to a stop near the gateway through our lilac hedge. In this Ford convertible sat uncle Ole in the front seat with Reuben driving. Wallace was in the back seat. They had come from their farm near Sherwood, a small town west of the Mouse River.

Uncle Ole is the eldest of the Olson brothers. His sons are much older than I am, being grown young men. The basic character of the Olson tribe, except for Cousin Reuben, was to be easy going, "laid back," in current idiom. Though they worked hard when necessary, they were unexcitable to the extreme, not given to talking any more than absolutely necessary. They let others carry on with animated conversations or to get upset. This characteristic, a laudable quality to most people, drove my mother absolutely nuts. She was of the Krogen clan, folks definitely excitable, full of nervous energy, and talkative.

The first thing I did when the car had pulled in was to run inside the house and tell Ma. Lena did not take the news well. She swore quietly, using her favorite Norwegian cuss words. "Now I've got to make dinner and I haven't got any meat – you've got to kill and pluck a chicken." I agreed to this task but first I went out to observe the meeting of brothers who had not seen one another in a long spell.

Upon hearing the sound of the car, Carl had slowly rolled out of his hammock and was now standing. Jake, who had stretched out on the lawn was just sitting up and scratching himself. Excitedly, I told them Ole was here. No answer other than a grunt of acknowledgement. Then I ran through the gate in the Lilac hedge to the waiting car.

Ole, Reuben and Wallace were still sitting in the old car as if they were unsure of any real need to get out. Only Reuben seemed to be alive enough to say, "Hello Jackie, your folks home?" "Yeah, they're coming," I answered.

Carl and Jake finally emerged from the gateway and slowly walked toward the car, looking not directly at the occupants but the car itself. Reuben said "Hi Jake, Hi Carl." No answer, but a half wave of the hand. Then my mother came through the gate, vigorously wiping her hands with a dishtowel. Reuben said "Hello Lena, how are ya?" Ma answered something appropriate and suggested that since they had come so far it might be a good idea to get out of the car and come inside. She turned to go back to the house and Reuben opened the slab-like car door, climbed out, and followed Ma down the flagstone walkway. He was asking her about the flowers she had planted, and Lena was beginning to act a little less agitated.

In the meantime, no words had been exchanged between Ole, Wallace, Jake or Carl. Instead, Carl and Jake slowly circled the car and looked at the tires, kicking each in turn. Then Carl eventually said, "Left rear tire looks a little low."

Ole replied, "Slow leak, – pump'er up every fifty miles."

No answer. Carl then walked to the front and opened the hood on the right side and looked at the engine. Without saying what he saw or didn't see, he carefully reclosed the hood and secured the snaps.

Wallace finally spoke up. "Looks pretty dry around here."

After a minute Carl asked, " Any rain out your way?"

Another long pause – "Naw, just a sprinkle."

Jake still hadn't said anything but had unscrewed the radiator cap. He left the cap sitting on the hood and turned to walk slowly to the auto shed rain barrel and filled a sprinkler can with water. He returned and poured about half the can into the radiator, replaced the cap, and set the can down by the gate. Then Jake knocked the ashes out of his pipe on the gatepost, refilled it, and lit it with a kitchen match struck on the thigh side of his overalls. After filling the summer air with a cloud of Prince Albert he looked, not directly at Ole, but at the drifting smoke and said: "Well... you better come in."

Ole and Wallace slowly dismounted, stretched, and walked through the gate, down the walk and into the house. Lena and Reuben were in the kitchen having an animated discussion about Roosevelt's latest speech and politics in general. To be polite, Ole said a few words to Lena and she, of course had a lot of reasonable questions about weather, crop prices and "Have you heard froms." He answered with minimum expenditure of syllables: "Dry-low-letter from Selma." She then told them to sit down and have a cup of coffee and some cookies because it would be a little while before dinner *(lunch)* would be ready. Again to be polite, Ole went through the socially acceptable, expected verbal ritual of saying, "Don't bother with dinner, we don't need to eat." In gratitude that this was at least approaching a normal extended conversation, Lena was content to be able to say, "I can't let you go all the way home without dinner for heavens sake." (In general, the community rule was to decline twice and accept with humble reluctance the third time.) Turning to me, Ma then told me to get on with killing the chicken. Though I was still curious to know if my mother could extract two sentences in a row, I headed out to find a non-laying hen.

After I caught a fat chicken I went to the woodpile and grabbed an axe. Then cleaned and plucked the still warm bird. Upon returning to the house I saw that Carl, Jake, Ole and Wallace had gone outside. They were all stretched out on the lawn in the shade of the maple tree, straw hats covering their faces and snoozing. Obviously they must have been exhausted from all the conversation. Clearly, for them, there was nothing else of sufficient interest that couldn't wait till after dinner. Inside, Reuben and Ma were still talking and looking at some old photos, identifying relatives. There wasn't anything for me to do just then. Studying a bunch of sleeping men didn't appeal to me, so I went to a model building project that I had going on in the blacksmith shop.

About an hour later, Carl's loud whistle told me that dinner was ready. I put aside my project and went back into the house to join the taciturn crowd at the table. Taciturn except for Ma and Reuben chattering away. After dinner, the men shoved back their chairs, creakily stood up, and very slowly walked back out to the car. First checking the tires they took their time getting back in. After Ole settled back into the front seat, he looked across the yard and said to Jake, "I see you built a new granary." Jake shoved his hands into the depths of his overall pockets, looked in the direction of the new building and sighed – "Yah – don't know why, with no rain it'll stay empty."

Meanwhile, seated behind the steering wheel, Reuben set the throttle and spark levers, then pulled the choke rod. Wallace, at the front of the car, leaned over with one hand on the radiator and with the other, turned the crank. The Model "T" rattled back into life. Wallace then smiled and made an eloquent farewell speech consisting of: "Well…see'ya next year." He then climbed into the back seat. Jake and Carl stood by as the car moved forward, wheeled around the driveway loop, and headed back west. Lena, who had come out, just waved goodbye with her dishtowel.

Ole and his sons had visited. Jake, Carl, Ole, and Wallace hadn't spoken a dozen sentences the whole time. Yet, as Carl was walking down the pathway behind my mother he quietly said, "It was sure good to see Ole again." Lena stopped suddenly and turned to Carl, her face displaying total uncomprehending astonishment, if not anger.

"Good to to see Ole! – Good to see Ole!?.. Some dumb visit, Jake and you spend all afternoon with your brother and nephews, family that you haven't seen for a year and you didn't talk to each other at all!"

Carl totally surprised at her attack—"Talk" – "Talk about what?"

LO, THE MIGHTY HUNTERS

This story is true. It is about real people who lived in a place no one ever heard of, except for the people who once lived there many years ago or still live there. The location is northern border of North Dakota, a place no author has written about. The time period: The era of the Dust Bowl, 1930's. This story is about hunters, the hero, my father who hated hunting. The moral: make up your own mind.

Puberty rites, initiation rites into manhood or womanhood seem to be a bizarre ritual invented by sadistic adults in various societies around the world. At about 'thirteen summers' Native American boys had to endure an ordeal of some sort like lying naked on top a certain hill without food or water for a couple days until finally from exposure, thirst; hunger, mosquito bites or other misery he would hallucinate. During his self-induced delirium he was to receive an important vision or insight into the meaning of life. Some of the Plains Indians apparently didn't learn much the first time around because the next thing a young man might do is volunteer to take part in a "Sundance" ceremony. This extremely painful ritual, which lasted for twenty-four hours or more, is about as masochistic as it gets. The initiate went through this ordeal to prove his manhood and get him officially into the brotherhood of warriors. If he passed out and flunked the course, the poor slob would wind up washing dishes and carrying out the garbage doing 'woman duties.'

In Africa, young girls may have to go through an ordeal involving shamans and a dull knife. This brutal procedure was to eliminate the pleasure potential of sex and thereby ensuring faithfulness to a future husband. Sick.

The initiation ceremony, many still being practiced, may vary from one tribe of people to another but it is usually not pleasant for the youngster who has enough problems already. It doesn't seem to matter whether the nation is a primitive one or a technological country having cultured and educated people who attend ballets and appreciate operas, some dumb mumbo-jumbo event has to happen before one can call themselves a man or woman.

Thankfully, in North Dakota the first step into manhood was, for most young boys, actually pleasant--that of being given his first gun. Usually this would be a 'twenty-two' rifle. Another ritual involved 'reading for the minister.' Bible studies. This was even worse than going to grammar school.

At the age of twelve or so, introduction to manhood and expected **responsibility** normally occurred when the young lad had been confirmed at church and/or when he got his first gun. Usually both happened, as in my case. Most boys simply endured the church ordeal and eagerly looked forward to the gun present as a pay-off for pious obligation and obedience.

Unlike the other boys in my part of the county who longed for a real gun that could kill, I would have preferred something else--a pile of lumber or a model kit with which to build something. To the other farm boys in my part of the country this was heresy worthy of exile to a big city. "...don't want a gun? What are you – some sort of a queer?" All real boys wanted a gun! "Why, with a rifle, a fella could blast a big hole through the skull of a deer or pulverize a gopher. With a shotgun, a kid could knock a prairie chicken or duck into a cloud of feathers." Despite their enthusiasm I couldn't understand the supposed fun of changing a live animal into a dead one. As far as I was concerned, chopping the head off a chicken for our supper wasn't exactly a joyful experience. Actually I never did get the full ecstatic enjoyment out of killing things that a red-blooded boy is expected to get. When I told my sister, Luella, that I didn't particularly want a gun she called me a sissy! The only comeback that I had for that insult was to say, "Oh yeah,! – You read love-mush in TRUE STORY magazine."

Nevertheless, whether I wanted one or not, at the age of twelve I got my first and last gun, a "410" shotgun with a very small bore. Luckily for the wildlife, it was a miserable fowling piece. 'Fouling' piece would have been a better description. The small caliber and scant shot of this midget shotgun puts it in a category as the "Edsel" of firearms. To be fair, in some ways I finally did get some enjoyment from it--shooting tin cans.

Uncle Carl, who lived with us, was a typical "sport hunter." He enjoyed hunting, as did all our neighbors. He was very good at it. Carl, who later at the age of eighty still didn't need eyeglasses, brought down a deer at a hundred yards or more with a single shot. Oddly enough, my father Jake, who was actually a better marksman than Carl and probably the best shot in the whole state, disliked hunting and seldom did it.

Personally, I never did get very good at hunting by Dakota standards. In fact I was lousy at target shooting. By all odds I may have been the poorest shot in all of Bottineau County. However, after I joined the Army ten years later, I scored expert in all weapons from .45 Colt handgun to fully automatic rifles and wound up on a competitive rifle team. This might seem to be contradictory to what I have just said. To tell the truth, it wasn't that I excelled at firearms,--the U.S. Army had low standards compared to the local hunters' back home.

It was Carl, who for all practical purposes was my second father, who said he was going to buy me my first gun. He asked what I would like to have and I said I would like a single-shot twenty-two like my cousin Virgil had. However, Carl had seen this new small caliber shotgun in the gun catalog, called a "410."

As the number .410 implies it had a bore less than a half-inch in diameter using a miniature shotgun shell about half the size of a twenty gauge. He talked me into selecting it. I didn't really have much choice. The gun store in Bottineau had one and so the next Saturday I became the owner of a "410".

After blasting away a box of shells at tin cans I soon concluded that shotgun shells were too expensive and decided that for target practice I would borrow either Carl's or Pa's .22 rifle from now on. Carl decided that I needed to experience the joy of the hunt, so to encourage practice on live targets and, at the same time reduce the number of Flickertail gophers that were ruining our pasture, he offered to pay me a penny for every gopher that I shot. Since the cost of bullets equaled almost a penny a cartridge, the idea was to break even. This never happened. I never did break even. Hunting the gophers and getting paid for it seemed more like a chore than fun. Jerking the tail off a dead gopher as proof of kill was unpleasant. Target shooting was more fun, but even less profitable. In short, if I had a choice, I would rather build things in our blacksmith shop.

Apparently as a status symbol, it was very important to my folks that I become a good hunter, even my mother ganged up on me. She said it was my 'duty' to learn... Someday it might be up to me to go out and get the makings for dinner if my family was hungry. This notion must have been a holdover from her childhood in primitive North Dakota. One day she told Jake to take me out and teach me the art and science of hunting. Jake teach me hunting? He seldom hunted. Why not Carl? To me, Uncle Carl represented the real, genuine, classic hunter. He looked like a hunter, talked hunting, read hunting magazines, and had the best guns. On the other hand, my dad certainly didn't impress me as a hunter. He sure as heck didn't look like those guys in Carl's sporting magazines. Jake with his dumb straw hat, baggy overalls, blue denim shirt, frayed long underwear sticking out of his sleeves, tar stained corncob pipe stuck in his mouth, looked as much the part of a real hunter as Pope Pius XI. "Why Pa instead of Carl?" I asked in total disbelief. "Because Jake is a better hunter, even though he doesn't like it," she answered in a matter-of-fact voice.

This was too much. "Carl hunts all the time, Pa never, ... if he's so darn good, how come I ain't heard it before?" I demanded with more than a little derision in my voice. It seemed incredible to me. After a short lecture on respecting ones parents, she went on to explain:

"The first years for the Lars Olson family were very hard. They couldn't afford to kill their few cattle or pigs and the only way to get meat on the table was by hunting. They didn't even have up-to-date guns, only muzzle loaders. With only single-shot guns, the hunting duty had to be given to the best shot in the family. After sending one boy after another to hunt it became obvious from the game returned that Jake was the only one who never came home empty-handed. Since most people like to eat, especially the Olsons, it was decided that it was up to your Pa to do the hunting." This still didn't answer why he didn't like hunting, so I asked Ma for the reason why. Ma, who more often than not had some complaint to make about her husband, now seemed almost pleased to have something prideful to tell about my Pa. "A deer can be killed with one shot and it can feed a family for a few days, but the same old thing every day would get tiresome. Sometimes a duck or prairie chicken would be a welcome change for the supper table. Of course it took more than one duck to feed a family. When he had only a single-shot gun, it meant having to get more than one duck with every shot. To do this he would go to a slough with lots of reeds on the shore, then wade into freezing water and hide in the reeds or cattails until the ducks swam by. When they lined up just right, Jake could sometimes hit two or three at a time."

"But that's pot-shooting Ma," I protested.

"Tre hude – *(wooden head)*, he wasn't doing it for sport, he had to put food on the table. Imagine what it must have been like to stand in that cold water, waiting and freezing? It is hard enough to hold a gun steady even if you aren't shivering. After he had killed the ducks he would have to wade out and get them. Then he would have to walk home in wet clothing. He didn't dare to come back empty handed. Your Pa just has too many memories of being cold, wet, and miserable from having to hunt. Besides that, Jake loves animals, he hates killing." For Pa, hunting wasn't a sport it was an unpleasant necessity. A job he was very good at.

After my ma's story I took a little more interest in learning the skill of hunting from my father. My first lesson was soon to come.

One sun radiant fall day, a day filled with the herb tea smells of autumn, Lena told Jake she wanted a couple pheasants. Pheasants had been introduced to the Great Plains and had taken to the Dakotas as if they were on their favorite stomping grounds in China. They were very abundant in the 1930's and for my taste, good to eat--almost as good as domestic chicken.

Jake went to the gun cabinet and much to my surprise, took out two "22" rifles, the small Remington semi-automatic for himself and a single shot for me. I couldn't believe it! Suddenly I lost confidence in my father again. 'Real' hunters always use <u>shotguns </u>for bird hunting. That much anybody who reads sport-hunting magazines knows.

"Why not a shotgun?" I disgustedly inquired.

"Won't need a shotgun, we're out to get clean meat, not hamburger," Pa answered. "Also, with a .22 there won't be any BB's to bite on."

I wasn't sold. The hunters on calendar pictures and magazine covers had well-trained dogs, engraved shotguns and shot birds as they were flushed from a bunch of weeds by some magnificently trained Pointer. This business with 22's seemed really stupid to me. Typically, I didn't keep my opinion to myself. If anything, Jake was patient.

My opinion ignored, we went outside, and Pa said the best spot today would be across the road along the fence line of our neighbors' field. This led a half-mile north to the Canadian border. Across the road? I had been expecting to jump in the car and drive to the foothills to where the scenery looked like the pictures in FIELD AND STREAM. Across the road? Some dumb hunting trip this was going to be.

We had been walking along the fence for just a short distance when Jake quietly said: "Two pheasants have been running, keeping low, just ahead of us in the weeds. When we get near that open spot where the gate is, we will sit down." "Sit down!?" I exclaimed.

"Ya, sit down – one pheasant will stick his head up to look for us to see if it's safe to run across the opening. When it does, I'll shoot the first shot so you see how it's done and you shoot the next time." Then it dawned on me; "Pa wasn't going to shoot the bird on the fly like it shows in the pictures. Some sportsman – nuts!"

We walked a little further, then Pa motioned me to sit down slowly, and I did. He sat alongside me and looked toward the gate. Sure enough, the head of a male Ringneck pheasant stuck its head up. Jake slowly raised the 22, took aim, fired and the head of the pheasant jumped a couple inches, neatly removed from its neck. Jeeez!... That was an incredible shot, I had to admit--but it still wasn't like 'hunters' are supposed to do it. The image of cover illustrations didn't match what I had just seen.

"Pa, this isn't sporting, why don't we shoot them on the fly like sport hunters?" As usual, Jake was patient with my brat questions. He lit his pipe before answering and said: "We're out to get two pheasants for supper. We're not doing it for play. This way there isn't any torn up meat--and sometimes in trying to shoot a flying bird with a shotgun it will get away with pellets in it only to die later. What's the sport in that?" He continued, "This way if we miss, the bird stays healthy, if I don't miss, it's dead."

The other pheasant had flown but not far. Pa said pheasants are lazy and prefer to walk. It wasn't long before the opportunity came for me to try a neck shot. Jake said it would be OK to aim for the head, it was a bigger target. I did. No matter, I missed anyway. I missed at the second and third chance too. We were now at the Canadian border, which is nothing more than a neutral strip of native grasses and buckbrush about ten feet wide. On pastureland there will be a barbed wire fence. Here and there a cast iron marker may denote Canadian soil from the USA. After walking a half mile east along the border and seeing no more pheasants, Pa said one pheasant might be enough for supper and we would head for home. We walked back south along another fenceline, then next to the road passing our farm. About a quarter mile from home another pheasant was seen furtively sneaking along in the weeds. My chance came. I shot, a micro-second later, so did Jake. The head came off. Pa said I hit it, I pretended I believed him.

Just as we were about to walk into our yard, a female pheasant appeared in the shadows of our box elder trees. I brought my rifle up to aim. Pa said "Neyda" and gently pushed the barrel of my gun down. "Save her for another day."

When Jake handed the birds to Lena she looked briefly and knowingly at the neatly severed necks and asked if I had learned anything. I had, but it still didn't seem sporting as in FIELD AND STREAM.

By 1934 not only had the great depression wiped out the life savings of a lot of the farmers but the Dust Bowl era was at its worst. The total precipitation for that year on our farm, and that includes snow as well as rain, was only four inches. That meteorologically qualifies as desert conditions. The only vegetation that can grow with that little rain is Russian thistle (tumbleweed) and cactus. We weren't poor; we just didn't have any money. An opportunity to earn money came in the winter of '34. A fox farm somewhere, probably out of state, was offering ten cents apiece for jackrabbits to feed foxes they were raising for fur. The hares could be sold to the fur buyer in Bottineau, the county seat, and big city of eighteen hundred people. Since a .22 cartridge cost about a penny, this could mean a nine-cent profit with every shot, assuming no misses. Pa assured me that 'no-misses' were definitely assumed.

Jack rabbits, zoologically classified as a hare not a rabbit. They are larger than rabbits and a lot more elusive. For one thing, they have keen eyesight and can run fast enough to make a Greyhound dog appear to be going backwards. They live on the plains. In 1934 the farms were not the sterile, weedless, barren landscapes of today's high-tech farms. There were fence lines where weeds grew and Russian thistle piled up. Even though the prairie lakes and sloughs had mostly dried up, there had been enough moisture left over from previous years to have reeds, grasses, and standard weeds. Wildlife abounded; jackrabbits abounded, bounded, and rebounded everywhere. The problem was, they would usually bound when they saw you coming a quarter mile away. A jackrabbit hiding in a depression in a snow pile with its head sticking out in constant lookout was hard to see. Wearing its winter coat of white fur, this fleet footed bunny would suddenly burst out like a streak of white lightning before the hunter had spotted it. The hunter's best chance to shoot one successfully was when the jackrabbit had run about a tenth of a mile. Invariably, it would stop; stand up on his hind legs to see if it was being pursued or out of range. A hunter with a "22" and iron sights had to be damn good to nail a hare at that distance. The prospect of earning money, shooting jackrabbits seemed challenging to say the least. The miles walked didn't justify the worn-out shoe leather. I was about to learn another lesson in hunting, again **practical**, as opposed to **sport**, hunting.

One December afternoon Pa said we were going hunting that night and be sure to have more warm clothes on than usual, as it was going to be a long night and damn cold. Hunting at night wasn't normal in my mind. None of my friends had bragged about night hunting, though I had heard tales about some miserable, low-life deer hunters using a spotlight at night to blind and confuse the deer into a state of immobility.

"Are we going to use a flashlight and shoot them like damn deer spotting poachers?" I asked.

"Full moon tonight, won't need a flashlight," Jake replied.

Coaster sledding at night with my "Flexible Flier" had always been the most fun. Under a full moon, one could see almost as well as in daylight, and the icy snow seemed to be faster. Therefore the idea of hunting at night stirred my curiosity, although I couldn't imagine how it would work very well. Jackrabbits are hard enough to see and shoot in the daylight. This time I was told that Carl was coming along so I assumed that <u>since he was a real sport</u>

<u>magazine style hunter</u>, this was going to be a legitimate, valid and approved, hunting method.

Night comes early at 49 degrees N latitude in winter. Still, it would be a while before the moon came up. After the cattle were milked, chores done, and supper over, I was told that we were to wait until shortly before moonrise to leave the house. It was my job to go outside occasionally and check if it was almost time to go. Each time I stepped outdoors I got bit in the nose by the stinging cold air, and had second thoughts about hunting at night. The night sky, as if to compensate for the cold, had its own reward. Ever since the first stars had appeared, the Aurora Borealis had been swishing its brilliant darting curtains as if signaling the opening of a grand event. The wide, smoky vapor trail of the Milky Way arced overhead. The stars seemed exceptionally clear. Next to Mizar, the second star in the handle of the Big Dipper, was its companion star, Alcor. Alcor, a much smaller and dimmer star, was supposedly the eyesight test star for Arabian sharpshooters. Tonight it was easily visible. I even believed I could see the moons of Jupiter. After about my third time outside, a glow appeared over the Turtle Mountains indicating that it wouldn't be long until the moon would be floodlighting our killing field. Faintly, the northern lights were swishing their curtains as if the play was about to open. Going back into the house, I announced that moonrise was soon going to occur. It was time to go.

Carl and Jake went to the gun cabinet, Carl took the twelve gauge, Jake the twenty gauge, and I of course, got stuck with the stupid "410." Knowing what a single shotgun shell cost, I was wondering why we didn't use the .22's and save money.

"How come we ain't gonna use the 22's," I asked. *(Though I was already struggling to learn to speak proper English, it would take more years for my oldest sister, Evelyn, to beat the use of "ain't" out of me.)*

Carl seemed puzzled that I should be so dumb until he tolerantly remembered that I was a novice. "If you think you can clearly see the front sight of the rifle in the dark, go ahead and take the "22." Well, that made sense but I still wanted to know how we could make much profit at ten cents a rabbit. The answer was to be revealed in a straw stack.

It may have been nine o'clock, I don't know, but it was way past the Amos and Andy radio program when we walked out of the house into the brisk air of December night. "Where the dickens were we going," I wondered as Jake and Carl walked down toward our barn then turned east and cut across a corner of our pasture to go into the bordering field. I didn't know what was going on exactly but one thing I had learned was to shut up, follow without asking more dumb questions.

After pushing down the barbed wire of our pasture fence, we crossed over into the stubble field. This field had been planted for barley and although the previous summer's drought had reduced our wheat crop to nearly zero, there had been enough barley to be worth threshing for feed. Mostly it had been just straw with empty heads, but enough to leave a straw stack[18] about fifteen to twenty feet high.

It was a characteristic of Jake and Carl never to talk to one another. Actually, all the brothers of the Olson tribe were very close. They didn't need to have a conversation to work together or enjoy each other's company. Even a long afternoon visit to Carl and Jake from their brother Ole, who lived way out beyond the Mouse River near Sherwood, would involve maybe eight spoken sentences. These strange visits are worthy of another story in itself. *(See Uncle Ole Visits)* As usual, Jake and Carl knew what was going to be done without any needless talk. Trying to fit in to the family mold without any stupid questions on my part, I just followed along, holding this idiotic, ineffectual, "410" in my mittened hands.

My mittens, like all the mittens Lena knitted, for Jake, Carl, or man-gifts, had a special separate trigger finger so the mitten wouldn't have to be removed to shoot. This she claimed was her invention; perhaps it was I never saw any store bought ones to have a separate trigger finger.

Most of 1934's precipitation had been in the form of snow. Snow trapped in the stubble; weeds, and Russian thistle of the barley field made a mystical dimly white plain beneath the stars of the Milky Way. As we neared the straw stack, the moon was just beginning to rise above the Turtle Mountains. The snow brightened and the stack cast a long shadow toward us in the snow.

We walked, following a rabbit path beaten in the snow that seemed to lead directly to the straw pile. Pa finally spoke up, "We are going to dig a hole close to the bottom of the straw pile, crawl in and wait for the rabbits to come to us." I might have known another hunting method not covered in FIELD AND STREAM.   So, it was here that we were going to spend the night. The straw pile consisted not only of straw but uncollected barley and weed seeds that the threshing machine had failed to sort out. In short, it was a winter cafeteria for wildlife. Pheasants, Prairie Chickens, Hungarian Partridges, which came to scratch, sort and peck like hungry chickens. Hares came at night to feed on what the birds had missed. Predators--coyotes, fox, and Arctic owls came to feed on the seedeaters. A balanced world.

---

[18] *Straw stacks, also known as Straw piles, were the result of using threshing machines. Following harvest, the prairie lands were dotted with thousands of them. On The first calm evening, farmers would burn them because they were valueless except as bedding for the cattle and horse stalls in the barn. They would leave one or two for that purpose. At least one evening of the year we would drive up into the Turtle Mountains, high on the Indvik road, just to look out over the prairie to see the hundreds of stack fires burning to the far horizon. Truly, a wondrous sight. One could imagine lights from the world's largest city. After World War II, combines would replace threshing machines and as a result, wildlife was greatly reduced.*

Straw piles had been havens of food and shelter for little critters to winter over.

Radiating from the straw stack like spokes on a wagon wheel were rabbit paths of previous visits to the bounty of the straw. Carl leaned his gun against the north side of the straw pile and proceeded to dig out a cave in the straw. Jake took me to the south side, facing the aspen grove in the distance. He pointed to a spot and told me to start digging. He dug a hole close to mine, saying he wanted to be close enough to tell me what to do.

The firmly packed straw from months of settling wasn't all that easy to remove, yet in a short while we had dug out a hole big enough to crawl in. It was cozy inside but poking the gun barrel out seemed awkward and I said so. Pa then said, "I had dug the hole too horizontal – my feet should be a lot lower than my head."

"Pull some straw from above and make a pile so when laying on your stomach you will be slanting upwards then make a pile in front of you, put a hard snow-cake on top of it to rest your gun on." This meant practically doing the whole job over again. I not only had to crawl out of my nest but also had to search for a suitably hard snow-cake. Finally, much to Carl and Pa's relief, I settled in and kept quiet. Then came final instructions from Pa:

"Keep looking down the rabbit paths to your left and I'll keep an eye on the right. When we came here, every rabbit was scared away. It'll be an hour or so before they come back again. When they do, they will all come together from east, south and north."

"Why not west," I asked.

"We just walked from there and it's too close to home and the dog." he said. Then he added, "When they do come, usually one follows another, so try and shoot the one in front and the one behind at the same time." The old ducks-in-the-lake ploy.

"When will I know when to shoot?" I asked.

"If you see one coming, just point your gun at him and wait. At the same time, there will probably be some coming toward Carl and me too. When you hear our guns go off, the noise will make you jump and pull the trigger. If you have kept aiming right, you'll hit 'em."

"What if one comes up my side and not yours?"

"In that case wait till he sniffs your gun barrel," Pa replied. "Now be quiet and wait." After about fifteen minutes later, a blazing streak sliced a magnesium flare sliver of light across the star-sky. "A shooting star, did you see it Pa?" "Ya, I saw it, now because you talked we will have to wait even longer, so shut up."

Straw and chaff kept finding its way down the back of my neck but other than that, the insulating straw made my "cave" warm and cozy. If it hadn't been for the bitter cold piercing my nose and ears, I would have fallen asleep. To the southeast, I had two paths to watch.

Perhaps it was close to ten-thirty, I was never any good at moon-time, when I thought I saw something moving toward us on the rabbit trail. A white hare against a white snowfield isn't all that easy to see, even in daylight. It was its moving shadow, rather than the actual jackrabbit that I saw first. Sure enough, a victim was nearing our ambush. Jackrabbits are built for high-speed flight. Now as it slowly and cautiously came on the bunny trail it moved somewhat awkwardly. Closer and closer it came, moving forward a few feet then pausing to rear up, look around, then forward again. There was another one some distance behind.

"Are there others coming toward Pa and Carl," I wondered. Doing as I was told to do, I slowly aimed my gun at the unsuspecting creature. Despite the brilliance of the moon, I couldn't really see the front sight of my "410." It really didn't have much of a front sight in the first place, but like some jungle native with a blowgun aimed at a Toucan, I knew I had it nailed. I waited for the doomed hare to get closer and the nerve-jolt blast of Pa's, or Carl's gun aimed at other hares to remotely fire my peashooter. "Dammit—the on-coming 'bunny' looked so appealing, so innocent. Damn, why did I have to prove myself as a mighty hunter? Damned if I do, damned if I don't. As if sworn to defend the flag, God and country, I keep my miserable '410' pointed at the almost ghost-like white hare. Damn his rotten hide, I feel like a dastardly villain waiting in ambush."

KAPOW, BANG, BOOM, BANG. Whether Jake or Carl shot first, I didn't know. I had twitched and my gun had been fired--remote control. I saw my quarry twitching on the narrow path. A combination of joy and guilt enveloped me as it slowly quivered to stillness. My reaction, "A baby '410' just isn't fair to the rabbits. Carl's 12 gauge would have killed it quicker."

Jackrabbits had been killed, Pa said to go out and get them. First, I was to get the dead hare on my path. Carl had gotten two; Pa had gotten three, two with the first shot, one with the second. Six rabbits, four shots. The 'profit margin.' Not exactly filled with the joy of victory, I wanted to go home and call it a night. Instead, Pa said, "pile the rabbits on the path home, far away from the straw pile and get back into the straw hole."

Moonlight had dimmed the viewing of the Northern Lights. Even the stars were harder to see. After a quick look at the Big Dipper to get an idea of what time it was, I crawled back into my nest. We waited again.

This time, no jackrabbit came down my path--at least any that I was aware of. Morpheus had claimed control of my senses, I was asleep. Silence of the winter night and my failure at watch was broken with the loud sound of gunfire. Two more hares had been turned into fox food. Failing at my post, I hadn't fired a shot.

After gathering the last of the lately ambushed creatures, Pa said, "Now we go home." Eight jackrabbits would bring eighty cents from the fur buyer.

Deducting the cost of ammunition I wondered if it had been worth it. My folks seemed to think so. Last fall we had sold a cow for $3.00. Eighty cents would be equivalent to over ten dollars in the 1990's. We really needed the money. Ma assured me that it had been worth a night in the straw stack – besides, wasn't that a fun time?" Well yeah, I guess it was.

The next summer I was still trying to please my parents by improving my marksmanship. However, even the fun of target shooting turned sour when I tried to compete with my cousin, Virgil Moody. He was two years older than I and lived a mile and a half east of our place on what had been my grandfather's farm. Compared to him, I couldn't shoot worth a plugged nickel. We didn't have a nickel to plug but he could hit a small can tossed high in the air with his bolt- action, single shot .22 without a miss. He knew he was a skilled marksman and told me so, frequently. To take him down a peg, I told him he had to go some to be as good as Annie Oakley. According to what I had read, she had put on shows shooting tiny glass balls thrown high in the air. At a demonstration she had consecutively hit over seven hundred without a miss.

"Oh yeah?" he says, "I could do it but we don't have any little glass balls." I then suggested we try it with some old washers I had seen in a can in the auto shed. It seemed like a good idea to him, so I fetched the can and pulled out a washer about an inch and a half in diameter.

"Toss it up spinning so it doesn't flip over and I'll hit it."

"OK, here goes!" I sent one spinning in the air and he shot. It was knocked out of the air and fell in the weeds about forty yards away. We looked for it but couldn't find it.

"Throw another one!" I did. Same result.

"Throw another one." I did. This time the washer came down untouched.

"Ha! You missed!" I yelled.

He looked puzzled for a minute before he gave me a defiant look and said, "No I didn't miss. The bullet went through the hole!"

I couldn't prove it didn't and I knew better than to argue with Virgil or he would beat the tar out of me. Besides, he was probably right.

Washers were OK but his favorite targets were coffee can lids. Coffee can lids about four inches in diameter had a narrow rim about three-eighths inch wide. When thrown they behaved aerodynamically like our modem day Frisbee, but would go farther and faster. When thrown as hard as I could, it would sail very far. He would wait till it just about hit the ground and then shoot a hole in it. After the washer demonstration and the bit with the can lids, I just had to think of something to deflate his ego. "OK Virge, if you are such a sure shot, why don't you shoot a bullet straight up, reload and shoot the returning bullet as it comes down?" Instead of deflating his ego, for a moment he seemed to think it was a good challenge. Then shook his head and said: "Naw, I won't be able to see it coming down." Honest to God, he had actually considered the idea! No wonder I felt discouraged.

It was obvious that I could never be as good as my cousin at target shooting, much less ever be a mighty hunter. Now I don't mind being beaten by a small margin, but this was ridiculous. If I were ever going to be better at anything than Virgil it would have to be something other than sharp shooting.

A couple years later, Virgil would be shooting rabbits while galloping full tilt on horseback using a miserable single-shot pistol, homemade from an old Stevens's .22. It had no trigger, a finishing nail for a firing pin, and he had used an innertube rubber band for a hammer spring. He simply pulled the hammer back with his thumb and released the hammer to shoot. Usually the jackrabbit would be running at an angle away from his horse. He never seemed to miss. Tall tale? Nope.

In 1936, at the age of thirteen it was time for me to enroll in high school. This meant I had to live in Bottineau, staying in a small single room with a hot plate for cooking. Weekends I would come home. From living in town I learned that a many city kids were nuts about hunting too. They talked hunting and made it seem glamorous and exciting. One weekend I was home when duck season opened.

Uncle Carl had been talked into being a guide for some big-city hunters. Probably Minot or Grand Forks. They came out to see Carl on Friday evening, arriving in a shiny new, wood-paneled, station wagon. Their clothing matched the pictures in the sporting magazines. Red hunting caps, tan hunting jackets with little pockets for holding shells, wading boots, binoculars, engraved shotguns with checkered stocks, varnished wooden duck calls, thermos bottles, manly looking lunch buckets, whiskey. They even had retriever hunting dogs ...Man; this was the real stuff! All of a sudden I wanted to go along to see some fancy sport hunting.

The season was to begin at nine o'clock the next morning. Since Carl was going to drive his pick up and lead the way to the best spot on the Mouse River, I thought there may be room for me to go along and so I asked Carl if I could go. He kindly understood but said I couldn't. Lena had overheard my asking and after the city hunters left she said: "A couple ducks would be nice for dinner, I'll ask Jake to take you." Jake?.. Jake, the pot shooter? Dad sure wasn't my idea of glamour hunting. *(City kids called their father "Dad," so would I from now on.)* I wondered if he was going to expect me to wade into some mud hole slough and shoot swimming ducks. Anyway, I had learned by now that my father did know something about hunting, even if it didn't jibe with FIELD AND STREAM. Jake agreed to take me hunting. "We'll go tomorrow morning."

Morning had brought an eye-squinting bright day with almost no wind. No wind blowing is unusual in North Dakota. At 8:00 I had my little "410" ready but Jake came carrying an extra gun, a twenty gauge, double barrel. He said it would do a better job than a 'toy' gun. This made me feel a whole lot better. He had his Remington pump shotgun, also a twenty gauge. I started walking towards the auto shed and Dad asked: "Where you going?"

"Aren't we going to take the car and drive to some lake?"

"No," he answered, "We're going to walk."

"Walk? – There's no duck-lake around here that we can walk to." This was too much, even though we had some late fall rain, I knew there wasn't any lake or slough within miles of our farm. The draught had taken care of that. "Is my father balmy," I wondered. He didn't answer, just pointed northwest.

"Past Backmans – towards Canada?"

He just nodded. I had never walked far in that direction but couldn't believe there was a lake would be there since there wasn't any other lake or pond near our place.

We walked west down the road, across the creek bridge, past the Backman home place and when we had gone about a half-mile; we left the road, walked down and up the ditch, and crossed the barbed wire fence. Now we headed northwest across the stubble field. The light musty smells of sun-warmed earth and stubble made the walk very pleasant. There, close to the ground, a small, scraggly, prairie Wild Rose, more weed than shrub, held a single flower.

"Hey dad, – here's an idiot rose that doesn't know summer's over." Squatting down, I plucked the flower. "Here, let me stick it in your hat." Jake stopped for a moment and I poked it through one of the many holes in his beat up straw hat. It gave him a jaunty appearance, worthy of the day. It was the sort of thing a hunter of Jake's style would wear.

As we came close to the Canadian border the field ended at the base of some small hills. Just as we came over the crest of a small rise, there in front of us was a big round pond, no--a small lake. What a pleasant surprise! However the body of water should be classified, to my mind, it wasn't a slough. Sloughs are muddy, shallow, have lots of reeds with muskrat piles, and smell sloughy. This body of water was clean shored with surrounding low hills sloping to the water. It was a big, plate glass mirror reflecting the deepest blue of the morning sky. There were just enough cattails to edge the pond in a golden rococo frame.

"Why hadn't Dad told me about this pond? I could have learned to swim here." Then my enjoyment about this discovery turned to disappointment when I saw there weren't any ducks in the picture. Just as a light breeze was breathing color changes on the glass, I turned to my dad. "We should'a gone to the river, no ducks here." Jake relit his pipe again before answering, "There will be soon after the season opens," saying it so matter-of-factly, I had to believe him.

"There ain't – aren't, any reeds or brush to hide in. We need some kind of a blind."

"Don't need a blind, we'll just sit down by that rock and wait for them to come. Ducks have better eyes than we do. A blind would only make'em suspicious. It's almost impossible to hide from them on shore or anywhere. The thing to do is look like we belong here, just resting and looking peaceful as a cow chewing cud."

We sat down by the boulder. Jake leaned his back against it and laid his gun down and started covering it with dry grass. He said for me to do the same. "Guns are what the ducks are worried about, cover yours the same way."

"How can a duck tell a gun from a plain old stick?" I wanted to know. "Dunno – good eyes – sticks don't glint in the sun – maybe a good memory of just having been shot at..."

"How do you know ducks will come here – when will they come?"

Jake finished refilling his pipe before he answered, "This ain't a breeding lake – just a safe, stop-over resting lake. Haven't you noticed the ducks that fly past our farm are either headed to, or coming from, this direction?" To think of it, that was true. "When the first shots are fired by the river or other sloughs far from here, this will be one of the few places they can come to. Teal will be the first to get here, 'cause they're fastest. Then the mallards will come, then the pintails or canvasbacks." This sounded logical and exciting. Then another concern came to mind.

"We're not going to pot shoot them on the water, are we?"

"Not unless you like wading and swimming in cold water." Much to my relief, we would be doing as other hunters do. Almost.

Waiting and watching the pond was almost hypnotic. Every now and then a zephyr would swoop down to the smooth surface of the water, and with the single stroke of a wide brush, paint a different shade of blue.

We hadn't been sitting very long when, faintly heard, the distant booms of gunfire marking season opening. Dad said it wouldn't be long before we would see some action, and to get ready to grab my gun fast when he said so. He told me that I would be shooting first and to be sure and lead the bird enough.

"How much lead?"

"More than you would a coffee can lid," he said. Now I knew exactly how much.

From the west, three ducks, wings beating rapidly, came in low and very fast over the far hill across the lake. I reached for my gun. Jake stopped me, "Not yet, let'em start'a circle to land."

Circle they did, partly over the land partly over the pond Three,--four seconds later Dad said, "Now get the gun." Quickly, I grabbed my gun, grass, and all and took aim. Wait, or they'll fall in the water – NOW!"

The kick of two successive shots slammed into my shoulder. I missed; the Teal went looking for another lake. "Not enough lead but close," offered my dad.

"Now what?" I asked.

"Wait for more."

About ten minutes went by and then, somewhat higher, from the southwest came some more ducks. Their wings not pumping as rapidly as teal now stopped beating, and they started a wobbly glide for the lake.

"Mallards – wait, they don't like the look of us, they'll pull up to think it over and circle." They did. It looked like they were going to make a wide circle before landing. It was like watching an English horse race, clockwise on the track.

"Now the gun, aim, wait or it'll fall in the water – NOW." I fired. A Mallard plummeted to thud into the ground just a few steps from the water.

"Pretty good," that, coming from my dad, constituted a great compliment.

Proudly, I picked up the duck and admired the brilliant blue wing feathers and chatoyant green head. We had one duck and needed one more. Jake hadn't even lifted his gun from its hay hideaway. Barely had I sat down again when some more ducks came our way, again from the southwest. This time I was going to do it all myself without any instruction and said so. They circled, I waited, picked up the shotgun, took aim and fired twice. Missed both times. The ducks scattered in the general direction of Manitoba. My gun was empty. Then as if to demonstrate that all is not lost, Jake knocked his pipe out on the boulder he was leaning against, picked up his gun and just as the last of the ducks was disappearing into the distance, much too far away to be hit, he fired. At first I thought he missed, then the duck stopped flapping as if someone had hit pause on the video tape player. It plummeted to earth to crash on the upslope of the other side of the lake. "Got goose-shot in my shells – bigger BB's – carry farther." That was all he said.

If only my high school friends could have seen it. I was so proud of my dad. He sent me to pick it up. When I returned he said we would go home now. By now I was so excited about duck hunting the thought of going home seemed crazy. "Why not stay and shoot some more?"

"Two's all we can eat, no icebox to keep more," Dad said as he tried to light his pipe again.

When I brought the duck back from the other side of the pond, Dad said we could wait a while and watch the other ducks land. Reluctantly I settled for that and sat down to watch, still wishing I could shoot some more. It had been a lot of fun. Sure enough, here came some more Mallards then some Pintails. We still kept our guns hidden as a sign we weren't hunters. Jake must have been right about hiding the guns. The ducks would circle the lake once or twice, then in a tumbling, gliding maneuver, would skim over the water to water ski, wings up to a landing.

Calming down from the excitement of the hunt, it was relaxing to watch the ducks paddle around, and squabble about water space rights. After the time required for Jake to finish a new load of Prince Albert in his corncob pipe, we headed for home with our two prizes. "What'll we do with the ducks Carl brings home?" I asked.

"Oh, he'll probably give whatever he got to the hunters."

Our ducks had been plucked and already in the oven, when Carl's pickup came into the yard. Hurrying out to meet him, I couldn't wait to hear how many they had gotten. His door cracked open, he slipped one foot out onto the running board. He seemed tired so he waited a bit before stepping out.

"How many did you guys get, Carl?"

He smiled, spit out a small gob "snoose" on the ground before answering. "Skunked! – "They shot up a lot of ammunition – didn't hit a damn thing. Well, I got a few but I gave 'em away."

"How come you gave 'em away?" I questioned, even though I remembered what Dad had said.

"Didn't you and your dad go hunting today?" I nodded yes.

"We don't need any more," he replied. Brother knows brother. He knew Jake was never skunked.

Though I personally don't enjoy hunting very much, I do not want to put down those who do. I also recognize that my perspective and attitude was shaped by my father, a gentleman who loved animals.

THE LAKE

When the Midinakwadshiwininwak, Native Americans living in the Turtle Mountains, decided to name their favorite fishing lake, you can bet it didn't turn out to be something simple like "Tahoe." Lake Metigoshe (a shortened name), is **the** weekend Retreat Lake for North Dakotans eager to get into it all. It has been that way for a hundred years--and about the only thing in northern Dakota that hasn't changed much.

METI-GO-SHE-SAH-HE-GUN, METIGOSHE WASHEGUM,
Fish Lake and finally: LAKE METIGOSHE (Metty go she)

Meti-go-she-sah-he-gun? Funny name? What else would you expect when the Native Americans (a tribal branch of Chippew/Ojibway), who probably named this lake called themselves the Midinakwadshiwininwak? Since I'm not fluent in Midinakwadshiwininwak, I'll just have to take somebody else's word for it that it means "A body of clear water surrounded by oak trees."

How the Midinakwadshininwak wound up holding on to the Turtle Mountains in the middle of hostile Sioux country ought to baffle any anthropologist. The Sioux weren't just a bunch of choirboys. The great number of stone war clubs and arrowheads that have been found in the foothills all around the territory suggests that some pretty heavy arguments had been going on for centuries. Either the Midinakwadshiwininwak were the meanest, cussedest, bunch of hell-raisers or the Sioux decided there ain't no way you can make war against somebody whose name you can't even pronounce.

Finally, "White Eyes" came to the Dakota Territory, beat up everybody that wasn't articulate in French or English. It wasn't firearms that done in the Indians. It was germs and viruses. Even measles was deadly to a people who had not been exposed to it before. In the Turtle Mountains, smallpox wiped out nearly all the natives. The few leftovers who didn't die--Midinakwadshiwininwak, Sioux, Cree, etc., were then herded onto reservations. For the local survivors, one small reservation was set aside in the hills for the "Chippewa," because Chippewa is pronounceable. The government then claimed the rest of the Turtle Mountains open for settlers. Ashes of Indian lodge fires were still warm when some immigrant, still with the scent of the sea in his woolens, found "The Lake." First thing he did was to build a cabin on the shore and wait for somebody to invent the outboard motor. Thus, to this day and tomorrow, Lake Metigoshe remains the premier resort lake of North Dakota.

North Dakota is not well known for its awesome scenic wonders. A lake, after all, is quite an ordinary occurrence almost anywhere in our land. However, there is a certain charm and magical quality about this lake that would make it popular even in Minnesota which has 11,413 lakes of its own.

The Lake

First, I'll have to try to unravel the mystery of why nearly everyone who has lived in North Dakota will spend at least a little time on it, in it, or by it--some even live there year around.

What makes Lake Metigoshe so special? It isn't the only lake in the state. Surprisingly, North Dakota has a great number of lakes. It isn't a big lake, since it is nestled within a three square mile area. Garrison Lake is over a hundred miles long. Metigoshe isn't the only body of water with fish and wildlife. At least two hundred lakes and ponds offer more waterfowl for hunters. It isn't the only lake surrounded by forest. There are about a hundred lakes and ponds in the Turtle Mountains, all surrounded by trees.

Part of the appeal is that it is a goofy shaped lake. The land, which cradles the lake, is as wrinkled, dented and bumpy as a prune. Therefore the lake has more bays, points, coves, peninsulas, and channels for its size than any lake in the known world. Because it is shaped like a Rorschach inkblot, the length of the shoreline, if straightened out, would stretch half way to Peoria.

Other lakes are either round, square, oval, angular, or shaped like the outline of a knobby potato. Stand on the shore of one of these lakes and you have seen it all at a glance. Stand on the shore of Lake Metigoshe and you would be lucky to see a small percent of it. This makes it fascinating because one can spend a lot of time exploring all its nooks and crannies.

Essentially it is two lakes, divided in the middle by a causeway road, and a bridge. Most lakes are lucky to have an island. This one has five. Though the lake is not very large, the long convoluted shoreline makes it possible to have hundreds of lake cottages, still within a relatively small area.

One end of the lake extends a short distance into Canada. This, plus the many bays to hide in, made it convenient for bootleggers during the prohibition years, and who can deny that the bootleggers stirred some excitement?

People don't really go on outdoor outings to get away from it all. They go to be around other people getting away from it all. Pack a bunch of folks into a small, intimate, local area, and things tend to get interesting. In the thirties there were two rival commercial recreation resorts each trying to outdo the other. That made the lake even more appealing.

Even while the prairie was being homesteaded, resort hotels, and cabins, were being built to lure the pioneers to its irresistible waters. There was even an enterprising outfit in Souris building rowboats, sailboats, and power launches. Advertisements extolling the attractions of the lake reported that an easy stage ride from the railroad in Bottineau through the forest would get the traveler to the lake in short time.

About the only thing that hasn't changed in the rest of Bottineau County is activity at "The Lake."

Circa 1930-1940

In my boy-mind, there was nothing better than going to Lake Metigoshe. Sure, going to town was fun, especially on Saturday night. However, city lights and pleasantry of movies and ice cream cones paled in comparison to a chance of going to "The Lake."

Lake Metigoshe was a strong part of the environmental geography, which led to my developing such a keen sense of direction at a very early age. All kids who grow up on a farm or ranch soon learn the cardinal points of the compass. Learn or get lost. The whole state of North Dakota is like one gigantic compass card. Roads and farms are precisely laid out with great regard to being aligned with north-south, east-west orientation. In my case a special awareness grew because the **north** property line of our farm was on the Canadian border. Visually, this was a narrow strip of native grass and weeds, which ran **east** and **west** forever. **North** of the border lived Scottish and English farmers who spoke English with a strange foreign accent. **South** of the border were Norwegian or Swedish immigrant farmers who spoke a language everybody could understand, except maybe the Canadians. No wonder a kid growing up with such powerful references would develop an awareness of directions.

One day I asked my folks where I would wind up if I walked **west** along the border as far as I could, they answered:

"In the Pacific Ocean"

"How about **east**?"

"In Lake Metigoshe."

That direction appealed to me. The imprint was permanent. From then on, **north** – Canadians, **west** – Pacific, **south** – civilization, **east** – "The Lake." **East** is where the sun rises over the wondrous lake, tauntingly inaccessible because when I was nine there was no short road to the lake. Walking to the Pacific seemed easier. From then on, if someone would say the word east, my first flashing image would be 'that's the direction of "the lake".'

In later life, my obsession with compass directions will sometimes irritate strangers and friends alike. If asked directions to someplace, I have never learned to say: "Go back to 1st. Ave., then take a left to 188th, then turn right. Go two long blocks to Memorial Drive, then left about 14 blocks until the street makes a "Y" – take the one to the right..." My directions will more apt to be... "Go back to big street with all the mercury lights, go north .6 miles, turn east .3 miles, then north 1.3 miles to the "Y," use the road going northeast." The listening and nodding person being directed will then turn on the dumbest look you ever saw, vaguely point southeast and say "By the way – is that north?"

"On second thought... Go back to 1st Ave., Take a left to 188th..."

The poor about-to-get-lost-again soul, answers "Got it."

Now that I have explained the importance the lake had in establishing my awareness of direction, I'll get on with some of my happy days there.

The Passion to Swim like Tarzan

By the age of ten, I was greatly lured to any body of water bigger than a bathtub. In fact, I was obsessed with the need to be involved with water. Perhaps the onset of the big drought, beginning the Dust Bowl Era, had something to do with it. It didn't matter if it was the horse trough, the creek, or a musty smelling slough, it was water, and I wanted to be on it, or in it. Actually, North Dakota is surrounded by water. Unfortunately, the water surrounding it is over fifteen hundred miles away in each direction. Obviously the oceans were too far away to be of much comfort to me. Realistically, I would have to settle for whatever water I could find more than knee-deep.

To me, the creek running through our farm was the greatest thing that could happen to a kid, even though it was shallow and devoid of deep swimming holes. However, I had learned at an early age about Lake Metigoshe and this was really big-time stuff. We, that is my folks and I, had been to this lake a few precious times. Though this lake was only ten miles east of our farm, there was no passable road at that time through the hills and forest that could be driven with the family car. There was only a meandering trail through the oak and aspen with deep ruts and oil pan ripping rocks lying in ambush. The only alternate way to get to the lake was to go southeast by south eighteen miles to Bottineau and dogleg northeast another thirteen miles. Once there, winding roads around the lake would burn up three or four miles more. By the time we returned home, my dad would have driven seventy miles for a string of perch and a picnic. No wonder we didn't go often. True, we didn't go often, but how I cherished the early few times we did.   The passion to become a great swimmer began when I saw a Tarzan movie. From then on I had wanted to learn to swim as well as the movie guy. Anyone who could swim was, in my mind, a cut above mere ordinary mortals. The creek on our farm was too shallow and confined for a serious swimmer. In desperation I had tried to build dams to create swimming holes with deep water, only to have the dams wash out. *(This pitiful story of frustration is covered in another tale, which I call "Dust and Hard Times..")*

"Buck," Harold Backman, five years older than I, my local hero, guru, man-talk confidant, could swim, but not like Tarzan in the movies. Johnny Weissmuller could out swim, outfight African crocodiles. I could outfight a newborn calf, but I couldn't swim. In shallow Boundary creek all I could do was stir up mud from the bottom. There I was, manhood a few years away and still unable even to dog paddle. Then came a solution in the mail. It was an article in some, now forgotten magazine that my folks received. The article title is not forgotten. "LEARN TO SWIM" subtitled "The Basics of Swimming Made Easy." Never were pages scrutinized more avidly. There were instructions and diagrams.

The article called for some on-shore preliminary practice. Learning the basic strokes was to be done by utilizing something like a piano bench. Great! We had a piano bench.

Positioning the magazine on the floor at one end of the piano bench, I assumed a prone position on the bench so I could read and follow the instructions. First, the dog paddle, simplest of all basic strokes. Next steps, the sidestroke and backstroke. Then finally, the overhand stroke, known as The Australian Crawl. All these strokes after a few minutes of concentration and practice, I found were extremely simple. It was so logical, why hadn't I learned this on my own? After a half-hour I had learned to swim. I was ready for "The Lake."

At this point in my story--after learning to swim on the piano bench--it is important to introduce my brother-in-law, Arnold.

Arnold Wunderlich, married to my oldest sister, Evelyn, was old enough to be my father. Evelyn and Arnold were the parents of my precocious nephew, Gene, only five years younger than I was. Arnold's original home state was the 'eastern' state of Minnesota, land of ten thousand plus lakes.

First, a few words are needed to explain the characteristics of people born and raised in Minnesota. These people are, without exception, all alike in one certain way. No, I don't mean racially pure. Blonde hair and blue eyes is not the distinguishing base line. A Scandinavian accent, though common, is not the universal marker--however, the ability to swim is.

Every person raised in Minnesota, without exception, can swim. This is not the result of a state law. The reason can be traced to an insect, the mosquito *(order Diptera, family Culicidae)* In summer, the eleven thousand lakes and equal number of ponds and sloughs of Minnesota breed mosquitoes in numbers surpassing the stars of the universe. Minnesota mosquitoes will attack anything that moves, whether it be people, bears, moose, dogs, turtles, automobiles, etc. Their favorite lunch menu of all is hide of human being. The only escape is a lake. In summer, once a person leaves the hermetically sealed offices of Honeywell or 3M, the only option is to immerse oneself in a lake with mosquito netting over the head. Since there you are, already in the lake, there is little to do except learn to swim. In fact, a sub-specie of the human race has evolved: *Homo sapiens piscatorallis*. Minnesotan.

In addition to Arnold's ability to swim like a barracuda, or being good enough at baseball to pick up a few dollars as a catcher now and then, he had another characteristic which set him apart a little from most of the local farmers. It wasn't that he had jet-black hair and brown eyes--so did a few Indians and one Armenian. It was how he dressed--like a big city dude. On the farm doing farm duties he dressed like any other farmer. However, whether it was Saturday night, Sunday, or any special occasion, he would dress in the latest style suitable for the event. Never was my sister Evelyn embarrassed because Arnold had failed to pick out the right tie.

One special Sunday my parents and I were going to the lake. Arnold, Evelyn, and Gene, traveling in a separate car, were also going. Several neighbors and we were going to the lake to enjoy a picnic and a general social gathering. Arnold was dressed in his finest natty attire, blue coat, white polo shirt, white slacks, and straw boater hat. My sister Evelyn was wearing a modestly stylish nautical dress, sailor collar, which would have been acceptable at any fancy eastern yacht club. My mother, Lena, had also taken some time to look her best, if not fashionably nautical. For the occasion, I had been given a new bathing suit. Of course, Ma, Arnold, and everyone else had assumed I would only go wading in the water up to my waist or something. What they didn't know was that I had learned to swim on our piano bench. I was withholding a great surprise for my folks. How proud they would be.

Finally, after many tortuous miles over washboard gravel roads, we arrived at the lake. Near the beach, a short distance from the Dygert's Eastside Hotel, Arnold found a place near the swimming beach to spread the picnic blankets. In the back of Pa's car, I was squirming and hiding the best I could from prying eyes to put on my new bathing suit. It wouldn't be long now for my debut.

Confidently I walked down to the beach. Now the moment had come to impress the folks, especially my well-dressed brother-in-law from Minnesota. I would amaze them all that I had learned to swim. I would demonstrate the breaststroke, backstroke, Australian crawl, and more.

There were a lot of folks, mostly young people, swimming, or wading in the water. In easy view from our picnic spot and a few yards from the shoreline was a swimming and diving platform built on small piling. A swimmer could wade to the near shallow waterside. At the far end was a diving board. The diving platform was my first goal, easily attained by wading. The depth only reached my chest. I climbed the ladder on the side and walked to the deep-water edge where I was sure I could be seen by my folks. To make sure they were looking, I checked it out by waving and waited for the answering wave. They seemed to have a concerned and curious look on their faces. Good, the surprise would be even more effective than I had hoped.

There were some big guys using the diving board, but I chose not to join them because I hadn't read an article on diving yet. It was a wise decision. Other kids were simply diving headfirst from the platform, or just plain jumping in. It looked easy either way. Diving headfirst would impress my onlookers the most.

Recalling my swimming lessons, I took a deep breath and plunged forward into the deep. My folks may have been surprised, but not as much as I was. Karoomph! GLUG! Water closed over my head and body. I couldn't see anything but dark-green water, I didn't know which way was up. I flailed the Australian Crawl, sidestroke, backstroke, and dog paddle all at the same time. Somehow I had missed an important point: It is very necessary to continue breathing occasionally while swimming. I tried to inhale, which is very difficult under water. The thought of yelling for help occurred to me, but since I was underwater, only the fish heard my bubbly yell for help. Choking and gasping, I realized that I must have missed a lot of information in my instructions. Things were getting mighty grim when, suddenly, I felt a hand under my chin and my face being turned up to blue sky. At last, I inhaled air instead of water. I was being dragged back to shore. My rescuer was Arnold.

Oh, the embarrassment of it all! There stood Arnold, his natty attire a wet soggy mess, my mother about to pass out, Evelyn questioning my sanity, my little shrimp nephew, Gene, giggling his damn head off, totally pleased about my discomfort. If there had been a badger hole nearby, I would have crawled into it.

Oh the humiliation! The rest of the day was the most miserable time of my life. Ma was still upset and fretted as expected. The worst was how every neighbor laughed when Arnold and Evelyn told about my folly. On my ride home, I swore an oath to myself never to trust a how-to-do-it magazine article again.

Despite my ill-fated swimming adventure, the lure of the lake and swimming was stronger than my humiliation. It was maddening to be stuck on the farm on a warm Sunday afternoon and look to the east. There, just ten miles away, was paradise. Only ten miserable, impenetrable miles away was warm, almost clear, deep-enough-for-swimming water, water with live fish. A few more years of frustration getting to "**The Lake**" would have made a total babbling idiot out of me I am sure. However, the Lord works in mysterious ways. I owe my sanity to FDR.

First came the depression, then Franklin Delano Roosevelt was elected. FDR then invented the WPA. Some inspired local person then decided that a cross mountain road was needed. The WPA needed useful work. I needed a shorter road to Lake Metigoshe. The WPA was put to work building the Peace Garden Road and outdoor privies. So, because of the depression, FDR, and the WPA, my road got built. The trip to Metigoshe was shortened to eighteen miles. Divine intervention! Who says there isn't a God?

Yes, I learned to swim but Weissmuller never had to fear much competition from me.

Resort Rivalry Heats Up

The rivalry between Dygert's East Side Hotel and Burnett's West Side Hotel was wonderful. In addition to rooms and cabins for rent, each place had a restaurant, and what we now call a convenience store. To lure customers, they were always installing added attractions-- like the water-slide.

Every time we went to Lake Metigoshe, as we neared our destination I would sit staring through the car windows to catch the first glimpse of blue water through the trees signifying that we had finally arrived at "The Lake."

One Sunday, as we came within a mile of the West Side Hotel, a strange white structure could be seen. It was taller than the trees. *(This doesn't mean a whole lot; trees around the lake are seldom more than thirty-five feet high.)* This structure, which at first looked like the start of the construction of a roller coaster, turned out to be waterslide built on the beach. In a way, it was very similar to a one-hill roller coaster. It was built in shallow water parallel to the shore. There was a tower accessible by a stairway along the side. From the top, a track curved downward to a steep slope, similar to the first precipitous drop of a roller coaster. This track ended in and slightly under the water's surface. The ride down was to be done on an aquaplane; a short planing board fitted with wheels. These wheeled boards could be rented on an hourly basis. The user would climb to the top of the tower, fit the board onto the rails, and then take off, rolling down the slope. When board and rider hit the water, the board and rider would plane on the surface for several yards before sinking. The rider would swim or wade back and then take the board back to the top for another run.

At first, the beginning riders would just go in a straight line before sinking. As skill levels rose, the riders would practice turning and weaving about. It was super fun. The slide was a great success. Then Dygert's Hotel, stung by the West Side attraction, built a slide as well, only taller. Now young folks went to the "Eastside" slide. The westside establishment wasn't going to stand for that, so by next summer's swimming season, the tower on the west side had grown. The slide had become much more exciting. Then followed another upward surge on the eastside. In the process, both resorts had shot themselves in the foot. The slides had become so tall that none but the bravest would dare to ride them and business fell off drastically. The whole dilemma was solved by Mother Nature. One day a powerful wind, perhaps a tornado, came along and blew them both down. End of waterslide era.

The rivalry between the two lodges never died. Eventually the depression plus low water level due to the drought brought an end to the glory days. The Eastside hotel burned down. Old folks now still alive get misty eyed as they recall days of romantic youth spent at the lake with either lodge as meeting places.

The Maid of Moonshine

Now I'll get to a certain artifact, unsigned artistic graffiti done by an unknown artist. It was simply known as "The Maid of Moonshine." It didn't need a signature for me to know who did it. There was only one possibility, my older cousin-Levi "Pat" Moody. Because some prudish folks were upset about this painting I decided to keep the name of the culprit secret forever.

Near the Canadian border on the northeast side of the "North Lake" was a combination dance hall and boxing arena. It was called the Darling-

Amsbaugh Camp. For a time, boxing and wrestling matches were held there. Boxing and wrestling appealed to Uncle Carl, so I got to go to see at least two.

What boxing or wrestling events need is promotion. Promotion means exciting lies and good artwork. My cousin Levi Moody did the poster art.

One morning, people driving on the cross-lake road were surprised to see on one of the concrete wings of the bridge, a large, billboard size painting of a woman in bathing suit. The suit, even for the modem times of the thirties was perhaps a bit sparse. The bathing beauty was seated on the horn of a crescent moon and lettered were the words, "MAID OF MOONSHINE." So there, in broad daylight, glowed a Flapper hussy with breasts, thighs, and the forbidden word "moonshine." The lake already had too much notoriety concerning moonshine. That and the girl were too much for some people. As in any community our area had a few people who were, well, to put it nicely, rather prudish and judgmental. A woman shown on a billboard, poster, or magazine that wasn't decently attired from the chin down was considered improperly dressed and sinful. Divine punishment for an evil artist portraying otherwise was certain.

The only conclusion that seemed logical was that Levi, who designed and drew the fight promotion posters, had done the deed. He had the gift of sketching likenesses of people that bordered on genius. Considering that Levi was the most talented artist in the community and that he, like the other young sports, hung around the lake a lot, it was obvious to me who the culprit was. It was wonderful to have a rascal relative. So, from then on until recently, I assumed that the titillating artwork on the bridge was his.

Actually the painting was very nicely done. Even at the time, most folks generally considered it innocuous. Sixty years later as I am writing these tales of the past, I send certain stories back to old friends still living in North Dakota to check on my facts. One friend, Helen Molberg, upon reading THE LAKE, made a long distance call to inform me that her friend, an old-timer, Olive Benson **knows who really painted** the "Maid of Moonshine." She said it was Jules Krogen. My uncle! Uncle Jules never struck me as a roue or 'ladies man'. In fact, my cousin, John Sigurdson, informed me that our uncle had touched it up at least once. Oh well, despite my mistake I can rest a little easier. Pride in family notoriety can continue.

(The original concrete buttress has crumbled and painting with it. An attempt to replace the art with a painted panel was a noble thought--but it fails. In the interest of historic preservation, hopefully from a photo of the original, the concrete retaining wall and painting should be restored as exactly as possible. If the Vatican can restore DaVinci's Last Supper, Local Lutherans should do a little bridgework at the lake.)

Short Road to Lake Completed

Their dirt-worn shiny shovels put away, the WPA workers celebrated the completion of the road. The Peace Garden Road extending all the way to the International Peace Garden was finished. It passes very close to Metigoshe and from then on, getting to the lake became easy. As I was only thirteen years old I was not allowed to legally drive the car, so I was still dependent on my folks, but it was a heck of a lot easier to talk them into going to the lake.

An added attraction about going to the lake was a chance to visit "Happy" Thomas. He was a man of medium height, wiry-thin, and always wore a captain's hat and quizzical smile. Happy ran a small marina with rowboats for rent, fishing equipment and bait for sale, in addition to the launch excursion rides he gave. This character didn't fit the local norm. He never seemed depressed, despite all the good reasons he justifiably could be. Each year during the drought, the lake level dropped a few feet lower. The lake shrank drastically in area so each year Happy had to move or rebuild his dock to accommodate the lower level. Though the lowering level of the lake, plus the nation-wide depression threatened his business, he seldom complained. The only reference hinting of concern that I can recall him making about the shrinking lake was: "The crick's gettin' lower – fishing spots are getting so small the fish have to take turns swimming – ought to be able to spear 'em with a pitchfork."

His launch, the "Neptune" could hold about twenty passengers who had paid 25 cents each for a half-hour or so of seafaring adventure making a round trip to Canada. On the way to Canadian waters, Happy would give a tour-guide speech to impress the dry flatland tourists. "On the right is Masonic Island, annually visited by Masons – here they hold secret ceremonies invoking mystic rites." Later on course – "we are now passing Squaw point, site of an early grist mill and the deepest clear water in the crick." Three quarters of a mile later – "On the left, Bear Island, where Ludvig Larson saw a three hundred and twenty-two pound black bear. We are now approaching Canadian waters, get your visas out in case Canadian Custom agents are checking up on foreigners." Passengers had a hard time sorting out truth from imagination, but they got more than their moneys worth of entertainment.

Coming to the lake on a weekend, in the time during the drought and dust storms of the prairie, the sight of the stately canvas covered launch, including a fringe on top, stirred a longing in me for a big boat of my own someday. Happy was more than just a marina operator--he was a character with a very colorful way of expressing things. It was fun just listening to him talk. He made it a point not to use the proper word for any thing or event. The lake was "the crick," minnows – "fish food," fishermen – "fish feeders," outboard motors – "iron oars." It wasn't just his unique choice of words. Everything came out with a chuckle as if life was good all the time. His nickname fit perfectly.

One year Happy added a powerful Chris-Craft speedboat to his marina. With this new boat, the rides became much more exciting. It was a fast and attractive boat. It had two cockpits, one mid-ship, one aft. Topsides were decked with mahogany strips about two inches wide with white caulking. A lot of brightwork and a windshield made it the classiest powerboat I had ever seen. The powerful engine would make the boat plane and stir up an impressive wake. A trip to Canada took about four seconds. While other local farm boys wanted to own a speedy car, I wanted a boat like Happys. The truth was, if I were ever to own a boat, I'd have to build one. I did. It didn't match Happy's.

Shipyard--The Blacksmith's Shop Behind the Auto Shed, Summer 1938

As I was home for the summer vacation from high school, I decided I could wait no longer to own a boat. Not having the hope of ever having the money to build a powerboat, I decided a sailboat would be the next best thing. In the school library I had found all the information about boat building I could.

Except for pictures of clipper ships, schooners and the various winners of the America's Cup, there were no designs for small sailboats. I would have to design my own from scratch. It would have to be made from whatever I could find on the farm. Looking around for what was available, there wasn't very much that I could use. In the comic strip "GASOLINE ALLEY," Skeezix had a flat-bottomed scow he floated in some lake or swamp and had a lot of adventures. This looked easy to build. With some improvements, it could be fitted with a sail. I drew a lot of plans utilizing a minimum of material. Then, plans in hand, I showed them to my dad, Jake. He said that on the next trip to Souris we would get what I needed: two 1" x 12" x 10' pine boards, one sheet 4' x 8' plywood. I needed two more feet of plywood to cover the bottom but there was a scrap left over from some other farm project that might serve.

For two weeks outside our blacksmith's shop, I sawed, cut, bent and fastened wood, and plywood, none of it marine material. It wasn't to be just a slab-sided scow. To make its line more fair, I had bent the sides as much as I could. The bow did not come to a sharp point. Unknowingly, I had built the best shape for a flat-bottomed sailboat slightly less than ten feet long. Racing scows, the fastest single-hull inland lake boats, are made without a pointed bow. For a mast, I used a fir 2 x 2, rounded at the corners with a hand plane. Since I had designed a lateen rig, I used two more 2 x 2's for spars. The sail was another matter. I didn't know how to sew. With my boat, sitting forlorn and sail-less by the shop, I pointed the problem out to my mom. Lena said that the next Saturday when she would be in Bottineau she would buy enough canvas duck-cloth, whatever that was, to make a sail. I needed enough cloth for about seventy-five square feet.

The Monday after we got the material she sewed the sail on her sewing machine. The deal was, to cover the expenditures of the boat; I would have to work hard helping with farm work. Total expenses came to nine dollars and forty- three cents, a staggering amount of money in 1937.

The boat was ready for sea trials. Pa, Carl, and I loaded the boat onto the back of Carl's pickup and went to a reservoir about five miles away on Boundary Creek. We launched the boat. I put up the sail. There was a slight breeze blowing. The boat skidded sideways more than forwards. It was a failure. Undaunted, I spent a few days pondering the problem. I needed something to keep it from skidding sideways. I thought of a vertical board in the center--a centerboard, but that was too difficult to build. Instead, I built a board that could be quickly slipped onto the side of the lee side of the hull. The Dutch had been using them for centuries, but I didn't know that. Installing the larboard solved my problem. From then on, the boat would go like blazes. I could even tack upwind. Lake Metigoshe, here I come. The Peace Garden road had been built. I would explore the whole lake.

A Typical Sunday Sailing, Summer 1939

06:00, Sunday, another day at the lake ahead. The folks were still in bed and I couldn't wait for breakfast. I got out of bed, pulled on my faded blue jeans, and headed for the auto shed where I kept my boat. There I loaded my boat onto the back of Carl's pickup; its use OK'd by Carl the previous evening. After pulling a few carrots to eat from the garden, and in my pocket two bits for a couple of hamburgers at Dygert's, I drove up the road headed for Lake Metigoshe.

Pulling alongside Happy's landing I unloaded my scow sailboat and rigged her up. Happy always had some laughing comment about the untraditional look of my creation. This Sunday two other sailboats appeared on the lake. They were Star-class sailboats operated by boy scouts from Minot. They were much larger than my little boat and designed by some marine architect of considerable fame. There was a stiff breeze from the west. I raised sail and headed toward Masonic Island hoping to have a closer look at those elegant boats. Much to my surprise, I passed them easily, rounded the island, and came skimming back to Happy's Landing. Happy grinned at me and said something to the effect that the "Star boats must be dragging an anchor." He made my day.

Even on calm days, exploring the lake was fun. One time, while rowing the boat I had entered a bay on the northwest end of the lake. It was fall, one of those September days when the air is so transparent one can almost see the stars in daytime. The aquatic weeds were dormant and algae gone. The water was so clear I could see to the bottom anywhere. Now and then I would stroke the oars and coast. Near the reeds I had startled a Teal duck. It had dived and I could see it darting under my boat. I was surprised that Teal could swim so fast underwater.

Later as I slowly drifted with my head over the shadow side peering at the muddy bottom of the lake I spotted something unusual. There, about ten or more feet below the surface were the outlines of six canoes, all grouped together in orderly formation. They were sunk deep in the muddy bottom, with only the gunnels showing. Because none of them were exactly the same size or form, they probably were Indian canoes, why were they there? I later told a lot of folks about my discovery of the sunken canoes, including my parents, but nobody had an answer or even seemed curious. Even Happy didn't seem surprised when I asked him. "Who knows? Lake's been here a long time, Injuns a long time before us, 'wharf rat." I was never to learn the answer. It still remains a puzzle unanswered.

Cousin Stanley and The Lake, 1939

In high school I had established a close friendship with my cousin, Stanley Norell. During the last school year, I got my room and board at his mother, Aunt Selma's home. What I liked about Stan was his wry sense of humor. It was primarily based on observing the foibles of human beings, the odd flaws, the dumb things we all do. Stan could manage to notice something funny or humorous in the most common occurrence or characteristic of someone's behavior. He would notice and make some comment that would make me chuckle or laugh--not so much **at,** but **with** the person observed, and in general the person observed was one of us. In short, he was interesting and someone I could be comfortable with.

Neither Stan nor I could financially afford a girl friend. On the rare occasions when we had met at the lake we would try to find out where the Sloan sisters were. Not to actually talk to them, just so we were where we could gaze and marvel at their amazing lines and superstructure. As for approaching them in hope of dating, they were, in our minds, way beyond our reach, even with the lure of my yacht, the scow.

The Great Camping Adventure

One day while home on the farm, I happened to see something on the overhead cross beams in the auto shed that I hadn't noticed before. It looked like it might be a camping tent. I crawled up and dragged it down. Sure enough, here was an old umbrella tent. Then came a great idea involving visions of great outdoor camping. Generations of mice had used the old tent for nesting and had gnawed many holes in the canvas. Never mind the holes, they could be patched. There was no great need for it to be waterproof, considering that it seldom rained anyway. I wanted to use it for a <u>whole week</u> at the lake. It was mid-summer. No farm work needing my help was scheduled. It wasn't necessary for me to stay home. Excited about my find and my idea about going to the lake, I decided to tell my mother. I found her making dinner in the kitchen and told her I had found the tent and wanted to take it to the lake for a whole week.

Mom commented, "That old thing? It has been there since 1924. It must be full of holes and rotten all through." commented Lena.

"I can patch the biggest holes myself and sew up the little ones."

"The mosquitoes will eat you alive."

"Not many mosquitoes at the lake, minnows eat 'em all."

"I worry you'll upset and drown, the way you sail that little boat."

"I've upset it a couple times already, full of water it still floats."

"Now you be sure to take a lantern."

"I don't need a smelly old lantern because I'll be in the tent right long before it gets really dark."

"It wouldn't hurt to take it – you never know when you might need it."

"I'll just have to suffer then – I won't need it."

Lena dropped the lantern argument and brought up a new subject.

"Why don't you ask Stanley to come along – he might like to go too."

"I was just coming to that."

It had been easier than I thought it would be. Not only was I going to the lake, but even better, Stanley might be coming along. Now I'd better get at fixing that old umbrella tent. There were some scraps of duck cloth left over from making the sail and so I set about patching the tent. It was a slow process. After the tedium of stitching a few patches, I decided that extra ventilation from leaving the rest unpatched would be a desirable option and left the small holes unsewn.

Saturday night in Bottineau I met Stanley and told him about the adventure we were about to have, That is if he wanted to come along. Stanley was enthusiastic. "Maybe we can find a place where we can sit and watch the Sloan sisters jiggle by." A real sailing buff that Stanley.

For our trip, Mom had packed a cardboard box with a lot of food that would keep for a week and some food that had to be eaten within two days. Included were some cooking utensils and a small crock half full of butter. The crock of butter seemed incongruous. Real outdoorsmen wouldn't be taking a crock of butter along, but I didn't want to argue with my mother. She had gone to a lot of trouble for me, so I shut up. Lena hadn't been on any camping trip that I had heard of and yet she was telling me what to do. She told me to be sure and keep the food covered and in the tent, or animals would get into our supply.

"For crying out loud, Mom! There aren't any bears, wolves, or mountain lions at the lake."

"Never mind – just do it."

Uncle Carl couldn't spare the Ford pickup for a whole week so he took me, with the boat in back, first to Bottineau to get Stanley, then drove to the lake, and dumped us off at a spot we had picked. It was close to some trees on sloping land, which only a few years ago had been under water, but was now covered with reeds, weeds, and tall grass. "Happy's Landing." was across the water about a half-mile away. Carl left us. He said he was going to try a little fishing with a casting rod before he took off for home.

Aunt Selma, Stanley's mother, had also packed food for us. We now had enough food to feed an army platoon. That was just about the right amount for Stanley and me. There was a pile of gear around us that had to be attended to. He and I then set about setting up the tent, then finally stuffed the food in what we hoped would be the coolest corner--safe from mountain lions. The butter crock would be the biggest problem. It needed to be cool as possible. Since the tent had a few big holes in what was supposed to serve as a bottom, I found a hole near one corner. I then dug a shallow depression in the cool dirt and planted the butter crock in it. The crock had been neatly covered by wax paper tied in place with string. We had no cots so we would sleep, padless, on the floor. In case the temperature fell below ninety, we had old blankets if we should need them.

We were set. After admiring our official looking camp we went to explore the lake in my sailboat. The lake level had now dropped to the point where Lake Metigoshe was two separate lakes connected only by a canal scooped out under the bridge. We sailed about on the North Lake until sunset. At 49 degrees North Latitude it doesn't get dark immediately when the sun sets. For a long while, Old Sol is just skimming along barely below the horizon. Stanley and I headed for "Happy's Landing," but the wind had quit and we had to row. We tied up at the dock and then went up to Dygert's hoping to see the Sloan sisters. To our surprise, we found that there was a new waitress serving tables. She had even more superstructure than both the Sloan sisters put together. "She wouldn't need any hands to carry that tray." commented Stanley. We completely forgot the Sloan sisters for the time being. During the rest of the week we kept thinking up excuses to go back into the Eastside Hotel to see her again and again.

That first night, Stanley and I got back to the tent long after sundown. Stanley said that we should have brought a lantern. I didn't want to admit that my mother had tried to talk me into bringing one. Fumbling around in the dark we finally found a place that seemed relatively smooth to lie down. Something else we learned about camping is that it is prudent to <u>clear</u> a place for a tent, including the removal of any rocks bigger than a baseball.

  Finally, despite the discomfort, I fell asleep with my head near the butter crock. At dawn I was awakened by the loud sound of wax paper rustling. I opened my eyes to see the source of my disturbance. There, almost too close for me to focus clearly, I saw a big squirrel sitting in the butter crock, its face smeared with butter, its head stretching wax paper like a tent pole. In each paw was a gob of butter. Seemingly unconcerned about my proximity, the idiot squirrel was looking at me with a happy Bugs Bunny expression. I yelled and swatted at the little thief. It took off like buttered lightning. Stanley, the sounder sleeper, had missed most of it. Oh well, a little squirrel hair in the butter, it can be scraped out. Resolution: "Today I'll find a short, heavy board to cover the crock." After a canned hash breakfast, I found a board that would do.

  Next evening, after a day of intensive sailing on the waters of the North Lake, including exploration of Masonic Island and its big trees, we were back at Dygert's--checking to make sure the girl with the incredible anatomy was still there. Unfortunately, considering our aching frustration, she was. Oh, how we longed to say something appropriate like, "Hello 'Super-boobs', let me introduce myself," and still have it understood as an expression of great appreciation. Choice words failed us. Courage failed us. Instinctively Stan and I both knew we couldn't think of anything to get her attention. It was very depressing. Here we were, with an overload of hormones, surplus physical energy, great appreciation regarding the exquisite contours of her female body, and totally innocent of carnal pleasures. With no money for a seductive treat, all we had to offer--she wouldn't want. Even my sailboat, cruising in the moonlight, would not be sufficient lure for the Goddess of Dygert's. We were late getting back to the tent again. By feeling around in the inky blackness, I checked the butter crock to determine if the board was still securely in place. Dammit! It wasn't. It had been rudely pushed aside. Obviously, there would be more squirrel hair to remove in the morning. Reaching as far under the tent as I could, I found enough rocks to weigh down the board. Luckily, most of the rocks I found were under where I was to sleep. Settling down to sleep, I told Stanley that we sure could use a lantern.

  Again, at dawn, I was awakened by rustling noises of frantic activity. Opening one eye, I saw the darn squirrel trying to lift rocks. Eye to eye, that squirrel was giving me a very dirty look. Intimidated by the accusing squirrel, I decided that when I scraped the hair-butter out of the crock, I'd have to leave some where it could get at it. The squirrel would damn well have to sort the hair out of it by itself, or wind up with a hairball. My conscience would be clear.

  That day we decided to explore the "South Lake." After sailing to the Westside Hotel we went south as far as we could. The lake had become so shallow that reeds were growing in some parts near the middle. Algae was covering some of the smaller bays. As we came back along the east side, Stanley suggested we beach the boat and explore an island we were passing. He thought he had spied a structure on the island. None of the islands in the lake have cabins on them since there is so much accessible shoreline around the rest of the lake. There shouldn't be anything other than trees on that island.

We beached the boat and walked through the grass and reeds, which covered the now wide beach surrounding the island. We then walked up the shallow bank of the former shoreline and into the trees. There, completely surrounded by small aspen trees, we found a huge double-ender passenger launch. At least it was huge for Lake Metigoshe. It was an enclosed excursion boat, having a long cabin with big viewing lights (windows) on all sides. It was a lot bigger than Happy's launch, the Neptune. It was set up on blocks and propped with small logs. Since many aspen trees had grown completely around it, the boat had obviously been there a number of years. Except for the checked and peeling white paint on the hull and badly checked varnish on the cabin, the big boat was in excellent condition.

The double-ender passenger launch

First, we just walked around it looking at the brightwork. There were brass fittings everywhere, cleats, bollards, cabin trim, ventilators. Even after many years, the brass, though now a dark patina, still gleamed in the dappled sunlight. A big bronze screw, which was about 18 or 20 inches in diameter, was enclosed by a bronze frame holding a bronze rudder. Stan and I wondered why we had not heard about this remarkable vessel. Why wasn't it in the water where such a fine craft belonged? Though we felt like trespassers we climbed aboard near the pointed stern. The jack staff for the flag was badly checked and needed replacement. The aft deck was not very large since the enclosed cabin took up most of the space of the boat. In the center of the aft deck was a box-like housing about twenty inches high, which had wooden seats around its edge. We assumed that this covered the engine. The rear door to the cabin had a big oval window with decorative etching on the edge. The door was not locked so we went inside.

If the outside had been a surprise, inside was even more so. The cabin interior was like a plush railroad car. A broad aisle separated two rows of double seats. The seats were not bare wood as one would expect, but cushioned and covered with burgundy-colored mohair. All woodwork was some kind of rare, to us, red hardwood. The only wood like that, that I had ever seen, was on a grand piano. Despite the years of neglect, the varnish was good as new. True, there were spider webs here and there, and if one banged a seat, a cloud of dust would result. In general, a little cleaning and the boat would be ready for passengers. We discovered that not only were there big windows on all sides, but smaller ones overhead at each of the double seats. The overhead windows could be raised by a brass linkage and fitting attached to the mullions separating the side windows. A person could raise the overhead windows with barely getting off his seat to do so. Up forward, a ship's wheel, compass, and throttle quadrant made it evident that this vessel was never intended to be confined to a small lake in North Dakota. This boat was more suitable for rich tourists in Venice. Personally, I thought if Stan and I had it, fixed up and in the water, we might stand a chance of inviting the Sloan sisters to go for a ride and have them accept. Stan and I would have to ask Happy about this boat when we got back.

Happy grinned when we told him what we had found. "Oh that old tub – so you 'wharf rats' found it."

"Yeah – what's the story about it – why isn't it being used?"

"Belongs to Captain ret. XXX (real name forgotten), he bought it in New Orleans, cruised it upriver to Minneapolis, had it freighted to Bottineau, hauled it up to the lake, put it in the water, and then parked it on the island where nobody could fool with it. It was fall and he said he was gonna float her come spring. Spring came, summer and fall came, and he never got'er in the crick. Lot of guys tried to buy her, includin' me, but the answer would always be: "Come spring, I'm gonna float'er." That tub has seen a lot of springs – a few more and the only thing it will be good for is a chicken coop!" Well, that answered our question except for why on earth would a person go to all that trouble and not cross the last inch across the finish line. The boat mystery settled, we then forgot all about the launch because the sun was low, almost time for Dygert's. We could buy a Coke and split it--an excuse to see "Miss Astonishing."

Blast! She wasn't there. We decided to wait. It cost us another Coke before we gave up. Since the sun was down, we decided to do some nighttime skinny-dipping. We went to the swimming beach and peeled off our clothes. The water was still warm from the heat of the day. It was a fine time to swim. After an hour of diving off the float and splashing around we swam back to the beach. Unknown to us, a car with its headlights off had quietly pulled in close to where our jeans had been left. Some one must have heard us say we were going skinny-dipping. We were standing there, naked as noodles, trying to locate our clothes in the dark when the headlights of the car about twenty feet away came on. The surprise stunned us so much we didn't think to simply run out of the glare. There we stood, trying to cover our private parts. Then the laughter of girls assailed us. Girls! Oh God! How embarrassing! This was during a time when innocence was still in vogue. The car then backed up and pulled away with laughter echoing through the woods. The problem was that we never found out who the girls were. We imagined having to sit in some stupid class in high school this fall and never know for certain if the girl sitting next to us was one of the laughing idiots in the car. Damn!

Camplight Problem Solved

The squirrel problem as far as the butter was concerned had solved itself. The butter, after melting each day, had finally become rancid. In the meantime the squirrel had found other food. He had developed a fondness for bread. If the squirrel failed to unwrap the towels that our bread was kept in, it managed to make a hole big enough to help itself. No matter what we did, we couldn't outwit that insistent rodent with the big fuzzy tail. The problem of lighting our tent remained.

Stan and I first spent the late morning visiting the Westside Lodge that had installed a roller rink, also used for dances now and then. We watched the few skaters until we became bored and left. We continued exploring the lake and went swimming in the clear water off Squaw Point. About an hour before sunset we were back at Happy's. I don't know if it was Stan's idea or mine but one of us came up with a proposal that might bring light into our tent without a lantern. As it turned out, the notion was so stupid I would like to blame Stan for thinking of it.

Anyone, who spent evenings at Lake Metigoshe during the thirties when the lake level was so low, was aware of the extraordinarily great number of fireflies, lightning-bugs around the shore of the lake. *(actually a beetle, family Lampyridae)* They seemed to be numbered in the billions. Apparently the low waterline, allowing many kinds of weeds, reeds and grasses to grow, was ideal for the breeding of these luminary insects. At night, the reedy beach sparkled as if a demented person had decorated the lakeshore with a million tiny flashing white lights. One of us *(Stan, I hope)* said—"If we could only catch a few thousand lightning-bugs and put them in a Mason jar, then we could light our tent."

"Hey – yeah, but how do we catch 'em?"

That stopped us for a while. In the first place, we could only see one when it flashed. The flash only lasted a second or so and then the bug would not be seen until it flashed again. Even if we could see it, it would be very difficult to catch in our bare hands. Devious minds can solve anything. The solution turned out to be simple--Happy's minnow net. This was a net a little smaller in size than a tennis court net. It had a very fine mesh to trap minnows. For a dime Happy would hire a couple boys, us sometimes, to wade out hip-deep in the water with the net stretched tight and walk parallel to the shore. Normally, a bucket of minnows could be filled in about five minutes.

"Hey – I got it! Why don't we borrow Happy's minnow net and run through the weeds where the bugs are blinking?" This idea did not need to be explained. We had empty mason jars. Some of our food had been packed in them. We hurried to the tent to get them. After getting the jars we both took off for Happy's dock. Happy was still there. He was fooling around with some outboard motor clamped to the dock.

"Well, what are you two wharf-rats up to now?"

"We'd like to borrow the minnow net."

"Don't need any shiners."

"We aren't going after minnows."

"I'm not lending a net to a couple of knuckleheads without knowing what you intend to do with it."

"To catch some lightning-bugs."

"Lightning-bugs? Lightning-bugs! – that's the lousiest bait idea I ever heard of."

"Not gonna use 'em for bait."

"What are you going to use 'em for?"

"An experiment. We are going to put 'em in a mason jar and see if they light up enough to make a light."

Happy almost fell off the dock from laughing. "That has to be the most stupid idea I have ever heard. It's so damn dumb it might work."

"Well – how about it?"

"Go ahead – the net's where it always is, hanging in the bait house."

We took the net and hurried out to where the beetles were blinking most. It worked! With each pass through the weeds we got a lot of fireflies. In the net, a few of them kept flashing. Getting them into the jar wasn't easy. A lot of them got away. When we thought we had enough we put the net back in the bait house and showed Happy our catch. The flashing had stopped. We were about to accept it as a failure and dump the beetles out when Happy suggested, "Maybe they're just upset, maybe the flashing is a mating signal *(It is)* and the bugs are having an orgy. If they aren't blinking by the time you get back to your tent let 'em out. Just don't let 'em out here, I got enough bugs as it is."

We took the jars to our tent and were about to dump them all out when a couple of flashes came from the jars. "Maybe if we just let the jars remain still for a while they will all start blinking again." They didn't. Obviously being cooped-up in the jar they weren't going to flash. One of us suggested that since the fireflies we caught had been all near the top of the weed they were clinging to, perhaps they needed space and elevation to light up.

"That's it, we will let them loose in the tent, they will crawl up to the ceiling and blink." *(I hope this was Stan's idea.)* We then took the lids off the jars; set them close to the inside tent wall and let them crawl out. Swarm out, is more like what happened. Some went to the ceiling, most just found space wherever they could. Apparently they were not the type to hold a grudge about being cooped up. The fireflies turned the circuits back on and began to flash like crazy. Soon, seven thousand blinking beetles lit up the tent. Fluorescent lights couldn't have done better. We could have read a paper in the scintillating glow. The problem was that they were everywhere--on the walls, on our blankets, pillows, supply boxes, and on us. Despite the discomfort from luminescent critters crawling all over us, we declared the experiment a success. Our idea worked! Except for a few 'bugs' it was a great invention.

Stan and I just sat and stared at each other with a self-congratulatory satisfaction. For a while we endured the itchy-crawly feeling of blinking beetles stomping on our skin and through our hair as a price for our success. Finally the stupidity of our brilliant idea sunk into our thick skulls. We had learned a fundamental difference between a lantern and fireflies--a lantern can be turned off when darkness is desired. Now we had problem we hadn't foreseen.

We could tolerate our invention no more. The bugs were driving us buggy. Bolting for the tent flap, we escaped the tent and into the night. Brushing most of the beetles off our clothing and out of our hair, we stood a short distance away and looked at our tent. Actually it was kind of pretty glowing like that in the dark. The small holes I hadn't patched shone like stars. Then Stan started to laugh and I did too. We deserved our predicament.

There are experiments that work, there are experiments that don't. This one had worked too well. Here we were, standing in the dark while thousands of lightning bugs were enjoying a luminescent orgy in our lodge. If we were going to get any sleep we would have to get rid of the fireflies. We went back to the tent and with pieces of cardboard ripped from our supply box, started scooping beetles off the walls, ceiling, and blankets to shake them loose outside. Then we would repeat the process. Getting rid of the first five thousand went fairly well, but the more we threw out the darker the tent became. Ok, that was the general idea, to darken the tent. Unfortunately, as the tent became darker the fireflies became harder to find. Only when little beetle flashed could we spot its location. After what seemed hours of searching for the remaining few, we quit. Those damn insects were playing a hide-and-seek game with us. Stan and I never did get them all. Even after shaking out the blankets, some were still hiding to do mischief. By now we were tired and sleepy. Stan and I groggily tried to get comfortable by finding some flat space between the rocks under us. Just when we would just get settled down, a bug or two would glide out of ambush to sit on the blanket near our faces and light up. I tried sleeping on my back and had just dozed off when suddenly one nervy bug landed on my nose. Before I could swat it, it blazed away! Reacting to swat it, I accidentally hit my nose a solid whack, enough to make it bleed. Eventually I fell asleep only to be awakened again because one stupid firefly was perched on my pillow about a half-inch from my eye. It was like trying to sleep with a malfunctioning neon sign in my face.

The next morning we were too tired to plan any exploring. We stumbled out of the tent only to sit down again immediately. If the Sloan sisters had come along and invited us to join them, we would have said, "Some other time." We were too tired to talk much. Though I do remember Stan insisting, "Next time we go camping, we bring a lantern."

When normal yearly rains returned and the lake again rose to its pre-drought level, many of the old commercial establishments were gone. The Eastside Hotel burned down, the Westside business also crumbled into oblivion. Many cabins and lake cottages were deserted. However, the lure of Lake Metigoshe remains constant. It is an interesting body of water because of its tortured shoreline. After World War II, new businesses and activity again flourished. My personal encounter with the lake is but one story as experienced by an awkward farm boy. The lake has character and attracts characters. A historian with a gift of prying tales from old-timers could probably fill a thick book of varied stories. As one nice older lady wistfully put it, "When I think of the lake, I remember romance." Well, when I thought of the lake I remembered a lot of things, but somehow I missed out on the romance stuff--unless you can call my unfulfilled yen for the Sloan sister's romance.

During World War II, high prices were being paid for scrap metal, premium prices for brass or bronze. Somebody besides Happy, Stanley or I, obviously knew about the launch on the island. Every piece of metal was stripped from the elegant boat. Perhaps rotting remnants of the vessel can still be found.

THE BEAST OF BIG SANDY

Loch Ness has its monster. Lake Osoyoos in British Columbia has "Ogopogo." In North Dakota, Lake Metigoshe had only Uncle Carl futilely seeking a monster that would take his lure while fishing. In 1937 he encountered a "nautical beast" in Big Sandy Lake, Saskatchewan or maybe it was Manitoba. What he found was ugly, awesome, and frightening, but it was mechanical not mythical.

This is a true fish story – yes, true, perhaps it is true only because I'm not a real fisherman.

Unlike Jake, my father, who regarded hunting or fishing as simply a chore to provide food, Uncle Carl was an avid sportsman who pursued both with optimistic passion. Hunting, whether it be big, medium, or small game, was Carl's primary avocation. However, fishing came in a close second. He was a sucker for any new tackle gimmick or magic bait that would ensure a catch of record size or amount. His tackle box was loaded not only with every new plug, wiggler, or spoon known to man, but also with jars of potions and scents appealing to the libido of over-sexed piscatorial creatures. Though he studied the sport magazine articles about the secret methods used by famous fishermen, his favorite reading was the book "THE COMPLEAT ANGLER" *by Izaak Walton.*

Carl had told the story so many times to anyone even partially interested that he came to believe it himself. Perhaps I was nine or ten years old the first time I heard it. It was inconceivable at the time that Carl would tell anything but the absolute truth; but as I grew older I did notice that the fish increased a little in size every time I heard it repeated. Oh it wasn't that the story didn't have an element of truth in it. Carl probably did have an exciting encounter with a big one. After all, there actually were some big lunkers in Lake Metigoshe. Once somebody had caught a Northern pike that weighed over forty pounds. However, Carl's story created an image in my mind of a monster so large it could have swallowed the mounted record fish--board, brass plaque and all.

Essentially the story was that he had been bait fishing on Metigoshe with no luck. As he was about to call it a day, he caught a small Walleye. Just when he had it to the side of the boat and about to haul it in, a silver-speckled monster fish flashed to the surface and swallowed his Walleye. The fish roared away breaking his pole and line.

The first time he told it, the mouth of this fish was bigger than his hand. Later, it was bigger than his hand with fingers spread. Finally, it was as big as a garden spade. By this time, even I couldn't swallow his 'swallowing' story.

Eventually it came to the point where the listener's eyeballs would swing upwards or sideways as he told the tale. Carl couldn't help noticing that look of incredibility. Rather than downsize the ravenous fish, he then became obsessed with the goal of catching a fish so big that no one would doubt him again.

Carl started falling for any ad in sporting magazines, or store display claiming this so and so "Boundtogettim" lure was guaranteed to catch the most or biggest fish in the pond. It never worked out that way but Carl kept trying.

Before the Peace Garden road was built we didn't get to Lake Metigoshe all that often. Sunday was our day of rest and recreation. Whatever was planned for that day was seldom relayed to me. I had to look for clues. If Ma was baking an angelfood cake on Saturday it meant we were expecting company. Rats! If Carl was oiling his Shakespeare reel or fooling with his tackle box, it meant we were going fishing on Sunday--hopefully skipping church. Fishing appealed to me only to a limited extent. The problem with fishing was that we sometimes caught fish, which meant a chore of scaling and cleaning. For me, the appeal of going to the lake offered an opportunity to go swimming in water more than hip-deep. Going to the lake meant speedboats, ice cream cones at the Eastside lodge, and people having fun. Fishing? Yeah – OK for the old folks.

By the time I reached high school age, Carl still hadn't caught the big one but hadn't given up either. One Saturday Carl surprised me by asking if I'd like to go fishing with him out on the prairie. Carl had heard that the fishing in Mouse (Souris) River was great and no boat was needed. It sounded like a new adventure to me so I said, "Sounds swell to me." So, late Sunday morning I happily rode along with Carl in his Ford pickup to the river.

The land to the river is almost lake-bottom flat, broken only with a shallow runoff ravine. Near the river, the land drops about forty feet over a hilly east bank which, runs north and south. A flood plain about a quarter mile wide is filled with a marsh of reeds and ponds. Then the west bank climbs again to the elevation of the prairie. Upstream from where we crossed the river are several CCC built dams impounding water to a depth ideal for waterfowl. The Mouse River waterfowl refuge is the largest in the country. There are only a few stretches where the river runs untouched in its natural state.

Today, where we are going fishing, the water runs free until it crosses into Canada, here the name of the river changes again to the Souris River. Carl found a road on the bottomland firm enough to drive upon. He parked the truck near some large old willows. We climbed out and got the tackle out of the back of the truck. He had an extra rod for me.

Carl had said that the sure-catch lure for river fishing was to be the famous "Daredevil" spoon. This time the black and white striped version was recommended instead of the standard red and white design normally used for lakes. For some mysterious reason black and white worked in rivers but not well in lakes.

We found a dry grassy bank on a bend where the sun glazed river emerged between a long double lane of willows. Barely had we made a few casts when we started catching "Northerns." It was almost too easy. It seemed that every time we cast, there would be a darting silver flash and a fish would seize the end of our line. We wondered why everybody didn't fish here instead of the lake.

Almost disappointed because it had been so easy we took our catch and went home. After cleaning the fish we waited for Ma to work her culinary wonders in the frying pan. I refer to her cooking non-secret as a culinary wonder because she used bacon fat for frying. Therefore the fish never tasted like fish. This suited me just fine; I didn't like fish all that much in the first place. To tell the truth, even when she cooked chicken, the tang of pork fat prevailed.

Though Lena normally had the ability to make fish taste more like pork chops, this time her magic failed miserably. The "Northerns" we had brought home tasted very bad. Though I have never actually tasted the rotten muck of a stagnant slough, I have smelled it. These fish tasted like that foul odor. This catch of pike from the "Mouse" had apparently absorbed every putrid stink of some sluggish side pond of the river. It was so bad that even a passel of French chefs, who can normally make snails palatable, couldn't have made these fish taste remotely edible. No wonder local fishermen preferred Lake Metigoshe.

Disappointment resulting from our Mouse river adventure and futile years of trying to catch the monster of Metigoshe was gnawing at Carl's self-image. His obsession to catch a record-sized big one festered. Then one day he came home from town with some important fishing news. The word was out that some storeowners from Bottineau, wealthy people who could write a check for ten dollars without even consulting their checkbooks, had been up north to Flin Flon, Manitoba. They had experienced fantastic fishing. Fish had been so ravenous they had been caught with almost any kind of lure, even no lure... just a colored hook. By the look on his face, I could tell Carl had been hooked too.

Carl could not shake this report from his mind. Flin Flon was out of reach, he couldn't be gone from the farm for a week and he would have to do with limited resources. Yet, he was determined to catch something big enough to brag about, staying within a two hundred miles radius. The limit of his time and wallet.

The next time Gustav Dalen and his wife, Sigurd came for a visit, Carl and Gust had just stood by the car politely talking crops, but Carl couldn't wait to relate the fishing news. Carl told him about what he had heard in Bottineau about the fabulous fishing up north. *(Incidentally, the way local folks pronounced "Gust Dalen" it sounded like "Gus." so that's how I'll write it.)*

Gus listened to the whole story, thought about it a while before he spit out a big brown blob of "snoose." (chewing tobacco) He stared downward at the ground as he pondered the information. Then he looked up at Carl as if he had just remembered something of significant importance. Projecting a matter-of-fact look in his eye to Carl, he says, "I've heard that Clear Lake, in the Riding Mountains is just as good as Flin Flon – and a hell of a lot closer." A person didn't need to be a mind reader to tell that Carl was interested.

That night, after company had gone home, I told Mom about Gus' idea. *(As a cultured sophomore in high school I had stopped calling Lena "Ma".)*

Her reaction was typical of my mothers thinking. Her logic was, "With a perfectly good lake in the Turtle Mountains, why would anyone need to drive four hundred and twenty miles, as-the-crow-flies, north into Canada to go fishing?" Lena should have known better. She, of all people, had told me the old saw about the grass being greener on the other side.

About that old adage, I knew from personal experience that it was based on raw fact. Once I had seen two cows in a lush meadow. These cows were separated by a sturdy barbed wire fence. No.1 cow was straining against the wire on one side trying to reach the grass on the side of No.2 cow. No.2 cow was likewise straining the wire on its side, trying to reach the grass on No.1's side. Apparently the steel barbs painfully sticking into their hide didn't deter either of them from the notion that grass was bound to be better on the other side. Therefore the saying is 100% valid as observed in the psychological behavior of cattle.

It was plain to me that North Dakota fishermen had a lot in common with cows. Perhaps they didn't have a barbed wire separating them from fishing heaven but the Canadian Border made a good substitute. In reality there was a great deal of truth in the concept that fishing was better in that direction. Up there were pristine lakes and few people. It was the dream of every angler in Bottineau County to go "Up North."

One weekend uncle "Sig," pharmacist in Bottineau, married to my aunt Mena *(Minnie)* came out for a visit to our farm. He had been to The Pas, Manitoba, another fishing paradise. In the surrounding lakes he had caught huge fish. He said they were biting any kind of lure offered. For the novelty of it all, he claimed to have caught a twenty-four pound "Northern" using nothing more than the lid improvised from a "Velvet" tobacco can. To the attentive ears of my Uncle Carl, that did it. Fishing heaven was across the border. Nothing could stop him now. In his mind he could see his trophy mounted on a mahogany plaque.

Carl, driven by his obsession and flaming desire to go north, already knew the most likely candidate to accompany him on such a journey to Canada. He drove up to Gus's place. It wasn't a hard sell.

The die was cast. Carl and Gus both were determined to go fishing in Canada. Both retold fish-tale stories to each other, stories which made claims that fish in certain Canadian lakes virtually jumped into the boat as soon as a person opened the tackle box. These fabled fish of great variety were real fighters, born and raised in the purest waters. As for flavor, they were culinary treasures that would please the most demanding gourmet. Best of all, they were very huge. However, there was one nagging problem the anglers had to face.

The dilemma was that neither Carl nor Gus had a boat, a very necessary requirement for a serious fishing trip. Guess who had a boat? Me! *(As mentioned in the story called, "The Lake.")* I had never seen a real sailboat and couldn't have afforded to buy one if I had, so I had built one. It was more scow than boat, however it worked very fine as a sailboat. Mast removed, it could be rowed without a sail. In short, I had a boat of sorts and they needed a boat. Carl and

Gus probably felt guilty borrowing my boat without asking me to go along, so I got asked. Vern Dalen, my age and Gus' son, should have been asked to go along too, but probably wasn't because Carl's pickup would only hold three riders. The trip would be too long to expect someone to ride in back. I felt somewhat guilty being invited to go and when my friend Vern couldn't--but what the heck, I had the boat. It was my ticket for a trip to a Canadian lake.

A week later Carl and I drove up into the Turtle Mountains to Dalen's place. The garish sun had been up about a half-hour. Gus came out of the house with a blanket roll, a thermos of coffee and a cardboard box of camping vittles.

As soon as the stuff was packed in back, off we went, heading for Clear Lake in Riding Mountain Provincial Park, Manitoba. The first town we passed was Deloraine, then Boissevain, then the 'big' city of Brandon, a town with a population of almost five digits. As we drove through Brandon I was treated a sight I had never seen before, a horse pulling a milk wagon, delivering milk house to house. I marveled at the conveniences offered in a big metropolis. The milk bottles reminded me that I was very hungry. I hoped we would take a lunch break in the big city, but we didn't. We continued north along the flat road of the prairie, which I found interesting only because I hadn't been there before.

Approaching Clear Lake, we still had over forty miles to go. I was starving and said so. Thankfully, by now, Gus and Carl were hungry enough to consider stopping for lunch. They said we would look for a place to eat in Minnedosa, a pleasant small town in a valley with a river. When we came into town we had discovered that finding a restaurant wasn't easy. In the "States," advertising signs were big and garish, so we were accustomed to large signs that would say **"X's" Drugstore, "Y's" Hardware, Eat!** Here signs were modestly conservative and small--"X. Jones," Chemist, "Y Ltd.," Iron goods, Mrs. English's Tea Room. Looking in the windows at the tables it had looked like a restaurant. Baked bread odors wafting through the screen door made it smell like a restaurant, therefore, it must be a restaurant. So into this dainty little place with petite tables covered with lace-like linen tablecloths, clumped two husky farmers wearing rough work clothes, and tagging behind, a gangly kid in denims. It didn't take long to realize that they had picked a place requiring some refined customers.

Too embarrassed to admit they had probably made a mistake and just gracefully walk out, Carl and Gus sat down on the spindly little chairs and looked as if they had been caught in the ladies underwear department at Chamholms Dry Goods store. Before either of them could think up a good excuse to leave, a sweet scented, petite, middle-aged lady wearing a lace doily for an apron came to the table. She handed us a menu neatly encased in a leatherette hardcover folder. The menu, written in the most elegant Spencerian script didn't have one item suggesting a hot roast beef sandwich with potatoes and gravy. Instead were lists of pastries I had never heard of. Carl and Gus hadn't heard of any of them either. To stall for time they asked for coffee while they thought it over. The lady smiled ever so nicely and informed us that she only had tea.

"Oh... aw'right, bring us some tea then" Carl said.

"What kind?" says she.

"Black tea" says Carl.
"What kind of black tea? We have several kinds and blends."

"Lipton's" said Carl. The lady looked pained.

"I'm sorry, we don't have – Liptons. What I am referring to is what variety of tea do you prefer? ...Oolong...Darjeeling... I have the choices listed there on the menu."

At this, Gus, looking as bewildered as Carl, leaned back in his chair, slowly shoved his hands into his pockets and said, "Just bring us whatever's most popular around here."

The enigma of the other unknown items on the fancy menu remained. What to order? Finally Gus or Carl asked if she had some sandwiches.

"Oh yes, all of these," she offered while delicately pointing to one side of the page. Except for recognizing a few words like rye, white and pumpernickel it was still foreign to all of us. We just poked our fingers randomly at the menu and hoped for the best. The lady left our table, leaving only the scent of lilac or something. Later she returned with a silver tray, silver teapot, and miniature cups thin as eggshells and decorated with tiny rosebuds. There were napkins encircled with a silver ring, normal spoons, dinky spoons, and a silver sugar container with the dinkiest spoon I ever saw and a silver cream pitcher. Doll toys. She returned to the kitchen. We just sat there inwardly knowing we didn't belong here.

After what seemed an eternity she came back pushing a little cart holding little sandwich plates. To working men, normally accustomed to a half pound of roast beef and equal amounts of potatoes, gravy and beans just for lunch, the little plates held only what must have originally been a small sandwich even before it had been quartered. Each quarter was the size of one healthy bite, a four-bite meal. The sparse plate didn't hold much promise of satisfying a normal appetite. Each sandwich quarter had been speared by a toothpick for some reason. In some cases the toothpick had also speared a black olive, others a sugar cube size chunk of cheese or a pickle. The end of the toothpick had some sort of a colored paper wrapped around the end of it. What was the purpose of these toothpicks? To hold the sandwich together while she quartered it? To hold the olive tidbit in place so it wouldn't roll off the plate? Perhaps, to use as a handle while eating the sandwich?

Gus seemed to know what to do. He yanked the toothpick out with one hand, stripped the pickle off in his mouth and picked the sandwich up in the other and added that bite to the pickle. Four such deft maneuvers emptied each plate. It was allover too fast.

The lady again appeared at our table. "Do you gentlemen care for anything else?"

"Got any pie?" Carl asked.

"No but I have some pastries."

We all guessed, without saying so, that considering the size of the sandwiches, the pastries would only fill a canary. Either Carl or Gus said, "No thanks," and we got up from the table. Carl and Gus paid the bill and we left, still as hungry as when we came in. Before we left town, Carl stopped at a butcher shop and bought a big hunk of sausage. Gus got a loaf of bread at a bakery. Back on the road again, we finally had a real meal while rolling along in the truck.

The flat prairie had ended at Minnedosa. The land was gently rolling with spruce and pine trees appearing more and more frequently. It was the first evergreen forest I had seen since I was four years old. These road sights helped the time to quickly fly and it wasn't long before we saw the entrance to Riding Mountains Provincial Park.

We hurried to have a look at the park's main attraction, our fishing destination--Clear Lake. This, as we viewed it from a large dock, was a large lake with incredibly clear water. Through many feet of water I could see pebbles and rocks on the bottom. As I saw Carl standing midway on the dock staring at its broad open water, I knew what was going through his mind. The truth of the matter was that the deep water frightened Carl. Also, the lake was too big to suit him. Though Carl could swim, the thought of rough water and overturning in a boat scared the hell out of this otherwise courageous man. He confirmed my guess when he said the chance of big waves on Clear Lake swamping our little boat would make it much too perilous. This beautiful lake appealed to me, swamping threats or not. Gus didn't say anything. He knew what was worrying Carl too. Carl then said he would like to go to Moon Lake instead, a lake which he had seen on the map. It was nearby and much smaller. By fishing reputation, Clear Lake would have been a far better choice, but Moon Lake became our destination--much to my disappointment. We all walked back to the truck.

Moon Lake at last. The name fit. It was shaped like a crescent moon and small in size. We pulled the boat out of the back of the pickup, then Carl and Gus went fishing. They didn't get a nibble; the only bites were from mosquitoes.

They pulled the boat out of the water and remarked that since there wasn't another fisherman in sight, we must be the only guys stupid enough to try fishing here. Except for bugs and mosquitoes no other form of life could be seen, not even a mud hen. Carl said we would go to back to Clear Lake and rent a traveler's cabin for the night if we could find one. *(The word "motel" hadn't been invented yet.)* Then we would ask around about other possible places to fish in Canada. We then drove back and found a place that had small one-room cabins.

The little buildings were not much larger than our milkhouse. They were painted white with red trim. Inside was a gas cooking stove of sorts, a small chipped enamel table, and two beds. The sagging spring and mattress on each bed resembled a thick hammock more than a bed. Gus said that he would cook supper on the stove if Carl would hunt up a local person and ask where we should try fishing. That suited Carl so he left and I followed.

"Big Sandy, is where they're biting," said the friendly Canadian. "It's just a few miles northwest of here." Carl got directions and we went back to the cabin, ate supper and went to bed. Despite Carl's snoring and the beds, we slept.

Next morning we got up at dawn, which must have been four-thirty, got dressed, and left for Big Sandy. The "few miles" turned out to be a considerable distance--like Saskatchewan maybe. I had no idea where we were.

The lake turned out to be a big one, bigger even than Clear Lake, the size of which had originally worried Carl in the first place. It was a huge open prairie lake apparently without any sheltering bays or islands; obviously even a moderate wind could kick up big waves. By the look of disappointment and despair on Carl's face, I knew he considered it much too big for my little boat and its ten-inch freeboard. However, Carl had come too far to go back without trying to find a way to catch his dream-fish.

There were many fishing boats pulled up on shore and a few idling about in the water with fishermen fussing around with their tackle. Adding to Carl's frustration, the fish oriented activity made it seem very promising. Along the beach were bait shacks, also rental places for fishing boats that appeared very seaworthy. After the long drive to get here, Carl screwed up his nerve a notch or two and said that we would just have to rent a fishing boat--one with a lot of freeboard. Gus thought it a good idea, so rent one we did. Carl then asked the man at the rental landing about where we should go on the lake to catch fish.

"Fishin's no good this side, far side of the lake is where to catch'em," replied the boat renter.

The far side of the lake seemed about seven miles away. Carl and Gus looked at each other, then across the lake and their shoulders sagged at the prospect of rowing that far.

"By the way" spoke the boat renter at last, "You don't have to row over, there's a tow boat that'll take you over and pick you up again this evening. I also sell box lunches, lemonade or tea ready to take along. There's a tug launch just about ready to take three boats over right now." Carl then said we would wait and watch to see how the operation goes.

A natty nautical appearing, power-launch pilot, wearing a white captain's hat, authoritatively strode along the shore. He cupped his hands and called out to the three rowboats already in the lake and told them to pull up to the dock nearby. Once the boats were at the dock, he played out a line about thirty feet long from the stem of one boat and tied it to the stern of another boat. He then tied the second to the third, and finally, the first boat to his double-ender launch. This launch was covered with a big red and white striped canopy with a fringe.

After climbing aboard his launch, he then eased his boat gently forward taking all the slack out of the lines. Slowly the string of boats moved out to open water before he increased speed slightly. The train of boats took off at about six or eight knots, leaving a considerable but not threatening, wake. It seemed very gentle and orderly to me.

Apparently to Carl, it didn't appear gentle. His sad face told all. The launch was too powerful and fast. It stirred his fear of foundering. As much as Carl was afraid of water, he was even more afraid to admit it. Gus seemed serene and content about the whole operation. He was somewhat surprised when Carl motioned for Gus to join him in a short walk and a conference.

"Let's look for a slower boat," Carl suggested. "I don't feel like rowing over." Gus, already guessing Carl's real problem, nodded and gave approval by saying, "Whatever you think best is OK by me. Lets walk down the beach a ways, I think I see some other fishing places."

We had walked perhaps a little more than a hundred yards when Gus spotted the sign on a weather beaten bait shack: TOWS! OVER AND BACK $1.50. He and Carl ambled toward it. Next to the rough door of the shack was a window-like opening. A large wooden panel, which could be swung down to cover the opening at lockup time, was propped up with two braces.

In the unpainted shack, sitting on a stool, was a slim, tall young man reading a magazine. As we came near, his freckle-face suddenly lit up with a smile of dazzling white, big teeth. His head carried an explosion of curly and unruly red hair. Red hair in itself wasn't unusual, but this was the age of hair oil. All young men wore their hair in the greased-back "George Raft" style of the times. Those with curly hair cursed their misfortune--curly hair is so difficult to plaster down. Therefore, ungreased unruly wild hair was unusual to the point of being abnormal. There were other things about this lanky mariner that didn't fit the norm. His attire wasn't nautical like the other boat operators. He was wearing a well-worn blue-denim shirt, patched faded denim trousers with no belt. This meager outfit hung loosely on a frame more bones than flesh. He was barefooted, which detracted even more from any semblance to a professional man of the sea. But his broad confident grin compensated for everything.

Something about him, perhaps his body language, said he belonged on the water--even more than the dude with the captain's hat and its scrambled eggs brim.

Carl walked up to the open side of the shack stood and planted his hands, palm down, on the narrow board counter at the window of the shack. He asked, "Are you the fella with the towboat?"

"You bet! Name's Frank but I answer to "Red." You're lookin' at the owner and operator of the best damn powerboat on Sandy." We were somewhat surprised by his answer. On the way to his shack we hadn't seen anything resembling a boat, a best boat or any boat for that matter. All we had seen out in the lake was what looked like a rusty metal swimming raft and that thing was listing as if it was about to sink. Carl then asked if he could see his towboat since there obviously wasn't any boat or dock in the vicinity that we could tell. The gangly red-head looked at us a bit quizzically as if we were blind, tossed the ragged magazine onto an old crate, slid off his stool, and walked out the door.

"There she is." Red said with pride as he pointed out into the lake. We looked and saw the hulk about forty yards out in the water.

"That's your power boat?" Gus asked incredulously. Until then, what we had thought only to be a rusty swimming raft about to sink, was his 'tow launch.'

"Yep, that's it – best damn boat in the lake!"

After walking down to the shore for a closer look, we could see it did indeed have a pointy-end, apparently the bow, and a square stem. The bow was about a half-foot lower in the water than the stem. Instead of being upset, Carl looked very pleased. I knew what he was thinking... "If that boat can move at all, it won't go very fast or it will become a submarine."

"You got a deal!" Carl declared, almost gleefully.

"How do we get out to it?" Gus wanted to know.

"Go get your rowboat and well row out."

"How will you get back to shore when the tow's over?" I asked.

"Oh I just swim or wade out and back when I need to."

Then I asked, "How come you don't have a dock?"

"Spent all my money on the boat," was his answer.

By the look of his launch, my unspoken thought was, "His fortune couldn't have totaled more than about three dollars – No wonder he didn't have any money for a dock."

Carl had gone to fetch the rowboat, Gus and I the fishing gear. Coming back to the shack we found Carl already sitting in the rowboat nudged up against the shore. We all got in and headed out to the powerboat. On the way

Red said that he would like one of us to stay in the rowboat to keep it from fishtailing as he towed it. Two of us were to ride with him. Less drag was his reason. Strangely enough, Carl volunteered to stay in the rowboat. I suspect he believed it had less chance of sinking than the rusty hulk we were approaching.

Carl eased the rowboat up to the 'raft' and Red agilely jumped aboard his boat. Gus and I followed and were told to sit down on the stem seats, which were wooden benches bolted to the sides and transom. Because he was facing the stem of his rowboat, Carl didn't see what Gus and I saw. It was just as well that he didn't or this story would end here. In the first place, the rust we had seen from the shore turned out to be mostly red-oxide primer. Inside, the entire hull of the hulk seemed to be filled with the biggest engine I had ever seen, including that of a Caterpillar tractor. Now I knew where Red had spent all his money and time.

"Back your boat up and take slack out of the line," Red told Carl. Carl, his back still turned to the view, immediately moved astern in his boat without ever seeing the monster engine. My attention was focused on the mass of machinery in front of me. Upon surveying the array of levers, switches and knobs, instruments, engine oil cooler, pumps, hard-line tubing, flexible hoses, huge flywheel, massive gear box, exhaust manifold pipes leading to a homemade muffler, I realized that this was not going to be an ordinary ride. My worst suspicions were confirmed when Red opened a small hatch and took out a pair of aviator's goggles.

Coming out of my stuporous state of fascination with the engine I suddenly remembered poor, innocent, unsuspecting Uncle Carl. I had a moral obligation to warn him that this towboat was much more than it had appeared from shore and offer to take his place. Actually, I was afraid he might say yes. I wasn't so sure I really wanted to be out there in that little rowboat either. Then again, he might take one look and cancel the whole trip and I didn't want to miss the ride. If I didn't warn him, or something like it, he would certainly be justified in doing me great bodily harm later. Gus wasn't about to warn Carl. He seemed complacent about the whole deal. Perhaps he hadn't recognized the significance of the huge engine. It was up to me to inform Carl, if not a clear warning, some weasely thing to get me off the hook later.

"Carl- – --Carl! – I think you ought to ride here in the towboat!"

"Naw, I'll be just fine right here," he yelled back.

Red, who had ignored the whole exchange, was proudly extolling the magnificence of his creation as he scrambled about flipping switches, pulling knobs and turning valves. "Built the hull myself – haven't made a windshield yet." He paused to study and tap a gauge. "Got a real good deal on this old war-surplus airplane engine. It's a V-twelve Liberty, 420 horses..."

Carl was still back in his boat, fooling around with his tackle box.

Seeming satisfied with his pre-flight of the machinery, Red pulled out what appeared to be a long crank and inserted it into a hole in the side of the engine. "Inertia starter, put'er in myself, modified everything for boat use, had to add a flywheel." He started to turn the crank. After a lot of effort and a slow windup process, the crank turned faster and faster. After the inertia flywheel was whining to his satisfaction, he removed the crank, turned on the master switch, yelled **"Contact"** and pulled a ring. The inertia starter engaged gears, the gears ground away thus turning the crankshaft. Then **BAROOM!, BANG!, BOOM!,**--loud explosions from a few of the cylinders. Suddenly all twelve cylinders caught, the whole boat was roaring and shaking. The sound was deafening.

Looking back to where Carl was sitting, he had already turned and was now seated, facing forward, in the rowboat when the engine started. The sound of the engine got his instant attention. I didn't know he could open his eyes that wide. His mouth hung open as if he had been told to say "Aaah" by Doc. Johnson. His white-knuckled hands were grasping the gunnels on both sides of his rowboat.

Red, completely oblivious or unaware of our apprehension was still shouting the merits of his creation. **"Tried to make my own mufflers! – Don't work too good yet!"** Red then eased the throttles back a notch and grabbed a long lever, which I assumed to be the clutch. The warmed up engine of the powerboat, now idled back to a very low RPM was rumbling a deep throaty sound as if some drummer was doing a drum roll on a bass drum. The clutch was eased forward and the "Beast of Big Sandy" began to plow forward slowly.

Carl seemed to relax somewhat. I supposed he was thinking that, despite the noise, perhaps we wouldn't be going any faster. Then Red moved the throttle ahead a couple notches. The sound level jumped a few decibels, the line to Carl's boat tightened. Carl tightened. The bow of the powerboat rose slightly. Red, now wearing goggles, advanced the throttles even more.

The bow of Red's boat rose higher and higher out of the water, the rumble of the engine became louder, the throttle was advanced another notch or two. The Beast, now roaring an ear-splitting din, leaped out of the lake shaking water like a wet dog. We were suddenly planing. The primary bounce-wave rose behind our stem. Carl's rowboat riding just behind the crest had become an aquaplane. Only about two square feet of its bottom sizzled on the lake. The line back to Carl's boat stretched hard and stiff as a steel rod. It sliced through the top of the standing white wave in front of Carl's boat. Carl could be dimly seen through the fine spray-fume. His hands were locked to the gunnels, arms outspread and rigid. The brim of Carl's felt fishing hat was folded back to the crown by the wind. It revealed a face of pure terror that was awesome. Red, wearing his goggles, red hair streaming back in the blast of airflow occasionally looked back and seemed satisfied that everything was going

OK. He leaned over to yell in my ear: **"Can't open'er up any more with that boat back there – in fact I've never opened her up all the way but I bet she'd do ninety – maybe hunnerd, easy!!"**

It wasn't long before we crossed the lake. Actually we zoomed past the first launch, <u>the one that Carl had thought too speedy</u>. We went by so fast that it appeared to be anchored. Only close observation would reveal that the launch and its train of three boats were still sedately moving toward the far shore.

The once far-shore, was now near. Slowing down had to be done as gradually as the speeding up. Red couldn't just pull the throttle all the way back or the bow of the **Beast** would have suddenly dropped and plowed under like a diving walrus. With great timing and skill, he accomplished the deplaning. *(The word deplaning now has a different meaning in the jet age.)*

Soon Red's boat slumped down into its bow-down attitude with a little wash sliding over its nose then it wallowed in the following wake. Inertia brought Carl's rowboat to gently clunk 'thump' at the stem of our steel hulled wonder. Carl, with his hands still gripping the sides of his boat was rigidly motionless. His eyes were staring nowhere as if in a state of total shock.

Gus had noticed Carl's emotional state. "Somebody hand me a crowbar – looks like I gotta pry Carl's fingers loose from the boat!" Carl did not seem to hear his amusing remark. Not until we got into the rowboat and Red was preparing to head back did Carl move. When Red said, "I'll be back at eight to pick you guys up," Carl was startled out of his stupor and suddenly let go of the gunnels and wildly waved his arms. In his hurry to yell, Carl jumped up and almost fell out of the rowboat while screaming,

"NO, for Chrisake, No!! – We'll row back Goddammit!"

Gus didn't dare to laugh out loud. Later he did say quietly aside to me, "I didn't know Carl could cuss so forcefully."

After the beast had roared away in a flurry of misty spray, Gus seated the oars in the oarlocks and said we might as well get started catching a bunch of lunkers. Since I was along in the boat, I would try fishing. Gus and I selected our lures and tied them on. Carl just sat there. Gus tried to get his attention. "Hey Carl! tie on a lure, the fish are starvin'." He still didn't move.

Gus and I started fishing by casting with different lures, spoons and plugs, but no luck. Only when we tried trolling did Carl half-heartedly join the lack of action. All the rest of the afternoon we trolled. Even still, fished, with if-all-else-fails live bait, in different areas. We didn't catch any fish. Carl couldn't care less about fish. His dream trip had become a disaster. His heart wasn't in it.

The sun neared the horizon. We guessed that the sun would be setting in an hour or so. It was time to give up and head for home but had underestimated the time it would take to get back. Though we rowed hard, the sun set before we touched shore. Gus and I packed our gear in the pickup and

Gus offered to drive. On the long road to home Carl did not carry on a lively conversation as he had on the way up. He spoke hardly but few sentences. It was almost dawn before we got back. The customs office was closed so we just went home. The customs matter could be handled next day.

Back on the farm Carl never mentioned the ill-fated fishing trip to anyone. I told Mom not to ask anything about it. She guessed why. He not only didn't talk about it; he never mentioned this particular fishing trip again. He never mentioned going up north again either--and either did we.

Since writing this story I dug out a map of Saskatchewan, also of Manitoba. Though I remember approximately where in the vast area this lake was, I'll be darned if I can find a lake named "Big Sandy." It may have been a lake nick- named such by the local folks and not officially on any map. Anyway, I like the

named "Big Sandy" so it stays.

ENTERTAINMENT, 20 BCT

(**B**efore **C**ommercial **T**elevision)

Before **C**ommercial **T**elevision became a part of our national lifestyle, people entertained each other. Entertainment did not come from a one-eyed plastic box in the corner of our living room. Now as we are about to close the twentieth century, a sense of loneliness pervades our crowded suburbs. Am I suggesting that living was more fun in 1930? Yes! Not more easy or comfortable, but more fun.

Citizen Kane's fondest memory was of a sled named "Rosebud."
The name on mine read "Flexible Flyer."

As I am writing these tales and remembering what life on a farm was like sixty years ago, one thought pervades my mind--how much more fun and entertaining life was then. As we live now, trapped by our television sets in our homes in the suburbs, townhouses, or ghetto apartments we are, in reality, living the loneliest time of human existence. I can recall a time when people entertained each other rather than to watch a box of heartless electronic wizardry. I can recall a time when people played a game of baseball rather than watch a ball game. I can recall when real people danced rather than watch images on MTV. Wishful, nostalgic sentimentality? You bet! Sure, life was real and damn hard, but entertaining and having fun with neighbors was also real.

Winter Sports

As I write these stories I mention playing outside at night in winter. This may seem rather strange... perhaps it would be appropriate to give a dull explanation.

A coaster sled having flexible steel runners to enable steering was, in my kid-opinion, one of the world's great inventions. Using these sleds to slide down the icy slopes was the favorite pastime for children lucky enough to live where there were hills. The slender steel runners were no good for soft snow. Luckily there seldom was soft snow in North Dakota. Any snow that fell didn't remain soft and fluffy very long. Strong winds would soon pack the snow into hard drifts. Sometimes the drifts were so hard packed that footprints would barely show, an ideal condition for coaster sleds. Often the bright sun and mild weather would thaw the upper surface of the snow, and at night the bitter cold would freeze the moisture, thereby forming an icy crust on the surface. At such times sledding was superb.

Because of the short daylight hours of winter, it would be dark by the time we came home from school. Therefore, most of the time sledding was done at night when the moon was up. Even a quarter-moon would light the slopes enough to see where we were going. Where there were well-traveled roads going up into the hills, automobiles would sometimes pack the snow and then we could sled for long distances at great speed following tire tracks.

Ice skating was second in popularity to sledding. Early winter, before snow fell, ponds, lakes, and streams would freeze thick enough for skating. Our skates were of the kind that fasten with clamps, using a skate key, to ones' hard soled shoes. Primitive equipment, to be sure, but it worked. Again, night was the best time for skating. The best place to skate was up in the hills on smaller ponds. Here there were trees to shelter us from the wind and trees to provide wood for building a warming fire on the shore. The moon provided more than enough light to see any hazards frozen in the ice. For these trips into the hills I was dependent on my brother-in-law Arnold and my sister Evelyn. Their son Gene, my nephew, was my playmate for these adventures. My mother and father hadn't learned to skate so they were duds when it came to enjoying ice.

One evening sticks in my memory. Arnold, Evelyn, Gene (Pete), and I went to Seter Lake *(now Strawberry Lake)* for an evening of skating. There had been a very light snowfall leaving a thin layer of snow on the ice. The trees bore a heavy load of white frost crystals. The only contrast to the white landscape was the black trunks of the oak trees. The moon was full; shadows of the trees and branches drew long dark lines over the undulating slopes and banks.

Arnold built a fire on the shore and we skated. At the time I had acquired my first pair of shoe skates, hockey style, and they sure beat using clamp-ons. Even skating seemed better at night. The only element missing was an orchestra playing "The Skaters' Waltz." No indoor rink will ever match night skating on a mountain pond.

Skiing

Scandinavians are born to ski, right? Well, either the Scandinavians in North Dakota didn't get the word about this mythical tradition or just decided the little hills weren't worth skiing. It seems that I was almost the only young person to ski much. Gene, my nephew, was my only skiing companion. No Olympic class skier ever came from our part of the country. The North Dakota mountain removal project has been too successful I guess.

Now that you know all there is to know about Turtle Mountain winter sports, lets get on with slightly more interesting stuff.

Dance at Moody's, Winter, Probably 1931

By the sound of it, either Pa or Carl was coming in from the cold outside. First came the sound of the door in the small storm porch opening, then the sound of overshoes being pulled off, to be followed by the sound of the sun porch door opening. Now footsteps across the linoleum of this sun-filled room and the kitchen door opens. It's Pa, breath-made mini-icicles are hanging like ornaments on the woolen scarf wrapped around the lower part of his face. He heads straight for the baked enamel coffeepot lurking at the back of our wood burning, kitchen stove. He pours a black stream of coffee into his favorite cup. Lena, Ma that is, asks in Norwegian, "How cold is it today?" Jake doesn't answer right away. He is busy ladling sugar and thick-as-molasses cream into his cup.

Lena's coffee must be the worst coffee in the universe. It starts out as a full pot in the morning and by mid-morning it has simmered and condensed to a tar- black, acidy, thick fluid that could peel the paint off a tractor. Incredibly, Pa seems to like it. He finally answers Lena's question, "Don't know, didn't look." By then the answer has been so long in coming that Ma has almost forgotten what she had asked in the first place. She complains, "God forbid that I should have married such an uncurious and untalkative man." Ma is angry. I can tell by the way she opens and bangs the stove lid down again. A few minutes go by, Lena has calmed down enough to tell the latest news to Jake.

"Talked to Ella on the phone – she says there's going to be a dance up at Moody's Friday evening." Jake sips and answers, "Mmf."

A little later Carl comes in the house and goes through the same routine as Pa, except he wisely avoids the coffee, opting instead for a small shot of apricot brandy. Ma asks him the same question, "How cold is it today?"

"Minus thirty-two," answers Carl.

"There's going to be a dance at Moody's Friday," says Ma.

Carl thinks that over a moment before he answers, "It better warm up some or Moody's are going to be dancing alone just to keep from freezing."

After supper that evening, I know for sure that we are going because Carl opens the cabinet in the living room where we keep books and other odds and ends. He removes his violin from the battered leather case and starts to practice a few of the polkas and other tunes he knows. Even if the weather is worse than today, I know we'll be there. That I would be going along was certain as a Sunday sermon. Kids, babies, and doddering old folks, even the family dog would always be expected to be show up at a neighbor's dance.

Friday, after the chores were done, we started loading the wagon box, now on the runners of the sleigh. Ma had packed her food contribution of fried chicken in the turkey roaster around which she, in turn, had wrapped a blanket so it would stay reasonably warm. The sleigh box had been filled with clean straw to keep the folks warm as we drove up to Moody's. The weather was nice--it was almost up to zero on the thermometer. Moonlight lit the white breath of our horses as they stamped in eagerness to get moving.

The big treat for me was not to ride in the wagon box but to tie a long rope to the horse drawn sleigh and then to my coaster sled. I would be riding on my sled, which I could steer, in a weaving path behind. We wouldn't be going very fast but I could steer across the road, down and up the ditches and into the fields alongside if the rope was long enough, and it was. Ma, Pa, and Carl were sunk in the straw filled box before I had finished tying the last knot. When I had finished, Pa grunted a Swedish "Gidup" to the horses, slapped the reins on their rumps and we were on our way. As cold as it was, they didn't need much urging. We pulled out of our driveway onto the snowy, icy road to Moody's.

The moon was full and bright enough to see every hazard or interesting snowdrift to cross along the way. Once or twice as I swung out into the field by the road the rope caught on an icy projection in the snow, and the sled suddenly accelerated in an unpredictable direction and upset. Pa, alert to my yelling simply stopped the horses until I got my sled ready to go again.

We got to Moody's in much too short a time. Oh well, I still had the tow home to look forward to.

The dance was slow getting started because the folks were too busy laughing and visiting. There were still some Canadian neighbors to arrive. The kids had no problem getting started. Our business was to play outdoors on our sleds. We didn't go inside and take our winter clothing off. Instead we waited in the animal warm barn until all the boys we knew who were coming showed up. In addition to Virgil, who was the host kid, there would be Eugene Forsberg and Gordon Morrison from across the border for certain. Maybe Vernon Dalen would be coming if his folks up in the hills had gotten the word about the dance. There would also be guys like Harold Backman who would be coming, but they would be at that awkward age--too old for sledding, too young for dancing. Some kids like my nephew, Gene Wunderlich, were still much too young to join us older guys. Girls were never expected to join 'boy stuff.' Girls--phooey.

We waited for Vernon until the strains of violin, accordion, and piano dance music came from the house. We could wait no longer, his folks must not have been told. They didn't have a telephone. There were snow covered hills to be tried, time to start the search for the iciest slopes and snowdrifts.

The moon was so bright it seemed like sledding in daylight. We sledded for hours, going down the hills, trudging back up hills to zoom down again. We would fly into the air over found natural snow jumps. There would be spectacular crashes and notable mishaps. One time "Gordy" Morrison impressed us all. Though he wasn't any older than the rest of us, he paused once on top of a hill to light up a cigarette he had rolled. He had been sneaking and smoking since he was about six years old. We already knew that. (This matter will be exposed later.) It was the strange sight we saw as he slid down the hill with the lit cigarette in his mouth. He went over a jump and when he hit the icy ground--oof! A huge puff of smoke and the sparks of the cigarette burst from his mouth like a fireworks sparkler. We agreed that was funny enough to remember for a long time.

After trying out all the hills we were tired, and hungry, and headed for the party. We leaned our sleds on the outside of the house, unbuckled our overshoes, and walked in. Furniture had been moved or removed to provide space for dancing. The dancing, polkas, schottisches or whatever they were doing, was still going full blast but dancing didn't interest us all that much. Food was our goal. Some of the food was already gone but there were plenty of bowls and pans of chicken, ham, sausages, mashed potatoes, fresh rolls, cake, and JellO to eat until we were stuffed. Sated, we looked at each other as if trying to figure out what to do next. My Aunt Anna (Moody) solved that problem. "You boys go upstairs and lay on the beds and tell ghost stories to each other... take your shoes off before you get on the bed...put the top scrap blanket (patchwork quilt) over you to stay warm..." We happily did as told.

I don't think Virgil even finished his version of a ghost story before we were all sound asleep. Much later, only vaguely do I remember getting up to put on my cap, overcoat, and overshoes to crawl into the straw of the wagon box to ride home. The coaster sled was put in with us. I had no intention of riding it. I buried myself deep in the straw and fell asleep again on the way home.

My folks were late getting up to do the chores. I guessed that even Pa had danced a bit too much. I had trouble imagining him being that active.

Country dances seemed to occur frequently except during the really busy seasons like spring plowing, and planting, or threshing time. Country dances were always held in people's houses or rural schoolhouses, <u>never in a barn</u>. We had heard of barn dances elsewhere in the nation but couldn't understand how those folks did it. They sure couldn't do it in any barn we knew about. The lower part was full of stalls, cows, horses, and manure. The hayloft usually full of hay starting in summer and through the winter, dust and chaff in the late spring.

Before I became old enough to go dancing I was already in high school and country dancing had started to wane. Even in my late teens I was too shy, awkward or broke. Learning to dance had to wait a long time.

Whist

Whist is a card game that was the rage when I was growing up. Not being a card player, I have no idea about the rules or how it was played. All I know is that, like Bridge, it took four people with partners sitting opposite to play. It involved deciding to play "Grand" (high) or "Nullo" (low) and take "tricks." Poker was never played. Poker involves gambling, which, of course, is sinful. Farmers had enough problems dealing with the gamble of farming.

Playing whist was more than just a card game. It was a social event.

Neither Sleet Nor Snow...

It had been the normal kind of an evening we all shared during a medium gale force blizzard. The storm had started first by a buildup of clouds in the west after a warm spell. That is, the thermometer had read above zero. The clouds came over and huge snowflakes started to fall. We expected a storm, and had plenty wood for the kitchen stove, and coal for the brown, baked enamel, simulated brick, living room stove.

Carl had sat in his chair near the new six-volt "A" battery operated Atwater-Kent radio with the ten-inch speaker. All evening he had tried to find a clearer static free station to hear the AMOS AND ANDY show and other favorite programs. The storm or perhaps the northern lights had raised heck with the signal, which they frequently did.

Jake, as usual, had fallen asleep on the sofa in the darker part of the living room.

Lena had sat in the easy chair by the piano and attended to her nightly relaxation knitting. She had the only light on, this measure to 'save the juice' in the batteries of our 32 volt light system. Her floor lamp with the 25-watt light bulb made a warm glow in her corner. Every now and then she had suggested to Carl to try KFYR, Bismarck or WCCO, Minneapolis, etc. If he answered at all, it was to say, "That station is too far," or "That's what I'm trying to do." Eventually we all had to settle for a static punctuated radio drama.

As for me, I had been carving yet another solid wood airplane model. This I had to do in the middle of the floor using a big sheet of corrugated cardboard to catch all the wood shavings. With the light flickering through the small mica windows of the simulated woven stick frame of the stove it had been a cozy evening. Cozy except for the shuddering rumble as a gust of blizzard wind shook the house.

09:00 PM bedtime. Carl turned off the radio and stood up to pull the chains of our cuckoo clock to raise the simulated corncob weights to wind the clock for another day. Lena put her knitting back in the big picnic basket she used for storing her yarn, needles, and unfinished work. Then she walked over to wake Jake to go upstairs to bed. I slid my piece of cardboard holding shavings and parts under the sofa. Ma said, "Don't do that, put the shavings in the stove."

Carl had just barely started up the stairs to bed, I was still putting shavings into the stove, Ma and Pa were in the kitchen when there came the sound of loud knocking on the door of our storm porch. Lena, startled, said, "Who, in heaven's name can that be, somebody in trouble in this storm?" She and Jake hurried out the kitchen door to look. I followed.

"Come in, come in for Heaven's sake!" Ma shouted to the sound of knocking as she turned on all the indoor and outdoor porch lights. We opened the storm door. There stood our Canadian neighbors, The Stewarts. From head to foot, a thick layer of snow was packed on the right side of their heavy woolen clothing. Lloyd and his wife, Jean, were grinning ear from to ear as if it were a balmy summer evening.

"Hello Jake, hello Lena – how about a game of whist?"

Ma was struck too dumb to speak. She started to drag them into the house while trying to find the proper words of astonishment. She couldn't believe anyone would deliberately go out in a storm like this. Jake was just smiling, perhaps a little baffled himself. They took their time beating the snow from their clothes and removed their overshoes before coming in. From the outside porch light we could see the snow outside streaking horizontally. Snowdrifts were piling up in the sheltered places. I too, wondered how, not to mention why, they had made the trek from their place, a mile north, in such bad weather.

In the kitchen, the Stewarts sat down by the kitchen table while Jake opened the draft on the stove. Lena fussed around to make a pot of coffee and then brought out the cookie can full of Scandinavian pastries. Lena kept up a steady conversation asking questions about their crazy adventure.

Lloyd explained: "Before this storm came up we had been talking about coming over to visit and have a game or two. Then the snow came and so we thought better of it. Later on, as I was looking out the window, this thought came to mind, 'Am I going to let a little storm stop us? Wouldn't it be a surprise to you folks if we were to arrive in a blizzard, eh?' So, I talked it over with the missus – she thought I was balmy. I said to her, 'The Olsons live directly south, the wind is straight from the west. All we got to do is keep the wind to our side and we can't go wrong – besides, we will have the Backman fence line between their pasture and field to follow, it ends right across from the driveway into Jake's. Jean still thought I was out of my head, but was game to try. So, here we are."

They were dealing cards as I went up the stairs to go to bed. I knew it was going to be a long night of card-chatter coming from downstairs.

Whist and "Wee Gordy"

There will be a hole in this very short tale because I can't remember all the circumstances or the proper names of Mr. and Mrs. Morrison; but I do remember Gordy because of his habit of smoking at the age of six or so.

Gordon Morrison was all of six years old. He had come with his parents to the Moody's where they had been invited to play whist for the evening. My folks had been invited too. Lena loved the game. Uncle Carl enjoyed it somewhat, Jake would rather pass--pass out that is--in other words, take a nap.

We children were left to entertain ourselves. In our case, Virgil and I could always think up something to do. "Wee" Gordy Morrison, younger than us, had to shift for himself. He decided to just watch us.

Before President Roosevelt's Rural Electrification Administration (REA) brought electricity to farm homes, most families had to do with oil or Aladdin mantle lamps. At Moody's, the card game was lighted by an oil lamp in the center of the dining room table, the largest room in the house. This left the rest of the room very dimly lit. The shadow of the head and shoulders of each adult at the table plastered the surrounding walls. We, the kids, had our own lamp in the parlor where the piano was. The sparse lighting was perfect for an escapade of Gordy's, as we found out later.

Virgil and I were having a great time drawing pictures of guys doing stupid crazy things, things we thought were very funny. Things an adult wouldn't think funny at all. Gordy didn't think them funny either. It was obvious that he was bored, but that was his problem, not ours.

Virgil and I paid little attention to Gordy as time went on. We had barely noticed that he kept slipping out of the room now and then. Then finally something caught our attention. As he came back into the room from one of his surreptitious ventures he blew out a long puff of smoke. Virgil gave me a surprised what-the-heck's-he-up-to look. The next time Gordy left the room we went to the door and watched.

Gordy, with all the stealth and cunning of an Indian, using the shadows of the room for cover, crept toward the table of card players. Apparently his goal was an ashtray near the edge of the table. In it was a lit cigarette, its smoke trail weaving to the ceiling. Gordy, crouched, waited below the level of the table. At the precise moment he thought everyone's attention was diverted he carefully reached up and deftly removed the cigarette from the tray. He took a long drag on the butt; his eyes somewhat crossed as he watched the ember glow. A comical sight. Then he quickly returned the cigarette to the tray.

This time he was caught. Somebody had noticed and told his mother. He tried to contain the smoke but couldn't. Virgil and I thought now he was really in for it. Well he was scolded, but not to the violent extent we would have been. Instead, his mother, with some exasperation and in a strong voice, admonished him, "Aii – nae, Gorrdy – y've gut to stup smookin', else it'll stoont y'r grrooth!" (If the reader can mentally roll the "R's," – you'll get the idea.)

Gordy, hopefully if you are still alive and read this story, you'll back me up won't you? Tell folks that I didn't lie excessively...eh? – and by the way, did you ever reach normal grrooth?

Baseball

My brother-in-law, Arnold, was a baseball nut and brought a bit of minor fame with him from Minnesota as a catcher. It was his idea that our community should have a baseball team. My mother, Lena, for some strange reason, considering the little exposure she had to real games, followed the World Series every fall by listening to the radio. She backed Arnold's idea full bore.

The concept of forming a ball team out of a bunch of local farmers, men or boys was about as ambitious as forming a yacht club. That didn't keep Arnold from trying to get a team together in our neighborhood. Oh, he did some serious catching from time to time and got a buck or two for his expertise from some of the clubs in local towns like Bottineau and Dunseith.

One of the obstacles he had to cope with was that this was occurring during the Dust Bowl era. A baseball cost a fortune--almost a dollar. Gloves were so scarce that I never saw a new one or one with padding still in it. There were two bats, these to be shared by Haram and Dalen townships. 1st, 2nd, 3rd and home plate were boards cut from a pine plank. Uniforms? Huh? The biggest hurdle of all--there was a full scale drought in effect. There wasn't a patch of meadow grass big enough for a grass diamond in the whole county, much less Dalen township.

Not to be daunted, Arnold drove his Model "A" Ford around to various neighbors seeking young men who might be interested. Some were, most weren't.

No game with nine players on each team ever occurred that I could recall. If ten guys showed up they would have to split into two groups of five each. This does not constitute regulation baseball.

One poignant memory comes to mind. For some reason Uncle Carl had to go to Souris and I went along. We walked into Frykman's Auto Garage. They had a huge metal lathe suitable for repairing railroad locomotives. As we neared the monster lathe we saw, mounted between the headstock and tailstock, a piece of Turtle Mountain ash. A mechanic was shaping a baseball bat. Perhaps Souris would have better luck organizing a ball team than Arnold. If they had no paying work for the magnificent lathe, at least they could make their own bats.

Country baseball was not found to be one of the great sources of entertainment in our part of the county.

Pie Social 1931

My sister Luella is all excited about a notice that came in today's mail. It read Pie Social, Carbury Hall, (and the date, probably a Saturday), 1931.

Carbury Hall is actually an abandoned hardware store that the Community uses for a gathering place. The small Carbury high school uses it for a basketball court, about three-quarters the size of a regular sized court.

The way Luella is carrying on you would think she had just won a thousand dollars and has to dress up to get it. The first thing she does is complain that she doesn't have a dress to wear. Ma says she can alter one of the ones she has already. It seems to me that the dresses she wears to dances are too tight to be comfortable. They ought to be let out a foot or two. The notice said, pie social, but Luella is behaving like she thinks she is going to a dance. Pies and dancing don't go together, or do they? I'll ask Ma to clear this matter up. I don't want Luella to find out that I am too dumb to know what a pie social is, so I'll wait till I catch Ma alone and ask her. I do.

"A pie social is a dance party where girls can meet men who are otherwise too bashful to ask a girl out," Ma tells me.

"What's a pie got to do with it?" I ask.

"The girl bakes a pie and brings it to the social, then they hold an auction and the bachelor men bid on the pies."

"So what's that got to do with dancing?" I'm still baffled.

"The highest bidder for the pie gets the girl that goes with it for the dancing," replied Ma.

"Is he stuck with the same girl all night?"

"No."

"What kind of pie is Luella supposed to bring?"

"Any kind."

"Is Luella really gonna bake it?"

"Well, I'll probably do it for her."

"Good – otherwise she'd probably get stuck with some bum."

"That's no way to talk about Luella, she's a good cook. Anyway the men are really bidding on the girl not the pie."

"Luella's gonna be stuck with some bum for sure."

"Jackie! Shame on you!"

Saturday evening came and Luella was struggling mightily to get into something she called a girdle. Of all the dumb things that women wear, this takes the cake. A girdle looks like a section from a big pink inner tube. Maybe it is a form of armor. A guy would have to use a tire iron to get that thing off.

Luella finally got all gussied up and we all got in the car to go to the social. Ma balanced the pie in her lap. Pa drove at his usual breakneck speed, pushing thirty-five. We were going to stay only long enough to see how the bidding went and the dance got started. "How's Luella gonna get home?" I ask.

"The man who buys her pie," Ma answered.

"Bad deal," I replied. Luella hit me.

"Serves you right," says Ma.

The social had been slow getting started. Folks spent more time greeting and visiting than getting the party going. Finally every thing was ready for the auction. The bidding was interesting for the first two rounds, and then it got boring. A couple of other boys and I raided the coffee and cookie table. Then we went outside to count cars. I came in just as Ma and Pa were fixing to leave for home. Luella was already dancing up a storm. As she swirled around, her butt packed in that girdle looked flat as a board and hard as oak. Her virginity was going to remain intact for another night for sure--unless the guy had a tire iron.

Saturday Night in Town

By the time I was in my early teens most of the farmers in the county were going to Bottineau, the county seat, for their Saturday night shopping. It was far more than just a weekly shopping duty. In summer it was the weekly entertainment event.

Since I had had to live in town during the winter months to attend high school I soon learned that "Ma and Pa" were 'country hick' words. From then on I called Lena "Mom" and Jake "Pop" or "Dad." At school I established a close friendship with my cousin Stanley. Stanley Norell was the son of my widowed Aunt Selma. Stan, by coincidence, bore a physical resemblance to Stan Laurel of Laurel and Hardy fame, and he took advantage of this to mimic his appearance and clownish behavior. He could have earned money doing this in a nightclub, if there had been a nightclub. As it was, he entertained me sometimes until my stomach ached from laughter.

Stan's forte was the art of people watching. At this he was a master. By observing the subtleties of body language or overhearing some tidbit of conversation he would know enough about the observed person to predict what they would do before the night was over. Saturday night provided ample opportunity for this harmless and inexpensive form of entertainment.

Work on a typical Saturday during harvest season would end an hour or so earlier than usual to allow the harvest hands a chance to shave, wash and get dressed-up for a night on the town. For most hands, dressed-up would mean a white shirt, if they had one, 'city-dude' slacks, if they had a pair, or unfaded blue jeans--and sometimes, a felt hat. The common final crowning touch for the Saturday night reveler would be to douse himself with shaving lotion and put about a quart of 'rose' hair oil in his hair and slick it down into a shiny imitation of Rudolph Valentino. This means hair combed straight back, contrary to natural grain.

For the men, especially bachelors, this duding-up activity took place outdoors by the old milkhouse. There, next to the north wall, was a bench with a washbasin, hog bristle brushes for scrubbing, and homemade lye soap. On the clapboard wall hung towels on a nail, a mirror for primping stray hairs into oily order. On the corner of the milkhouse, a rainbarrel full of water. These basic supplies, plus the would-be-Lothario's private supply of aftershave lotion, were the materiel requirements for preparation of a night on the town.

For the women, Mom or Luella, my sister, ablutions took place in the house, our kitchen. A galvanized sheet-metal washtub in the middle of the floor constituted our bathtub. For grown men, including my dad, our kitchen was 'no- mans-land.' For me, regarded as a brother or son-eunuch, it was considered no more than 'hand-me-the-soap land.'

As usual, on the way to Bottineau, Jake did the driving, never going any faster than thirty-five mph. Even at that velocity the washboard gravel road would rattle anything not bolted down. Lena wouldn't trust me to drive because I would probably speed over thirty. On the way we had to patiently endure the endless chatter of my mother talking about the condition of so and sos's crop. If we had only one hired hand he would usually ride with us. If he 'got lucky' and met some young lady, he would tell the folks not to wait for him; he would walk the eighteen miles home on Sunday, promising that he'd be there for work Monday.

Very few of the young men who worked the harvest fields during the years of the Depression owned cars. Those that did would pick up other hands with the intention of making a real party out of the occasion. At those times we weren't all that sure they would show up on Monday.

In town, the city rules were that everyone had to park their cars at a forty-five degree angle to the sidewalk. The second, but unwritten, rule was for everyone to leave their keys in the car. This was probably the most practical solution to the Saturday night problem of crowded parking. Farmers were a little careless about the angle or spacing. With the leave-your-keys-in-the-car rule in effect, the town's Sheriff could re-park cars otherwise carelessly parked to optimize parking space. All evening until store closing time Stan and I would watch our officer of the law patiently re-parking cars until they were in neat order suitable for a military review. Car theft? What?

We not only laughed at Laurel and Hardy movies but found humor in films not meant to be comedy, especially Gene Autry horse operas. We would go to his singing cowboy movies to laugh at the supposedly serious dialog or action. For example, I recall a memorable scene near the end of one movie. Autry, who to us looked more like a used car dealer than a cowboy hero, was gazing into the face of the rancher's daughter as if he had just realized he was supposed to say something romantic. Then, with a nasal, flat as a pancake delivery, he spoke the script line, "You have – blue eyes." A dumb line and very dismal acting. Of course, Stan and I broke up laughing. Carter Troyer, the theatre owner, came down the aisle and told us to keep it down or we would be asked to leave. Other moviegoers had not thought the dialog or acting to be so funny, but to Stan and I it had been hilarious. For weeks later we would occasionally repeat the line at opportune moments--such as to a dog which may have came up to us to be petted.

If we couldn't afford a movie, we would sit in the front seat of my dad's car and watch the parade of people. One of the first things that Stan pointed out to me was that married people walked in no specific direction on the sidewalk. However, young bachelors circled the block clockwise, young ladies of the dating age would go counter clockwise. This tactical maneuver provided maximum opportunity to look each other over. *(Many years later while visiting Oaxaca, Mexico, I noticed boys and girls in the soccalo using the same ploy in circling the bandstand.)*

Stan had a habit chuckling sometimes without saying anything. Then I'd ask, "What's so funny? For example, like the time he saw a local dude standing by Sig's drug. Stan had chuckled and I had asked, "What now?"

"See that guy standing there smoking a tailor-made?

"Yeah, so?"

"I've seen the guy before, he rolls his own when nobody's looking. Tonight, in addition to his new jacket he's bought ready-made cigarettes to impress the girls with what a big shot he is. Look at 'im now – he's sneaking a look at himself in the store window reflection. Boy, he sure thinks a lot about himself. Look at 'im pose. Wait 'til he discovers that he hasn't taken the price tag from the cuff of his new jacket – what'a Jerk." I laugh and we wait, hoping we can see what he will do when he discovers the tag.

Naturally, girl watching was very enjoyable. Stan and I would have liked to join the circle of guys, but we didn't have any money to date girls so we had to be content to just sit and watch.

(For the guys, the 'in' slang term of the year for a girl, pretty or not, was "scack." Disgusting as the word sounds it wasn't meant to be bad.)

"See that red-headed scack with the yellow blouse?" says Stan.

"Yeah? I see her."

"She must'a just discovered that she has boobs."

"Whys'at?"

"Seen her walk by before, notice when she comes by the drugstore window, she'll stick her chest out and sneak a look at herself. She wants to make sure they are still there I guess."

Just as Stan predicted she would do, she came by the window, threw her shoulders back, and sneaked a look. He looks at me and a self-congratulatory smile crosses his face.

Watching young ladies flirt and what young men did to get attention was very educational--probably worth two credit hours in a social science class.

It wasn't just young folks that we watched. Old folks, farmers, businessmen, all came under Stan's scrutiny. All the foibles, foolishness or strange behavior they exhibited was exposed. Even simple mannerisms were observed and sometimes predicted by my guru of people watching.

"Look'it that farmer with the big gut standing by the State Theatre with his mouth full of snoose. He's waiting for the show to let out. When his old lady comes out he'll walk to the edge of the sidewalk, let fly a gob of juice, then he'll pull his watch out of his bib pocket to show his woman how late it is. He hasn't had a good time tonight so he's gotta spoil hers." A few minutes later the show is over, people come outside and Stan's prediction is followed like a script.

Hard as I tried, I never achieved Stan's ability at truly observing people.

A Whale Comes to Bottineau

Saturday night was not the only form of entertainment in town. There was the annual county fair, carnivals, and the circus. Once there came a special exhibit on a railroad car--a whale. Yes, a whale. North Dakota is quite a distance from the ocean so seeing a whale would be a real novelty--at least some promoter had thought so. Its coming was advertised in the Bottineau Courant. So we went to town to see it. It was on a flatcar on a siding near the depot and surrounded by a tent wall enclosure, I was disappointed because it was so small. Obviously a whale small enough to fit on a railroad flatcar wouldn't be a standard size whale. Nevertheless, we had paid the admission fee and looked at the thing. It had been embalmed--sort of. There were tubes sticking out of its hide to replace the formaldehyde or whatever was leaking out of it. The embalming had not been totally successful; the gray mass of scrofulous flesh stank. The exhibit was not one of my great experiences.

Speaking of great experiences, the air show in Bottineau was a great experience. In fact, to this day I have never seen a better one nor will you or I ever again. Today such an air show would not be allowed by the FAA, for reasons of audience safety. I cannot recall the exact year that it occurred nor the name of the flying circus or the aircraft used. My guess is that the year was 1934 and the aircraft were similar to, if not actually, the sturdy Stearman biplanes used as primary trainers by the Navy in World War II.

The planes for the show were painted with a black fuselage, red cowling over the radial engines, and yellow wings and tail-feathers. I had never seen anything more beautiful. The pilots looked as if they had just stepped out of a Hollywood movie lot. Leather jackets, jodhpurs, white scarves, helmet and goggles, and of course each wore a pencil-thin mustache, the mark of the real aviator.

The primary reason the Bottineau air show was spectacular was because it took place at the fairgrounds. Normally a person would expect to look up at an air show. Not so this time. People had paid money to sit in the grandstand and by golly they would sit there with the overhead roof blocking any chance to look up. So, to accommodate the paying customers, aerobatic maneuvers took place in front of the grandstand just slightly over the racetrack. The deranged, insane pilots would roar by doing snap rolls so low that the folks in the upper seats were level with the airplanes. A cloud of dust would be churned up at every pass. The pilots then flew by in extremely close formation, three planes following the perimeter of the racetrack to pull up just high enough beyond the backstretch to clear the cottonwood trees as they did a slow-roll in formation. Then they came by again, two planes inverted and barely clearing the ground. Then they separated and came by again singly. A ribbon had been stretched across the racetrack about ten feet off the ground. The first pilot came by inverted and neatly picked up the ribbon with the rudder, The second pilot came by inverted and waved his arm at the audience, the last pilot came by inverted and <u>waved both arms</u> at the audience. The secret to this insanely awesome stunt is that the control stick must be held and controlled in forward position by clamping knees together and wedging the stick between them. This is very difficult to do, especially while hanging upside down in the seatbelt[19]. While two of the planes continued the show, one of them had landed to pick up some passengers, wing walkers--two young ladies in acrobat suits. This took place in front of the grandstand, too. They didn't have a safety line or any special gear to hold them in place. They just looped an arm around the wing struts and waved as they went by. All during the show the audience applauded. Why, I don't know, because with the roar of unmuffled engines there wouldn't be a chance of a snowball in Hades that the performers could hear the clapping of hands.

For the final act there was to be a special parachute jump. No one in our community had seen anyone jump from a perfectly good airplane. This stunt we were told would be something which could only be seen done by this particular flying circus. First the parachutist and his special outfit was shown to the crowd. Attached to the side of his flying suit was a pair of folded bat-like small wings. The wings had several stiff battens sewn in. The stiff leading edge of the wing ended at arms length with a husky leather loop for grasping. We were told that he would spread his wings and dart about the sky while falling before he pulled the ripcord of his parachute. The audience was told that to see this last act, they would have to leave the grandstand to look up.

After the demonstration the parachutist got into a car to be taken to the airfield which, at the time, was only a short distance from the fairgrounds. The people left the grandstand, and most stood on the track and watched as the jump plane climbed higher and higher. Then the pilot rocked the wings of the plane signaling that the jump was about to begin. Suddenly we could see a body falling. Then the parachutist started to veer from his downward path. He swooped from side to side then he made a spiraling turn. It didn't seem to slow his rate of descent very much but it was impressive. Then about the time we began worrying about the opening of the chute he pulled the ripcord and a big white canopy blossomed out. A wind had come up during the show and so the

---

[19] *Much later, when I was learning to fly in the Army Air Corps it turned out that my first pilot instructor in the U. S. Army had once been a flying-circus pilot. His philosophy was that a student should be as competent at flying inverted as right side up. We spent more time inverted than in normal attitude. Once I had soloed, I tried and learned to fly inverted using only my knees to control the stick. Part of the procedure requires the loosening of the seat belt a little to allow "swinging." However, I did this at high altitude. A reasonable amount of sanity is part of my psyche.*

'chutist' began to drift downwind. He drifted beyond the fairgrounds, beyond the School of Forestry, in fact he drifted out of town. There was no point in applauding. Strangely, nobody stuck around to welcome back the hapless parachutist. He likely landed miles away. The unsung hero must have wondered why he risked his fool neck for a bunch of folks that didn't appreciate his act enough to stick around.

Today's free-falling skydivers do wondrous things, but I haven't seen any of them use wings to zoom around while falling. The first one to do so will probably try to convince the world he invented it.

Like I said, there won't be any air show to top the one I saw long ago. Imagine how the Federal Aviation Administration people would now react to anyone doing aerobatics ten feet above the ground a scant hundred feet from a crowd.

Entertaining Liars

There are two kinds of liars. One kind is the despicable rat who lies to cover up his own sins or to get some innocent person in trouble. A liar of this miserable ilk should be eliminated from human society.

The other kind of liar is basically a harmless entertainer, the kind of a person that the author, Mark Twain, loved. Their lies are not meant to harm anyone and are usually so outrageously improbable that the listener instantly recognizes that he is being treated to an imagination free of boundaries. Strangely this liar seems to believe his own tales and will change them only if an improvement can be made. Another oddity--this seems to be a purely masculine characteristic. I have never met or heard of a female yarn-spinner.

Hyperbole should not be considered a lie. Stretching the truth to color a story is, in a sense, a way to be even more truthful about an otherwise dull story. To say that your dog was so fast he could out run the sound of his own bark, clearly informs the listener that your mutt is speedier than average.

There were a few liars of the entertaining variety in our part of the country but not enough to suit me. Luckily, my folks once hired an old farm hand that could really tell some whoppers. Unluckily for my folks, he proved to be such a distraction to the other workers on the field that they had to fire him.

He said he wanted to be called "Cap" Thompson. Claiming to have sailed clipper ships around the "Horn."

"Cap" Thompson came in with the rest of the threshing crew for dinner. He was about five and a half feet tall and a bit on the skinny side. His graying sparse hair would start to float around his head whenever the sweat from wearing his hat dried out. Cap's arms, bare to the fold above his elbow, were covered with king size freckles lurking under curly white arm-hair.

His job was to help load bundles as a field pitcher out in the field. My job was spike pitching bundles into the threshing machine. Therefore, the only chance I had to hear his wild yarns was at the dinner table. I listened intently, even encouraged him a little. The other men at the table had heard enough already. They would cough, scuffle around, roll their eyes in disgust, and try to change the subject.

Yesterday the subject had been Indians. "Cap" had claimed he knew famous Indian chiefs personally, including Sitting Bull. I immediately pointed out that Sitting Bull had been killed by Indian police, in 1890, much too long ago for Cap to have known him. That didn't faze Cap any.

"Didn't mean the old man, I meant his kid, Sitting Bull."

To this I replied, "I didn't know there was a Sitting Bull 'junior'."

"Indians don't call em 'juniors'," he quickly answered.

"What then?"

"His actual real name, Sitting Bull Calf."

Today, at the table, he was telling about the time he had astonished the archeological world by finding a cave full of petrified rattlesnakes near Tombstone, Arizona. When I had asked him what shape they were in, I had meant condition. The other hands were trying to keep from laughing. One of them rolled his eyes upward. Obviously he had gotten sick of these stories some time ago. Being a kid, I needed entertainment.

"Well sir, believe it or not, five of 'em were in a coiled shape as if to strike, life-like as anything you ever saw. Three of 'em in a natural crawling position – and you ain't gonna hardly believe this – four of 'em were stretched out straight as a ramrod." He was right; I didn't believe this either.

"How could that happen?" I asked, probing his imagination.

"Ever see a rattler die?"

"No,"

"Darndest thing you ever saw, when they figger they're goners anyway, rather than suffer a slow death they bite themselves to hurry it up, The pizen rigidizes em stiff and straight as a poker,"

"Why?"

"Ever been bit by a rattler?"

"No, there aren't any rattlers around here,"

"No wonder you don't know nothin', I got bit once, Leg straightened out straight as a fence post,"

First ramrod, then poker, now fence post, This conversation was leading away from the petrified snakes but I had to ask another question:

"How come you didn't die?"

"A desert-smart fella like me always carries a vial of an old Indian snakebite remedy, I drunk my vial and in no time I wuz cured,"

Now I had him... "I'd sure like to see your vial of snakebite remedy," "Didn't bring it,"

"Why not?"

"No snakes around here, you said it yourself,"

He had gotten away again, so back to the fossilized snakes.

"About when I asked about what shape the snakes were in, I meant what did they look like? Like petrified wood?" I waited for his answer. It didn't take longer than for him to swallow a sip of coffee,

"Just as natural as a live snake, even to the beady eyes, diamond pattern and working rattles,"

"What did you do with the petrified snakes?" By now even the other men at the table were quiet as they listened to the verbal duel, Cap didn't miss a beat,

"Sold the straight ones as fancy fireplace pokers."

"Of course, I should have thought of that myself, What about the others, the coiled ones, the crawling ones?"

"Gave 'em to a museum in St, Louis,"

"Glad to hear that, I'll make it a point that someday I'll go there just to have a look at them," Now he was cornered for sure,

"Won't do you any good, They won't let you see 'em"

"Why not?"

"Too precious, they won't show 'em to ordinary folks,"

"Are you sure about that? I don't understand,"

"Course I'm sure, just like they won't let you see the original Bible chapter writ by Mark in his own handwritin' either,"

"What original Bible written by Mark?"

"Proves my point, it's so secret that nobody knows about it,"

"How did you know about it?"

"Inherited the book from my gran'pa on my mother's side, I giv it to the museum too."

He had me whipped, there was no way I could trap him. Cap had an instant response to any question.

Other Entertainment

Hunting for most country people was, in general, not thought of so much as a sport but simply as a way of life. A man hunted to put meat on the table to end the monotony of beef, pork, or chicken; or sometimes for the simple need of fresh meat. It is true that hunting in the Turtle Mountain area was superb. Upland game and waterfowl abounded and to some extent still does, despite the loss of breeding grounds due to extensive farming. Deer hunting brought city sport hunters from great distances during the deer season. Some of the wiser farmers avoided hunting during season for a good reason--to avoid getting shot.

In my home it was a tradition on Thanksgiving Day for all the men to go hunting jackrabbits or pheasants while the women made a big company dinner. It was a relaxed form of hunting. If it was sunny (it usually was) we would walk for a few miles on the frozen ground of our fields and if a hare suddenly spurted from its hiding place we wouldn't try to shoot it on the run. We knew that, after running a distance, the jackrabbit would stop and stand on its long hind legs to see if it was being pursued. At that moment we would have only a second or two to aim and fire. Since we used rifles instead of shot guns the chance of a hare being only wounded was minimized. Whether or not we brought back any game didn't matter. The walk in the brisk air and bright sun did much to enhance the appetite for the feast we would have at the Thanksgiving table.

As for fishing, the universal entertainment, we had Lake Metigoshe. To tell the truth, fishing never was as good as in Manitoba but good enough.

I'd like to end this story about what folks did to make life pleasant long ago with something humorous or at least titillating. What can be humorous about the game of horseshoes? Sex tales can be titillating, but I was too young or too afraid--due to my mother's repeated warnings of the dreadful consequences of sexual adventures--to have any interesting thing to report on a personal basis. The local gossip I can only report as hearsay and that wouldn't be fair. However, sex obviously was as entertaining in our neighborhood as anywhere else.

As I said, my own sexual experiences were limited, if you can call zero, limited. Perhaps a person can count bawdy jokes as experience of some sort. This telling of the latest dirty joke among men folks was almost the first part of any man conversation after saying hello and "Have you had any rain out your way?" This form of entertainment was of course not unique to our community, nor is it new to the twentieth century. Cavemen undoubtedly told dirty jokes. The observation that I have made is that a dirty joke, next to pollen, is the most long-lasting life form. Occasionally I hear a so-called "new joke." With only a slight variation, change of name, etc., it will be essentially the same joke told to me sixty years ago.

THE GREAT WATERMELON HEIST

The degree of honesty in an individual seems to be inversely proportional to the value of the booty involved. The value of treasure is proportional to its rarity. In North Dakota, homegrown melons were rare indeed, and never so rare as in the times of the Dust Bowl. Since the intended victim of this tale is long dead, I can fess up to my role in this sordid tale. Who can question my veracity? I am the only surviving witness.

What can I say? In the hearts of the most puritanical, noble, and otherwise honest men, there lurks the thrill of larceny. Even I, though totally indoctrinated with all of the rules, cliches, morals, and virtues of my Lutheran up-bringing, once succumbed to the illicit lure of stolen booty--especially gastronomical treasure to be easily gained according to the plan described by my cousin Virgil. Actually, I had no choice in the matter. Considering my cousin Virgil, if I had elected not to join in his venture--he would have employed his fists and pounded me to lint.

Watermelons, Native to Africa, Do Not Flourish in North Dakota

There is quite a difference between the climate of Africa and that of North Dakota. This however didn't keep folks from trying to grow watermelons. Sure, the seeds would sprout and if watered, vines would spread dutifully in the patch. However they seemed to be reluctant about being in a Siberian climate.

Watermelons require warm to hot weather or they just mope around and won't grow much. During the Dust Bowl Era the climate was certainly hot enough but unfortunately there was no rain to water the patch. Even hand watering the vines every day brought little success. Just about the time the little melons were about to ripen, an early frost would put an end to dreams of home- grown watermelon. Typically, after a cold night in early fall we would walk out to the garden only to find all the watermelon leaves wilted and lying on the ground limp as wet dish rags. The growing season was just too short.

Rarely, but once in a while, some success was achieved. This was due to some determined, stubborn gardeners who would jump-start the season by planting the seeds indoors. When visiting some neighbors, say in late March, one might see on south-facing windowsills, a row of tin cans. In these cans would be tomato seedlings. Along with the cans of tomato starts might be included a few hopeful cans of sprouting melons. At night the seedling cans would be set on the lid over the warm-water reservoir of the wood burning stove to prevent freezing.

When danger of the last spring frost was over, the plants would then be set out in the garden patch. Even then, just to be sure, little tents made of newspaper would be set over the plants for the night in case we were wrong about the frost season being over.

If these plants were so difficult to grow you may wonder why anyone would bother to try growing melons in the first place. For one thing, to us the taste of that exotic fruit from the outside world was a treat beyond compare. For another, who could possibly afford to frivolously pay **fourteen cents** for a store-bought melon? Nobody in our neck of the prairie. Store bought melons from the foreign country of Texas were reserved for 'spare-no-expense' special occasions-- church picnics or wedding parties. Otherwise, if one were to have melons it was a case of grow your own or go without. However the real reason for trying to grow melons was the challenge of it all. Successfully growing a fat melon in our county would assure the grower horticultural fame.

Lena often claimed that the year before I was born she had grown a crop of good melons in a patch near the creek. It was hard to believe, but a story so wonderful, occasionally needs repeating. She had tended the patch, which ideally sloped slightly toward the sun. Ma had hand watered it with countless buckets from the creek. By late summer the vines were long with rhubarb sized leaves. The melons were a foot long and plump. One day after thumping one she had cored it to remove a plug to check if it was ready. It almost was. In just two more days it would be.

The very next day she went to the patch only to discover that all the big ones had been stolen. Bitterly angry, she tried to think who the culprits might have been. "The Backman boys? – some Canadian hoodlums? The Norman brothers? – etc." The answer was never resolved. To hear her tell of this loss, I wondered how my mother could have stood it. Forget skulking pickpockets, beady-eyed bank robbers, demented murderers--the most despicable low-life of all would be one who would stoop so low as to steal watermelons. Hearing my ma and her tale of woe was an object lesson in morality--an insight to the pain a thief could inflict on decent people. Of course, I, boy-Lutheran, would never, never-ever, be so bereft of honesty, as to do a deed so mean as to steal a single watermelon. Oh yeah?

Each year my mother tried to repeat her 1920 success of growing melons. Each year, just as the small melons were about to ripen, a night frost would end our hopes. Disappointed, we would try to make the best of it and feed these miserable, green-on-the-inside melons to the hogs. The porkers would sniff this new addition of cut up melons to their normal oat-and-kitchen-garbage fare. Then they look up at us with their small accusative eyes as if to say, "What's this new crap you are expecting us to eat today?"

My folks never again succeeded in growing melons, but in 1936 Ole Indvik did. The same year my morality did a nosedive.

One evening after milking, Pa, Ma, and uncle Carl decided to give a call to the Moody's. I, as usual, both looked forward to and dreaded the visit. If my cousin Virgil were in a mood for exercise, he would urge me to defend myself the best I could. *(To give credit to his sensitivity, he was careful not to knock my teeth out.)* On the other hand, he sometimes had an unusual fun project in mind. This particular evening, he had a dandy idea he couldn't wait to tell.

Almost as soon as we had opened the doors of our car "Virge" came running up from somewhere I hadn't noticed and grabbed my arm. By the look on his face I knew he had something important on his mind. He was fifteen years old and about ten inches taller than I. At the age of thirteen I had just barely begun my upward surge of growth. I envied his gold-blond wavy hair, brutally hard muscles, and resented his total dominance of my destiny. What could I do but pay attention to him? It was obvious that he had something on his mind that was of great and secretive importance. He tugged me to one side, away from the folks.

With a conspiratorial voice he said, "Follow me to the shed, *(auto shed)* I gotta swell idea."

"Yeah?"

"Yeah."

We headed for the privacy away from parents. We left Jake, Lena, Carl, Aunt Ann, and Victor who were engaged in the usual folksy palaver of visiting. Even from a distance we could hear them exchanging the standard litany of hard times. "When do you think we are going to get some rain? Crop prices are so low it doesn't matter if we get a crop or not – grasshoppers are really bad – so hot the hawks are walking… cominahouse n'havvacuppacoffee."

Virgil squatted on the ground inside the shed where the dirt was smooth. It was also blotched with dark patches where oil had leaked. He had a stick in his hand and started to draw a map.

"Here is the Border. *(Canada)* Here, is the turn-off to Gustafson's – Here about a mile east and north of the road is a small slough, almost dry now. On the north side of the slough, where it slopes up the hill is where Indvik's have a patch of watermelons."

Skeptical that anyone could grow watermelons, especially during the drought we were having, I asked, "Are you sure they are watermelons and not squash or somethin'?"

Virge gave me an intense and forbidding look as if I had commited a sin to question him. "Damn right I'm sure – I seen'em yesterday. Ole and Oscar were tending them. I was hiding in the brush. They didn't see me. The melons are almost as big as those in town… The Indviks place is a mile or two away… They drive down to the place in their jitney and the old man always has a double-barrel with him. This means they must really be worth something – it ought to be easy to take a couple if we get in fast and get out fast – I gotta great plan. You come up tomorrow around ten o'clock and we'll help ourselves to a couple."

Virgil was actually expecting me to help him steal watermelons! The most despicable dastardly deed I could imagine. I remembered how my ma never forgot about the melons that were stolen from our mythical patch. What's more, the idea of stealing melons scared hell out of me. It was a terrible crime Virge had in mind. I looked Virgil straight in the eye and said, "All right, I'll be here at ten or earlier." Considering the taste of watermelons, morality can be so fleeting.

Virge then said, "Be sure your folks don't get some idea that you're up to somethin' out of the way – jus' tell'em we're going to look for pin cherries."

"OK."

At about nine the next morning I walked up to Moody's and was looking around the place to see if I could find Virgil without his folks learning that I was there. While I was lurking in the shadow of the milk house by the cottonwood trees I heard the screen door of the house slam shut. Virgil had just come out and headed my way. He was eating a monster-size peanut butter sandwich and hadn't seen me yet. As he came closer I loudly whispered, "Hey Virge – I'm over here."

Virge didn't change stride. A real cool guy. As he came up to me he only acknowledged my presence by saying, "You're early – can't wait huh?"

"Couldn't sleep."

"Whatsa matter...scared'a the Indviks?"

"Who me?!! naw."

"Bullshit!"

Virgil then said we were going to go behind the barn and he would fill me in on the details about the theft that was going to take place. He was being more secretive about this affair than I thought necessary. When we got behind the barn he looked for a clear patch of dirt whereupon he could draw more maps and diagrams. I had no idea that stealing watermelons was so complicated.

"This is no different than if we were planning a bank-job...we gotta plan everything..." Hearing Virge talk, I got the impression he had been listening to too many radio dramas about Jesse James, Baby-face Nelson or Dillinger. He continued to draw a detailed map of the watermelon patch area and commented about every feature of terrain, including dimensions. He drew a better map than I had ever seen him do in school.

"Here is the road to Indvik's. The patch is partly on the edge of the slough bottom and slopes up this rise." I'd heard this part yesterday. He continued, "The water in the slough is gone but it is still too muddy to walk on. The Canadian border is about a third of a mile north. There used to be a small field or pasture surrounding this patch – so, there aren't any trees except in clumps. That means we can't sneak up on it through the woods. To get to the melons we will be in the open for a while where it will be easy for old man Indvik to see us if he should be coming down the road. He just might be able to see it from his house."

"Hold it Virge – If old man Indvik is watching this patch at odd times and it's that far from the woods to the patch, we are gonna be easy to see –"

"Shuddup and listen, I ain't finished yet."

I shut up. Virgil at times was more to be feared as Ole Indvik and his shotgun.

"We're gonna use horses," Virge stated assertively.

"Horse – horses? "

"Riding horses, stupid!"

"Oh," – not daring to question further.

Virgil continued, "I'll take Lily, the white horse and ride bareback. You'll ride the roan and get the saddle." I was wondering why Virge was being so nice to me as to let me use the one-and-only saddle when he explained: "That dumb roan follows Lily wherever she goes. If Lily walks, he walks. If Lily runs, he runs right behind her like he was being led. All we got to do is ride into the patch. We stop, then you hang the reins over the pommel and wait. I'll jump down, grab a couple big melons and toss'em up to you. Then I jump back on Lily and I'll take off for the border. You just hang on to the melons. The saddle will hold you in place. Your dumb horse will follow Lily. All you got to do is hang on to the melons – the easy job." No wonder Virge was letting me use the saddle. Virge said that the only problem was that his brothers Levi or Everett might see us getting the horses and ask questions. He said that if they did, he would lie.

Catching the horses was easy. They usually came to the trough when fresh water was being pumped. No need to use a lasso. In a short while we had saddled the stupid roan and were on our way. We rode through the ravines and away from the Indvik road as if just our being on horses would indicate that we were up to no good. The distance wasn't far enough for me. The whole operation had taken on a magnitude I hadn't anticipated. Ole Indvik was a big man with big husky sons who dearly cherished their garden patches, whether it be potatoes, tomatoes, or cabbages. I could only imagine how they must feel about their ripe melon patch. Perhaps I could outrun the Ole and his sons but Ole's shotgun was another matter. The dread of this journey was balanced only by the thought of eating the fruits of their labor.

Virgil pulled Lily to a stop under some aspen edging the open area around the patch. He waited for me to stop alongside before he pointed and spoke. "There, do you see it, the patch?" I looked and sure enough, there about two hundred yards away I could see the patch, the Indvik road, exactly as Vigil had drawn the map.

"Yeah I see it – tell me the plan again."

"You're stalling, I told you enough already. Lets go!" Virgil leaned forward and whacked Lily with his rein ends. She bolted forward in a gallop and my stupid roan followed without any encouragement from me. Through the underbrush, across the road, around the slough, we rode at full tilt until we came to the patch. Virge slid off his horse and started looking around at the melons. Instead of just picking the biggest ones and tossing them up to me he looked uncertain as to which ones to grab.

"Hurry up," I yelled.

"Gotta make sure we get ripe ones," he yells back.

Then, unbelievably, he starts thumping them seemingly dissatisfied with the resonance of several. This procedure is taking hours. I keep looking up the Indvik road. Then I think I hear the sound of a jitney coming. The dirt road to Indviks across the clearing disappears into the forest as it starts up the hill beyond the slough. My hearing is excellent, now the sound is unmistakable. A Model "T" is buzzing its way to our fate.

"Virge! I hear a car coming!" He pauses to listen. Just then we see the hulk of the topless jitney come out of the woods. Virgil frantically grabs a melon and tosses it up to me. He grabs another and tosses it up then runs for Lily and jumps on. I can see the driver and one of Ole's sons. I see Ole, looking like a big squat frog beside him. My God! He has a shotgun cradled in his arms. The jitney is bouncing toward us over the rough road. Ole seems to be hopping up and down in the seat of the car.

In a wheeling turn, Virgil on Lily took off and headed for the border. Then my horse finally wakes up as my heels rapidly pooch his ribs. Gathering galloping catch-up speed he follows Lily--but not exactly. There is a clump of oak trees between Virgil and the border. Virgil and Lily speed around the clump giving the low branches of the oaks wide enough berth to avoid the foliage. My damn horse decided to cut the corner to catch up. Desperately I hung on to the watermelons when common sense should have prevailed. I should have dropped them and grabbed the reins and steered the horse to avoid the long oak limb extending out from the big tree. I should have--but didn't. In a glassy-eyed helpless state, I saw the long extended oak limb approaching at breakneck speed. It seemed to be coming at the speed of sound, a vengeful God-sent arm to smite me for my sins. Disaster was eminent. The roan's head ducked under the limb. I couldn't duck. AAARRGGH! ! The limb caught me in the middle of the melons. They burst on impact. The saddle back held me firmly in place for a moment as the limb yielded and swung. Yielded--but only so far. A stout oak limb is stronger than boy or saddle. At the maximum allowable swing, the branch jolted me out of the saddle and propelled me backward at the same velocity as I had first struck it. Whoosh!

Hitting the ground must have hurt but I didn't feel anything. I was too shocked, too scared. Even before I stopped rolling I was trying to run. No one ever got up on his feet and ran as fast as I did. I headed for the border. Virgil, Lily, and the roan were almost to the border and I was catching up. My shirt was covered with bits of melon and black seeds. My face and arm had many scratches apparently leaking blood but I didn't know it. I wasn't aware of anything but the border, woods, and the safety of impenetrable-to-jitneys wilderness.

Even when I crossed over into Canada I kept running, running, running. Then ahead of me I saw Lily, dappled white in the shadows of a clump of aspen. Virgil was yelling "Here, over here." I was still a few yards away when he saw the black seeds, red melon bits, and blood. He mistook the seeds for shot holes from the shotgun.

"Jeeesis, you been shot!" I shook my head no – I couldn't talk. I hadn't taken a breath since I hit the ground and was now gasping for breath. Virgil then saw that the holes he had seen were black seeds stuck to my shirt. It was a while before I could tell what happened. Virgil seemed as scared as I was. Finally, when I told what had happened, he just lay on his back and started to laugh, not only because of my accident but from hysterical relief of escaping a very angry melon grower.

"What are we going to tell the folks?" I asked.

"Tell'em nuthin."

"What about my scratches?"

"Tell'em you fell outa'a pin-cherry tree."

"What if the Indviks talk to the folks and say we did it?"

"We'll say it wasn't us, musta been some Canadian guys."

"Virge."

"Yeah?"

"Stealin' melons was one dumb idea."

For once he didn't argue about a contradictory opinion.

255

BUCK FEVER

Buck fever is a strange malady that affects some would-be hunters. It can strike the young and old alike. Immunity is sometimes achieved with the experience of a few tough lessons. During the 1945 hunting season in the Turtle Mountains, I decided to be helpful. Since negative experience is so valuable, I added a stone to the road of hard knocks.

In Oct. 1945 the Air Corps allowed me to leave the military service. I was no longer needed to win the war. It happened to be fall when I arrived home at the farm. My applications to colleges were still in the works. A four-day deer hunting season was coming up. Hunting is supposedly a sport. Since I was in a sporting mood I decided to participate--only my game would be hunters instead of deer. Somewhat in sympathy for the deer, it only seemed fair to me.

Hunters tend to be normal people in most of the ways we consider average human beings to be normal. However, when deer hunting season begins, <u>some hunters</u> go through a metamorphosis that would baffle a psychologist. Normalcy goes out the door at the moment he buys a license. A strange, temporary illness, commonly known as "Buck Fever," takes over and warps a part of the mind of the would-be hunter in a very bizarre way. A person stricken with this malady may appear outwardly normal in every respect except for his eyes. Though he may be looking at your face, you get the feeling that he is not really seeing you. His pupils will be mere pinpoints; eyelids will be wide open exposing the whole iris. Even in brown-eyed people, the eye will seem to have a strange blue glaze.

The eerie thing going on behind these eyes is the real problem. Once out in the woods something occurs between the eye and the brain of the hunter, which will cause him to see a deer where no deer exists. To a non-hunter a cow will appear to be cow, a stump will appear to be a stump. However, a person afflicted with buck fever a hallucinatory disorder takes over. Once his rifle is in his hand and license in pocket, a neophyte hunter will mistake a full-grown cow, horse, dog, skunk, raccoon, or stump for a deer and blast away. Owning cattle in deer country can cause considerable worry for the owner of the herd. Seeing your prize cow, wrong side up and riddled with bullets is not a pretty sight.

My brother-in-law, Arnold Wunderlich, had his farm in the foothills, a prime hunting area. In an effort to save a cow or two, his son, Gene, once took a measure to combat buck fever by painting the word "COW" in whitewash on all the cattle. Personally I felt this would be futile, because a person with buck fever would simply read the word "COW" as "DEER" regardless--then shoot to kill.

In addition to eye problems, there are other strange characteristics as well. Reliable witnesses have reported seeing a real deer, in plain view, serenely walking fifty feet away from a stricken hunter without a shot being fired. The hunter just stood there, frozen in motion like a statue. A pigeon could have landed on his head and left its calling card. He might continue to stand there, transfixed, frozen, until found by one of his hunting buddies.

Sometimes, despite hours of practice and simple logic, the hunter will forget the simple sequence of events required to fire his rifle and bring down game. For normal hunters, after spotting a deer, the standard logical sequence is to accurately aim the rifle at the vital area of said quarry and smoothly pull the trigger. Unfortunately, the hunter with buck fever will sometimes get the order mixed up. **First**, upon identifying the cow as a deer, the afflicted hunter pulls the trigger. **Then** he aims the gun. This is lucky for the cow, but unlucky for the hunter. He now has to make a fast trip to the nearest doctor to get the big hole in his foot attended to.

No psychologist or psychiatrist has, to my knowledge, affixed a proper medical name to this strange illness, so I'll invent one. How about *Manic Bambi halucinosis?* MBh for short.

The malady "MBh" occurs only in a relatively small percentage of hunters. What about 'normal hunters'? Even the normal nimrods of November who are not afflicted with buck fever sometimes appear to be caught up in a state of emotional intensity that alters good judgement. Hunting seems to bring out the best or worst in people.

So it was, during a four-day deer-hunting season 1945, I had a rare opportunity to observe *MBh* at its best or worst for that matter. Had I been a student studying psychology I could have written one hell of a great term paper or thesis based on what I witnessed. Had I already been a professional head shrinker, I could have delivered a paper at a national convention of brain-manipulators that would have brought a standing ovation requiring an encore.

To bring some clarity to the following story I must present a little background. As a twelve-year-old farm kid I had a pet deer named "Buck." *(Ref: "The Buck Stopped Here")* To me he was as lovable and close to me as our dog "Tootsie." Therefore, I personally relate to killing a deer as akin to killing a puppy. Whether it be people or animals, the idea of a high-velocity metal slug exploding living bones and tissue bothers me. Let me make it clear, it is not my intention to put down hunters who get enjoyment out of sport hunting, something has to replace the missing natural predators. It's just that hunting and killing is just not my idea of great fun. However, being aware of the MBh factor I will admit to the desire of having some fun at a deer hunter's expense. At this particular time, conditions for my idea were ideal because of the recent war.

December 7, 1941 caught the USA flat-footed at Pearl Harbor. Our country was so ill prepared that even in Feb. 1943 I was issued a wooden rifle for drill practice in the USA Aviation Cadet Corps. If the US Army was in short supply of rifles and ammunition, imagine what it must have been like for the deer hunters at home. These folks, who, for one reason or another, were not qualified for military service, still had the urge or necessity to hunt and provide meat for the table. Times were tough. The tail end of the Great Depression had overlapped our entrance into the war.

During World War II the supply of civilian hunting rifles and ammunition dried up. All the arms factories had concentrated their effort on making guns and ammunition for the war. Whatever hunters had in their gun cabinets at the outbreak of hostilities would be all they would see for the duration. At the end of the war, hunters new to the sport or experienced hunters just wanting a new rifle, were stuck with a very meager supply. So desperate were some of the would-be hunters that they would buy almost anything capable of discharging ammunition. The few gun shops in Bottineau had a steady clientele clamoring for any gun or ammunition they could buy. If the shop had some weird size ammunition left over from the Boer War, somebody would buy it in the hope he could find a gun to match somewhere.

Adding to the pressure of the firearm shortage, the Turtle Mountains were teeming with deer. The foothills with immense natural browse of underbrush and lack of human predators during the war years indicated a potential banner harvest of Virginia White Tail deer. Deer were everywhere in great numbers. They were almost a nuisance, getting into haystacks, gardens, and whatnot. There was about a foot of new snow on the ground to make tracking easier. The prospect of great hunting held much promise. The best year ever was about to begin.

On the evening before the hunt, Arnold came over to our place to talk hunting with Uncle Carl. Sitting at the kitchen table, they were planning what they would do to get the first deer when the season opened tomorrow. They had talked about who would join them in the hunt. It would probably be Oliver Magnuson, Hilman the hardware dealer in Souris and Doc McCullough from Bottineau. Getting the first deer, as early as possible, was a local challenge among friends. This, in Carl and Arnold's case, was usually a matter of minutes rather than hours. Of course this skill had its drawback. For them the season would be over almost as soon as it started unless they could find some poor shot and help him bag his deer.

It wasn't Carl or Arnold or any other experienced hunter that intended to play the joke on. All of these fellows were not only capable of identifying a deer for a deer but would not shoot unless the deer was of the correct age, sex, and properly fat. The kill would be quick and accurate so as not to spoil the meat. It wasn't this group of deadeyes I had in mind. It was those out-of-county-crazies with buck fever that bothered me. It was this odd bunch that I intended to ambush. However, I had little time to put my plan into action and, considering my lack of ideal supplies, the task might be difficult to accomplish. Nevertheless, tomorrow I would build a fake deer for the potential suckers from Minot, Bismarck, or Devils Lake.

In the morning hunting season had already been open a couple hours and undoubtedly Carl, Arnold, and the rest of the gang already had their deer. I was still rummaging around the blacksmith shop and auto shed trying to find something from which I could make a dummy deer. At first I thought of making one out of burlap sacks stuffed with straw, but that would take too much time. Then I remembered the symptoms of buck fever and decided realism wasn't all that necessary. Almost anything resembling a deer would do. Even so, material for making even a low-quality deer seemed scant. There was a corrugated cardboard box in the back of the auto shed. It was beat up and had some grease stains, but it would have to do. It didn't seem remotely big enough. However upon opening it and undoing the places where it was glued together, then flattening it out, I saw that it was big enough to do the body and head. For legs I would have to think of something else. Drawing the profile of a deer was easy enough. Then I cut it out with some tin snips. Even considering how easy it would probably be to fool a guy with MBh, it still needed some painted details. I looked for paint but all I could find was a can of black enamel. It was stiff as molasses due to the cold. For a paintbrush I found an old used one, also stiff, not only from the cold but also from old paint not thoroughly cleaned out. It was all I had so I used it more like a palette knife to smear the paint in place. The result looked like a very mangy, beat-up doe with no legs. For legs I cut two, not four, leg sized sticks and nailed them on. The results were not impressive. This cardboard deer should fool only the dumbest of hunters. How wrong that proved to be!

Though the season had started at 6:00 A.M., it was noon before I finished. I borrowed Dad's car, (Jake never hunted) and headed for the hills. Driving up the Peace Garden road, the thought occurred to me that it was dangerous enough to be walking around the woods without a warning red hat, but to be carrying a deer would be stupidly dangerous. Another thought, "Where would I set the thing up? Oh well, I'll know the right place when I see it."

About two miles up the winding road I came to where the road straightened out for a short stretch passing a small lake on the north side. The small lake, or pond, was frozen over and covered with about a foot of packed snow. On the far shore glowed the golden colors of a clump of small willows and tall reeds. There, I thought, would be the typical natural setting where one might logically expect to see a deer. After stopping the car on the grade I got out and listened very carefully for the sound of approaching vehicles. Except for the distant sounds of rifle fire, it was dead quiet. I scanned the surrounding woods for any hunter who might be there. It seemed a good time to risk carrying the fake deer.

Holding the cardboard deer in a flat horizontal position so it would not expose its deer profile to anyone unless they were in an airplane, I set out to cross the pond and set it up. The road had recently been scraped relatively free of snow. The scraper had left a snow bank on both sides. The grade passing the lake was about eight feet higher than the lake. Scrambling over the bank I found that the soft snow came up to my hips. Plowing through the snow required some effort. Needlessly, as it turned out, I worried that my telltale path through the snow would tip somebody off to the scam. However, the circuitous route around the small lake meant going through snow covered brush so I chose to go directly across the ice. Much to my surprise, I found that the ice in the reedy edge had not frozen solidly; a startling discovery made as I broke through and ice-cold water and mud leaked into my overshoe. The ice on open water must have been six inches thick or better and I had no problem crossing the ice. If I heard a car coming, my plan was to drop the fake flat deer, and wave nonchalantly at the driver and passengers. None came. So that I wouldn't leave a track directly to the deer, I took a dogleg route getting to the place I intended to place the deer.

After selecting the best spot I jammed it upright in the snow, and ran back to the car before anyone came and started firing. Getting up on the grade where the car was parked meant plowing through the deep snow again so I deviated my return path somewhat to avoid the problem. The next move was to get the heck away before somebody came. The deer wasn't immediately easy to see, but to a hunter it would be exactly in the right place. It didn't seem wise to hang around so I left for home, preferring to think about what would happen rather than actually witnessing it. That night I went to bed with a feeling of great satisfaction and anticipation, anxious to see how many guys I had suckered the next day. Tomorrow I would count the bullet holes. I also decided I would watch the action, if any; so I needed to find a place to hide and watch the circus.

The next morning I packed wieners, rolls, a can of corned beef hash, a can of beans, along with coffee and coffee can into a basket. As long as I was going to sit there in my hideout I might as well have a picnic in the snow and be comfortable.

When I got back to the place where I had set up the deer I stopped the car and listened to make sure no one was coming before I got out. There was a small knoll to my right opposite the lake, which might provide a good watching place. I checked it out and sure enough, it proved to be perfect. It was covered with a stand of aspen trees and, in places, clumps of covering underbrush, chokecherry and highbush cranberry shrubs. There was sort of a dent in the ground, which was just deep enough so my body would be completely hidden from the road should I choose to duck out of sight. Hurrying back to the car, I gathered up my picnic supplies and stowed the basket in my hiding place. Then I went back to the car and drove it up the road about a half-mile and parked it in an open spot just off the highway.

While walking back to where I had stashed my stuff, a single car passed me. Wondering why I hadn't heard a sucker shot from these guys, I simply waved hello as they passed. Thankfully they didn't even slow down to ask questions. Maybe they hadn't seen my 'deer.' When I got back to the lake I decided to check up and see how many bullet holes there were in my target. Again I listened before crossing the pond. What would happen, I wondered, if a car should come along now with me between the deer and the road? No time to dwell on that prospect. Risks sometimes must be taken.

As I approached the fake deer it looked more intact than I expected. On closer examination, it had only one bullet hole in it. One miserable hole!

Obviously nobody but one guy had even seen it. I would have to move it, but where? In the middle of the pond it couldn't be missed, but that would be an idiotic place for an alert and intelligent deer to be. At first I dismissed the idea as being too unnatural when I remembered buck fever, the condition where logic and sanity departs an otherwise logical brain. So holding the deer in an edge-to-the-viewer position, I went to the center of the pond and set it up in the packed snow and got the heck away from there. It looked dumb and out of place there on the ice. Only the most stupid of hunters would take it for a real deer. Except for MBh.

Back at my lookout post I had gathered enough tinder-dry sticks to make a smokeless fire. Before I got the fire started I heard the sound of a truck grinding up the gravel highway from the west. Time to see what would happen, I ducked down in my shallow depression and peeked around the lower trunk of the aspen tree shielding my head. Soon the truck, a green pickup, could be seen through the scattered underbrush. In a moment it would be in position to see the fake deer. All at once the driver slammed on the brakes and sled sideways on the icy road and came to a sudden stop, nosing into the roadside snow bank. Both doors opened simultaneously and two local hunters leaped out. The man not driving was first to take aim and fire once, then fire again. The deer didn't fall down. Obviously it wasn't a real deer. Before the driver could fire, the first guy said, "Don't shoot – Hell, it's a goddamn decoy!" The driver put his gun down, studied the target a moment and turned to hunter number one and started to laugh boisterously. "Lets have a look at the sonavabitch!" He started to climb over the snowbank and upon seeing the deep snow I had plowed through, thought it better to reconsider. These guys weren't so dumb after all. Sound carried reasonably well up to my knoll. I could hear them without much of a problem when they talked loudly.

"Hey – I got a better idea." one of them said. "Lets go up the road to where Gus is waiting for us and tell him and Norvil that we spotted some deer down this way. They'll go for it, sure as hell."

I couldn't hear what the other hunter said but I could hear him giggling at the prospect of a practical joke. After they backed the truck around and headed up the road again, I got back to building my fire and waiting for Gus and Norvil. The fire had just barely started to crackle away when I heard another vehicle coming up the hill from the west. This time it turned out to be a car full of a whole family. There was a man, wife, and a bunch of kids. The car slowed down weaving like a snake, but didn't stop. It was plain they had seen it but weren't hunters.

My fire was in need of more fuel so I piled on a few dry sticks. Not even a wisp of smoke curled up from the fire. The sun was bright and hardly dimmed by the overhead branches of the aspen trees. The smell of thawing twigs faintly hung in the air. It had a musty odor mixed with a balsam-like scent- very pleasant. It was a perfect day for anyone who liked the outdoors and winter picnics. I had forgotten to cut a green stick for roasting hot-dogs so, after listening for an approaching car I went over to a bush of the kind that make good fire resisting roasting sticks and cut a couple. It was about noon and this was the slow time of the day as far as traffic was concerned. I had filled the coffeepot with snow and set it on the fire before I heard the sound of another car coming. This time it was from the east. It could be that person called Gus and Norvil somebody. I knew it wouldn't be Gust Dalen, a local. Gust didn't hunt during deer season. A smart decision.

The car came at a speed more than prudent considering the slick road. Coming to where he should be able to see my 'decoy' I saw the car suddenly brake, skid, unbrake, roll to regain control, brake, skid, unbrake, roll, brake, etc. all the way past the pond and down the road for about seventy-five yards and slide past the deer. Then the driver did something really goofy. He started to back up as if a deer would be stupid enough to stand and wait to get shot. Sure enough, my cardboard deer hadn't budged an inch. The driver managed to back right into the snowbank with a sudden thump! Undaunted, he jumped out of the car and blasted away. KAPOW, KAPOW, KAPOW, KAPOW, KAPOW! Obvious misses, he batted at his sights, reloaded and KAPOW, KAPOW! Then came the dawn. He suddenly realized he had been suckered into making holes in cardboard or something. In the meantime the other rider had climbed out of the pickup and just stood there. He had caught on early. After the driver put his gun back into the car he turned to go onto the frozen pond and demolish his tormentor. Thank goodness, floundering in the hip-deep snow discouraged him and cooled him off to the point where he changed his mind.

The two of them got back in the car, turned and went back east where they had just come from. It must have been Gus and Norvil. Norvil, maybe Gus--I didn't have any way of knowing which one of them must have been forewarned because he seemed to be laughing his head off. In the meantime, the snow in the coffeepot had melted so I packed in some more which melted rapidly. It wouldn't be long before I could add some ground coffee. The day and entertainment had been wonderful so far.

Some time had passed before the next car came along. In fact, my coffee was brewing, adding to the pleasant fragrance of thawing twigs and aspen bark. Then I heard engine sounds heralding the approach of another car. This one also made a skidding slow-down but didn't stop. Another non-hunter. After jamming a couple frankfurters on my roasting stick, I then poked it into some packed snow so the end with the wieners on was near, but not over, the fire. That way they would thaw and bake slowly, hopefully without splitting open. Opening the can of corned beef hash, I then set it near the fire to heat. The coffee was ready. It smelled good. Is there anything better than a cup of hot fresh camp coffee on a sunny winter day? If there is, I'd like to know what. Even coffee grounds getting stuck in one's teeth somehow add to the taste.

At the sound of the car coming I flopped into my viewing position. It was a 'woody' station wagon--outsiders for certain--hunters that I hoped, were from Minot. This car managed to make a complete slow spinning circle before it plowed into the snowbank. The three men in it had, for some reason, put their guns in the back behind the rear seat. The sight of three grown men trying to dive over the rear seat to get their guns was worth all the trouble I had gone to. It seemed to me that they could have saved time by just going outside and opening the rear door in the first place, but then like I said, even normal hunters behave strangely during hunting season.

Finally, the trio got their guns out of the car--except there seemed to be a mix-up about whose gun was whose. It was better than watching the Three Stooges, Larry, Curly and Moe, whom they resembled. For the following account, I'll borrow their movie names as a convenience.

After a flurry of gun swapping the Three Stooges ran to get a clear shot at the extremely patient 'deer.' All of them had trouble trying to keep their footing on the slippery ice-snow. Two of them managed to collide and fall down. The one who remained standing, I'll call him Moe, must have realized he would get the first shot. He became so excited he started firing immediately. That is too immediately--with the gun barrel pointed at the sky, pointed at the woods, pointed at the reeds, pointed at the pond ice. Puffs of snow jumped from the ice in various locations around my 'deer.' He emptied his gun. Then he stood there, working the action, trying to get ammunition from an empty magazine. Jerk, pull, click, jerk, pull, click.

In the meantime, Larry and Curley had slipped and fallen on the icy snow. Scrambling to regain footing, they were still slipping and skating around trying to maintain balance and aim at the same time. Larry steadied himself enough to take careful aim. Then he discovered his gun wasn't loaded.

Moe, had already skated back to the car to get more ammunition. Again, instead of opening the rear door, he was climbing over the rear seat to look for his ammo box. Just as he found it, Larry, who had tried to fire an empty rifle joined him bending over the seat frantically seeking his ammunition. Moe, trying to get out, Larry, trying to fish out his supply, created a lot of jostling activity. It never occurred to Moe to go out the other door.

In the meantime, Curley had at last steadied himself. In fact, he had steadied himself to the point of being motionless. There he stood facing the deer, transfixed. His gun was only halfway to an aimed position. MBh had taken over. We now had a statue of a hunter on the Peace Garden road. Both Moe and Larry were frantically loading their rifles when Moe took a closer look at Bambi of the pond. *Something was wrong.* That damn deer should have made tracks by now. All at once his shoulders sagged as he stood there staring. Now there were two motionless hunters. Curley in a trance. Moe about to cry. Larry had his gun loaded and was about to aim when Moe quickly put his restraining hand on Larry's gun while yelling, "It's a God – damned fake, a damn dummy-deer!" Larry seemed irritated for a moment and then the truth sank in. Both of them first looked at the deer, then at each other for a moment. One of them said something I couldn't hear. Moe returned to the car and came back with binoculars. Then he noticed their other partner, gun still at half-mast.

"Frank – Frank? Frank! Hey Frank! Curley's name turned out to be Frank. Its nothin' but a dummy!" Frank's gun then suddenly snapped up a few degrees and fired, lifting another clod of ice and snow from the pond. He relaxed then and sheepishly put his gun down.

Moe then brought his binoculars up to his eyes for a closer look.

"Sheeeeit! Its nothin' but a piece of cardboard, nothin' but a piece of f---- cardboard – sheeeit."

Angry at having been suckered, Larry headed over the bank but Moe yelled at him. "Forget it, you'll be over your head in snow." Larry then paused, thought it over, and turned back. Frank, obviously humbled by his lack of hunting prowess just slowly walked back to the station wagon, put his gun in the back, sat in rear seat and looked stonily straight ahead.

Larry and Moe got back in the car and started the engine. The rear wheels spun on ice going nowhere. Frank and Moe had to get out and push. Eventually the snowbank released its hold and the car backed up, Frank and Moe got back in. Then the mighty hunters continued fishtailing up the highway.

In the meantime my wieners had fried on one side. I had been too fascinated watching to laugh at the time, but I found myself wishing I had a movie camera so I could see the comical antics again. My corned-beef hash was ready. Lunch was greatly enjoyed. As I sat drinking coffee and eating, I found myself hoping the Three Stooges were from Minot.

If the station wagon bunch was a comedy team, the next guy was Ivan the Terrible. Eventually I learned that he had good reason to become hopping mad. A couple of years later, my old friend, Oliver Magnuson, who knew the man, told me the story. To prevent getting sued, I'll call him Percy. (There isn't a single "Percy" in the whole state of North Dakota that I know of.)

It seems that Percy could find no ammunition for the one rifle he had, so he had gone to Bottineau to find a rifle and ammunition. He would settle for anything, and did. He came home with a German Mauser, a relic from "The Great War," World War I. Unfortunately, there were only five bullets available this side of the Atlantic. It was OK with him. He considered himself a good shot and five bullets ought to be enough for not only this year, but next.

Percy was driving his pickup truck up the Peace Garden road to a spot he knew was good hunting. His untried rifle was ready by his side. Through no fault of his own, he was late getting started. There had been some last minute trouble at home he had to take care of and he was still irritated about the whole deal. Oh well, bringing home a fat doe would make everything all right again. Still, it was hard to relax. He couldn't afford to miss.

His pickup was only a few yards from where he would see the 'deer.' I had heard it coming and was waiting.

Percy couldn't believe his eyes. There in the middle of a frozen lake stood a doe. It didn't make any sense for a deer to be there, but Percy was not one to be judgmental about the lack of brains in an idiot deer. He slammed on the brakes and turned off the ignition instantly. "This doe has had it. No way can it sprint away on ice."

From my watching post I saw the truck come to a sudden stop. At least this fellow had put on chains. In a few quick steps Percy got to where he had a clear shot. He then flopped against the snowbank where he could steady his aim. KAPOW! The deer didn't fall. KAPOW! KAPOW again. Surmising that there must be something wrong with his sights, Percy checked the elevation on his rear sight and re-aimed. KAPOW, KAPOW! The deer slowly tipped over backward to lie flat on the ice. Then Percy became painfully aware he had fallen for a piece of corrugated cardboard. I have never before heard a man scream with such rage. He threw his rifle into the snowbank and crashed down over the bank. He went through the deep snow like a racing snowplow, slowing down only a little as he broke through the ice at the edge of the pond. He sank into the cold mud. Charging out of the shards of ice he left a trail of muddy tracks as he ran to the fallen 'deer.' First, he tore the legs off and threw them shoreward. Then he violently started ripping cardboard. All the time he kept yelling words vile enough to make a marine sergeant blush.

"My God!" I thought, "What if this maniac should see me." I hunkered down, flat as a shadow, in my dent on the hill. If there was a time to pray that a madman would leave the area before he found me, now was the time. I didn't dare look to see what was happening next. Though he might be out of ammunition, that wouldn't prevent him from bludgeoning me to death with his gun butt. Only when I heard the engine of the truck roaring and chains clanging against the fenders did I hope to move. Even then, I waited about fifteen minutes before peering over the edge of my nest. A thought plagued me; "He might come back looking for me." Flying Army airplanes had been a chancy business, but this was scarier. Coals in my fire were starting to smolder, thus advertising my position. In my eagerness to douse the smoke signal, I dumped gobs of snow on the embers only to have it steam and smoke all the more. Two or three more cars came by and my heart stopped beating until they were out of earshot. *Years later Oliver Magnuson told me he knew who the man with only five cartridges was and that he had vowed to beat the crap out of the perpetrator if not kill the SOB.*

The sun was getting low before I dared to leave my hiding place. I carried my picnic basket to where I had left the car. Then I drove back to the pond where my fake deer lay in pieces. I followed the Percy's muddy footprints

266

to the middle of the pond to where the parts lay scattered and picked them up. I had no need to worry that it looked like a deer anymore, I was just a guy carrying an armload of corrugated cardboard scraps.

Once again safely at home I set about repairing the deer. Luckily my mom, Lena, had a roll of Kraft carton tape so I was able to repair it. Cutting new legs would be no problem. As I was repairing my bullet ridden Bambi, Dad and Uncle Carl asked me how my day had gone. Both were highly amused at my story. Mom was not amused. Carl, after hearing about the madman, said I probably shouldn't risk hanging around if I set the deer up again tomorrow. I agreed. Incidentally, Carl had gotten his deer in the first hour of the season, but would continue rejoining his buddies for the fun of sharing the hunting season.

Next morning I set the deer up again and then drove back home. I returned that evening to see if the deer was still standing. It wasn't, but it had an amazing number of holes in it and needed a new leg again. The snowbank on the edge of the road had a few more dents in it. Skidmarks and spent cartridge casings littered the road. Why hadn't the hunters seen these and concluded that the deer was a fake? Buck fever could be the only answer.

The next day I set the deer up again at dawn and returned at noon. The fun of seeing the circus was worth the risk of staying a while. My hideout hadn't been discovered. The only tracks to it were mine. This time I had brought sandwiches, coffee and the reliable dented coffeepot. The sky had a thin layer of cirrus, which diffused the sunlight somewhat. It would make viewing even better, bright sunlight on pure white snow is hard on the eyes. It had been my plan to stay only a short while because I didn't believe I could see anything to top what I had already witnessed. To tell the truth, I was feeling a bit apprehensive after the antics of Percy, the mad maniac.

The sound of a car or pickup suggested that I had better get down in viewing position. It was a pickup coming along at pretty good clip--two guys this time. When they reached the critical point, again the sudden braking and skid. They skidded so far they passed the point where the fake deer could be seen. There was a clump of willows and brush, which blocked the view. Instead of backing up, the two hunters had grabbed their guns and ran back to the vital area. One of them spotted the skid marks and brass cartridge casings glittering on the road. He quickly held his arm out in a 'hold-it' position, then pointed the evidence out to the other guy, who at first reacted irritably. Reluctantly trusting his partner that something was amiss, he took another look at the 'doe' and then came to the same conclusion as his more alert friend. He appeared relieved and disappointed at the same time. They both stood and studied the target for a half a minute. Then the driver walked back to the pickup and returned with binoculars.

These two were not given to talking or yelling a lot. The driver studied the target a few moments before he handed the binocs to his friend. I could barely hear what he said. "Must be a hunnerd holes in that thing…" After his buddy confirmed the sight, both of them then went back to the truck and continued on. My thought was that the cartridges and evidence on the icy road would put a damper on further activity. But, as it turned out, it didn't.

There didn't seem to be much traffic this day, so it was a long spell before another car was heard coming. This time it was a sedan full of hunters, six of 'em, all stuffed in like a six-pack. Another skid making a graceful, one-turn pirouette to a crunching snowbank stop. All four doors opened at once. It seemed like an explosion of people. The men were trying to hurry to the trunk of the car where their guns were. Their feet were having a hard time getting footing on the icy surface. With all the slipping and sliding, yet staying relatively in place, it resembled a bunch of clowns doing a frenetic dance.

All of them arrived at the trunk at once. All of them tried to open the lid at once. However, only the driver had the key--or did he? He kept frantically sorting out keys to find the right one. The other guys made the job harder by yelling at him, "Try the other key again!" "Try that key!" Lucky for them, the patience of a cardboard deer is outstanding. Finally, the lid opened and guns were being handed out. It was a replay of the Three Stooges act. Swapping guns or rather parts of guns. Some of them had been broken down to fit the trunk. Now the action speeded up to match a Keystone Kops comedy.

One fellow, the coolest of the bunch who already had his gun assembled, ran to the snowbank, flopped down and started emptying his gun, pausing only to bat at his rear sight a couple of times. He then became aware that his target was a phony. He turned on his side and waved to stop the others. He started to get up, but quickly figured that by the look of them, that this might be a dangerous move. They had that "MBh" look.

Sure enough, in a matter of seconds the five hunters were pumping bullets as fast as they could work the action. Some of them might actually have hit the deer but, in general, ice and snow explosions were popping up all around the target. The war-like scene reminded me of newsreel pictures of an airplane strafing a submarine. The hunter who had fired first remained lying down against the snowbank. He was on his side with his head propped up on one arm; elbow in the snow, watching his comrades' fire away knowing it was hopeless to stop them. He had wisely chosen to wait until all ammunition had been fired. Some folks are apparently very slow to catch on, because one of the men had run back to the car and was actually looking in the trunk for more ammunition!

When it was all over and cease-fire in effect, the overall reaction of this crew was strange. They didn't seem to know how they were supposed to react. Each had been taken in by a fraudulent deer, making them all gullible equals. They walked rather aimlessly back to the car, put their rifles away and slowly drove up the road. The skidding arena now had a new coating of shining brass.

One thing I had overlooked was that not all hunters would be in vehicles driving by. Although I had picked a spot not considered very good for hunting, it didn't mean that there were no deer, or that there would not be hunters on foot looking for them. I was about to learn the psychological difference in people.

Sitting with my back leaning on the trunk of my peek-around aspen tree, I was facing south, opposite the highway. Cars could always be heard in time to warn me of another potential victim. Then I noticed him. There was a trail coming from the south passing the east side of the knoll I was on. It was a pretty trail with a foot of unbroken snow through the aspen. No one had walked this path for a spell. There was not even a suggestion of old tracks. Because I was screened by a clump of highbush cranberries, he had not seen me. Slowly I slid down to become more invisible. Totally hidden by some underbrush close to me, I had a good view. He was coming closer. If he stayed on the trail he would pass less than sixty feet away.

The hunter looked familiar, but I couldn't place him. He was definitely a Turtle Mountain man. He had the easy smooth gait of people used to walking the hill trails. Wearing a patched blue denim jacket, heavy dark wool pants, fur-lined cap with flaps up, marked him as a person whose home was somewhere in this forest, not Minot. When he was close enough for me to get a good look. I could see he was carrying a double-barrel shotgun. This meant that he probably was using a shell with a solid slug. It also meant that he could only be using one barrel since most double-barrels choke one barrel and a slug shouldn't be used in a choked barrel. All the signs added up--this gentleman was a real hunter. I wondered what would happen when he came to the road and saw the deer. I also had a hunch he would spot the empty cartridges on the road and not waste a shot. Only he didn't get as far as the road. Somehow he spotted the fake deer through a lot of brush while still short of the road. He made one smooth side step to get a clear shot through the shrubbery and fired. BOOM! The deer flopped over backward, flat as a pancake.

"Oh – oh," I worried, "Here we go again – another damn angry hunter." Instead, this unknown man that I have admired ever since, instantly recognized that he had been suckered into falling for a fake deer. Instead of raging angrily, he slapped his thigh and started to laugh. He was laughing at his own error! Here he was, supposedly alone and laughing at himself. It was so infectious that I almost laughed out loud myself. It was hard not to. The hunter then broke the breech of his gun and removed the empty shell and inserted another.

Still chuckling to himself, he continued walking to the highway. Once on the road, he saw the empty cartridges and laughed again. Then he looked to where the 'deer' had fallen and seemed to be studying the situation. He was picking the best way to get to it. He skillfully managed to avoid the deep snow, to avoid breaking through the ice and was soon looking down at his cardboard quarry. He held it up briefly and discovered that he had broken the front wooden leg in the back where I had nailed it to the cardboard--approximately where the heart would have been. It figured this man was one hell of a shot.

With the side of his foot, he kicked snow aside, making a clear space on the ice and laid the 'injured deer' down flat. Then he walked to the shore and drew his knife. "Now what's he up to?" I wondered.

He had cut a stick and returned to the wounded target. He used his knife to split the broken stick and remove the small shingle nails I had used to fasten the cardboard. Lacking a hammer, he pounded the nails back in with the metal butt end of the hunting knife handle. He had repaired it!

After he looked around to make sure no idiot would fire at him while holding a deer, he set it up again and hurried away. Once back on the road, he took one final look at it again, shook his head, chuckled and walked up the road. Oh how I admired that man and wished that I could be that kind of a person.

Nothing could top what I had just seen, so I decided to go home.

Sometimes, when I need to remind myself that there really are some well- adjusted, wonderful people out there in our world, persons who can privately laugh at their own errors or folly, I get comfort in remembering the laughter of that man alone in the woods. Heroes sometimes come in a patched blue-denim jacket.

A BRIEF VISIT HOME, 1944

One bright summer morning in 1944 there came an opportunity to make an unauthorized visit home in a B-24 Liberator bomber. As the pilot-in-command I gave my "passengers" a sales pitch and they agreed to keep their mouths shut in exchange for a little adventure.

At the sound of a distant rumble, Lena paused washing dishes to listen. She recognized the familiar sound of an airplane, but it was somewhat different this time. During the past four years she had become accustomed to the sounds of single and twin engine 'visiting' military aircraft from Canada. This time it was unlike any engine sound she had heard before--different even from the sound of a formation of aircraft. It had to be some kind of airplane she hadn't seen. A sudden thought came to her mind--by some motherly instinct, she knew her son was coming home for a visit in that B-24 bomber he had written home about. She flung the dishrag splashing into the dishpan, grabbed a towel, and ran outdoors. She hurried down the flagstone path through the lilacs, then stood in the driveway where she could get a view of the sky in all directions. Lena's hopes were dashed. The sound seemed to be coming from the north--Canada. She felt a surge of disappointment because this is the opposite direction from Lowry Field, Denver, where her son in the Army Air Corps is stationed. Nevertheless, since she was now outside she waited to see whatever the strange aircraft might be.

1940

In great haste, following the Battle of Britain, the RAP, as well as the RCAF, began building training fields for aircrew training in Canada. Many of these fields were within seventy-five miles of our farm. As early as 1940 we began to receive aerial visits by 'crazy' Canadian pilots flying DeHavilland Tiger Moth biplane trainers. This was to be expected. The easily recognized Turtle Mountains, the highway crossing the border with its Canadian customs office made it an identifiable turnpoint for navigation training. Also, to the young lads from England, it was something to write home about... **"Dear Mum: Today I flew across the American border and paid some Yank farmer a surprise visit..."** Since our farm was only a short distance from the customs office, one of those farms frequently visited was ours.

The first time a Tiger Moth came to our farm I had been in the blacksmith shop and heard it roar over. I ran outside in time to see it pulling up in a gentle climb as the pilot rocked his wings "hello." To a seventeen-year-old farm boy, the sight of that agile yellow biplane buzzing our farm made my heart yearn to be a pilot. As a show-off gesture he made a beautiful slow-roll[20]. Then, wings flashing sunlight, the little plane banked into a turn. Then I noticed Mom standing beside me. She too had come outside to see the show. Again the plane came toward its appreciative audience of two. This time the pilot made a slow pass giving us a "so-long" friendly wave and swung again to the north from whence he had come.

What before had been but a yearning, the visit fanned the already smoldering embers of my passion to become a pilot into a raging fire. As the

---

[20] *A slow-roll is a seemingly simple but technically difficult maneuver in which the wings of the aircraft rotate relatively slowly about the axis of its straight-line flight path. Inverted, to coordinate the controls, the rudder must move in the opposite direction as compared when the plane is right side up. It is beautiful to watch when expertly done. At low altitude, it is also dangerous. One slip, goodbye.*

little plane disappeared into the blue void of the northern sky, an important decision became clear to me. I would just have to overcome my scholastic deficiencies and perhaps someday--miracle of miracles--I could play in the sky as well.

Considering the lack of family wealth, my only option to escape the farm and become a flier was the military. Then again, An older town-guy had said the only use the U.S. Army had for a dumb farm boy was for service in the mud-slogging infantry. The thought of being a private in the infantry made me shudder.

The biggest problem was that my mother, concerned about the inevitable involvement of the United States in the coming war, was paranoid about my going into the service. Even a Boy Scout uniform seemed ominous to her.

From the time Hitler had taken over control of Germany in 1934, Lena knew from the ranting speeches of "Der Fuhrer" that another terrible war was coming. In her mind, her son would be of just the right age when it came. The thought frightened her that I would be in it and get killed in some muddy trench. She expressed these concerns at the end of every newscast of things happening in Europe. In her raging heart she knew Hitler and Mussolini had to be stopped. She dreaded the oncoming war and what it would mean. All the older folks remembered the Great War of 1914-1918 and the losses it brought in men killed or crippled. My uncle Monte Woods, married to Aunt Ann, had been there in the worst of it, as an officer in the trenches. He knew best of all.

In my mind, my mother was probably right about the coming war and America soon being in it. I had mixed emotions. On one hand, being a mud-soaked soldier dying from mustard gas or hanging bullet-ridden on a barbed wire entanglement didn't appeal to me. On the other hand, the military, whether Navy or Army, was my only hope of learning to fly--to hell with the risk of being shot down in flames. There was one big catch. That was the requirement to qualify for acceptance into the Air Corps or Naval Aviation for pilot training--two years of college--minimum. The junior college in Bottineau, The North Dakota School of Forestry, could provide those minimum requirements. This time I didn't argue about going to school. In September I began college.

Even the School of Forestry wasn't immune to the buzz-job visits by Canadian pilots. The act of flying low and showing off over a small town or your girlfriend's house was an act subject to court martial or other punishment as much in Canada as with U.S. pilots. This apparently was no deterrent. The type of person willing to risk his neck in learning to fly would be very likely willing to bend the rules and risk dealing with a mere gravel-gripping officer authority later.

The aerial visits lasted only a moment. Most of the time I would be stuck in the classroom and miss the excitement. Once in a while I would be lucky enough to be outside when the buzz-job occurred. The planes weren't just slow moving Moth biplanes anymore. Now came Avro Anson twin engine bomber trainers, single engine Harvard advanced trainers, *(The familiar American AT-6, in Canadian colors),* and on one occasion, a plane very much resembling the twin- engine American built Cessna Bobcat, *(Air Corps designation-UC-78).* This plane came roaring overhead, at grain elevator altitude, at balls-out throttle. Then, just as he passed the high school, he pulled up into a gentle climb executing the traditional slow roll. A verrry slooww roll. Very impressive and superb job of flying--also very risky. This type of plane wasn't rigged for the stresses of aerobatics. By now, I knew enough about military aircraft to know that the Bobcat was not designed for inverted flight. Only the Harvard was stressed for aerobatic maneuvers, but these pilots were already risking punishment in what they were doing--so adding a little more risk to the list-- what the hell. As they came over town, all these planes would make only one quick pass in the hope that no zealous citizen or official would have time to take the aircraft's number and turn it in to the authorities. We couldn't fairly say that it was just crazy Canadians that performed these entertaining antics. Some of the lads were just as likely to be from England.

America Declares War!

One would have to be an alien from another planet not to know about Dec. 7, 1941 and Pearl Harbor. I was home on the farm for the weekend when the news came over the radio. America was suddenly officially at war. Lena was furious at the sneak attack. My dad didn't say anything, but I could see that he was deeply disturbed. In her loyalty to the U.S. Mom was torn between teaching those sneaky 'Japs' and evil German war mongers a lesson, and her fears about my being in the war and getting killed. Lena was a very upset woman. As for me, I wondered if the Army Air Corps or Navy might be desperate enough for volunteers to accept a farm boy for flight training.

Perhaps not just myself, but several young men in our county had been inspired by the aerobatic displays by our Canadian friends. A great number of them soon chose to enlist in the Air Corps. However, I had another year of college to go to be eligible.

As for the activity of our fliers across the border, the buzzing visits came to a gradual halt in the summer of 1942. The daring aviators had discovered a new thing to do with their planes--"forced landings." It started with a genuine forced landing at the Bottineau airport. Engine trouble had caused the aviators to land their Avro Anson at the small airfield north of town. The field was too small and some minor damage was incurred.

The Canadian repair crew came and in a few days had fixed 'the problem.' In the meantime, the dashing aviators had met some local girls. Awed by the uniforms, elan, and charm of the handsome young men--what girl could resist? The aircrew must have had a very fine time. Word across the border had spread through the ranks. There followed some more "forced landings" in the vicinity. This too, soon came to an end. The RCAF would pick up the crew immediately after the incident and return them to Canada. This spoiled their fun. There was one last "forced landing" at Bottineau. Perhaps this particular one also helped put an end to their adventuring.

A few other Forestry students and I had a job for the summer. This, our first government desk job, was calculating farm acreage from aerial photographs and on-field-measured maps for the AAA government office in Bottineau. Farmers were not allowed to exceed the allotted acres for planting or lose their Agricultural Adjustment payment. Rarely did we find that a farmer had exceeded his allotted acreage, but they seemed always to be within a frog's hair of penalty.

One day a fellow worker, Raymond Hanson, who had been calculating the acreage on my father's farm, jokingly yelled at me to say that my father had been farming three acres in Canada! It was not a deliberate misdeed on my dad's part. The Canadian border wasn't all that clearly defined and the north side of Jake's field bowed into Canada. The 'stolen' acres belonged to Harry Morrison, our Canadian neighbor. Raymond said that from the kindness of his heart he wouldn't turn my father in to the authorities. He added that all things considered, he couldn't count farming in foreign countries anyway.

Across the street from our office was a blacksmith's shop. The normal sound of the smith beating a plowshare into forged sharpness sounded like the lead-in to the Anvil Chorus by Geuseppi Verdi. However, one afternoon there came the unmistakable sound of an Avro Anson. We looked out the window of our second-story office and saw the twin engine plane making a slow pass as if it was intending to land. Strangely enough, either the pilot didn't see the airport or chose to ignore it. We all voiced an opinion, "Why doesn't he head for the airport?"

For whatever reason, his landing site turned out to be very badly chosen. We could see that in his final approach he had lined up for a landing in some field south of town. The landing gear remained retracted. This looked like real trouble. We couldn't see the actual landing because of trees and buildings blocking our view. This was too much for me to miss. Responsibility to my job ignored, I left my desk and headed outside to discover what had happened to the plane. It would be a long run to the location of the landing. Running on the way to the site I overtook a student nurse that I knew. She had just happened to be at that end of town visiting someone. Since she was very pretty I stopped running to walk with her. By the time we got to the crash scene, the crew had already been picked up.

No one apparently had been seriously hurt but the crash site was amusing in a disgusting sort of way. It had been a day of intermittent rain showers. The barley field that the pilot had selected for his landing was wet and the knee-high barley had been slippery as snow. The aircraft, wheels up, had slid like a toboggan across the field, through a barbed wire fence, across a small pasture and into the foul-smelling Oak Creek settling pond of Bottineau's sewage system. There, plunk in the middle of the reeking foul pond, sat the Avro Anson--about four feet deep in sewage. Through the ample side windows of the plane could be seen, hanging neatly on hangers behind the cockpit, dress uniforms appropriate to dazzle local damsels. The bottom part of the uniforms was soaking up all that 'stuff,' to put it politely.

There were no more 'forced landings' after that. Mentally I made a note that if I were ever to become a pilot, I would be very careful in selecting a field for a forced landing if the need should ever arise.

As the only son of a farmer, I knew that I probably could avoid the draft. I would also miss my only chance of joining that most esteemed awesome, wonderful legion of professionals--a pilot. So when I finished my required two years of college, I enlisted in the Army Aviation Cadet program. My mother's dismay was very apparent.

Supposedly these stories are about life in the Turtle Mountains, not my military career. However, a little background is necessary to understand how I could make an unauthorized visit home which will involve the local folk's back home. Admittedly the event was a stupid thing to do. However, as you already know, maturity, and responsibility develops late in some people.

Because so many men had enlisted, I wasn't called up right away so I continued college by going to the University of North Dakota, Grand Forks. There I waited for the orders to begin my service. The orders came in Feb. 1943.

Nearly every hopeful young man wanted to be a pilot. Only a few would choose to be a navigator, bombardier, or another aircrew skill. There had been too many volunteers, so the weeding process began early. Anyone weeded out had to go into the infantry. This was a depressing blow to the man who had hoped to become a pilot or other aircrew flyer. Even so, accepted cadets first had to go through the whole miserable torture of basic infantry training.

After completing basic infantry training I expected to start pilot training. It turned out that so many men had volunteered for the aviation cadet corps there was an overload waiting to start flight training. So believe it or not, despite the fact that I had already finished my two years, the Army sent me back to college again. Another six months down the tube in special college training for cadets in St. Louis, MO. This was to be followed by another three-month delay at ground school at Brown Field, San Antonio. Finally, Pilot Training.

Because of the many applicants, only a few would make it all the way through to becoming a pilot. Due to the surplus of applicants, we were told that the odds would be rough at the very beginning. The prospect was even worse than we were told. In general, here is a rough accounting of the washout rate on the way to receiving pilot wings. Of a sample thousand volunteers, the cadets in Class 44C, that went through the same various schools and training fields I did, only about sixty-five would have the silver wings pinned on their lieutenant's blouse. A 6.5% chance of success is damn poor odds. Despite a very close call of washing out due to airsickness, by some miracle I made it through Primary (80% washout rate) and Basic flight training. (20% washout rate) The next step would be Advanced, (10% washout rate)

Aerobatics was my strong suit, so after Primary and Basic training I was given a choice of becoming a fighter pilot or bomber pilot. Considering my getting this far despite the odds, I felt my incredible luck might just continue to hold and that I might even survive the war. The decision was difficult. Flying a nimble fighter appealed strongly to me. However, being raised by parents determined that I become a responsible wage, earning citizen and Lutheran had made a srong impression on me. After all, I had to consider the future. That is, if I had a future. Flying a fighter would perhaps be considered frivolous. Being a multi-engine pilot would give me a big advantage in getting a job flying a commercial airliner after the war was over. Responsibility being more important than frivolity, I therefore asked for bomber pilot training in Advanced and got it. The aircraft I would train in was the UC78--the same kind of plane I had seen doing a slow-roll over my hometown!

After successfully completing Advanced I was converted from being a mere cadet to the status of "Officer and a Gentleman." Big deal. The biggest achievement of my life happened when the coveted silver wings were pinned on my newly purchased uniform blouse. To me, the lieutenant's bars were ho-hum and incidental.

Winning one's wings was not the end of flight training. The next step was transition to heavy bombers. B-29's were almost secret aircraft and no fresh lieutenant would be training in those, so I opted for B-24 training, only because it was bigger than the B-17. My choice was honored. To B-24's I would go. The B-24 was a four-engine bomber weighing about 60,000 lbs. It had long slender wings, a huge double rudder and had a very boxy looking fuselage. All pilots assumed that it would be a clumsy clunk of a plane to fly and it was at first. Yet, when a pilot had a great number of hours in this bird and overcame inhibitions about being gentle as with normal aircraft, it could be a real tiger.

B-24 Transition and an Unusual Instructor

At Liberal, Kansas, A fellow student pilot, O'Brien and I were assigned to a maverick, aeronautically gifted, flight instructor, one of the best pilots I have ever encountered. *(Damn! I wish I could remember his name.)* He taught us to do things in a B-24 that can't be done in a heavy four engine, lumbering B-24. Somehow he could get that big sucker 5000' feet higher than its supposed maximum ceiling of 28,000'. He taught us how to hold altitude with three engines out. On takeoff he would pull three throttles off. With only one engine churning, we swept miles of Kansas grain fields at about fifty feet of altitude. Aerodynamically, we were flying in ground cushion effects. In formation flying he demanded we would get so close and hold steady, that the lead pilot would be having sweaty white knuckles on the control column. We did landings more befitting an aerobatic airplane than an otherwise clumsy brute of a bomber. We did forward slip, sideslip, short field landings, including a hair-raising maneuver he called the power off, overshoot, short field landing. Before he demonstrated this frightening approach and landing he had said, "Suppose just as you get back to your airfield and your last engine quits, there are clouds at pattern altitude, you spot the end of the runway through a hole in the clouds...you have no chance of a normal approach...what will you do? I'll show you."

Our instructor called the tower and told them he was going to make a high approach landing and entered the traffic pattern at normal altitude. He put the landing gear down and ten degrees of flaps. On the base leg he did not begin a let down but maintained altitude. Then he turned on what should have been a normal final approach to landing. In my mind it was impossible to land anywhere on the airport runway from our present altitude. The nose of our fuselage hid the sight of the end of the runway. At that point he cut the throttles of the engine back to idle and dumped the flaps to full down. Perhaps a single-engine fighter could have spiraled down. We weren't in an agile aircraft. What followed next seemed totally insane.

With the four windmilling propellers now acting as powerful air brakes what does he do but pull the nose up to a full stall position! The plane stalls and the nose plunges down. It will require at least 600' to recover and it appears to me that we are going to plow directly into the ground short of the runway. At just the right moment, having regained flying speed, he flares out in a graceful pullout just in time to make a feather-light touchdown on the end of the runway. We haven't used but a quarter of the runway and turn off at the first taxi strip. He says that tomorrow he will teach us how do this landing. My student buddy and I noted that the other guys didn't have to do these wild stunts.

In addition to strange emergency landings, he demonstrated every other kind of emergency that could happen and how to deal with it. He taught something else. He said that there were a lot of things he couldn't demonstrate in the air, but we could imagine. For example, he said, "Imagine that Number 3 engine has just been blown off your wing by anti-aircraft. Imagine the steps you would do to save the ship. Your brain will file such information for use later. You won't really ever forget it. When the time comes, if such trouble should occur, instead of being immobilized by panic you will do the right things to save 'er'." *Later his words proved to be correct, but that's another story that doesn't belong here.*

One day, as we were nearing the end of our training, he took my buddy pilot and me aside to where no one else could hear his confidential and cautioning words. Words, which are particularly, appropriate to the rest of my story.

"Misters, (ahem), 'gentlemen'...as you know, having been told many times, buzzing your girl friend's house or beating up your home town is not only frowned upon, but strictly forbidden."

"Yes – sir!"

"Such an offense, if you were caught, would lead to severe punishment – perhaps even court martial and loss of rank. What's more important, there is the risk of aircraft loss, the unwarranted frightening of civilians and disturbing the general peace. Furthermore – in addition to what I have just said about the official consequences, it is my opinion that no rational, sane, responsible pilot would ever do such a thing in the first place. Since none of you two brainless idiots fit that category, I feel it is my responsibility – in order to prevent future costly aircraft loss, that I must give you verbal instructions about how to do low-level flying in the safest possible manner."

We hung on his every word. We knew he was an expert on the subject. Didn't he, on our first indoctrination ride in the B-24, fly down the length of the Grand Canyon at about two hundred feet above the turbid water of the Colorado? Didn't he say that he knew where to make those violent banking turns because he, as a young man, was still one of those few men to have gone down that turbulent river in a boat? We nodded at each other in appreciation of his expertise. He went on revealing the details of a forbidden buzz job.

"Never buzz on a sudden impulse. The flight must be planned like any other mission. First check your aeronautical chart and note the heights of any local obstacles – radio antennas, lookout towers or local peaks. Expect the unexpected. A new tower may have been erected since the printing of the chart. Use your f...ing Goddam eyes! One of the dumb things stupid pilots do is to back off on the throttles to have more time to view the scene below. The airspeed drops and the moron stalls-in with no chance to recover."

My fellow student and I were spellbound at his wealth of logical information. Low flying was obviously an art filled with potholes of potential disaster. As for subconsciously reducing throttle, he explained that this is a psychological response to be aware of. "At high altitude the ground appears to be moving slowly. At low altitude the ground appears to be moving swiftly and the idiot pilot unconsciously reduces airspeed." To prevent this, he said to lock your throttles at cruise velocity. For the B-24, he recommended 165 MPH. Set flaps at ten degrees for max. aileron response...etc.

He covered all the fine points of buzzing which may never had occurred to O'Brien or me. When he had finished, these are the instructions he gave in closing, "Just remember what I told you – never, I repeat, buzz your girlfriend's house. Her father might just be smart enough to copy a number to identify your plane."

1944 Lowry Field, Denver

For some reason that I never found out, I was one of four people from the Liberal, Kansas group of pilots finishing transition not to be sent overseas. Instead, I was sent to Lowry Field, Denver, to be an instructor pilot. As it turned out, I was more often an odd-jobs pilot. One day I would be flying an indoctrination flight for a bunch of disgruntled ex-fighter pilots. Next would be flying a cargo version of the B-24 (C-87) converted to B-29 flight engineer training. *(Installed in this aircraft was six complete B29 flight-engineer control panels.)* Once, I even picked up a load of beer in Texas for the officers club in Liberal, **dry**-Kansas. Some of these flights would be boring. For example, the six-hour milk run to Rapid City, South Dakota then Billings, Montana and return. "Deac" Evans, a buddy fellow pilot, sometimes had to fly the same dull run. I don't know who thought of it, but we discovered we could spice that trip up by a low fly-by of Mt. Rushmore. Whoever we had on board always seemed to enjoy the quick fly-by of the granite faces of Washington, Jefferson, T. Roosevelt, and Lincoln. They always promised to keep mum in appreciation of our tour. Certainly we had to devise careful schemes to avoid getting caught by wary eyes and binoculars on the part of some ranger. To avoid being heard until it was too late, we had to come in with minimum noise. From considerable altitude we would glide in, engines idling with cowl flaps closed to keep the engines warm. At the right moment we'd open the throttles and roar by at low altitude. It was good training for my trip home to the Turtle Mountains.

Most of the B-24's at Lowry field had seen service overseas or somewhere else. They had been returned for modification, which meant that gun-turrets had been removed and the holes neatly faired over with aluminum skin. Bombsights, spare radio gear, etc.--any equipment not required for combat was taken out. As a result, the aircraft was tons lighter and flew faster. The lighter plane with four 1200 hp. Pratt and Whitney engines could climb like a P-47 Thunderbolt. A hopped-up ship was a condition we frequently took advantage of. Often we would rendezvous and fly in very close formation just for the fun of it.

Visit Opportunity Taken, Exact Date Forgotten

Arriving at flight operations one early morning I picked up my flight assignment. It was to be the milk run to Billings with a mixed bunch of men, mostly combat veterans back for reassignment. The only person I had flown with before was "Packrat," my favorite crew chief. He had a useful habit of collecting small spare parts, which he had scrounged and always carried with him in his tool kit. Somehow this was comforting, though I admit I was a little hard pressed as to how he planned to repair a plane in mid flight. When asked, his standard answer was, "Well, you never know, we might have to land at some dumb field in Nebraska or sum'pin."

My copilot was an ex-fighter pilot who was mad as hell that he had been relegated to flying in an ugly boxcar of a plane. He made no bones about saying that he would be ashamed to have any of his flying fighter buddies see him in it. It was my job to indoctrinate him. That I would. His attitude burned me. In reality, the copilot's duties were simple and could be performed very well by Packrat, the crew chief.

Two of the men were navigators who were just going up to earn their four hours flight time to collect flight pay. There was also a bombardier, a radio operator and a couple gunners, all getting their indoctrination flights. Why they need indoctrination flights I didn't know. A B-24 wasn't all that functionally different from a B-17. Another reason for the flight, a new engine had recently been installed and needed a checkout. With this mixed and motley crew the situation was ripe for my planned change of mission. One I would wait to explain when we were out at the plane.

Following the advice of my instructor at Liberal, I had planned ahead. I had rehearsed my speech several times before I presented it.

"Gentlemen – today, as you know, we are scheduled to go on the milk run to Billings. "Plan A." We can do this and it will be very boring. However, if you would like to have a more enjoyable and exciting trip, including a visit to Mt. Rushmore, I can deviate from the official plan. If you would like the deviation that I will propose – I want your word that what we do on this flight will be kept confidential." Not too surprising, they approved "Plan B."

"Navigators, I suspect that you already have in your flight cases the well- worn route to Billings. As an exercise to hone your navigation skills, you may keep track of where I've taken you today. If you are correct I'll give you top grades on the course of where we <u>supposedly</u> went on the way to Billings. Here are two charts you probably don't have in your flight case. (The Minot sectionals) The first leg to Rapid City, South Dakota, remains the same."

According to the milk run, the first leg to Rapid City was a 313-mile flight on a true course of 16.1 degrees. The second leg to Billings a 283-mile flight. Course 296.4 degrees. My proposed change: the second leg to Bottineau would be 82 miles further. 365 miles at 17.3 degrees. By pushing the throttle a nudge. I could make up the time difference and arrive back at Denver precisely on schedule. The flight would take 6.8 hours.

At 11,500 feet mean sea level we were approaching the first scenic tour flight, the Mt. Rushmore fly-by. I eased the throttles back and closed the cowl flaps to keep the engines warm at idle. The silent gliding approach began. The little mountain and its faces became visible in the down distance. On the flight deck, the waist opening and in the windowed nose of the navigator/bombardier deck everyone watched the approaching sculpture. My ship's numbers were painted on the sides of the fuselage and rudder. By going directly over the ranger station, it would be unlikely that a ranger could get my number. If I came in silently he wouldn't even have time to focus his binoculars if he had them. I kept the nose pointed down in the direction of the tourist center and ranger station. Airspeed 180. At just the right time, I eased the throttles forward again to full power and roared by the faces at the altitude of Washington's chin. The sight was appreciated by my passengers. Cowl flaps reopened, engines at climb power we climbed back to altitude and set the new course for Bottineau and my farm home on the Canadian border.

On the way to Bottineau I had a new idea--a dumb one. Completely forgetting the importance of remaining anonymous I thought it would be nice to drop a friendly note to Leonard Berg, the editor of the BOTTINEAU COURANT. In my School Of Forestry years, as a friendly gesture he had kindly loaned me his Speed Graphic press camera a few times to take home to the farm on weekends.

I called Packrat to the flight deck. I told him I wanted to drop a message that I would write to a friend. What I needed was something that would be more visible that a mere sheet of paper that would flutter away in the wind. He went to his scrounge kit and returned with a red mechanic's rag. This too, I thought might be too light and drift away unseen. He came back with a big 5/8" steel nut for a weight. I wrote the note and wrapped it around the nut, but I needed something to secure it. Again back to his trusty tool kit and he came with a short piece of wire. That wrapped around the folded cloth in the corner of the rag secured the note.

There would be no need to sneak up on Bottineau since there would be no National Rangers with notebook in hand. Halfway beyond Minot, N.D., I began the standard letdown, maintaining a 190-MPH airspeed. As Liberal instructor had advised to do on a forbidden buzz job, five miles from my hometown we leveled off at about 300' above the ground and reduced the speed to 165, put down 10 degrees flaps and locked the throttles. The town came into sight. It looked better from the air that I expected. It appeared as a pretty, very orderly, small town. White painted homes, clean business buildings, and colorful grain elevators sparkled in the sunlight near the foothills of the Turtle Mountains. Soon the town slipped below us. We roared overhead, rocking the wings as a "hello" gesture and continued in a gentle climb to clear the forests of the hills rising ahead. We didn't drop the note on that pass. First, I revisited the irregular goofy shaped lake of my youth, Metigoshe. Then a sweeping turn into Canada to pay back earlier visits from the Canadian pilots and now, on to the farm. Three minutes to home.

To my left, familiar scenes flashed by below. Still over Canadian soil I headed for Lloyd Stewart's farm, my folk's neighbor immediately north of our farm. Following my flight plan, just before his place, I would turn for my home. Hoping that my folks would be home I dropped lower--to about a hundred feet, less than the wingspan of a B-24. Our farm was just ten seconds ahead. The trees of the windbreak, the white house, red-painted outbuildings, and barn rushed toward me. There, in the driveway by the lilacs was my mother. She was wearing a blue and white patterned housedress. I had expected to see her in overalls and that white cotton jacket she liked to wear. But where was Dad? Where was Carl? As I thundered by overhead, Mom waved her towel.

No slow-roll was prudent in this big bird so I pulled up, made a tight circle over our pasture of startled cows. Then I began another pass from the opposite direction. Again Lena waved wildly, almost dancing. Even in a steep bank at low altitude, my turn carried me across the border again over Harry Morrison's farm. Then I headed for Arnold's, my brother-in-law's place, less than a minute away.

Wunderlich's farm was at the end of a ravine going into the hills of the Turtle Mountains. When we got there, Arnold was standing in the farmyard as I headed up the tree filled narrow ravine. I could see his upturned astonished face as we sped overhead. Some crewmember, looking backward through the waist window, yelled over the intercom that I had scared the hell out of a bunch of flapping chickens. The down wash from the plane had kicked up a maelstrom of dust, straw, and Leghorns around Arnold. I hadn't seen my sister Eva. Damn! I hoped she hadn't missed my visit. (To my disappointment, I learned later that she had.)

After swooping up out of the ravine, I made a gentle turn over the hills to head for another run at Bottineau, I cracked open the bomb bay doors about a foot in preparation for the message drop in my return pass over my hometown. In the meantime the intercom was busy with guys talking. They were spotting frightened deer running in the open glades of the forest.

"This must be great huntin' country!"

"Jeeze...lookit all the little lakes... How's fishin' up here about's?" I didn't have time to answer just then.

Three minutes to Bottineau. Following the north hill road which lines up with Mainstreet, I motioned to Packrat to come closer to where I could tell him to get ready to drop. He wasn't wearing a headset. Standing slightly behind my seat, he leaned closer to hear as I shouted instructions. Unlike stupid Hollywood movies where aircrews have almost normal communication, World

War II aircraft interiors were as noisy as boiler factories filled with demented workmen swinging sledgehammers.

"Stand in the flight deck well and throw the rag out when I turn and yell **now!**" With my hands busy on the controls, I couldn't just signal with a wave of the arm. Despite the engine noise he may hear me. At least he could see my mouth open. It was my hope that someone in town would see the dropping rag, find it, and deliver it to Mr. Berg. Considering our speed, using the verbal signal and response, I felt we would be damn lucky to get the message down within a half mile of the intended target--the newspaper office.

Packrat opened the flightdeck hatch and was already in place and poised ready to throw the message through the slightly open bomb bay doors. I lined up on Main Street for the final run. It would be five seconds to drop-time after passing the grandstand at the county fairgrounds. This time I brought the plane down to a level, which would be slightly below, but easily bypass the top of the highest obstacle, the town water tower. We were a mile away from the drop. My 'fighter-pilot' copilot looked very nervous. Good! He had complained that he had been missing excitement. This was good for his soul.

The fairgrounds slipped by. The street, directly below, was obscured by the long nose of the plane. By counting seconds without looking at my watch the moment to drop would still be a guess – 5-4-3 – I turned my head and yelled "**NOW!**"

Packrat dropped the message. I unlocked the throttles, opened them to max climb RPM, changed pitch and boosted the boosters. At the same time I flicked the switch to close the bomb bay doors and rocked my wings from side to side as a farewell greeting. Then we made a steep climbing circle over town before departing on our return to Denver. To give our navigators a chance to exercise their skills I had requested our return course. Once on the proper compass heading I gave my cocky copilot the controls for the whole distance back. Occasional turbulence kept it from being too boring. There were times he had to battle the controls, as I yelled at him to "Godammit stay on course." Control forces on the B-24s were not light and it took considerable effort to maintain a precise heading in rough weather. He soon learned not to be timid with the control column and rudder pedals for the big double barndoor rudders.

By flying a straight-line return, we got back to Lowry Field at the proper time equaling a flight to Billings. As usual, a number of B-24s were also returning from their flights. The landing sequence was supposed to be established by the control tower but when too many aircraft returned at once, the tower tended to just give up and let the airborne pilots sort it out by playing "chicken" and with sneaky maneuvering. This time was no exception. Gear down and 30° flaps set, I turned onto the base leg of the traffic pattern. Then I saw an extra B-24 who was dragging in on a long approach. That SOB would cut out my final and I'd have to go around again…unless? ... Yeah, there was a way to land behind the interloper. Better yet, here was an excellent opportunity for my copilot to experience a power-off, over-shoot, short-field landing. I informed my crew and passengers by intercom to strap-down and hang-on for an unusual but safe landing.

First we had to slow down to allow enough time for the plane on final to get ahead of us, so I throttled back. By maintaining altitude at reduced power the airspeed would drop off; however we would also be too high for a normal approach. As we turned onto final I turned to my fighter pilot in the right hand seat and loudly told him not to panic or try to take over the controls at any time. He looked quizzical, but pretended to be nonchalant. The other plane had cleared the end of the runway. Good time for special handling, an intentional stall on final approach to get rid of a lot of altitude in a hurry--back the throttles to idle, dump full flaps and pull the nose up. The propellers of the idling engines quickly become four big windmilling airbrakes. We can feel the forward surge in our seats as we rapidly lose our speed. It doesn't take but a few seconds to full stall, then the nose plunges downward, pointing at the trash dump at the edge of the airfield. What my colleague in the right hand seat yells as we plunge vertically is not fit for print. We are plummeting like a sash weight, his hands grip his seat, a real case of 'white knuckles.' Timing is critical. Airspeed regained, I ease the control column back to flare out. We are still a hundred feet high, perfect--the intended height-cushion for safety. Now a hard forward slip to quickly get rid of excess altitude and simultaneously slow down. It takes a lot of leg force on the rudder pedals to slip a '24. The boxcar fuselage sides create a hell of a lot of drag, the airspeed quickly approaches stall just as we clear the edge of the runway with five feet height to spare. The big bird responds beautifully as I kick her into alignment on the yellow line. Luckily, the touchdown can hardly be felt, a grease-job. We easily turn off on the first taxiway and have our ship parked before the B-24 who had been ahead of us has been able to return to the parking ramp.

Walking back from the parked airplane, everybody said they had had a good time but admitted to being a little shaky from the 'interesting' landing. One of the men told me he was going to write home and tell his folks that he had 'visited' Canada. This made me recall that first visit by a Canadian Tiger Moth. Wondering what my hotshot copilot was thinking I glanced his way. His cockiness somewhat restored, he actually had a smile on his face. Referring to our modified B-24, he said, "that fat ugly turkey ain't too bad a bird at that."

A week later I got a letter from Mom. I learned that my dad, Jake, had been in his car on the way to town and had missed the flight. So had Carl. As for anyone getting my number and turning me in, I need not have bothered using all that cautious flying technique to prevent identification while buzzing as prescribed by my instructor in Liberal. **Not when I was stupid enough to drop a signed letter.** In the next issue, the message to editor Berg was boldly printed in the paper for all the world to see. Luckily, it being a small town paper, it never reached the eyes of any Air Corps officer who could raise hell with my flying career. Luck of idiots!

That was not all of my dumb luck. In the local article the editor praised the ability of the U.S. Air Corps for its "remarkable bombing accuracy." The message had landed on a shed in the alley immediately behind the COURANT office! Fifty feet east and it would have landed at the front door. He actually believed we had come this close as the result of skill at precision bombing.

IMAGES

There are a bunch of scenes, things, and impressions that linger in my mind, leftovers from a feast of experiences more than a half-century ago. These moments were brief, too short to justify a long story, too demanding in my memory to ignore.

Being born and raised in the middle of nowhere isn't all that bad. Almost seventy years later, images of my boyhood remain--flies caught in the tangled web of my mind. These images recalled are included because for want of a video camera that long ago, it is the best I can do to picture the way it was. If I took the time, perhaps I could just weave the scenes into my Turtle Mountain tales to enhance the stories, but that would be a lot of work. Whenever possible, I do things the easy way. These are but single grapes, which may add up to a bunch.

SPRING (Early Boyhood)

Crocuses? Wind Flowers? Anemones?

Walking to school I must first cross our pasture. It is a sunny spring day. The sky, for now, is clear. By afternoon it will be filled with white gray-bottomed clouds. It is too nice a day to be wasted in school; I would rather stay home. The creek is filled with the last of the runoff from the Turtle Mountains. The cow path I am following is on the sloping side of our pasture hill. On either side of the path, crocuses are blooming again--pale-blue splashes on the hillside. Yesterday our teacher told us these flowers aren't crocuses at all, they are pasque flowers. *(Pulsatilla vulgaris)* Somehow the correct name doesn't matter to me, they are pretty and friendly. Furry petals, blue on the outside, cream-white on the inside, surround yellow-orange anthers and stamen. Like the petals, the flower stems and leaves are covered with delicate fur as if clothed against the chilling wind. The fine fuzz somehow brings to mind a kitten. After plucking a few flowers to bring to the teacher, I then cross the icy creek on the narrow plank.

At school, on the teachers desk is a tumbler filled with fresh crocuses, er-- pasque flowers. Those damn girls have beaten me again.

Crows

Gray gloomy clouds cover the entire sky. I'm a mile from home. A cold, raw April wind reinforces my desire to be sitting in our kitchen having a cup of warm chocolate milk. My attention is drawn to the black crow aloft. Not very high, it is pumping its way against the wind. It is followed by another crow about a hundred yards behind. Behind that crow is another, behind that another--a line of crows as far as I can see. All are going in the same direction on the same course, northeast. In a way it is an eerie sight. An odd way to migrate. Why don't they fly together in formation like the geese do? Strange bird, the crow.

Meadowlark

There, I heard it, "Yoo hee diddle de do," a meadowlark; spring is here to stay for sure. There will be no more morning frosts now that he's here.

Aspen

Downwind from the aspen grove we can smell that the pregnant buds have given birth again. Bottle that scent and make a fortune in the aftershave lotion business. Soon the crows will be building a nest in those trees. Crow babies are sure ugly, so ugly that I wonder why the parents don't abandon them. They are certainly nothing to crow about.

Spring Plowing

Carl's tractor is a two-cylinder John Deere. It has a large flywheel on the side. The cylinders are very large and it runs loudly at low RPM. A person could almost count the firing-stroke explosions of the engine. The neighbor's tractor is a McCormick-Deering, four cylinders. Nobody could count those explosions. In the early morning there isn't any wind and sound carries well. From all directions comes the distant muted clatter of two-lunges and four-lungers--all racing against the calendar to turn the loam in time for spring planting.

As the packed earth of last year's crop curls away from the three-bottom plow, gulls follow to see what turns up. I've seen pictures of gulls in a magazine but these must be a different kind. However, to me, the graceful creatures now flying behind the plow *(Franklin's gull)* must be the most elegant and prettiest of all the gulls.

With mewing laughter sounds, they hover, and make wheeling turns as they closely follow the plow. Unseen by human eyes, but to them a wiggling morsel is suddenly revealed in the inverted earth. In a twinkle, two, or three gulls swoop, dive, for same tidbit. It would seem impossible to avoid a midair collision. Yet they never do.

Relentlessly the plow plows on. The black-ribboned area grows larger. A big stone pile, a round mound of gathered boulders in the field means Carl has to depart the straight furrow, and swerve around it. When both sides have been plowed around, the stone pile is now an eye, blindly staring up into space.

Ice Breakup

Yesterday the runoff from the hills filled more than the creek. The big icy snowdrift under and over the bridge dammed the stream. A lake then filled the bottomland all the way to the neighbors across the way. Last night the lake froze over. Today the creek broke through under the bridge. Sounds of ice blocks clumsily jostling under the wooden span make rumbling sounds similar to the sounds of the railroad switching yard in Minot. Maybe the creek will warm up enough in a couple weeks to try swimming.

Wrens

A late spring day, Lena takes the washing down to the clothesline. Reaching into the clothespin bag hanging on the wire, she finds it full of twigs. She cusses in Norwegian. "Forbandet! *(dammit)* The wrens are back again." It is stuffed full of debris. Lena turns the bag inside out--twigs, pins, all fall on the ground. Carefully, she picks out all the clothespins and puts them back into the bag. She has an idea to put a stop to this desecration--a birdhouse compromise.

Jake has been ordered to build, and put up a nesting box to keep them from using Lena's pin bag. It doesn't work as planned. Oh, the wrens are using the nesting box all right--but that doesn't keep them from filling the bag again. Wrens are anti-social. They never want any other bird to move into the neighborhood. To prevent this, they simply plug up any potential cavity. Each year the same ritual occurs. Even Jake is not immune to wren trouble.

Late summer--time for Pa to get the reaper in order. On the back of the reaper is a twine can capable of holding two big rolls of binder twine. This can is about four-*gallon* volume in size. In the sides of the can are two holes to visually check the twine supply. Just like last summer, Jake opens the lid to find it stuffed to the brim with twigs. The wrens again! This is a very big container. A wren is a very tiny bird--talk about being an overachiever.

Berry Pickin' Time

Neighbor drops in to say hello. "Just got down from the hills...unless we get a late frost we're gonna have one hell of a crop of juneberries this year." *juneberries, a local term--also called shadberry, saskatoons, sarvisberry highbush blueberries, depending on where in North America one lives.)*

A few weeks later my 'old' sister, Evelyn, calls Ma up on the party line. She, being married to Arnold, lives in the foothills. A few berry bushes are in their farmyard. After a while Lena hangs up the phone. She has good news. "Eva says that the berries are ripe..."

We go berry picking. We get a few milk pails full. That evening we take off all our clothes in the yard and examine ourselves for wood ticks. In hidden private places we look for the secretive blood-hungry little bastards. We find a few.

During the next two days the kitchen is a mess of jars, rubber sealing rings, paraffin, strainers, and the odor of aspen-wood burning in our "Monarch" wood burning range.

Finally, on the pinewood shelves of our musty cellar rest a regiment of Mason jars holding blue-black berries waiting to fill a dessert dish, or piled on a stack of pancakes to brighten the gloom of a snowy winter morning.

SUMMARY (Early Boyhood)

Mirage

Pa called everybody to go outside this morning and have a look at Goodlands. "Look at Goodlands?" He must be joshing. Yet, we knew something special was occurring because Jake hardly ever got excited about anything. Goodlands, Manitoba is a small town about six miles north of our farm. We normally can't see it from our place because of a gentle roll of the land.

We all went outside to the driveway from whence we can look to the north. There, in the sunlight, we could see the whole village of Goodlands, grain elevators, trees, houses and all. Ma said it was a mirage. Well, I had seen mirages before on warm mornings in the flat country, but nothing like this. Those mirages looked like a silver lake in the distance. Once I had seen buildings that appeared upside down. Today Goodlands was right side up just as if it had been lifted into the air. I asked how this could happen. Even Carl didn't know. Goodlands didn't last an hour. It disappeared when the wind came up.

Circus in Souris *(my age? Too young to walk far, too old to be carried far.)*

We are in Souris today. Something about this day is going to be special. I can feel it, even though no one has said anything to me about it. Ma is buying things in the dry goods store. Pa is mostly talking to old farming friends who greet him and tell jokes I don't understand. After a while it seems like everybody in town is gathering to stand on the sidewalks. Pa tells me there is going to be a circus parade--whatever that is. We stand a long time on a board sidewalk. Nearby, a stout man wearing a town suit reaches into his vest pocket and pulls out a watch. He opens it, adjusts his wire-rimmed glasses and puzzles the big hand little hand, snaps the lid shut, and puts it back in the little pocket. He turns to a person staring glumly at the far end of Main. "Damn near a half hour late already."

Suddenly a loud sound assails my ears, **boom, boom, boom.** Then strange music is added to the beat. Coming around the hotel at the south end of Main are a bunch of men in formation wearing red, yellow and violet uniforms. When they come closer I can see gold braid on their sleeves. They are wearing strange hats with fancy feathers stuck on top. Cheeks puffed out; musicians are playing sun- gold instruments and marching at the same time. The small man with the huge drum pounds the cadence. A tall man with a little whistle tube is squeaking what seems to be a melody totally different from the others.

"Circus band," says Pa.

After the band come clowns. After the bulb-nosed clowns come white horses with fancy harness and feather plumes. They are pulling glittering golden animal cages. The first live elephant I have ever seen is pulling a fancy cage. Inside is a dull-faced lion. Young handsome men and women, aliens from some other planet amble by. They are smiling as if they knew everybody. Wearing colored sparkling long underwear, it seems to me that they should feel embarrassed--but they sure don't seem to be. The band walks to one side and continues to play exciting music. More wagons and more sparkling people pass by. The parade then turns the corner at the far end of Main Street near the high school and disappears.

Farmers, town folks, slowly go back to doing the normal things of Saturday. Saying "We gotta go home now and do the milking." Pa then takes me by the hand and we head for our car parked on a side street.

On the way home I try to understand what I had just seen. Circus parades are very wonderful and interesting, but what are they for? What's the point? No matter, I just hope I can see a circus parade again someday.

Thunder

A very huge cloud is building in the west. The sun from behind illuminates a crooked silver line on top. The flicker of lightning frequently lights the blue, dark bottom. Ma says to get some firewood for the stove. She is hoping it will rain, the crops need it. I'm hoping it will rain to fill the swimming hole, I sure need to learn how to swim. The rumbling distant thunder is music to all our ears. We hope it will continue getting louder and rain. Standing on our weather- watching knoll, we try to ascertain the path of the storm and hope it won't pass us this time--like last time. It does. Even late at night we can still hear the faint distant and dying rumble from the east.

Next day, Ma calls a neighbor to the south to ask if they got any rain. "Forty hundredths? I'm glad you got some anyway...no, we didn't get any." After a while Ma hangs up. I can tell she is envious as hell.

Frogs

Frogs in the creek are serenading this evening. Nice sound. The other night, that second storm? It didn't miss us. It filled a little slough out in our field that has been bone-dry for two years. Right away there came the croaking sounds of frogs. Where did they come from all of a sudden? Where there was dust is now water and mud complete with frogs. Frogs aren't like a magical weed-seed that can sprout and grow overnight years later. Or can they?

Mosquitoes

They are sure bad since that rain a couple of weeks ago. Pa had to build a smudge-fire out in the pasture. The dam mosquitoes were driving our cattle nutty. Ma said they wouldn't give much milk at milking time.

Jake first gathered up a lot of damp green stuff--ragweed, green Canadian Thistle, green Russian thistle, green anything. Then he built a scrap wood fire on the gentle side hill sloping to the creek. When he dumped the green stuff on it, a dense white cloud of smoke drifted along the ground up the slope. For some strange reason the cattle knew what the smoke was for and headed for it.

Now, Whitey, our boss cow, is the one closest to the fire where the smoke is most dense. She, with her Viking horns, made certain of that. Whitey sure looks strange with nothing but her head poking out of the smoke cloud and feet poking out the bottom. It's amazing how stupid a cow can appear, but I know better. They are not as dumb as they look--an expression we've heard before. However, it's sure true when it comes to cows. When they give us that stupid looking stare they are really thinking we are the dumb ones, having to take care of them seven days a week all year. To the herd we are their slaves.

Watermelons

Carl came home from town with a big watermelon today. It was the first one I had ever seen. Ma said that after supper we would go outside for a watermelon treat--a place where we could spit the seeds on the ground without having to wash dishes.

Carl sliced it up on the picnic table under the box elders. Hard striped-green rind yielded to the big butcher knife. An inch of white-green and then the bright- red cells. In a very short time we were devouring sweet, watery chunks out of the slices. Up until now I thought pin cherries had the best taste in the world. The taste of this delicacy from a foreign land is beyond belief. Everything about this oversized berry is a treat, not only its cool, sugary flavor, but like seeing how far you can blow the black seeds onto the lawn. I make a decision – "Someday I'm going to live where fruit like this can be grown."

Ma says that the Indviks can grow them up in the hills. Well?--she lied to me about Santa Claus--so this I've got to see for myself. Ma said that she even grew some--here on the farm in a patch near the creek.

"What? – Here, on our own farm?" Unbelievable.

She went on with the story claiming that just when they were about ripe, somebody stole them. She said she knew who but didn't want to cause trouble. Cause trouble? I thought she should have killed 'em.

Gypsies and Puppy Love

Saturday evening, after supper, we are on our way to Souris to visit relatives. In the front seat, Pa is driving. Ma is looking left and right out of the side windows at the grain fields we are passing. As usual, Pa isn't talking while Ma chatters endlessly. Her favorite subject, verbally judging the neighbor's crops, usually with the comments "wooden head...he should have done... instead... (Etc)"

After a mile and a half west over the roller coaster dirt road, we approach the corner where we will turn south. Coming over the last hill before the turn, we see that there are people and objects gathered around a bonfire. They are on that grassy patch of ground where some optimists had tried to drill and find oil a couple of years ago[21]. There are four, no--five, strange wagons there. They look like covered wagons except the tops aren't made of canvas. The tops and end panels are solid, made of thin curving wood or something. As we get closer I can see that every available space is covered with painted flowers, small scenic panels surrounded by vines and other ornate stuff.

Ma, with a derisive tone, said, "Gypsies are back again... Well Jake, you think maybe we should go home and guard the chicken coop?"

"Neyda," Jake answered, "If they come they won't take more than one or two." Ma thought about what he said for a while before she muttered, "Well – mmm, ya – I guess you're right. They don't have much, being always on the go like that. Maybe we should just give them a couple?"

"Neyda – they might take that as an insult. Stealing isn't wrong to them, a present would be accepting charity."

I didn't understand what Pa meant by that.

As we turned the corner and went slowly by, I saw a girl about eleven or twelve years old. She was standing, staring into the small fire. The sun was low in the west and the bright fire lit her wistful dreaming face. She was there, yet somehow not there. Her hair was <u>unlike the hair of any girl I had ever seen</u>. **Black!** A cloud of black hair flowed back over her slim shoulders almost to her waist. I had never seen a girl with raven black hair before, just blondes. Her thin body wore a long dress, embroidered with more floral stuff. Her arms hung down, her hands clasped loosely in front. The adult women near the fire, and men attending to the horses looked at us but didn't wave a greeting. Ma waved

---

[21] *If the optimist's who tried for oil at that spot of ground had been able to drill another 800 feet they would probably have struck oil. Twenty-five years later, oil was found nearby and is being pumped today. My folks had a few shares in that first attempt.*

weakly, but got no return greeting. The little girl, lost in her own world, didn't even look at our passing car. The view lasted less than a minute. Though she must have been a head taller than I--I instantly fell in love with that little girl. Now, sixty-three years later, remembering and writing--I'm still in love with that girl and wonder if she ever got to the place of her dreams.

Next morning, Pa went to the chicken coop and counted chickens. He came back and reported they were all there. I felt sorry for the girl with the black hair. What did she have to eat instead of chicken?

Vaudeville and Moving Pictures

Saturday afternoon Carl got that "I've got a treat for you" look on his face. That look always signaled that a pleasant surprise was about to occur. My hunch was right, he said we were going to Souris tonight to see a vaudeville show and a cowboy movie. *(Carl, my uncle, who lived with us, was to me, such a natural part of our family, I didn't know then that it* was *unusual to have two "fathers.")* Carl didn't explain what a vaudeville show was. I was too embarrassed of my ignorance of vaudeville to ask. It didn't matter, tonight I'd find out for myself.

In town Pa and Ma went to visit relatives, Aunt Anna, Aunt Selma, and husbands Victor and Albert. After the obligatory niceties of relative greeting relative, Carl and I went to the Souris 'Opera house' to see when the show would start. We had to wait an hour. Since it is Saturday night most all the local farmers were in town, so Carl will do a lot of visiting in the meantime.

Nearing show time, it is obvious that tonight is going to be very special as more folks than usual crowd near the theater. People line up at the ticket booth and buy tickets, then head for the door. Over and around the ticket booth is a row of light bulbs flashing so they appear to be moving, lights endlessly chasing each other, Carl buys some tickets and we go in.

Inside, we look for a place to sit. The seats are hard benches with hard backs. Behind us, above the entrance hall, is the projection booth. On either side of the booth is an upstairs balcony with more seats. A bunch of young guys are scuffling around up there sometimes throwing peanuts at each other and other targets down on the main floor. Ignoring the rowdy guys, I stare ahead at the fancy custom-made flat curtain, which normally covers the movie screen. In the center is a painted scene inside a big oval, simulated gold, painted ornate frame. Carl says the picture is of some place in Italy. In my opinion the artist is good at painting buildings and the spouting fountain, but he didn't know much about painting trees. Even I know what the real shape of an evergreen is like from the pictures I had seen in NATIONAL GEOGRAPHIC. The trees the artist had painted were very skinny, sharply pointed, and stood apart from each other like a row of soldiers. For another thing, nearly all the buildings had marble columns. It didn't seem logical to me that every building in Italy would be a bank.

Surrounding the oval scene are painted advertisements for the local stores in Souris. "E.L.Garden FURNITURE AND HARDWARE – Quality merchandise at fair prices." "MONKMAN'S CONFECTIONERY – *Sweets for your sweety.*" "STATE BANK OF SOURIS" – Etc. Surely one of those merchants who had paid for the painted curtain should have complained about those dumb trees.

"Time for the show to start" said Carl as he slid his big Hamilton watch back into the bib pocket of his for-town-wear-only overalls. Shortly after he says it, the piano player comes out from a side door and starts putting sheet music on the upright piano. The piano player is followed by a tall, gaunt man with long hair. He is carrying a violin and trumpet. He in turn is followed by a short guy in strange shiny suit with big lapels who sits down behind an array of drums and cymbals.

It is certain that tonight really is going to be different--a show with three musicians had never happened before. A few moments later, the seated piano player nodded to the drummer who then started a drum roll as the painted curtain rolled up.

There, in the lights and standing still as a fencepost on the small stage is a dude in a fancy black-tailed suit and top hat. He tips his hat and bows to the audience as if we were the most important people in the world. He also has a cane, the kind that old folks hobble around with, except he isn't very old. He bows again with a sweeping exaggerated flourish. The audience claps, glad the show is finally getting started.

The city-dude smiles and looks at everybody. Then he makes a short speech about how glad he is to be in this fine city. I think he is lying. He says he is the master of ceremonies. He then walks over to an easel on the side of the stage and removes the first card which has the name of the vaudeville show on it. The next card has the name of a person in the opening act. For those whom he guesses can't read, he announces in a large pompous voice – *"(Name long forgotten)* Vaudeville Company is proud to present..." and leaves the stage.

Drum roll again, followed by piano and violin. A man in a disheveled red and white checkered suit came on stage pretending to be drunk. The violin makes sounds that mockingly make him seem even drunker. Actually he is a skillful juggler doing impossible things with his derby hat, tossing a bunch of empty bottles, billiard balls, and other stuff he keeps finding in that baggy suit of his. The drummer bangs time to match all the movements. The violinist switches instruments as needed. Folks applaud at each change of flying objects and when the juggler-drunk is finished, clap hands like crazy.

Following the juggler comes a comedy skit involving a pretty lady with a sparkly dress, much too small for her. She meets the sharp city-guy and the very stupid acting person. They are asking dumb questions, giving answers that made no sense to me at all, doing goofy things and talking, yelling, in general saying nonsensical things. All the grown-ups are laughing. I ask Carl, "What's so funny?"

"I'll, ha, ha, ha, tell you, ha, ha, later," laughing until tears stream down his cheeks.

There were a few more acts. Then that curtain painted with the grotesque trees came down. Then it went up again and the actors stood holding hands and bowed as people applauded. That part of the show is over. In some ways vaudeville is really very silly.

Now for the Tom Mix movie following the vaudeville show.

The curtain came down again for a while. The drummer and trumpet/violin player left. The pianist stayed and brought out a booklet of sheet music for the movie to follow.

When the curtain went up again, the old familiar white screen for movies was up. The movie started with piano accompaniment. The picture show is about a cowboy out to get even with bad guys. The actor's name is Tom Mix. He wears an oversized white hat that must be glued to his head. He never takes it off. It never blows off in the wind. It never falls off when he gets into a fistfight. Even so, I get involved with the action and hope the bad guys will get what's coming to them.

The shoot-ups disappoint me. Even as a kid I know that Six-guns normally have a load of six cartridges. The cowboys seem to have revolvers with a hundred bullets in them. The pistols puff big clouds of white smoke when they fire. Our guns at home don't puff white smoke. Neither the bad guys nor good guys can shoot worth a damn either. Most of the shots miss. My pa wouldn't miss. At the end of the movie some moon-eyed girl who looks like she is about to cry sags against a porch post as Tom rides away on his horse. Thank God, the ending is OK. I'm so glad he doesn't get stuck with that dumb girl.

Later, on the way home, I think about the great time I had. Well, now I know what a vaudeville show is, and have seen a Tom Mix movie. Then I remember the vaudeville comedy act and the jokes I couldn't understand. Carl had said he'd tell me later what was so funny, so I ask him to explain. Carl starts to say something, hesitates, then has a lapse of memory or something...says he can't remember.

FALL (Later Boyhood)

Farm Auctions

Ma sees a notice in the BOTTINEAU COURANT. Another farmer has gone broke. An auction will be held somewhere close to Kramer. She said it wouldn't hurt to look around, so we go. The day is going to be another dusty, hot one. Not a cloud in sight.

As at other auctions, the men folk look at the animals and machinery. The women folk look at household furniture. They examine kitchen junk, dishes, and odd objects stuffed in boxes. No selection allowed--you gotta buy the whole box.

There is a picnic bench outside with a blue-and-white-speckled enamel coffeepot--the big kind folks use for the threshing crew. It is full of steaming coffee. Cream and sugar jars, coffee mugs, and cookies are there. Help yourself.

Nearby, sitting in a rocking chair up for sale is a very obese woman holding a red-faced, squinty-eyed, squalling, fat baby. The floral print dress that lady is wearing is stained with sweat under her armpits. Downwind from this sight I can smell that the baby has fouled its diapers. This disgusting odor mixed with the sweat and rose oil scent from the mother makes me want to throw up. Why do some people like babies? Ugh.

The auction begins. The rapid-fire singsong spiel of the auctioneer riddles the small crowd. Nobody seems to be bidding up or bidding at all. Like us, no one has much money. It isn't going well for the farmer selling out. His wife is standing outside the kitchen door fighting tears and losing.

Ma had said that it wouldn't hurt to look around.

Well, she was dead wrong about that.

Time to Stop Squabbling

All summer the blackbirds couldn't stand to be together. In the tall reeds of the sloughs they would argue about who owned what perch. The crows were no better, fighting over who owned what tree. Ducks, neck, and flat beak extended, fluttered, and splashed about the pond claiming water rights.

Now that the reeds have turned to the color of buckskin, everybody wants to be sociable again. A cloud of blackbirds drop into our wheatfield to see if we missed a few grains. A bunch[22] of crows play aerobatic games over the aspen grove. The ducks are strictly formal about their get-together. They can't seem to fly anywhere without a regimental formation.

The wrens however, will have none of this reunion business. They just head south as unsociable as ever.

---

[22] Yes, to write "a bunch of crows" is technically wrong. To be correct, as the collective noun for crows it should read as "a murder of crows." I'll stick with bunch. After all, what does a kid know?

Fall – School Again – Curses!

Carl is cleaning and oiling his rifles and shotguns. Hunting season must be coming up soon. Oh, oh. This above all, is a sign that summer is over and I know what that means. School starts about the same time as the bird-hunting season. Doggonit! Any day now, Lena will tell Jake that she has to go to town and buy some new clothes for me to wear to school. Damn! Damn! And this day had started out so bright and warm, a new empty day to be filled with fun things to do. Soon I will be faced with the prospect of seven months of humiliation by a bunch of girls who are smarter than I. Another fall, and winter of walking to that lonesome building without trees or garden. How bleakly depressing.

Perhaps at the right time, when Ma is in a reasonable mood, I will be able to talk some sense into her--that is, about the profound futility of sending me off to school. Of course, I will back up my objection with a list of sound, logical and practical reasons.

Eventually, what I guess to be the right moment comes along.

It doesn't work this time either.

WINTER (Later Boyhood)

Morning

Holy gee-whilickers it was cold last night. Woke up to the downstairs sound of Pa rattling the grate of our kitchen stove. My pa has to be the bravest man in the world to get out of bed, and endure the frigid sting of our house.

Uncle Carl and I share the same bed. On the hair of the horsehide blanket[23], that has covered us during the night, is a lot of frost from our moisture-laden breaths. Ma is still in the next room. She doesn't want to get out of bed either--and she won't until the aspen wood fire Jake has started will ease the chill. We all know the litany of sounds and smells that will follow. The crackling of the fire, the grinding of coffee in the grinder, the metallic clink closing of the coffee pot lid. Next, up our stairway will waft the pleasant scent of Prince Albert tobacco freshly lit in Jake's pipe. A few minutes later comes the odor of fresh coffee brewing. Carl whispers to me, "Now Lena will get up."

Ma left her bed; hurriedly added layers of woolens over her nightshirt then fled downstairs to the warmth of the fire. As usual, on such a cold morning, her first words to Pa were:

---

[23] *Horsehide blankets were not uncommon. When a man's favorite horse died he would sometimes have the hide sent to a special tannery that would turn it into a blanket. The hair would be left intact and the inside lined with a fine mohair-like material. The edges would be trimmed with colorful satin. The blankets in our house retained the name of the horse. Carl and I slept under "Minnie." (I still have Minnie.)*

"What did the thermometer say?"

"Didn't say ennyting, its just hangs there."

"You know what I mean, – oh never mind, I'll go see for myself!"

But Lena can't see our outdoor thermometer. It hangs on a bracket outside our living room's north window. There is too much frost on the panes.

Upstairs Carl flops the near corner of the heavy hide blanket off from the other layers of blankets that cover us and rolls out of bed. A blast of cold air comes in to chill the warm spot he left. Even my long underwear is impotent to stay the onslaught of cold. Carl puts on his woolen shirt, flannel-lined britches and felt boots. As he heads downstairs he says to me, "I'll go outside and check the thermometer to see if you have to go to school today." I hope it will be more than thirty below. That is the magic number. It has been agreed by the school board that if it is colder than thirty below, school is called off for that day.

At the smell of bacon and pancakes, it is my turn to get out of bed. Rather than dress in that frigid bedroom, I grab all my clothes into a bundle and race for the warmth of the kitchen. The doors to the kitchen are closed to confine the heat to that room until the coal-fired living room stove can heat the rest of the house.

As I am putting on my clothes in the kitchen, I can hear Carl stomping snow from his feet outside the storm porch. Then I hear him walking through our sun porch. He opens the kitchen door and looks at me in a teasing way, thus prolonging my agony of anticipating the good or bad news about whether or not I have to go to school. He is mighty slow about telling me.

"Come on Carl, do I gotta go or not?"

"Well, I really hate to tell you this – I'm terribly sorry but you don't get to go to school today, it's thirty-six below."

Unbounded joy! I am extremely grateful for our little cold snap.

A Close Call

Today I was sure I didn't have to go to school. Last night seemed about as cold as the day I didn't have to go. When I came into the kitchen to put on my clothes Ma said the thermometer read only twenty-seven below. It wasn't thirty, so I would have to face another day in school.

Lena had this old fashioned idea that anyone who had to face a day in sub- zero temperature would need a small shot of brandy. After a normal breakfast of a pork chop, fried potatoes, and eggs, she made a hot cup of honey-water *(mead)* spiced with cinnamon and laced with peach brandy.

My unfinished arithmetic homework stuffed in the pocket of my flannel-lined coat and my head stuffed in the flannel-lined contours of my "Lindy Airplane" helmet I head for school. It is just a little over a mile away. First, I have to go over the rolling hills and creek of our pasture, then across the narrow field of Ole Thorsgard's place.

There is a wind blowing, making rivulets of snow that curl downwind from my feet. Wind is unusual in weather this cold. I haven't even crossed Thorsgard's small field yet and I already feel the stinging cold biting into my windward side. I turn around and walk backwards to let the lee side warm up. It doesn't warm up. Ow – ow – ow, it's cold.

How far to the warmth of the bleak little school on the prairie? A half mile to go. The snow is drifting harder now. It is hard to see the small white building. Above the ice fog and drifting snow I can see the sun and its companions--the sundogs. Of my direction I am sure, but where, oh where, is that damn schoolhouse? Then I see it dimly outlined as a ghostly silhouette.

There is no smoke from the chimney. I run over the hard packed snow to the south side of the combination woodshed and entry to where the door is. The damned door is frozen shut or locked! Oh God, what am I going to do?

The school barn! I hurry to the school barn. Maybe I can bury myself under some hay in the manger. The door won't slide open but a few inches. However, I manage to squeeze through. There is no hay in the mangers. Snow has sifted inside through the crack in the door. What now? Perhaps I can throw a rock through one of the school windows, climb up, and build a fire in the school stove. No dammit! It's a stupid idea. There is no way I can find a rock or even a pebble in this snowfield; even if I could, how could I ever jump high enough to get in the window? Intuitively I know that I can never make it home alive.

My toes are stinging from frostbite. My body is shuddering from cold. Despite the flannel-lined "Lindy" helmet, my ears feel as if someone shoved a ten-penny nail through them. Think, Think, What can I do? Every neighbor is too far away. I go to lee side away from the wind. Here the steps lead into the corner of the entry. Scared of freezing to death I hop from foot to foot to keep circulation going. At every hop my feet sting with pain.

Then I hear sleigh bells. Tinkling, jingling harness bells. Maybe I am saved! Someone is coming with horses. Hurrying around the corner toward the sound I see the dark mass of the team driven by Ole Thorsgard through the screen of driving snow. On the board seat, he is huddled in his big overcoat. The team comes right up to me. "Get in the box," Ole says. He didn't need to tell me twice.

Mr. Thorsgard had seen me through the unfrosted clear spot of the east kitchen window as I walked over the hill of his farm. He had said to himself,

"That boy is in trouble, I'd better harness the horses, there isn't any school today according to our thermometer."

Ole, in the bitter wind of a Canadian arctic air mass, headed his team and bobsled for the lone schoolhouse on the prairie. He drove his team to rescue the idiot little boy from freezing to death. Upon his arrival it didn't take two invitations for me to climb into his rig. Under the longhaired buffalo robes in the box of his sleigh I snuggled and shivered.

Mama was surprised as Ole delivered me home and to the warmth of our kitchen. When she heard his story she was really upset. Ole said that he thinks he got there just in time. I knew he was right about that. I knew that I could never have made it home without his rescue.

Mama says that the thermometer read only twenty-seven below.

Ole shakes his head no, "Ours reads thirty-one."

Later, Lena called some other neighbors to hear what their gauges had indicated. Ole was correct. Our thermometer was off by four degrees.

Jake had to buy a new thermometer the next time he went to town.

Firewood

Not only am I old enough to help fell aspen trees for our wood burning stoves but I have been bitten by the camera bug. Today, Carl and I are going up into the hills to get some firewood. It is cold, perhaps thirty below. We are riding on the bobsled behind our team of Clydesdales. I have a Brownie camera in the pocket of my jacket. It is loaded with a roll of precious film.

We get to the aspen grove at the side of a small meadow, once a pond until the Dust Bowl. The sun is low, even at noon. Ice fog now turns the frost-covered forest into a mystical landscape. Near-things are clear. Far-things fade into the whiteness. Directly overhead the sky is blue. I tell Carl that I'm going to take a few pictures before I can help with the axe.

There is Carl, the team, and sleigh making fuzzy shadows across the meadow snow. Behind him is a row of frost-laden aspen, decorative like a Japanese screen. Behind the aspen are more trees, oak, and ash only dimmer in the ice fog. Behind that is the bulk of the forest barely seen in the hard sparkling light. The simplicity and design of the view is wonderful. I compose and snap the shutter until all eight exposures are used up. These pictures, I am sure, will win a prize in the amateur photo contest in the CHICAGO TRIBUNE.

Now to help Carl. At the first blow of my axe, a heavy shower of long needles of frost falls from the overhead branches and down the back of my neck. I quickly learn to keep my collar buttoned tight. Oddly enough, it is fun cutting trees. Despite the cold I work up a sweat under my woolens. Within two hours we have cut, trimmed, and loaded almost two cords of wood. This is enough for the rest of winter and following spring

At home, in the cellar of our house, I prepare the developing solutions. We don't have a red light bulb as specified in the developing instructions. Jake, my father who had once worked in a photo studio in Souris, said that any red light would do. He said that the red wrapping paper around apples from Washington State would work if I wrapped it around the twenty-five watt light globe in the cellar. It didn't.

The film negative is almost solid black. To say I am disappointed is an understatement. I am angry with my dad for false information. I am angry with myself for not following recommended instructions to the letter. This was a photo opportunity of a lifetime blown to smithereens.

To purchase a red light bulb for a thirty-two volt system requires a staggering forty cents. Eventually I hope to able to buy one.

Threshing and the World Series

Poor Ma! It's threshing time and she is going batty again. She has to cook for the whole crew--a dozen or more very hungry men. She hates cooking under normal circumstances. She detests and dreads cooking at threshing time and lets everyone know it. She especially hates cooking on schedule, and I don't blame her. Her task is to prepare breakfast by sunup, lunch at 09:00 A.M., dinner at noon, lunch again at 04:00 P.M,. and supper at 08:00 P.M.

What she really hates is the added complication. The World Series is being broadcast over the radio. Between keeping the wood stove going, boiling food, baking bread, basting chickens, washing dishes, and the clanking of her own labor, she is trying to listen to the game and remember all the details. Lena is a baseball nut; this rare interest aids her memory. Memory is important because when the men come in to eat, they, especially Arnold, will want a complete rundown of hits, runs, and errors. Between serving food, bringing in new plates, carrying out the dirty ones, Ma is expected to give a recap of the game as best she can. One of the hands asks:

"Who did you say was pitchin' when Ott got that run?"

Ma tries to answer, "I think it was...well I don't know for sure...I had to go to the woodpile and when I got back the inning had already started."

"Lena, don't go to the Goddam woodpile tomorrow."

Everyone laughed but Ma--she was miffed at the lack of appreciation and left. She had to think up a fitting, fighting comeback. Lena returned from the kitchen with a fresh bowl of mashed potatoes and an answer. She said as she clunked the potato bowl down in front of the offending wise guy, "Ya... well you can come carry wood, cook lunch, dinner, supper make dessert, and wash dishes for me tomorrow and I'll sit and listen to the whole game, and keep notes."

Some of the men laughed. One of them spoke up in a loud voice, "That's a hell of a good idea, Lena – he ain't worth a damn on the field anyway!"

"Hee, hee, hee..." from a few appreciative fans. Then another voice, "Forget it, he can't cook worth a fart either." "Har, har, hars," filled the room.

Now Lena laughed.

A Threshing Tradition

Every year the same thing occurs. As the time approaches for the last bundle to be thrown into the chomping crocodile maw of the threshing machine, the threshing crew stand around with their hands raised and ready to protect their hats. Then when the last bundle is about to disappear under the steel teeth of the choppers, a wild melee breaks out. Men grabbing for each other's hat raise lot of dust as they scuffle about. The object of the sport is to throw the other fella's hat into the machine where it will be chopped and ground into shreds before the thresher can be shut down fully. Not even the 'boss' is exempt from the fray. It is not a day to be wearing your best hat.

Farm Boy and World War II

Snow was gently falling in large quarter-sized flakes. It was early in February 1943; about eleven o'clock AM at the Bottineau railroad depot. Big snowflakes are uncommon in the semi-arctic climate of North Dakota. This was not a common day in any way. The Army Air Corps had finally given notice that I was to report for duty in Minneapolis, then on to training at some unknown destination. I was about to board the Galloping Goose, the local name for the little train consisting of a diesel electric locomotive, one passenger car, a mail and baggage car, and sometimes freight car. Through no fault of its own the Goose got its local and cherished name from coping with a roller coaster track. At Rugby, fifty miles away I would transfer to the Empire Builder, the important and famous Seattle to Minneapolis passenger train of Jim Hill, king magnate of the Great Northern Railroad.

There in the falling snow about six feet away stood my parents who had dressed up as if to go to a funeral. My father, Jake had on his best, actually only, suit and hat. My mother, Lena was wearing her navy blue dress and despite the temperature declined to wear a coat, which would hide her best dress. The snow on their shoulders and hats was in stark contrast to the dark colors. Apparently they wanted their son to have the best memory possible of them--a last look. Jake's face, normally sad anyway, had the look of a man about to lose his son forever. Tears were streaming down my mother's cheek. Her dire

305

predictions of many years were finally coming true. In my growing up she had always fretted that there would be another war with Germany and that her only son would be in it. Sure to be killed, gassed or maimed for life. She was even bothered when I wanted to become a boy scout because being a boy scout involved wearing a uniform. So now another war was in full swing and I, as a farmers only son, could have been given an exemption had I not only insanely volunteered to join the army, but intended to seek the perilous duty as an airman, hopefully as a pilot, the worst of all.

Hugging one's parents is not a Scandinavian thing, even though I very much wanted to. I just politely shook hands with mom and dad, and said goodbye. With a small suitcase in hand, I got on the train at the conductor's call, "All aboard." The view through the window as I departed was of two lonely people on the platform with hats and shoulders covered with snow.

THE TURTLES NOW
(IT AIN'T THE SAME AS IT USED TO BE)

The hills are still there--the lake still sparkles there--but much else has changed. Only a third as many people now live in the area as there were in 1930. Some villages have disappeared entirely. Yet the urge to revisit the place once called home causes people to come from Florida, Arizona, California, and elsewhere to again explore "The Lake." Perhaps to remember the time…some, tired of the rat race, come back to stay.

It isn't enough to say that the place has changed dramatically in a mere sixty-eight years. Since the change has happened so gradually and steadily, most people, especially the folks that still live there, would say that the area hasn't changed all that much, if at all. Oh, they might say that they have electricity on all the farms now and that they have TVs, VCRs, ATVs, a cabin up at Lake Metigoshe and that all the state roads are paved. Other than that, Bottineau County hasn't changed much. Those who lived this time may, however, recall an image a lot different from what can be seen now. True, the land is still there and no developer has yet built shopping malls or business parks along the Peace Garden Road, nevertheless, the change has been significant.

A person, driving along a road in the countryside, now might be bored with the tidiness of it all. It isn't unreasonable to imagine that the traveler may even feel a twinge of loneliness, and hope that there wouldn't be any car trouble because it may be a week before anyone would come along to offer help. The tourist will pass mile after mile of drab agricultural perfection. Fields sterilized with herbicides to prevent anything from growing that hasn't been planted. The few farms that still have people living on them are far apart. No more can the farmer just walk over and visit his neighbor. He or she, unless being some sort of a health nut, will need to use the family car. Once, a neighbor was someone who lived a half mile away. Now, even the old farmsteads are gone. House, barn, well, windmill, and windbreak--razed, burned, bulldozed, and buried. As for wildlife, a robin would starve to death looking for a worm.

To give a brief general view of what it was like in the twenties, to live up by the "line," I will say that to be in the country was not a lonely life. There were three farms per square mile of land. This simply because the first homesteads consisted of one hundred and sixty acres, plus in some cases, forty additional acres of "Tree Farm" land. (A strange story in itself--I may get to it later.) This works out to three farms per section. Now, in some parts of North Dakota, it is almost the reverse; three square miles per farm!

In the nineteen-twenties, farms did more than just grow wheat, oats, and barley. There were horses to pull the machinery, cattle to look contented while we stole their milk, chickens to cluck, turkeys to act stupid, and pigs building pork chops for your breakfast plate. We even had marginally useful animals, like a dog to lay on the front porch for stumbling over and a few cats to sit on top of the horses in the barn in the wintertime. One farmer even dared to bring a few sheep into the county but he couldn't stand the loss of friends, so he got rid of them. I even had a pet deer, long before they invented Bambi.

To visit a neighbor was a short walk, which we did often because visiting was the number three occupation. Farming of course was first. Speaking about number one was number two pre-occupation. There were lots of other children to play with. However unfortunately for me, our near neighbor, "The Thorsgards" just had a bunch of girls for children. Admittedly, they were all flaxen haired, blue-eyed and in retrospect, pretty as the minnows in Boulder Creek, but still, dammit, girls!

So how did this practice of diversified farming affect the local scenery? For one thing, when a farmer has horses and cattle, he needs a pasture. A pasture is more than just acres of grass. A pasture is a patch of wild onions, a clump of aromatic, scrubby Silver Willow. In the spring, a pasture is a place to find blue and white Pasque flowers, defying the last snow in April, and in the summer, Flickertail gophers squeaking "all clear" air raid warnings. A pasture is where one finds a small pond with melodious frogs, a nest of Burrowing Owls, and sometimes a Killdeer faking a broken wing to lure you away from the little ball of fluff on toothpick legs. In the fall even the Goldenrod is dry, and fluffy stuff from some unknown plant drifts in the wind. A pasture is where some lucky kid can find the bleached skull of a cow and pretend it to be the skull of a buffalo, probably killed by Crazy Horse. Here is where our Percheron draft horses grazed. Here is where I found flint arrowheads confirming my opinion about Crazy Horse. In the low spots, where moisture was held, were Buttercups of yellow flowers of plastic sheen, and in the shade of the little willows by the creek, wild strawberries, tiny but pungently sweet. Up in the shallow draw, at the edge of the pasture, in a grove of aspen, lived the resident crow family. In the nest, three ugly fledglings and the sparkling foil from a pack of 'Tailor made cigarettes'. As any farm kid knows, crows have an innocent habit of stealing such 'objets des art,' discarded by some unappreciative farm hand.

Pastures need fences to keep the cows out of the crop of barley or wheat. The barbed wire did more than just separate the cattle from the chaff. The fences stopped the roll of tumbleweeds. It made a place of untrodden ground where wild roses could grow. Chinese Pheasants would stupidly try to hide from the hunter by running in the tall weeds of the fence line. Fence lines bordered not only pastures but also country roads and neighbors fields to keep the cattle where they belonged. Now, not only the fence lines are gone, but so are most of the pastures. Hunters complain about the disappearance of game birds.

All is not lost, where the fence lines and pastures once were have been added more acres of weedless land producing weed free Durham wheat, at thirty bushels to the acre.

Undoubtedly, if you have been told anything of North Dakota at all, you have been informed that it is the treeless state. This is another myth, like Columbus discovering America. Nothing could be farther from the truth. Trees generally grow where the soil is too poor for grass. True, trees grew in the Turtle Mountains in glacial moraine but not to the exclusion of hundreds of little islands of aspen trees on the plains or other trees following the course of creeks and rivers. My father's farm had at least three little groves of Quaking Aspen, complete with a crow or Broadwing hawk family.

These groves of trees with leaves trembling in the wind were a delight to visit. Actually, they were usually a ring of trees like a fairy ring of mushrooms. This was due to the nature of aspen tree propagation. A parent tree would take root; spread its roots outward, new trees come up and the parent tree die, leaving a space to be filled with a small glade of grass and wild flowers. While I remember the joy of visiting these groves of aspen, I guess I overestimated their value for they didn't last long. They took up an acre of land, which could be growing something useful. So a few strokes of the axe, a few stumps burned, a little leveling, and 'voila' another acre of wheat.

Prairie sloughs either just dried up in the Dust Bowl times or never came back or they were drained for a few more acres of wheat. In the twenties, it seemed that about every other ravine in the foothills had a spring and its trickling stream. Even out on the prairie, one would occasionally see a clump of willows marking the location of a clear water spring and brooklet. Oddly enough, my very earliest memory is that of a sun filled meadow that had it all; a little clump of willows, spring, brooklet, wildflowers, and my parents, Jake and Lena haying with the help of a team of horses.